Emil Brunner
A Reappraisal

Alister E. McGrath

WILEY Blackwell

This paperback edition first published 2016
© 2014 John Wiley & Sons, Ltd

Edition history: John Wiley & Sons, Ltd (hardback, 2014)

Registered Office
John Wiley & Sons, Ltd, The Atrium, Southern Gate, Chichester,
West Sussex, PO19 8SQ, UK

Editorial Offices
350 Main Street, Malden, MA 02148-5020, USA
9600 Garsington Road, Oxford, OX4 2DQ, UK
The Atrium, Southern Gate, Chichester, West Sussex, PO19 8SQ, UK

For details of our global editorial offices, for customer services, and for information about how to apply for permission to reuse the copyright material in this book please see our website at www.wiley.com/wiley-blackwell.

The right of Alister E. McGrath to be identified as the author has been asserted in accordance with the UK Copyright, Designs and Patents Act 1988.

All rights reserved. No part of this publication may be reproduced, stored in a retrieval system, or transmitted, in any form or by any means, electronic, mechanical, photocopying, recording or otherwise, except as permitted by the UK Copyright, Designs and Patents Act 1988, without the prior permission of the publisher.

Wiley also publishes its books in a variety of electronic formats. Some content that appears in print may not be available in electronic books.

Designations used by companies to distinguish their products are often claimed as trademarks. All brand names and product names used in this book are trade names, service marks, trademarks or registered trademarks of their respective owners. The publisher is not associated with any product or vendor mentioned in this book.

Limit of Liability/Disclaimer of Warranty: While the publisher and author have used their best efforts in preparing this book, they make no representations or warranties with respect to the accuracy or completeness of the contents of this book and specifically disclaim any implied warranties of merchantability or fitness for a particular purpose. It is sold on the understanding that the publisher is not engaged in rendering professional services and neither the publisher nor the author shall be liable for damages arising herefrom. If professional advice or other expert assistance is required, the services of a competent professional should be sought.

Library of Congress Cataloging-in-Publication Data

Names: McGrath, Alister E., 1953–
Title: Emil Brunner : a reappraisal / Alister E. McGrath.
Description: Malden, MA : Wiley Blackwell, 2014. | Includes bibliographical references
  (pages 239–241) and index.
Identifiers: LCCN 2013030735 (print) | LCCN 2014001115 (ebook) |
  ISBN 9780470670552 (cloth) | ISBN 9781119283416 (paper) |
  ISBN 9781118569245 (ePub) | ISBN 9781118569269 (Adobe PDF)
Subjects: LCSH: Brunner, Emil, 1889–1966.
Classification: LCC BX4827.B67 M34 2014 (print) | LCC BX4827.B67 (ebook) |
  DDC 230/.044092–dc23
LC record available at https://lccn.loc.gov/2013030735

A catalogue record for this book is available from the British Library.

Cover image: Emil Brunner at Princeton Theological Seminary, c.1938. Courtesy of Special Collections, Princeton Theological Seminary Library

Set in 10/12pt Sabon by SPi Global, Pondicherry, India

Praise for *Emil Brunner: A Reappraisal*

"McGrath's consummate skills as both a theologian and an historian are masterfully at work in this penetrating and highly illuminating study arguing for the importance and continuing vital relevance to current theological and cultural debates of one of the twentieth century's largely forgotten major theological voices. Exhibiting the same sagacious understanding, balanced discernment and astute critical insight that we have come to admire and value so highly in McGrath, this intensively researched and captivating book brings together for the first time an enormous wealth of original source material yielding important new insights and contexts for a compelling reassessment and reappropriation of Brunner's legacy. The book will serve not only as an inspired catalyst for renewed attention to Brunner but also as an indispensable resource base for further research, whether on Brunner himself or on the doctrinal and cultural issues that animated him and to which he continues to contribute so richly and relevantly."

Paul Janz, King's College London

"Professor McGrath offers us a brilliant reassessment of a theologian who has for long languished in the shadow of Karl Barth. It needs no less than an author with the wide-ranging skills of a theologian, intellectual historian and expert in the interface between science and religion to bring to light the neglected contribution of Emil Brunner to the theology of the twentieth century. Brunner's comprehensive vision for doctrine, theology of nature, missiology, ethics, practical theology and apologetics is exposed by an author who has himself produced formative work in all these areas. Neither simply a biography nor a mere introduction to Brunner's theology, this deeply-researched and engaging study traces the emergence of Brunner's thought in its cultural context, recognizes its flaws and yet recovers a challenge for the involvement of theology in the culture of our present time."

Paul S. Fiddes, University of Oxford

"Professor Alister McGrath's meticulously researched and lucid exposition and assessment of Emil Brunner's legacy is a landmark publishing event not only for the better understanding of modern Reformed theology but also of twentieth-century theology at large. More than just a theological biography or an introduction to Brunner's theological writings, this monograph helps us rediscover the critical and constructive role this Swiss theologian, too often left in the shadow of Barth, played in the wider theological world on both sides of the Atlantic. The book serves not only theological scholars and students but also a wider Christian audience interested in the development of contemporary theology"

Veli-Matti Kärkkäinen, University of Helsinki

Also by Alister E. McGrath from Wiley Blackwell

The Intellectual World of C.S. Lewis (2013)
Christian History: An Introduction (2013)
Historical Theology: An Introduction to the History of Christian Thought, second edition (2012)
Reformation Thought: An Introduction, fourth edition (2012)
Theology: The Basic Readings, second edition (edited, 2012)
Theology: The Basics, third edition (2012)
Luther's Theology of the Cross: Martin Luther's Theological Breakthrough, second edition (2011)
Darwinism and the Divine: Evolutionary Thought and Natural Theology (2011)
The Christian Theology Reader, fourth edition (edited, 2011)
Christian Theology: An Introduction, fifth edition (2011)
Science and Religion: A New Introduction, second edition (2009)
The Open Secret: A New Vision for Natural Theology (2008)
The Order of Things: Explorations in Scientific Theology (2006)
Christianity: An Introduction, second edition (2006)
Dawkins' God: Genes, Memes, and the Meaning of Life (2004)
The Intellectual Origins of the European Reformation, second edition (2003)
A Brief History of Heaven (2003)
The Blackwell Companion to Protestantism (edited with Darren C. Marks, 2003)
The Future of Christianity (2002)
Reformation Thought: An Introduction, third edition (2000)
Christian Spirituality: An Introduction (1999)
Historical Theology: An Introduction (1998)
The Foundations of Dialogue in Science and Religion (1998)
The Blackwell Encyclopedia of Modern Christian Thought (edited, 1995)
A Life of John Calvin (1990)

Contents

Preface	ix
A Note on Translations and Editions	xiii

1 Emil Brunner: The Origins of a Theological Mind, 1914–1924   1

Theological Studies at Zurich	2
Pastoral Ministry and Contacts in England	4
The Swiss Crisis of Identity, 1914–1919	6
Brunner and Dialectical Theology: The Origins of an Ambivalent Relationship	9
Brunner in America, 1919–1920	12
Brunner, Barth, and Thurneysen: Continuing Debate	13
The Quest for Recognition: *Erlebnis, Erkenntnis und Glaube* (1921–2)	16
Brunner and American Psychology of Religion	18
The Limits of Humanity: Reflections on Revelation and Reason (1922)	22
The Critique of Schleiermacher: *Die Mystik und das Wort* (1924)	25

Part I The Making of a Dialectical Theologian   29

2 Brunner's Theology of Crisis: Critique and Construction, 1924–1929   31

The 1925 Inaugural Lecture at Zurich: Revelation and Theology	32
Reason and Theology: An Ecclesial Engagement (1927)	34
The Mediator: A Manifesto for Dialectical Theology (1927)	39
The Trinity: Dogma, not Kerygma	50
The American Reception of the "Theology of Crisis" (1928)	54

3 Reflections on the Tasks of Theology, 1929–1933 — 61
Crisis: The Rise of Ideology in Western Europe, 1920–1935 — 62
Brunner's Challenge to Ideology: The "Other Task
of Theology" (1929) — 66
Presenting Dialectical Theology in Britain:
The Word and the World (1931) — 74
A Theological Ethics: *The Divine Imperative* (1932) — 78
A Problematic Liaison: Brunner and the Oxford Group — 85
The Work of the Holy Spirit:
The Copenhagen Lectures (1934) — 87

4 Natural Theology? The Barth–Brunner Debate of 1934 — 90
Natural Theology: A Contested Notion — 94
Karl Barth's Views on Natural Theology, 1918–1933 — 101
A Game-Changer: The Nazi Power Grab of 1933 — 105
Brunner's Public Criticism of Barth: *Nature and Grace* (1934) — 113
Brunner's Later Views on Natural Theology:
Revelation and Reason (1941) — 121
Barth's Response: *No!* (1934) — 127

5 Brunner's Theological Anthropology: *Man in Revolt* (1937) — 133
The Need for a Theological Anthropology — 134
The Impossibility of an "Objective" Anthropology — 136
The Dependence of Humanity on God — 140
The "Contradiction" within Humanity — 142
The Image of God and Human Identity — 145
Humanity and Evolution: The Limits of Darwinism — 148

6 Objectivity and Subjectivity in Theology:
Truth as Encounter (1937) — 154
Object and Subject in Theology:
The Context to Brunner's Thought — 155
Objectivity and Subjectivity:
Brunner's Criticism of Existing Paradigms — 161
Overcoming the Object-Subject Impasse: Brunner's Strategy — 166
The Implications of Brunner's Notion of "Truth as Encounter" — 169
America: The Call to Princeton
Theological Seminary, 1937–1939 — 172

Part II Consolidation: Brunner's Vision for Post-War Theological Reconstruction — 179

7 Brunner's Vision for the Christian Community:
The Church, State, and Culture — 181
The Ideological Origins of Totalitarianism — 182

	An Antidote to Totalitarianism: The Renewal of Natural Law	185
	The Need for Theological Reconstruction: *Revelation and Reason* (1941)	190
	The Christian State: A Modest Theological Proposal	195
	Rediscovering the Church as Community: Brunner's Ecclesiology	199
8	**Teacher and Preacher: Brunner as a Public Intellectual**	205
	Rector of the University of Zurich, 1942–1943	206
	The Catechist: *Our Faith* (1935)	207
	The Fraumünster Sermons: Brunner as Preacher	210
	The Public Lecturer: *The Scandal of Christianity*	214
	Theological Education: Brunner's *Dogmatics*	218
	Tokyo: Brunner's Engagement with Asia	221
	Final Illness and Death	223
9	**Legacy: The Contemporary Significance of Emil Brunner's Theology**	225
	The Reformed Tradition: A Richer Range of Possibilities	228
	A Theology of Nature: The Basis of Natural Law, Theology, and Science	229
	Cultural Engagement: The Theological Foundations of Apologetics	231
	Personalism: The Defence of Relational Identity	232
	The Trinity: A Plea for Theological Modesty	234
	Conclusion	237
Works by Emil Brunner Cited in This Study		239
Index		242

Preface

In his time, Emil Brunner (1889–1966) was acclaimed as one of the greatest and most influential theologians of the twentieth century, especially in the United States of America. From the 1930s to the early 1960s, it is arguable that no single theologian exercised so extensive and pervasive an influence on American and British theologians and preachers.[1] It is easy to see why Brunner garnered such acclaim and gained such a following. Few have failed to notice his grace and clarity of theological exposition, his easy familiarity with the ways and concerns of British and American Christianity, and his clear commitment to the life and witness of the church.

His rise to fame in the English-speaking world was as inevitable as it was justified. Brunner spent two year-long periods as a visiting professor at seminaries in the United States, and delivered the prestigious Gifford Lectures at St Andrew's University in 1946–7. In the period of post-war theological reconstruction in the 1950s and 1960s, he was widely seen as offering the church a defensible and positive platform from which to begin its reconnection with society and the world of ideas. Austin Farrer (1904–68), perhaps one of the finest Anglican theologians of the twentieth century,[2] was one of many English-speaking theologians of the 1930s to recognize Brunner's merits. After reading Brunner's *The Mediator*, he commented in a letter of March 1931 that Brunner "is Barth with the rhetoric pulled out and thought inserted in its place".[3]

Yet today Brunner is largely forgotten. Even in his native Switzerland, interest in him is dwindling. The Emil Brunner Stiftung, founded in February 1973 to promote interest in Brunner and produce editions of his works,

---

[1] J. Robert Nelson, "Emil Brunner – The Final Encounter." *Christian Century* 83, no. 16 (1966): 486.
[2] Robert MacSwain, "Above, Beside, Within: The Anglican Theology of Austin Farrer." *Journal of Anglican Studies* 4 (2006): 33–57.
[3] Cited in Philip Curtis, *A Hawk among Sparrows: A Biography of Austin Farrer*. London: SPCK, 1985, 79.

x   Preface

was dissolved in November 2011.⁴ What was once a torrent of publications concerning him has dwindled to a trickle. Rarely is he the subject of theological monographs or articles; he is more often used to provide an angle of gaze or point of comparison from which to assess and understand others – most notably, Karl Barth.⁵ Brunner is often read through a Barthian interpretative lens, and found to be wanting by Barthian standards – especially in relation to their controversy of 1934.⁶

Brunner's complex relationship with Barth remains incompletely understood. Some have suggested that Brunner had an "inferiority complex" in relation to Barth,⁷ which led him to cultivate Barth's personal acquaintance and seek his theological approval for his projects. Brunner wanted to be affirmed by Barth and at the same time felt threatened by him. For his part, Barth never had a particularly high regard for Brunner, and gradually came to see no reason to conceal this.

Although this tension in Brunner's attitude towards Barth is probably best seen in the years immediately preceding the 1934 controversy over natural theology, it had clearly developed earlier. In the autumn of 1927 Barth was invited to explore the possibility of returning to Switzerland from Germany to take up a chair in dogmatics at the University of Berne. He mentioned this to Brunner, and asked what he made of the possibility.⁸ Brunner's reply, though positive in some respects, indicated unease over the move, partly because of the potentially negative impact on his own reputation in Switzerland, and partly because of its implications for student enrolment at Zurich.⁹ In the end, nothing came of the move; yet this development presaged similar anxieties when Barth eventually left Germany to

---

⁴ The Stiftung was founded and supported by the Evangelisch-Reformierte Landeskirche des Kantons Zürich. See Handelsregisteramt des Kantons Zürich, record CH-020.7.900.670-0.
⁵ See, for example, John C. McDowell, "Karl Barth, Emil Brunner and the Subjectivity of the Object of Christian Hope." *International Journal of Systematic Theology* 8 (2006): 25–41. A further point to be noted here is that Brunner often stands in the middle of complex theological debates, and thus tends to be excluded from consideration by those who find it easier to adopt or defend their extremes: see Mark G. McKim, "Brunner the Ecumenist: Emil Brunner as a *Vox Media* of Protestant Theology." *Calvin Theological Journal* 32 (1997): 91–104.
⁶ Claus Westermann, "Karl Barths Nein. Eine Kontroverse um die theologia naturalis. Emil Brunner–Karl Barth (1934) in perspektiven des Alten Testaments." *Evangelische Theologie* 47 (1987): 386–95; Klaus-Peter Blaser, "Communiquer l'incommunicable révélation: Le conflit Barth-Brunner revisité à la lumière de leur correspondance." *Etudes Théologiques et Religieuses* 78 (2003): 59–67; Gerhard Sauter, "Theologisch miteinander streiten: Karl Barths Auseinandersetzung mit Emil Brunner." In *Karl Barth in Deutschland (1921–1935): Aufbruch – Klärung – Widerstand*, ed. Michael Beintker, Christian Link, and Michael Trowitzsch, 267–84. Zurich: Theologischer Verlag, 2005.
⁷ See, for example, Eduard Thurnseysen's letter to Barth on this point, written on 21 October 1930: *Karl Barth–Eduard Thurneysen Briefwechsel*. 3 vols. Zurich: Theologischer Verlag, 1974, vol. 3, 56.
⁸ Barth to Brunner, 30 October 1927: *Karl Barth–Emil Brunner, Briefwechsel*, 159–60. See further Eberhard Busch, *Karl Barth: His Life from Letters and Autobiographical Texts*. London: SCM Press, 1976, 175–6.
⁹ Brunner to Barth, 1 November 1927; *Karl Barth–Emil Brunner, Briefwechsel*, 160–3.

return to Switzerland in 1935 as a result of his opposition to National Socialism. Even in the 1920s, Brunner realized that he was overshadowed by Barth, and eventually learned to live with this, however reluctantly. As one of Brunner's more perceptive colleagues remarked in 1933,[10] Brunner's troubled relationship with Barth was a "totally personal cross" that Brunner would have to learn to bear.

It has long seemed to me that there is a need to reappraise the theological legacy of Emil Brunner. He may have fallen out of theological fashion; he nevertheless offered, and continues to offer, a vision for Christian theology and the life of the Christian church which resonates with the concerns of today. Brunner has not been refuted; he has been neglected.[11] More than a generation has passed since his death, and such a reconsideration is clearly overdue.

This work is not primarily a biography of Brunner, nor an introduction to his theology. It is an exploration of the development of his thought, primarily in the 1920s and 1930s, set against the intellectual and cultural context of the age, leading into an assessment of his theological vision, and an attempt to make connections with our own context. In the course of the volume, I shall consider traditional questions of historical importance (such as Brunner's place in the development of dialectical theology, and the historical emergence of his theological vision) and theological interest (such as his complex – and generally misunderstood – views on natural theology). Yet Brunner's comprehensive vision of the tasks and possibilities of theology allowed apologetics, mission, ethics, social responsibility, pedagogy, practical theology, and preaching to be woven together as interconnected aspects of a coherent and greater whole, rather than forcing them to be seen as isolated and independent themes. It is a powerful, compelling account of the theological enterprise, which cries out to be engaged, assessed, and applied.

This book has taken a quarter of a century to write. Much of the research originally underlying it was undertaken at the University of Zurich in 1986 and 1989. My primary reason for visiting Zurich on both occasions was to make use of its research archives specializing in sixteenth-century intellectual history, especially in the University of Zurich's Institute for Swiss Reformation History. The university's Faculty of Theology was located in the same building, allowing me to begin a serious and extended engagement with Brunner's works, and the secondary literature concerning him.

It took a long time to reflect on my initial readings of Brunner, setting them against the context of the intellectual history of western Europe in the twentieth century, and my own reflections on the tasks of theology. The

---

[10] Frank Jehle, *Emil Brunner: Theologe im 20. Jahrhundert*. Zurich: Theologischer Verlag, 2006, 295.

[11] See the comments of Cynthia Bennett Brown, "The Personal Imperative of Revelation: Emil Brunner, Dogmatics and Theological Existence." *Scottish Journal of Theology* 65, no. 4 (2012): 421–34.

recent publication (2006) of Frank Jehle's reliable and thorough biography of Brunner[12] prompted me to bring together some lines of thought that had been preoccupying me for more than two decades, leading to the present study. This extended process of reflection has allowed me to understand and appreciate Brunner more deeply, and suggests that the time has come to reconsider his significance for the challenges facing both the academic discipline of theology and the needs of the churches in the twenty-first century.

Alister E. McGrath
King's College London, 2013

---

[12] See n. 10 above.

A Note on Translations and Editions

Brunner's works, listed in the bibliography at the end of this study, are referred to by their short titles, in English or German.[1] Where a work has been translated into English, the English short title has been used within the text to refer to it. Thus *Der Mensch im Widerspruch* is referred to as *Man in Revolt*, despite the failure of this English title to reflect Brunner's key anthropological theme of "contradiction", which is explicitly stated in the original German title. (Brunner occasionally expressed irritation and frustration over the English titles of his works.)

Unusually for a German-speaking theologian of that period, Brunner was perfectly comfortable lecturing in English. As a result, several of his major books, which were based on lectures originally delivered in the United States and Great Britain, were published in English, and never appeared in German during his lifetime – most notably, his Gifford Lectures at St Andrew's University. Some of his works originally published in German were never translated into English, and are referred to only by their German short titles.

Although Brunner has been fortunate in having many English translators,[2] this has led to a certain degree of inconsistency in rendering his often dense German prose, occasionally made worse by the decision to omit material deemed to lack interest to English-speaking readers. There are also points at which Brunner's theological intentions have been rendered opaquely, and occasionally inaccurately. Given these difficulties, I have made my own translations of his original German works throughout this study, and refer readers on to the appropriate place in existing English translations. Brunner's German, especially in his early writings, is not always

---

[1] Unless otherwise indicated, Brunner's shorter publications are referred to in the collected edition *Ein offenes Wort: Vorträge und Aufsätze 1917–1962*. 2 vols. Zurich: Theologischer Verlag, 1981.

[2] Most notably, the formidable Olive Wyon (1881–1966), but also including A. J. D. Farrer, John Holden, H. A. Kennedy, Harold Knight, Amandus W. Loos, John W. Rilling, and Bertram Lee Woolf.

easily rendered in English, forcing his translators to use paraphrases and circumlocutions more frequently than many would like. In translating, I have tried to be consistent wherever possible, while bringing out the theological sense of the original German.

The author and publisher gratefully acknowledge the kindness of TVZ Theologischer Verlag Zürich AG in permitting the reproduction of copyright material originally published in German.

1
Emil Brunner: The Origins of a Theological Mind, 1914–1924

Emil Brunner was born on 23 December 1889 in the Swiss city of Winterthur in the canton of Zurich.[1] His father, Heinrich Emil Brunner (1859–1926), was the youngest of six children, born into a "totally unbelieving family" in Oberrieden, on the south shore of Lake Zurich. This was a period of considerable political and social tension in German-speaking Switzerland, with liberals pressing for the secularization of the region's educational system, and conservatives wishing to retain its religious orientation. To his family's dismay, Brunner's father decided to attend a Protestant teacher training school (*Evangelisches Lehrerseminar*) in Unterstrass, also in the canton of Zurich, which had been founded in 1869.

The *Evangelisches Lehrerseminar* at which Brunner's father studied during the period 1874–8 had gained a considerable reputation as a centre of pedagogical and spiritual excellence under Heinrich Bachofner (1828–97). After qualifying as a teacher, Brunner secured a position at a Protestant school in Winterthur. Bachofner's strongly Pietist spirituality had a profound influence on Brunner's father, which was further consolidated by his marriage in 1884 to Sophie Hanna Müller (1862–1934). Sophie's father was the pastor of the village of Dussnang, in the canton of Thurgau, noted for his emphasis upon biblically grounded theology and preaching. The couple had four children: Hanna Sophie ("Hanny", 1886–1961), Maria Lydia (1887–1968), Emil (1889–1966), and Frieda Emma (1896–1964). In April 1893, the Brunner family left Winterthur to settle in the city of Zurich, where Brunner's father had been appointed as primary teacher at the Gabler School House in the suburb of Enge.

[1] Frank Jehle, *Emil Brunner: Theologe im 20. Jahrhundert*. Zurich: Theologischer Verlag, 2006, 19–32.

Emil Brunner: A Reappraisal, First Edition. Alister E. McGrath.
© 2014 John Wiley & Sons, Ltd. Published 2016 by John Wiley & Sons, Ltd.

2   The Origins of a Theological Mind, 1914–1924

Theological Studies at Zurich

Brunner's childhood was deeply shaped by his parent's strong religious beliefs, and their growing involvement in the Religious Socialist movement. Like many in Zurich at this time, Brunner was influenced by the pastor and writer Hermann Kutter (1863–1931), who developed a vision for a religious socialism that was both politically engaged and religiously grounded. Although Kutter argued that the essentially secularist Social Democrats were far more alert to social issues than their Christian counterparts, he insisted that a strongly Christian foundation was essential for any viable programme of social reform. Brunner was instructed and confirmed by Kutter at Christmas 1905.[2]

Yet although Brunner would remain concerned with political and social questions for the remainder of his life, it became clear to him at an early stage that the questions that really interested and concerned him were theological in character. In October 1908, aged 18, Brunner began to study theology at the University of Zurich.[3] His key concern was to find an "intellectually satisfying statement of his faith".[4] Initially, he appears to have been particularly attracted by Zurich's church historian, Walter Köhler (1870–1947), a specialist in the thought of the Reformation. Brunner's prize-winning early essay "The Religious Ideals of Erasmus of Rotterdam" (1910) clearly reflects Köhler's influence.

Yet even at this early stage, Brunner had become aware of the importance of the English-speaking world. He attended the eighth conference of the World's Student Christian Federation held at Oxford from 15 to 19 July 1909,[5] at which he met leading figures in the international ecumenical movement – including the American Methodist layman John R. Mott (1865–1955). Brunner's Oxford visit reveals two of his most distinctive characteristics, which mark him off from many other Swiss theologians of his age – an ability to speak English, and a willingness to engage directly with the ideas and movements of the English-speaking world, crossing the barriers of language, nationality, and denominations.

The most significant early intellectual influence on Brunner came from Leonhard Ragaz (1868–1945), a close associate of Kutter, who was Professor of Systematic and Practical Theology at the University of Zurich.[6] Critiquing capitalism for its commodification of humanity, Ragaz developed a theological foundation for a reaffirmation of the value of individuals in the sight

---

[2] For Brunner's relationship with Kutter, see Jehle, *Emil Brunner*, 90–8.
[3] Jehle, *Emil Brunner*, 33–47.
[4] "Intellectual Autobiography", 5.
[5] For the importance of this event and its immediate predecessors, see John R. Mott, *The Christward Movement among the Students of the World*. London: World's Student Christian Federation, 1909.
[6] For Brunner's relationship with Ragaz, see Jehle, *Emil Brunner*, 98–108.

of God.⁷ He reinforced Brunner's growing conviction that personal and social transformation was impossible without a foundation in the living reality of God. Like Brunner, Ragaz recognized the importance of English-speaking theology. During his 1907 visit to Boston, Ragaz became familiar with the writings of Walter Rauschenbusch (1861–1918), especially his *Christianity and the Social Crisis* (1907). Rauschenbusch's influence is evident in Ragaz's subsequent writings, particularly his sermons of 1909.⁸ In 1914, Brunner dedicated his first significant published writing, *Das Symbolische in der religiösen Erkenntnis* ("The Symbolic Element in Religious Knowledge"), to Ragaz.

So what does *Das Symbolische* tell us about Brunner's ideas at this time? Theologically, it positions Brunner neatly within the mainstream of Swiss liberal Protestantism in the period before the Great War. Brunner regarded Immanuel Kant and F. D. E. Schleiermacher as having inaugurated the modern discussion of central theological themes, particularly in shifting the emphasis from allegedly "objective" conceptions of religious knowledge to subjective religious experience.⁹ Religious knowledge is essentially experiential; "revelation" is essentially enlightenment.

The work echoes the anti-metaphysical approach to theology – especially Christology – characteristic of the liberal Protestantism of A. B. Ritschl and Adolf von Harnack.¹⁰ Jesus of Nazareth was to be regarded as a religious exemplar or prototype, embodying the ethical values of the kingdom of God.¹¹ "Brunner regarded Jesus as a man possessing special religious knowledge, not a God-man who is identical with God as an object of religious knowledge."¹² There is an obvious and significant soteriological deficit in Brunner's understanding of Jesus of Nazareth at this point, partly reflecting any sense of ontological distinction between humanity and Jesus.¹³ Jesus may clarify our understanding of God; he does not fundamentally alter our relationship with God. It is interesting to note that Brunner's Christology

---

[7] Leonhard Ragaz, *Das Evangelium und der soziale Kampf der Gegenwart*. 2nd edn. Basle: C. F. Lendorff, 1907. For a good account of Ragaz's ethics, see Robert Barth, "Leonhard Ragaz (1868–1945)." In *Schweizer Ethiker im 20. Jahrhundert: Der Beitrag theologischer Denken*, ed. Wolfgang Lienemann and Frank Mathwig, 9–32. Zurich: Theologischer Verlag, 2005.

[8] Leonhard Ragaz, *Dein Reich komme! Predigten*. Basle: Helbing & Lichtenhahn, 1909.

[9] *Das Symbolische in der religiösen Erkenntnis*, 2–3. For comment, see Yrjö Salakka, *Person und Offenbarung in der Theologie Emil Brunners während der Jahre 1914–1937*. Helsinki: Kirjapaino, 1960, 34–52; Heinrich Leopold, *Missionarische Theologie: Emil Brunners Weg zur theologischen Anthropologie*. Gütersloh: Mohn, 1974, 22–33.

[10] See Friedrich W. Graf, "Der 'Kant der Kirchengeschichte' und der 'Philosoph des Protestantismus.' Adolf von Harnacks Kant-Rezeption und seine Beziehungen zu den philosophischen Neukantianern." In *Adolf von Harnack: Christentum, Wissenschaft und Gesellschaft*, ed. Kurt Nowak, Otto Gerhard Oexle, Trutz Rendtorff, and Kurt-Victor Selge, 113–42. Göttingen: Vandenhoeck & Ruprecht, 2003.

[11] Stephan Scheld, *Die Christologie Emil Brunners*. Wiesbaden: Franz Steinbeck, 1981, 50–6.

[12] Scheld, *Die Christologie Emil Brunners*, 50.

[13] Scheld, *Die Christologie Emil Brunners*, 82–3.

seems to rest on his epistemological presuppositions, suggesting that his understanding of the role of Jesus of Nazareth was shaped by an essentially philosophical framework.[14]

There are aspects of *Das Symbolische* which merit further discussion, perhaps most notably the manner in which its ideas – especially the ethical role of Jesus of Nazareth – echo the views of Ragaz, and the manner in which Brunner draws on Henri Bergson to develop his notion of "intuition".[15] Yet for our purposes, the importance of the work lies in its illumination of Brunner's theological starting point. In his "pre-dialectical" phase,[16] Brunner is clearly deeply embedded within the liberal Protestant consensus, even if his ideas are tinged with the hues of the prevailing forms of liberal Protestantism at Zurich, rather than at Berlin. Yet this initial statement of Brunner's theological perspectives reveals someone who is at home with the ideas of Schleiermacher, Ritschl, and Harnack.[17] At this point, Brunner does not stand out from his cultural and theological background.

Pastoral Ministry and Contacts in England

Brunner – like his Swiss colleagues Karl Barth (1886–1968) and Eduard Thurneysen (1888–1974) – had little sympathy at this stage for the purely academic study of theology, or any notion of theology as an ecclesially disengaged activity. All three saw theology as linked to ministry, and above all to preaching. Brunner was studying theology in order to begin public ministry within the Swiss Reformed church. His initial pastoral responsibilities were in Leutwil, a small town in the canton of Aargau, some fifteen kilometres from the neighbouring village of Safenwil.

Brunner moved to Leutwil in September 1912 to deputize for pastor August Müller, who had become seriously ill. Following Müller's death in office on 3 October, Brunner was ordained on 27 October 1912 at the Fraumünster

---

[14] Scheld's puzzling suggestion that Brunner is quite close to Chalcedon at this point in his development seems to rest on a misunderstanding of Brunner's concept of "symbol": Scheld, *Die Christologie Emil Brunners*, 87.

[15] Salakka, *Person und Offenbarung*, 38, 40. Brunner's undated *Habilitationsschrift* at Zurich (1915?) concerned "The Significance of H. Bergson for the Philosophy of Religion": Jehle, *Emil Brunner*, 64.

[16] Brunner scholarship is divided over the periodization of his theological development. Salakka – writing before the publication of Brunner's *Dogmatics* – suggested that three phases could be discerned: a "pre-critical" phase (1914–20), a "dialectical" phase (1921–8), and an "eristic" phase (1929–37). Others have added a fourth: his "dialogical" phase, which is best seen in his later writings, particularly his *Dogmatics*. See Roman Rössler, *Person und Glaube: Der Personalismus der Gottesbeziehung bei Emil Brunner*. Munich: Kaiser Verlag; Leopold, *Missionarische Theologie*.

[17] For some divergences at this point between Schleiermacher and Brunner, see Salakka, *Person und Offenbarung*, 46–7.

in Zurich, and served as interim pastor (*Vikar*) at Leutwil until April 1913, when he returned to Zurich to complete his academic studies and examinations. Although Karl Barth was pastor of the nearby village of Safenwil throughout Brunner's Leutwil period, there are no indications of any direct contact between them. On 31 July 1913, Brunner was examined on his thesis "Das Symbolische in der religiösen Erkenntnis" – published the following year under the same title – and graduated *summa cum laude*.

Brunner's sermons of this period clearly echo the themes of the religious socialism articulated by Ragaz. In a sermon of 12 January 1913, Brunner played down any thought of Christianity offering hope in the face of death; its primary role was to transform the situation of the living.

> When [Jesus] speaks about the "Kingdom of God", he is talking first of all about this side of things. He does not want to bring a trusting hope for those who are dying, but speaks about a great future for the living. To put it briefly, the "Kingdom of God" will come on this earth – not as a rapture [*Entrückung*] into a better world through the entry door of death, but as a transfiguration [*Umgestaltung*] of our earthly life.[18]

Brunner was succeeded at Leutwil by Eduard Thurneysen (1888–1974), who served as pastor in the community from 1913 to 1920.[19] Brunner's close friendship with Thurneysen began around this time. A significant correspondence developed, indicating a growing restlessness with some of the conventional theological wisdom of their age, catalysed to no small extent by the outbreak of the Great War in the late summer of 1914. It was during his period as pastor of Leutwil that Thurneysen developed a relationship with Barth, which would prove to be so theologically significant.

By the summer of 1913, Brunner was fully equipped to begin professional ministry in the Swiss Reformed church. Yet he chose not to do this, believing that his vocation as a theologian and churchman – the two were closely interlinked in his mind – demanded that he become proficient in the English language, not least in order to sustain and develop the contacts that he had made at the Oxford conference of 1909. In an unusual move, without any real parallel amongst his Swiss theological contemporaries, Brunner spent the academic year 1913–14 teaching French and Latin at high schools in England.

Brunner's first such appointment was at Winchester House School in Great Yarmouth, a port in the East Anglian county of Norfolk. This beautiful Victorian building was set in extensive grounds on a cliff top on England's east coast, with impressive views of the sandy bays around. Yet Brunner's experience at Great Yarmouth was not a success in terms of its academic

---

[18] Text in Jehle, *Emil Brunner*, 54.
[19] Thurneysen had previously served as assistant secretary of the Zurich YMCA (German: Christlicher Verein junger Menschen) from 1911 to 1913.

outcomes. Winchester House seemed more concerned about the reputation of its sports teams that its examination performances in either French or Latin.[20] In December 1913, Brunner wrote to Thurneysen, admitting that his time in Great Yarmouth had been something of a "fiasco".[21] He resigned, and moved to London to consider his next move. Undeterred by his earlier unhappy experience, Brunner managed to find another teaching position – this time, as a teacher of French at West Leeds High School in Yorkshire. This proved much more satisfactory.

Brunner found his time in England to be politically stimulating, bringing him into contact with leading British socialists such as the future British prime minister Ramsay MacDonald (1866–1937) and the future chancellor of the exchequer Philip Snowden (1864–1937). At the more intellectual level, Brunner was "particularly impressed" by the "Guild Socialism" then being articulated by the leading young Fabian theorist George Douglas Howard Cole (1889–1959).[22] He also became acquainted with the future archbishop of Canterbury, William Temple (1881–1944),[23] whom he met through the "Brotherhood Movement", a British form of Christian socialism which flourished in the years before the Great War.[24]

However, the outbreak of the Great War in August 1914 forced Brunner to return to Switzerland as quickly as possible. Having already undertaken military training in the infantry at Zurich in the late summer of 1909, he was placed on active service until early 1915. He was posted to the 69th Fusilier Battalion (*Füsilierbataillon*), which was stationed close to the French border.[25]

The Swiss Crisis of Identity, 1914–1919

It is impossible to make sense of the emerging theology of the three great Swiss Protestant theologians of the twentieth century – Brunner, Barth, and Thurneysen – without understanding the nature of the national crisis through which Switzerland passed during the years 1914–19. Switzerland had expanded its territory after the resolution of the chaos resulting from the Napoleonic wars by the Congress of Vienna (1815), adding the canton

---

[20] For the origins of this emphasis on sporting achievement, see J. A. Mangan, *Athleticism in the Victorian and Edwardian Public School: The Emergence and Consolidation of an Educational Ideology*. Portland, OR: Frank Cass, 2000.
[21] Jehle, *Emil Brunner*, 52.
[22] "Intellectual Autobiography", 7. On this approach to socialism, see A. W. Wright, *G. D. H. Cole and Socialist Democracy*. Oxford: Clarendon Press, 1979, 72–99.
[23] For Temple's later links with Brunner, see F. A. Iremonger, *William Temple: Archbishop of Canterbury. His Life and Letters*. Oxford: Oxford University Press, 1948, 370.
[24] Paul T. Phillips, *A Kingdom on Earth: Anglo-American Social Christianity, 1880–1940*. University Park, PA: Pennsylvania State University Press, 1996, 148.
[25] Jehle, *Emil Brunner*, 59.

The Origins of a Theological Mind, 1914–1924   7

of Geneva; it also reaffirmed its commitment to political and military neutrality within the new European order then in the process of emerging.[26] It had no desire to become entangled in future European wars.

This doctrine was reaffirmed with the outbreak of war between the European Great Powers in August 1914.[27] Switzerland may have affirmed its neutrality; this did not, however, safeguard its territorial integrity. Pre-war strategic analysis had made it clear that the small nation was vulnerable to opportunistic territorial annexation by France, Germany, or Italy. Its neutrality had to be enforced through military mobilization.

Although Switzerland remained neutral during the Great War, it was profoundly affected by the conflict. In the west, the peoples of the Suisse Romande felt a natural affinity with France; the sympathies of eastern Switzerland lay firmly with Germany.[28] The fault lines reflected deep convictions about cultural identity between France and Germany.[29] Tensions soared. There was an open recognition of a massive gulf between the German- and French-speaking communities, which might easily have led to permanent fissure and national disintegration. At times, it seemed as if the nation would split, with the German-speaking cantons siding with Germany, and their French-speaking counterparts with France.

This tension expressed itself within the Swiss Christian socialist movement. Two of its leading lights – Hermann Kutter and Leonhard Ragaz – took very different positions on the "German question". Kutter openly supported the German cause; Ragaz argued that Swiss Christians ought to oppose the war without taking sides, developing an anti-militarist theme that would recur in his later writings.[30]

The impact of the war on Swiss industry and commerce was devastating,[31] paving the way for industrial unrest. Food rationing had to be introduced in 1917. The national debt spiralled out of control. A national

---

[26] Edgar Bonjour, *Geschichte der schweizerischen Neutralität*. Basle: Helbing & Lichtenbahn, 1978, 37–41.
[27] For a critical account of this development, see Max Mittler, *Der Weg zum Ersten Weltkrieg: Wie neutral war die Schweiz? Kleinstaat und europäischer Imperialismus*. Zurich: Verlag NZZ, 2003, 357–61.
[28] Jeannine Luczak-Wild, "Als der Graben aufklaffte: Vermittlung zwischen Westschweiz und Deutschschweiz? Das Scheitern der *Internationalen Rundschau* 1915." *Schweizer Monatshefte für Politik, Wirtschaft, Kultur* 4 (1997): 39–44.
[29] Gerd Krumeich, "Ernst Lavisse und die Kritik an der deutschen Kultur, 1914–1918." In *Kultur und Krieg. Die Rolle der Intellektuellen, Künstler und Schriftsteller im Ersten Weltkrieg*, ed. Wolfgang Mommsen, 143–54. Munich: Oldenbourg, 1996.
[30] See Dittmar Rostig, *Bergpredigt und Politik: Zur Struktur und Funktion des Reiches Gottes bei Leonhard Ragaz*. Berne: Peter Lang, 1991.
[31] For the economic issues, see Roman Rossfeld and Tobias Straumann, eds., *Der vergessene Wirtschaftskrieg: Schweizer Unternehmen im Ersten Weltkrieg*. Zurich: Chronos Verlag, 2008. For its religious aspects, see Christine Nöthiger-Strahm, *Der deutsch-schweizerische Protestantismus und der Landestreik von 1918*. Berne: Peter Lang, 1981, 69–206.

8 The Origins of a Theological Mind, 1914–1924

strike was called in November 1918, raising serious fears of a Bolshevik-type revolution in Switzerland, and causing a crisis within Swiss socialism.[32] Serious economic difficulties were exacerbated by political tensions. For Brunner, as for many others, the imperial German war policy called into question the basis and legitimacy of culturally assimilated forms of Protestantism.[33] Karl Barth and Brunner alike regarded ethics as grounded in theology,[34] and interpreted the *ethical* failure of the German churches in encouraging war through a *Kriegstheologie* (which often seemed to reflect pagan rather than Christian themes) as ultimately a *theological* failure,[35] demanding a radical theological correction.[36] So what could be done to recover from this theological crisis? How could theology recover its vision? This sense of unease is evident in the preaching of Barth, Brunner, and Thurnseysen during this period, reflecting anxiety about the present situation and uncertainty about what lay ahead.[37]

During the Great War, Brunner served in various temporary positions, including assisting Hermann Kutter at the Neumünster in Zurich during the summer of 1915. Finally, Brunner was given his own pastoral respon-

---

[32] Markus Mattmüller, *Leonhard Ragaz und der religiöse Sozialismus: Eine Biographie*. 2 vols. Zurich: Evangelischer Verlag, 1957–68, vol. 2, 502–34. The writings of Barth, Brunner, and Thurneysen from this period suggest they saw this strike as a social and religious watershed, forcing reconsideration of earlier social and religious assumptions. Barth initially supported Ragaz, where Thurneysen supported Kutter: for the issues, see Barth's letter to Thurneysen of 8 March 1915: *Karl Barth–Eduard Thurneysen Briefwechsel*. 3 vols. Zurich: Theologischer Verlag, 1974, vol. 1, 33.

[33] The term *Kulturprotestantismus* is often used to refer to this phenomenon. Recent studies have raised questions about whether this term is misleading, and suggested that it ought to be used with caution when referring to Wilhelmine Germany: see especially Friedrich W. Graf, "Kulturprotestantismus: Zur Begriffsgeschichte einer theologischen Chiffre." *Archiv für Begriffsgeschichte* 27 (1984): 214–68; Gangolf Hübinger, *Kulturprotestantismus und Politik: Zum Verhältnis vom Liberalismus und Protestantismus im wilhelminischen Deutschland*. Tübingen: Mohr, 1994, 26–262.

[34] For the context, see Folkart Wittekind, *Geschichtliche Offenbarung und die Wahrheit des Glaubens: Der Zusammenhang von Offenbarungstheologie, Geschichtsphilosophie und Ethik bei Albrecht Ritschl, Julius Kaftan und Karl Barth (1909–1916)*. Tübingen: Mohr Siebeck, 2000.

[35] See especially Karl Hammer, *Deutsche Kriegstheologie, 1870–1918*. Munich: Deutscher Taschenbuch Verlag, 1971; Günter Brakelmann, *Protestantische Kriegstheologie im 1. Weltkrieg*. Witten: Luther Verlag, 1974. For Barth's concerns about the apparent theological endorsement of militarism and nationalism in 1914, see Arne Rasmusson, "Church and Nation-State: Karl Barth and German Public Theology in the Early 20th Century." *Nederduitse Gereformeerde Teologiese Tydskrif* 46 (2005): 511–24.

[36] For a good account of Barth's view of the relation of theology and ethics around this time, see John Webster, *Barth's Moral Theology: Human Action in Barth's Thought*. Edinburgh: T&T Clark, 1998, 11–39, challenging contemporary suggestions that "dialectical theology" was morally vacuous – as found, for example, in John Cullberg, *Das Problem der Ethik in der dialektischen Theologie*. Uppsala: Lundequist, 1938.

[37] See, for example, Thurneysen's 1917 sermon, speaking of a pervasive sense of dissatisfaction and restlessness, and uncertainty about the future: Karl Barth and Eduard Thurneysen, *Suchet Gott, so werdet ihr leben!* 2nd edn. Munich: Kaiser Verlag, 1928, 133.

sibility. He was installed as pastor of the mountain village of Obstalten in the canton of Glarus, in eastern Switzerland, on 13 February 1916. One of most significant developments for Brunner around this time was his engagement to Kutter's niece Margrit Lauterburg (1895–1979) in May 1917, followed by their church marriage in October of the same year at Bremgarten, a small town near Berne.[38]

Barth served as pastor in the village of Safenwil from 1911 to 1921, and was a close neighbour of Thurneysen. Although it is impossible to establish either the date or the location of Brunner's first meeting with Barth, circumstantial evidence suggests that this probably took place at Thurneysen's home in Leutwil in the middle of February 1916. Thurneysen and Barth had studied theology together at the University of Marburg during the period 1908–9, and had developed a close friendship.[39] The two remained in close contact throughout the 1910s, and regularly met up. Brunner's first letter to Barth is dated 1 April 1916, praising a sermon of Barth's, yet registering hesitation over some of its theological gambits. It was a pattern of affirmation mingled with reservation that would continue over the coming years.

Brunner and Dialectical Theology: The Origins of an Ambivalent Relationship

It would not be until 1920 that Brunner began what could legitimately be termed a "dialectical" phase in his theological development.[40] Before then, he is best seen as remaining within the pre-war theological liberal Protestant consensus, despite his growing misgivings about some of its assumptions, and his increasing willingness to explore alternatives – including the ideas beginning to be developed by Barth and Thurneysen.[41] Although a cooling of the friendship between Brunner and Thurneysen in early 1916 is suggested by a somewhat belated invitation to Brunner to attend Thurneysen's wedding,[42] it seems that by late 1918 Barth and Thurneysen had come to see Brunner as a useful dialogue partner in their theological discussions. He was someone who needed to be kept on side, even if there were questions about his commitment to their vision of "dialectical theology".[43] Setting the

---

[38] For Brunner's period at Obstalten, see Jehle, *Emil Brunner*, 69–85.
[39] Bruce L. McCormack, *Karl Barth's Critically Realistic Dialectical Theology: Its Genesis and Development, 1909–1936*. Oxford: Clarendon Press, 1997, 38.
[40] For his theological development during the period 1913–18, see Walter J. Hollenweger, "Wurzeln der Theologie Emil Brunners: Aus Brunners theologischer Entwicklung von ca. 1913 bis 1919." *Reformatio* 13, no. 12 (1963): 579–87.
[41] Gabriele Lunghini, *Emil Brunner*. Brescia: Editrice Morcelliana, 2009, 27–39.
[42] For an analysis of the changing relationship between Brunner and Thurneysen around this time, see Jehle, *Emil Brunner*, 107–14.
[43] John W. Hart, *Karl Barth vs. Emil Brunner: The Formation and Dissolution of a Theological Alliance, 1916–1936*. New York: Peter Lang, 2001, 11–20.

Barth–Brunner correspondence alongside the Barth–Thurneysen correspondence for the period 1916–20, it becomes clear that Barth and Thurneysen saw themselves as sharing common themes, which they increasingly considered Brunner to fail to grasp.

Yet despite this incomplete harmony the three young theologians agreed to set out what amounted to a common public theological programme at a series of lectures, given at Leutwil from 4 to 6 February 1917. Thurneysen intended these lectures for his congregation to be delivered by colleagues who were sympathetic to a "new way" of doing theology. This "Bible Week amongst the People", hosted by Thurneysen, was addressed by Brunner, Barth, and Gottlob Wieser (1888–1973) – all younger theologians, representing an emerging school of thought (at present, without any agreed name).

On Sunday 4 February, Brunner delivered the opening lecture, on "Awakening the Bible". Wieser's lecture, delivered the following day, dealt with the theme of "Hope in the Bible". On 6 February, Barth spoke on "The New World in the Bible". Barth's lecture, now widely seen as a manifesto for his reforming theological agenda, seems to have generated the most interest on the part of the audience.

In a letter of 17 January, Thurneysen had hinted that he would prefer Brunner's talk to be entitled "The Word of God in the Bible".[44] In the event, Brunner's address was somewhat critical of any such idea, preferring to speak of the "Spirit of the Bible" rather than the "Word of God". Echoing the pre-war approach of Ragaz, Brunner called on his audience to allow the Bible to inspire and empower them, leading to the transformation of society:

> What we need now is the Spirit of the Bible [*Bibelgeist*], not the sayings of the Bible [*Bibelsprüche*]; God, not statements of faith; power, not doctrines. This living word and living power are asleep in the Bible. But we must try to wake them up, to draw them out . . . If the Spirit of the Bible awakes within us, there would be an earthquake, compared with which all revolutions are but a children's game. And the end result would be the kingdom of God on earth, the rule of righteousness, truth, and love.[45]

Brunner's lecture helps us locate him on a theological map at this stage in his development, not least in relation to his explicit distancing of himself from excessively cognitive approaches to doctrine or the interpretation of the Bible. Yet his approach was not what Thurneysen hoped for, either pedagogically or theologically.[46] As he later remarked to Barth, not only had the audience found Brunner difficult to understand; his proposals stood at some distance from their own.

---

[44] Cited Jehle, *Emil Brunner*, 88 n. 9.
[45] Cited Jehle, *Emil Brunner*, 88.
[46] Thurneysen to Barth, 20 February 1917: *Karl Barth–Eduard Thurneysen Briefwechsel*, vol. 1, 175.

The truth of the matter is that Brunner did not see himself as part of any theological alliance or axis at this time. There never was any close relationship, personal or intellectual, with Barth. There was a friendship, certainly, reflected in Barth allowing Brunner to read his landmark Romans commentary in proof in November 1918. As a result, Brunner's review of the work was the first to be published, attracting considerable attention for that reason.[47] Brunner rightly declared that Barth's approach opened the way for a "theology focused on the Word of God".[48] Yet it is not entirely clear whether, and to what extent, Brunner himself wished to be aligned with the specifics of Barth's approach. In reviewing Barth's Romans commentary, Brunner – much to Barth's irritation – presented himself as a neutral assessor of its approach, not as one who himself espoused and advocated such a position.

The simple truth is that at this stage Brunner was finding his own way, trying to reconstruct his vision of theology in the light of the trauma of the Great War, and the deep and fundamental questions about theological method that this had raised in his mind.[49] Given that the cultural ideology of an earlier generation could not be sustained after the distress of the Great War, what was to replace it? How would this affect his reading of the Bible? Of the Reformed tradition? Of his theological mentors at Zurich? He welcomed the stimulus of others – such as the little volume of sermons by Barth and Thurneysen (1917)[50] – while declining to identify himself with them.

Brunner's writings of 1918–19 indicate two main concerns with the approach of Barth and Thurneysen. First, although there are clear signs that Brunner was beginning to appreciate the problems associated with subjectivist theological approaches by the beginning of 1918, he had no time for a simple inversion of such an approach, focusing on the alleged objectivity of divine revelation. In a letter to Thurneysen of January 1918 thanking him for the gift of a copy of *Suchet Gott*, Brunner expressed concerns about its "almost dangerously one-sided" approach, which seemed to him to

---

[47] "Der Römerbrief von Karl Barth", 29–32.
[48] For reflections on the origins and significance of such approaches to theology, see Dietrich Korsch, "Theologie als Theologie des Wortes Gottes: Eine programmatische Skizze." In *Transformationsprozesse des Protestantismus: Zur Selbstreflexion einer christlichen Konfession an der Jahrtausendwende*, ed. Martin Berger and Michael Murrmann-Kahl, 226–37. Gütersloh: Gütersloher Verlagshaus, 1999.
[49] For the impact of the Great War on European thought, see Dietrich Korsch, "La modernité comme crise: Stratégies conceptuelles en philosophie sociale et en théologie au sortir de la première guerre mondiale." In *La théologie en postmodernité. Actes du 3e Cycle de théologie systématique des Facultés de Théologie de Suisse Romande*, ed. Pierre Gisel and Patrick Evard, 33–63. Geneva: Labor et Fides, 1996.
[50] Karl Barth and Eduard Thurneysen, *Suchet Gott, so werdet ihr leben!* Berne: G. A. Bäschlin, 1917. Thurneysen presented Brunner with a copy of this book as a wedding present. This collection of essays includes Barth's "New World in the Bible", which is mistakenly dated to the autumn of 1916. Following the inclusion of this lecture in Barth's *Das Wort Gottes und die Theologie*, it was omitted from subsequent printings of the sermons.

rupture any links between God and human morality.⁵¹ For Brunner, there was a "little spark" of divine truth in the world, "a seed of believing objectivity". Hints of his later notion of the *Anknüpfungspunkt* are found here, in an emergent form.

Second, Brunner was puzzled by the elusive theological substance of slogans such as "let God be God". Such an emphasis on the absolute priority of God seemed to him to be unhelpfully abstract, lacking content. Could such an approach be anything other than a *critical tool*, countering what could now be recognized as an excessively culturally determined vision of theology? Its iconoclasm might help identify and eradicate false starts; but could it function as a positive and constructive foundation for a theological programme? Could it bear theological weight? Brunner indicated that he had experienced such problems with such theological slogans back in 1916, when trying to absorb the theological significance of Hermann Kutter's slogan *Gott machen lassen* ("letting God matter").⁵²

Brunner in America, 1919–1920

Although Brunner continued to socialize with Barth, Thurneysen, and Wieser, his own horizons were being extended following the end of the Great War, when international travel became possible once more. The ecumenical pioneer Adolf Keller (1872–1963), pastor of St Peter's, Zurich, recognized the importance of developing international connections between Switzerland and the United States as a means of encouraging theological reconstruction and ecclesial reconciliation. As a result of Keller's initiatives, in July 1919 Union Theological Seminary, New York, announced that a one-year fellowship to the value of $1,200 would be offered to an outstanding Swiss Protestant theologian. Leonhard Ragaz had no doubt that Brunner was the ideal candidate, not least on account of his fluency in English, and approached him. Would he accept the award if it was offered to him?

Union Theological Seminary was then one of the most prestigious Protestant institutes of theological education in the United States, with an international reputation. Although it had been founded as a Presbyterian seminary in 1836, a series of controversies in the late nineteenth century led to the school divesting itself of its denominational links, and becoming a non-denominational seminary.⁵³ Its move to Morningside Heights

---

[51] Letter to Eduard Thurneysen, 30 January 1918: *Karl Barth–Emil Brunner, Briefwechsel*, 17–21, especially 19. The letter would be forwarded to Barth. For an assessment of the Barth–Brunner correspondence, see John Hart, "The Barth–Brunner Correspondence." In *For the Sake of the Word: Karl Barth and the Future of Ecclesial Theology*, ed. George Hunsinger, 10–43. Grand Rapids, MI: Eerdmans, 2004.
[52] Letter to Karl Barth, 9 June 1916: *Karl Barth–Emil Brunner, Briefwechsel*, 5–7, especially 6.
[53] Robert T. Handy, *A History of Union Theological Seminary in New York*. New York: Columbia University Press, 1987, 121–57.

in 1908, next to Columbia University, gave it a new academic status. By 1921 many regarded Union as one of the premier institutions of theological education in the United States – a "theological university", as some of its distinguished faculty put it.

Brunner realized that exposure to American theology and church life would enhance his own intellectual development.[54] Yet despite the attractiveness of the possibility, he was hesitant. It would mean being absent from Switzerland for eight months. How would his congregation cope without him? His first son, Hans Heinrich, was only a year old, and his wife Margrit was expecting their second child around Christmas 1919. And in any case, what would he gain from studying at an American seminary? Yet all these objections were overcome. Margrit insisted he should go to America. An extraordinary meeting of the Obstalten congregation granted him leave of absence, and arranged for his pastoral responsibilities to be covered initially by Ernst Stähelin of Basle, and then by Max Vatter of Lucerne.

Brunner accepted the invitation. He sailed from Calais, and disembarked in New York on 14 September 1919. He later recalled that this visit to New York established important contacts that he would maintain for the remainder of his life.[55] Yet his experience of American culture and church life seem also to have brought home to him that the European experience could not be absolutized as a theological norm. America offered Brunner a critical perspective from which he could see the European situation. There was no "crisis" in America, paralleling that which had overwhelmed Europe in the immediate aftermath of the Great War.

By the early 1920s, American philosophers and theologians had come to take an optimistic attitude towards industrial progress, scientific advancement, the efficiency of large-scale organizations, and the increased benefits of technology. There was no sense of an economic or political "crisis" arising from the Great War. The conflict had had surprisingly little impact on American culture and thought in comparison with western Europe.[56] There were religious tensions within the American context; yet these were quite distinct from their counterparts in Germany and Switzerland, and would express themselves in the emergence of "Fundamentalism" in the 1920s. If there was a cultural crisis in America, this did not arise directly from the Great War, but from the Wall Street crash of October 1929.

Brunner, Barth, and Thurneysen: Continuing Debate

Brunner returned to Obstalten in the summer of 1920, and resumed his pastoral ministry on 6 June. On 29 August, Barth and Thurneysen, who

---

[54] For an excellent account of Brunner's period in America, see Jehle, *Emil Brunner*, 123–44.
[55] "Intellectual Autobiography", 8.
[56] Lynn Dumenil, *The Modern Temper: American Culture and Society in the 1920s*. New York: Hill & Wang, 1995, 145–200.

were vacationing at the Bergli, paid Brunner a visit at Obstalten, and arrived in time to hear him preach at the morning service. They pronounced themselves unimpressed by his sermon, declaring his preaching to be "cheap, psychological, boring, and churchy".[57] Brunner was taken aback by both the substance and tone of his visitors' comments. Although he was careful to frame his subsequent extended letter of response in terms of grateful appreciation of doubtless merited and helpful criticism,[58] Brunner seems to have been wounded rather than enriched by their reactions.

By late 1920, Brunner seems to have come to the conclusion that Barth's approach to theology was becoming increasingly radical, accentuating rather than alleviating his misgivings concerning what he regarded as its excessively negative and critical tone. On this return from America, Thurneysen drew Brunner's attention to two important lectures given by Barth during Brunner's absence, in which he had begun to speak of God as "wholly other".[59]

These theological trends were given definitive formulation in the second edition of Barth's *Romans* commentary (1922). In this radical revision of his 1919 work, Barth argued for an "infinite qualitative distinction" between time and eternity, and God and humanity. This notion of "distance" is expressed both ontologically and epistemologically: God is in heaven, and humanity on earth; God can only be known through a sovereign and free act of self-disclosure.[60]

Brunner was profoundly uneasy about these developments, particularly when he got round to reading Barth's review of Franz Overbeck. Although scholars sympathetic to Barth tend to present Brunner's response to Barth at this time as muddled and compromised, lacking the critical brilliance and insight they hold to be characteristic of Barth, there is another way of understanding things. Brunner believed that the emerging "dialectical theology" was iconoclastic, not constructive, and that it failed to recognize the moral and theological complexity of culture and religion. How could such

---

[57] Jehle, *Emil Brunner*, 165–6.
[58] Letter to Thurneysen and Barth, 2 September 1920: *Karl Barth–Emil Brunner, Briefwechsel*, 42–5, especially 43, "Euer Keulenschlag war für mich etwas schlechterdings Wertvolles." Brunner's description of their comments as a *Keulenschlag* ("being hit with a cudgel", or "a crushing blow") indicates the ferocity of their comments.
[59] Jehle, *Emil Brunner*, 158. The two lectures were "Der Christ in der Gesellschaft", given at Tambach in Thuringia, Germany, on 25 September 1919, and "Biblische Fragen, Einsichten, und Ausblicke", given at Aarau, the capital of the northern Swiss canton of Aargau, on 17 April 1920. The "Tambacher Rede" is now seen as a milestone on the road to the formation of the "Confessing Church" in the 1930s. For the texts, see Karl Barth, *Das Wort Gottes und die Theologie: Gesammelte Vorträge*. Munich: Kaiser Verlag 1925, 33–69, 70–98. Barth's important review of Franz Overbeck's *Christentum und Kultur* (1919) should also be noted, particularly his suggestion that theology needs to begin all over again.
[60] See the analysis in McCormack, *Karl Barth's Critically Realistic Dialectical Theology*, 241–90.

a theology be lived out in the world? Surely theology could be both critical and constructive? Surely the Christian gospel had something *positive* to say, rather than offering aggressive intellectual and cultural negations?

Brunner is often accused at this point of wanting to have it both ways – to say both "Yes" and "No". Yet his position is completely consistent and principled. For Brunner, theology is "critical" in that it offers a basis for judging all things, affirming some and rejecting others. By its very nature, it must say "Yes" in some cases, and "No" in others. This is not about inconsistency, nor does it betray a muddled or subjective eclecticism. Brunner's approach is similar to the strategy of "critical appropriation" advocated by writers such as Augustine of Hippo, as the early church wrestled with its relationship with Roman imperial culture. Brunner's strategy of critical appropriation came to be placed on an increasingly rigorous conceptual foundation in the mid-1930s – as, for example, in the "law of the closeness of relation" (*Gesetz der Beziehungsnähe*), which we will consider later (pp. 137–40).

In his critical letter of 2 September 1920 to Barth and Thurneysen, Brunner uses the analogy of a watchdog (*Hofhund*) to make the point that his own approach, based on Kant's critical philosophy, allows him to discriminate between friend and foe; in marked contrast, the "dialectical" approach sees everything as a threat.

> For Kant, the "No" is critical, i.e., like a watchdog which barks at everyone except its owners, who belong in the house. The dialectical watchdog barks at everyone as a matter of principle. But Kant gets results.[61]

More fundamentally, Brunner queried whether the notion of God as the "totally other" compromised the crucial theological insights of the biblical theme "the Word became Flesh".[62]

An interesting and important divergence can be seen at this point between Barth and Brunner over the manner in which the Danish existentialist philosopher Søren Kierkegaard is to be interpreted and theologically appropriated. At this point, Barth tended to emphasize the critical side of Kierkegaard's thought, as in the famous preface to the second edition of his *Romans* commentary (1922):

> If I have any "system", it is restricted to bearing in mind, as much as possible, what Kierkegaard called the "infinite qualitative distinction" between time and eternity, in its negative and positive aspects. "God is in heaven, and you

---

[61] Letter to Thurneysen and Barth, 2 September 1920: *Karl Barth–Emil Brunner, Briefwechsel*, 42–53, especially 44. Brunner's important distinction in this letter between "Hofhund" and "Haushund" is difficult to render in English.

[62] Letter to Thurneysen and Barth, 2 September 1920: *Karl Barth–Emil Brunner, Briefwechsel*, 45.

are on earth." For me, the relation of this God and this person, the relation of this person and this God, is, in a nutshell, the theme of the Bible and the totality of philosophy.[63]

Brunner, in contrast, highlighted Kierkegaard's emphasis on the "subjective" aspects of truth, seeing this as an important corrective to purely objective understandings of the nature of theology.[64] Brunner's "dialogical" approach to theology, which attempted to provide a theological defence and contextualization for affirming both objectivity and subjectivity, can be seen as being partly rooted in his reading of Kierkegaard.[65]

Yet despite these clear points of divergence, both in theological substance and their reading of Kierkegaard, Brunner continued to engage in dialogue with Barth and his circle – including Friedrich Gogarten (1887–1967) – even though he was conscious of being seen, at least in some respects, as an outsider. His relationship with Thurneysen became formal and cool; at one point, the two did not correspond for over four months.[66] Yet Barth seems to have respected Brunner enough to allow him to see drafts of the revised version of his *Romans* commentary as early as May 1921,[67] which clearly stimulated Brunner in his attempt to forge his own approach. Barth, however, does not appear to have found Brunner stimulating; indeed, he eventually came to the view that he was simply wasting time in engaging him. With the benefit of hindsight, Barth later realized that he ought probably to have engaged more thoroughly and critically with Gogarten at this formative stage in his development.[68]

The Quest for Recognition: *Erlebnis, Erkenntnis und Glaube* (1921–2)

The published version of Brunner's *Erlebnis, Erkenntnis und Glaube* ("Experience, Knowledge and Faith") was completed in September 1921. An earlier version of this work, with the same title, was submitted to the

---

[63] Karl Barth, *Römerbrief*. 8th edn. Zurich: Zollikon, 1947, xiii. Barth's attitude to Kierkegaard is complex and ambivalent. For comment, see Lee C. Barrett, "Karl Barth: The Dialectic of Attraction and Repulsion." In *Kierkegaard's Influence on Theology: 1 – German Protestant Theology*, ed. Jon Stewart, 1–41. Aldershot: Ashgate, 2012; Philip G. Ziegler, "Barth's Criticisms of Kierkegaard: A Striking Out at Phantoms?" *International Journal of Systematic Theology* 9, no. 4 (2007): 434–45.
[64] See the 1930 essay "Die Botschaft Sören Kierkegaards": *Ein offenes Wort*, vol. 1, 209–26, especially 217–18.
[65] Curtis L. Thompson, "Emil Brunner: Polemically Promoting Kierkegaard's Christian Philosophy of Encounter." In *Kierkegaard's Influence on Theology: 1*, ed. Stewart, 65–103.
[66] For the points of tension, see Jehle, *Emil Brunner*, 168–70.
[67] Letter to Barth, 12 May 1921: *Karl Barth–Emil Brunner, Briefwechsel*, 58–9.
[68] Karl Barth, letter to Friedrich Schmid, 14 August 1964: Karl Barth, *Briefe, 1961–1968*. Zurich: Theologischer Verlag, 1975, 264.

Zurich Cantonal Directorate of Higher Education on 3 February 1921 as the basis of Brunner's second attempt at *Habilitation* – being allowed to teach or supervise research for the University of Zurich Faculty of Theology. This normally required the submission of a *Habilitationsschrift* – an independently produced piece of research, which would be defended before a panel of academic judges. The *Habilitation*, which has no direct equivalent in the British or North American university systems, can be thought of as a second academic dissertation, establishing a scholar's professional credentials for university teaching and research. Brunner's hopes of a future academic career depended on this work being well received.

Brunner's first (and unsuccessful) attempt to secure *Habilitation* took place in July 1915. Encouraged by Leonhard Ragaz, Brunner reworked his *Symbolische in der religiösen Erkenntnis* to serve as a *Habilitationsschrift* on the theme of "The Significance of Henri Bergson for the Philosophy of Religion".[69] Brunner seems to have assumed that his application to the Zurich Faculty of Theology *pro venia legendi* (a Latin phrase probably best rendered as "for permission to lecture") would be unproblematic. Yet Ragaz soon discovered that his colleagues at Zurich regarded any such move on Brunner's part as premature. There was clear resistance to allowing Brunner to teach on behalf of the Faculty. Some of Ragaz's colleagues had concerns about what they regarded as a superficial approach to theological issues. On 28 September 1915, Ragaz wrote a somewhat awkward letter to his protégé, suggesting that the time might not be quite right for Brunner to proceed with his case. Might it not benefit from further reflection and preparation?

Having waited more than five years, Brunner believed it was time to try again. Once more, Ragaz attempted to smooth the way for his protégé – this time, with greater (but not total) success. On 12 May 1921 Brunner wrote to Barth to inform him that his *Habilitationsschrift* had been accepted. "Yesterday I finally had notification that the Faculty at Zurich have accepted my *Habilitation*, although in the face of strong opposition from a minority."[70]

Yet the *Habilitationsschrift* was a necessary, but not a sufficient, condition for being allowed to lecture or supervise students at Zurich. The Faculty of Theology had to be satisfied on other grounds. And there was a problem. Brunner had made himself a controversial figure at Zurich, partly on account of an article he had published in 1920, calling into question the methods of academic theology and its relevance for clergy.

Although Brunner had originally suggested the somewhat pedestrian title "The Theological Preparation of Clergy and the Question of the Reform of the Theological Curriculum" for this three-page article, the editor of the journal to which he submitted it changed it to the somewhat more

---

[69] Jehle, *Emil Brunner*, 62–7.
[70] Letter to Barth, 12 May 1921: *Karl Barth–Emil Brunner, Briefwechsel*, 58.

provocative "The Poverty of Theology".[71] In this paper, Brunner made some fundamental criticisms of academic theology in relation to the needs of pastors, focusing especially on epistemological questions, such as the dangers of a false objectification of knowledge. Yet it seems to have been the title as much as the substance of the article that rankled some at Zurich – especially the New Testament scholar Paul Wilhelm Schmiedel (1851–1935) and the church historian Walther Köhler (1870–1946), both of whom were widely regarded as representing the classic liberal theology that had hitherto dominated Zurich's faculty of theology.[72]

Schmiedel and Köhler produced a highly critical minority report, alleging Brunner's work to be full of "misjudgements", to lack familiarity with recent developments in the philosophy of method, and to be disproportionately biased towards American scholarship.[73] Yet five of the seven faculty members appointed to reach a decision on the matter supported Brunner, even if they did so with qualifications, including concerns about the clarity of his writing. In the end, the decision was taken: Brunner would be granted *venia legendi* at the Zurich Faculty of Theology with effect from the academic year 1921–2.

We must linger over that criticism that Brunner made too much use of American scholarship in his *Habilitationsschrift*. The real issue seems to have concerned Brunner's interest in the "psychology of religion", a discipline which is widely conceded to have its origins in the United States in the final decades of the nineteenth century.[74] What seems to have irritated some of the Faculty of Theology at Zurich was that Brunner's criticisms of Schleiermacher were not primarily based on a detailed analysis of German-language theology and philosophy but on some empirical findings, derived from American psychology of religion, which called into question the reliability of Schleiermacher's approach. The problem was not that Schleiermacher was being criticized, but that he was being criticized on the basis of work that was, in the first place, *American*, and in the second, *empirical*.

Given the importance of this point, we must give further thought to Brunner's encounter with the psychology of religion during his time at Union Theological Seminary in the academic year 1919–20.

Brunner and American Psychology of Religion

It is clear that Brunner conceived at least some of the themes of *Erlebnis, Erkenntnis und Glaube* during his time at Union Theological Seminary.

---

[71] "Das 'Elend der Theologie'." The title parodies Karl Marx's *Das Elend der Philosophie* ("The Poverty of Philosophy"), first published in German in 1885.
[72] Jehle, *Emil Brunner*, 170–3.
[73] Jehle, *Emil Brunner*, 171.
[74] For its cultural significance, see Robert C. Fuller, "American Psychology and the Religious Imagination." *Journal of the History of the Behavioral Sciences* 42, no. 3 (2006): 221–35.

Brunner's critique of Schleiermacher's "psychologism" is partly based on the views of American psychologists of religion,[75] especially George Albert Coe (1862–1951), whom Brunner encountered at Union Theological Seminary.[76] In a letter of 8 October 1919, Brunner declared that the psychology of religion was the "most original" contribution that America had to offer modern theology.[77] He actively sought to pursue further studies under Coe's direction.

In early February 1920, he wrote to his wife telling her that, under Coe's direction, he had now acquired the resources he needed to begin his project.[78] It was not so much that Brunner believed that Coe could help him develop psychological resources to criticize the (somewhat tenuous) empirical foundations of Schleiermacher's notion of "feeling";[79] it was more that the sources that Coe encouraged him to read and study – such as William James (1842–1910) – seemed to Brunner to indicate the inevitable outcome of any psychological approach to religion: the elimination of distinctively Christian ideas about "God" in favour of loose talk about a generic notion of "the divine".

By this time, William James had a commanding reputation in Europe.[80] His works had been translated into German, and discussed at the International Congress of Philosophy at Heidelberg in September 1908.[81] While European scholarly interest focused mainly on James's pragmatic conception of truth, at least some of the wider implications of his psychological approach appear to have been appreciated.

Yet many would argue that G. Stanley Hall (1844–1924) did far more to establish the professional academic credentials of the discipline in the United States.[82] Hall's student James H. Leuba (1867–1946) published numerous articles and four books on the psychology of religion, and used his editorship of the *Psychological Bulletin* to ensure that articles concerning this field were published regularly. By the end of the Great War the psychology of religion was well established in American academic life, and

---

[75] See, for example, *Erlebnis, Erkenntnis und Glaube*, 52–3.
[76] Jehle, *Emil Brunner*, 135–8.
[77] Jehle, *Emil Brunner*, 136.
[78] Jehle, *Emil Brunner*, 137.
[79] There has been sporadic scholarly interest in Coe in recent years: see, for example, Ian Nicholson, "Academic Professionalization and Protestant Reconstruction, 1890–1902: George Albert Coe's Psychology of Religion." *Journal of the History of Behavioral Sciences* 30, no. 4 (1994): 348–68.
[80] Jaime Nubiola, "The Reception of William James in Continental Europe." *European Journal of Pragmatism and American Philosophy* 3, no. 1 (2011): 73–85.
[81] Theodor Elsenhans, *Bericht über den III. Internationalen Kongress für Philosophie zu Heidelberg, 1. bis 5. September 1908*. Heidelberg: Winter, 1909.
[82] Hendrika vande Kemp, "G. Stanley Hall and the Clark School of Religious Psychology." *American Psychologist* 47, no. 2 (1992): 290–8; Sheldon H. White, "G. Stanley Hall: From Philosophy to Developmental Psychology." *Developmental Psychology* 28, no. 1 (1992): 25–34.

was having a growing influence in mainline denominational seminaries. By the end of the 1920s, the movement was in decline, partly due to the growing influence of behaviorism.[83] Brunner studied in America when the movement was at its peak.

In the 1920s, Union Theological Seminary represented something of a theological laboratory, fusing together some traditional – and also some highly redacted – themes of Protestant theology with the pragmatism of William James and John Dewey. Dietrich Bonhoeffer (1906–45), who spent the academic year 1930–1 as a Sloan Fellow at Union, was puzzled, and even a little disturbed, by the dominance of pragmatic conceptions of truth, and their somewhat uncritical theological appropriation in the seminary.

> The destruction of philosophy as the question of truth, and its recasting as a positive individual discipline with practical goals – as most radically carried through by Dewey – alters the heart of the concept of scholarship, and truth as the absolute norm of all thinking is restricted by what proves to be "useful in the long run." Thinking is essentially teleological, aimed at serving life.[84]

This development was almost certainly under way during Brunner's time there, a decade earlier. Yet he makes little reference to it, apart from noting the general American tendency to emphasize practice over theory – a theme he would return to during his 1928 Swander Lectures at Lancaster Theological Seminary (see pp. 54–60).

The primary source for Brunner's reflections in *Erlebnis, Erkenntnis und Glaube* appears to have been Coe's *Psychology of Religion* (1916).[85] This standard text was widely used in American seminaries and colleges at this time, including Coe's own Union Theological Seminary. While Brunner clearly found much in this work to arouse his suspicions, he also found much to ponder, including Coe's analysis of the "social immediacy" of religion.[86] Negatively, Brunner reacted against what he regarded as the reductionism of this approach; positively, it brought home to him the distinctiveness of religion as a human phenomenon, and the importance of the theme of the "self-finding of the 'I' in the 'Thou'" (*das Sichfinden des Ich im Du*).[87] This emergent insight, only partly explored in *Erlebnis, Erkenntnis und Glaube*, required a more robust intellectual framework if it was to be

---

[83] Benjamin Beit-Hallahmi, "Psychology of Religion 1880–1930: The Rise and Fall of a Psychological Movement." *Journal of the History of the Behavioral Sciences* 10 (1974): 84–90. The movement recovered in the 1950s: see Kate M. Loewenthal, *The Psychology of Religion: A Short Introduction*. Boston, MA: Oneworld Publications, 2000, 6–11.

[84] Dietrich Bonhoeffer, "Report on My Year of Study at Union Theological Seminary in New York, 1930/1." In *Works*, vol. 10: *Barcelona, Berlin, New York: 1928–1931*, 305–22. Minneapolis, MN: Fortress Press, 2008; quote at 310–11.

[85] George Albert Coe, *The Psychology of Religion*. Chicago: University of Chicago Press, 1916. See *Erlebnis, Erkenntnis und Glaube*, 52–3.

[86] Coe, *The Psychology of Religion*, 246–62. See *Erlebnis, Erkenntnis und Glaube*, 53.

[87] Coe, *The Psychology of Religion*, 246–62. See *Erlebnis, Erkenntnis und Glaube*, 53.

developed further; Brunner would develop such a conceptual scaffolding a few years later through engaging Kierkegaard, Ferdinand Ebner (1882–1931), and Martin Buber (1878–1965).

The published version of Brunner's *Erlebnis, Erkenntnis und Glaube* (1922) was widely read, and attracted considerable attention, going through five editions. Brunner here offered a highly critical account of "earlier half-truths", aiming to retain what was valid in earlier approaches, and reject what was not, before coming to his final conclusion – namely, that some understanding of the "pure objectivity" (*reine Sachlichkeit*) of faith was fundamental to both theology and apologetics.[88] For Brunner, theology had to move on from Schleiermacher and Ritschl, and even more from the trends that he regarded as having so impoverished and misled theology in recent years: its historical relativism, its mysticism, Romanticism, and obsession with the "kingdom of God".[89] While some might feel that Brunner's critique of Schleiermacher and Ritschl is unduly dependent on Paul Natorp's neo-Kantianism at points, there is no doubt that Brunner has distanced himself from the hitherto dominant Schleiermachean tradition.

Although *Erlebnis, Erkenntnis und Glaube* was based on Brunner's *Habilitationsschrift*, submitted in the first half of 1921, the published version reflects a knowledge of two seminal works of the "dialectical movement", which Brunner read after completing the first version of the typescript – the second edition of Barth's *Romans* commentary, and Gogarten's *Die religiöse Entscheidung* ("The Religious Decision").[90] Brunner was clear that his developing views were not caused by his reading of such works, but that they represented parallel developments. His theological development was that of independent alignment with the emerging "dialectical theology" movement, not of being its "follower".

It is far from clear that *Erlebnis, Erkenntnis und Glaube* is a work of "dialectical theology". Barth and Brunner both criticized Schleiermacher; despite occasional convergence, however, the essential points of their criticisms were somewhat different. In particular, Brunner's criticisms of "psychologism" reflect a first-hand knowledge of American psychology of religion which is quite absent from Barth. Yet the difference between Barth and Brunner which is most evident relates not to their critique of Schleiermacher, but to their proposals for a positive alternative. Brunner remained convinced that Barth and Gogarten offered only a "No", where a partial "Yes" was clearly required.

Karl Barth had meantime left his pastoral ministry in Safenwil, having been appointed to a full-time position as Professor of Reformed Theology

---

[88] *Erlebnis, Erkenntnis und Glaube*, 89.
[89] *Erlebnis, Erkenntnis und Glaube*, 90. See particularly Coe's discussion of the differentiation of human experience into "I's" and "thou's" through social dynamics, enabling the affirmation of both: Coe, *The Psychology of Religion*, 256.
[90] *Erlebnis, Erkenntnis und Glaube*, iv.

at the University of Göttingen in Germany.[91] Brunner's role at Zurich, however, was more of an adjunct position. He remained as pastor of Obstalten, while becoming involved to a limited extent in the teaching and research of Zurich's Faculty of Theology. Brunner's correspondence of the period suggests he developed a sense of isolation in his rural parish, speaking of his "Obstalten Patmos", or his "long wait in Glarus".[92] Lacking a physical community of scholars with whom he could interact, he was forced to read books, and engage in discussion through correspondence.

The Limits of Humanity: Reflections on Revelation and Reason (1922)

Nevertheless, Brunner made the most of his situation. In May 1922 he delivered his *Habilitationsvorlesung* – his inaugural lecture as a *Privatdozent*. He used this lecture – entitled *Die Grenzen der Humanität* ("The Limits of Humanity") – to probe some aspects of his emerging understanding of theology. For Brunner, the limits of humanity are reflected in what can be known of God. His theme, although framed anthropologically, is actually about the need for revelation. A properly biblical theology, he argued, as reflected in the writings of the Protestant reformers, "is not orientated towards experience, nor towards humanity, but towards God".[93]

Brunner argued that the "crisis of humanity" is such that the grounds of true knowledge lie outside and beyond us. Human thought is ultimately an "after-thinking" (*Nachdenken*) that is determined and justified through a "pre-thinking" (*Vordenken*) that lies beyond us. We must, he insisted, recognize that a *Logos* underlies our own reasoning – a *Logos* that we do not establish and control, but which rather, as the "origin of all thought and existence", grounds and directs us.[94] The ultimate foundation and criterion of human thought lies beyond us, and is not subject to our control.

Knowledge of God therefore has a transcendent origin and foundation; it is something that must be mediated to us. Accentuating the "distance" between God and humanity, Brunner declared the centrality of the concept of revelation. What humanity could not know and could not achieve was disclosed by God.

---

[91] For the theological context Barth now encountered through this new position, see the masterly survey of Friedrich Wilhelm Graf, "Protestantische Universitätstheologie in der Weimarer Republik." In *Der heilige Zeitgeist: Studien zur Ideengeschichte der protestantischen Theologie in der Weimarer Republik*, 1–110. Tübingen: Mohr Siebeck, 2011.
[92] See his letter to Barth of 9 June 1923: *Karl Barth–Emil Brunner, Briefwechsel*, 73.
[93] *Grenzen der Humanität*, 7.
[94] *Grenzen der Humanität*, 12.

In this eternal instant, in this absolute moment the impossible happens, the wonder of faith. Here the barriers of time were broken down, here God – not humanity – speaks and acts.[95]

The idea of a "sense of distance" (*Distanzpathos*) is central to Brunner's analysis at this point.[96] "We gain a standpoint on the far side of humanity precisely because we recognize its distance, with unconditional awe and absolute pathos."[97] God's self-revelation allows human nature and culture to be "seen from there" (*von dorther gesehen*). It is the flash of light which shows us up as we really are. It is "divine illumination, not human knowledge", giving us an objective and external perspective on our own situation.

Yet even at this stage there is a clear divergence between Brunner, on the one hand, and Barth and Gogarten on the other. For Brunner, it is not enough to declare that "God speaks". Once the debate over the *possibility* of revelation is settled, the issue of its *substance* must be engaged. The question of the content of that speech is significant. It is indeed important that God speaks; but what does God say? To use a metaphor favoured by Brunner in *Der Grenzen der Humanität*, the flash of divine revelation is not merely something that is itself *seen*; it is something that makes it possible for humanity to *see*. Revelation discloses the way things really are. It allows us to see our world and ourselves from the divine perspective. Sometimes it may abolish false understandings, and demand that we say "No" to certain cultural norms or philosophical fashions – and here Brunner echoes Barth. But it also establishes the truth about things, offering a positive foundation for theological construction and cultural engagement. Revelation is about a divine "No" *and* a divine "Yes".

It is quite clear from the correspondence between Barth and Brunner, and from an examination of their published writings from 1919 onwards, that it is not correct to speak of the "development" or "emergence" of differences between the two thinkers – for example, during the important period 1929–31.[98] The two writers had quite distinct approaches to theology

---

[95] *Grenzen der Humanität*, 15.
[96] This idea – alternatively expressed as *Pathos der Distanz* – is an important theme in Nietzsche's philosophical writings, where it articulates primarily the distinction between those who rule, and those who are ruled: Volker Gerhardt, *Pathos und Distanz: Studien zur Philosophie Friedrich Nietzsches*, Stuttgart: Reclam, 1988, 5. It is easy to see how this notion could be transposed to articulate the "distance" between God and humanity. See further Peter Köster, "Nietzsche-Kritik und Nietzsche-Rezeption in der Theologie des 20. Jahrhunderts." *Nietzsche-Studien* 10/11 (1982): 615–85.
[97] *Grenzen der Humanität*, 14. Similar comments about the "pathos of distance" can be seen elsewhere in his writings at this time – for example, "Das Grundproblem der Philosophie bei Kant und Kierkegaard", 33–4.
[98] As rightly pointed out by both McCormack, *Karl Barth's Critically Realistic Dialectical Theology*, 327–74, and Hart, *Karl Barth vs. Emil Brunner*, especially 204–17.

from the outset. These differences still allowed them to collaborate programmatically in combating certain theological trends they both regarded as unacceptable, not least those which compromised their mutual insistence that "God is God". Yet such convergences often turn out to be opportunistic, lacking any grounding in a consistent and coherent shared vision of the nature and tasks of theology. They are to be seen as a critique of mutual enemies rather than an affirmation of a shared theological platform.

Furthermore, the term "dialectical theology" was used in several different senses by those emphasizing the priority of divine revelation.[99] It is historically improper to suggest that Barth was the proper claimant to the notion of "dialectical theology", with others deviating from, or fundamentally misunderstanding, its essential content. From the outset, "dialectical theology" was a porous concept, open to different ways of interpretation, both intellectually (in terms its core methods or ideas) and sociologically (in terms of who made up the circle of "dialectical theologians").[100] Paul Schempp (1900–59), for example, wrote of his perception of a "front" of dialectical theologians in 1928, whose leading members were Karl Barth, Emil Brunner, Rudolf Bultmann, and Friedrich Gogarten.[101] Theophil Steinmann similarly grouped Barth, Brunner, and Gogarten together, while recognizing that there were some significant points of divergence between them.[102] At this stage, "dialectical theology" was a socially negotiated, as much as a theologically determined, notion.[103] And, as we shall see, many chose to adopt Brunner's version of the notion – not least in the English-speaking world – unaware that this was actually a specific way of understanding the notion, which did not command universal assent with the movement.

The inherent theological tension between Brunner and Barth was unquestionably compounded by personal differences. Brunner, for example, was much more willing to seek common ground, both in his dialogue with other

---

[99] For a contemporary reflection on such terms, and their theological implications, see Ernst Neubauer, "Die Theologie der 'Krisis' und des 'Wortes': Ihre allgemeinen Voraussetzungen und Prinzipien." *Zeitschrift für Theologie und Kirche* 7 (1926): 1–36.

[100] For the complex reception history of this notion, see Dietrich Korsch, "Ein großes Mißverständnis: Die Rezeptionsgeschichte der eigentlichen 'dialektischen Theologie' Karl Barths." In *Karl Barth im europäischen Zeitgeschehen (1935–1950): Widerstand – Bewährung – Orientierung*, ed. Michael Beintker, Christian Link, and Michael Trowitzsch, 347–61. Zurich: Theologischer Verlag, 2010.

[101] Paul Schempp, "Randglossen zum Barthianismus." *Zwischen den Zeiten* 6 (1928): 529–39.

[102] Theophil Steinmann, "Zur Auseinandersetzung mit Gogarten, Brunner, und Barth." *Zeitschrift für Theologie und Kirche* 10 (1929): 220–37, 452–70.

[103] See Rudolf Bultmann, "Die liberale Theologie und die jüngste theologische Bewegung." *Theologische Blätter* 3 (1924): 73–86. Bultmann's reviews, especially of the second edition of Barth's *Römerbrief*, provide an illuminating account of his attitudes towards the movement: Matthias Dreher, *Rudolf Bultmann als Kritiker in Seinen Rezensionen und Forschungsberichten*. Münster: LIT Verlag, 2005, 151–86.

theologians and with representatives of secular culture. This willingness to accommodate – though within limits – is also evident at several points in the early 1920s, when Brunner appears to make use of some decidedly Barthian rhetoric in his writings, without actually commending or adopting Barth's theology. It is arguable that these tensions were only manifested – for they were not caused – by the appearance of Brunner's *Mediator* in 1927, when Brunner's positive exposition of his vision of theology enabled the fault lines with Barth to be more clearly discerned.

The Critique of Schleiermacher: *Die Mystik und das Wort* (1924)

Yet Brunner was not yet ready to begin to construct his own positive theology at this stage in 1923. Demolition work still remained to be done. He planned a "new attack" against the theology of Schleiermacher, seeing this as the final preparatory step for his own theological reformulation and repositioning. The resulting work, published in 1924, under the title *Die Mystik und das Wort* ("Mysticism and the Word"),[104] is a somewhat disappointing work, whose polemical agenda leads to oversimplifications which reduce its value as a serious piece of theological analysis.

Brunner's stated object in writing this work was "to uncover the opposition between what Schleiermacher aimed to articulate and the faith-world of the apostles and Reformers; the inner impossibility of an alliance between every kind of a mystical philosophy of immanence and the Christianity of the Bible". For Brunner, there were only two possibilities: "either Christ or modern religion".[105] Brunner here deploys a somewhat problematic dichotomist mode of analysis to assess theological strategies, in effect reducing these to what he considers as the biblically based Christianity of the Reformation and the subjectivist turn of modern religion, exemplified by Schleiermacher, which conceives divine immanence in mystical terms, and locates it in the immediacy of self-consciousness. For Brunner, such a "religion of feeling" (*Gefühlsreligion*) is ultimately nothing more than paganism.[106]

Brunner can be seen as partly echoing an established tradition of criticism of Schleiermacher's mystical turn. A. B. Ritschl, for example, was severely critical of those who allowed mysticism or metaphysics to intrude into theology.[107] Yet it is hard to avoid the conclusion that Brunner's polemical

---

[104] Lunghini, *Emil Brunner*, 39–45.
[105] *Die Mystik und das Wort*, 10.
[106] *Die Mystik und das Wort*, 386–7.
[107] Albrecht B. Ritschl, *Theologie und Metaphysik: Zur Verständigung und Abwehr*. 2nd edn. Bonn: Adolph Marcus, 1887. Max Reischle, *Ein Wort zur Controverse über die Mystik in der Theologie*. Freiburg im Breisgau: J. C. B. Mohr, 1886.

context of the early 1920s has shaped his analysis,[108] leading to a full frontal assault on Schleiermacher, when a more scholarly and reflective analysis would have been more productive and persuasive.[109] As Christine Helmer rightly points out, Brunner's criticism of mysticism actually reflects a lingering philosophical pre-commitment on his part – namely, a neo-Kantian trajectory deriving from Natorp and others, that "problematizes mysticism in the context of the neo-Kantian distinction between nature and spirit".[110]

It is also questionable whether Brunner's pitting of a "biblical-Reformation" conception of "faith" against Schleiermacher's category of "religion" is quite as straightforward as Brunner indicates, partly because it is not an appropriate or plausible comparison. Why did not Brunner compare what Calvin says about *fides* with what Schleiermacher says about *Glaube*? Or Schleiermacher's view of *Religion* or *Frömmigkeit* with Calvin's view of *pietas*?[111] Brunner's critique of Schleiermacher is clearly dogmatic, not historical, and seems curiously inattentive to the specific intellectual backdrop against which Schleiermacher developed his approach.

Despite the shallowness of his critique of Schleiermacher, Brunner's *Mystik und das Wort* articulated a fundamental distinction that would remain central to his theological development: namely, that there are only two ways of conceiving the relationship between God and humanity. This relationship either begins with humanity, and reaches out to God, which Brunner holds to be the way of philosophy; or it begins with God, who reaches out to humanity, which is the way of revelation.[112]

Brunner's thinking at this point was catalysed by his reading of Ferdinand Ebner's *Das Wort und die geistigen Realitäten* ("The Word and Spiritual Realities") in February 1922, a year after its publication, when it was recommended to him by Paul Walser, a pastor in the eastern Swiss village of

---

[108] See the points made by Stephan Gratzel, "L'importance de la théologie dialectique pour la philosophie de l'existence." In *Mythe et philosophie: Les traditions bibliques*, ed. Christian Berner and Jean-Jacques Wunenburger, 229–35. Paris: Presses Universitaires de France, 2002.
[109] This was Barth's conclusion: Karl Barth, "Brunners Schleiermacher-Buch." *Zwischen den Zeiten* 8 (1924): 49–64.
[110] Christine Helmer, "Mysticism and Metaphysics: Schleiermacher and a Historical-Theological Trajectory." *Journal of Religion* 83, no. 4 (2003): 517–38. Brunner, of course, had distanced, perhaps even dissociated, himself from neo-Kantianism in the 1923 article "Das Grundproblem der Philosophie bei Kant und Kierkegaard."
[111] See this comparison in Brian A. Gerrish, "From Calvin to Schleiermacher: The Theme and Shape of Christian Dogmatics." In *Continuing the Reformation: Essays on Modern Religious Thought*. Chicago: University of Chicago Press, 1993, 178–95, especially 180–1. See also the general study of Paul E. Capetz, *Christian Faith as Religion: A Study in the Theologies of Calvin and Schleiermacher*. Lanham, MD: University Press of America, 1998.
[112] See, for example, the clear formulation of this point in the 1925 essay "Gesetz und Offenbarung: Eine theologische Grundlegung", 53–4.

Hundwil.¹¹³ A year later, Brunner wrote to Ebner, thanking him for writing the book, explaining how it had helped him develop "greater clarity" in his thinking about Christ. Perhaps most importantly, it helped him distinguish *die Mystik* from *das Wort*, thus allowing him to develop a more sustained critique of Schleiermacher and his legacy than otherwise would have been possible.

By now, Brunner's theological programme was gaining wider attention internationally. In 1924, Hugh Ross Mackintosh (1870–1936), Professor of Christian Dogmatics at New College, Edinburgh, reviewed both *Erlebnis, Erkenntnis und Glaube* and *Die Mystik und das Wort*, suggesting that they marked the emergence of a new school of theology, capable of challenging and possibly overthrowing the predominant Ritschlian paradigm.¹¹⁴ He singled out four representatives of this school – Barth, Brunner, Gogarten, and Kutter – while indicating his own view that Brunner was the most important. Brunner's tone, Mackintosh felt, was unfortunately and unnecessarily shrill and loud. Perhaps, he suggested, "Brunner felt he could only get a hearing for certain truths by uttering them at the top of his voice." While Brunner offered what seemed to Mackintosh to be a "one-sided picture", it was painted with such "emphatic colours" that it could not but "catch the eye". It was only a matter of time, he suggested, before this picture was expanded and solidified.

By the time this review was published in December 1924, Brunner's life had taken a new turn, allowing him the opportunity to do what Mackintosh rightly discerned to be necessary. On 7 February 1924, Brunner was formally invited to accept the chair of systematic and practical theology at the University of Zurich.¹¹⁵ Brunner and his family initially moved into temporary accommodation in Zurich, before finally settling into 12 Klusdörfli, close to Waldrand am Zürichberg.¹¹⁶ Brunner now had time for writing, and a scholarly community within which to develop and test his ideas – both essential requirements, if he was to develop a positive statement of his own views, rather than critiquing those of others. It is at this point that his rise to international theological eminence may be said to have begun – and at which our examination of his theology becomes considerably more engaging.

---

¹¹³ Jehle, *Emil Brunner*, 191–2.
¹¹⁴ H. R. Mackintosh, "The Swiss Group." *Expository Times* 36, no. 2 (1924): 73–5.
¹¹⁵ The possibility of this move had been under discussion for some months. See Brunner's letter to Barth, dated 23 January 1924: *Karl Barth–Emil Brunner, Briefwechsel*, 87–93; and Barth's reply, dated 26 January 1924: *Karl Barth–Emil Brunner, Briefwechsel*, 94–6.
¹¹⁶ Jehle, *Emil Brunner*, 203.

Part I
The Making of a Dialectical Theologian

2
Brunner's Theology of Crisis: Critique and Construction, 1924–1929

Brunner's installation as Professor of Systematic and Practical Theology at the University of Zurich was a landmark development in his career. He would remain in this position until 1953, producing his finest work during this period. His lectures included:

Christian Theology in Context I–III
The Main Problems of the Christian Life: Christian Ethics I and II.
The Office of the Pastor and Contemporary Life
The Pastor and the Community
The Essence and Task of Preaching: Homiletics
The Main Problems of Religious Education, with particular reference to the instruction of Confirmation Candidates.[1]

Consistent with his vision of theology as an ecclesially engaged discipline, Brunner supplemented his academic work with preaching at churches around Zurich, and giving public lectures on aspects of Christian life and thought.[2] His reputation at Zurich grew steadily, culminating in the invitation to serve as rector of the university from 1942 to 1944. In this chapter I shall consider the development of Brunner's thought to 1929, culminating in *The Mediator* in 1927, and in a series of lectures given in the United States, published in English under the iconic title *The Theology of Crisis*.

The tone of Brunner's emerging approach to theology was set out clearly in his programmatic *Antrittsvorlesung* ("inaugural lecture"), on the theme

---

[1] Frank Jehle, *Emil Brunner: Theologe im 20. Jahrhundert*. Zurich: Theologischer Verlag, 2006, 211–12.
[2] Jehle, *Emil Brunner*, 204–8.

Emil Brunner: A Reappraisal, First Edition. Alister E. McGrath.
© 2014 John Wiley & Sons, Ltd. Published 2016 by John Wiley & Sons, Ltd.

of "Revelation as the Ground and Object of Theology", delivered on 17 January 1925. Such is the importance of this lecture that it merits close attention.

The 1925 Inaugural Lecture at Zurich: Revelation and Theology

Brunner's inaugural lecture at Zurich crystallized his emerging understanding of the nature of revelation, the central place of Jesus Christ within the Christian faith and theology, the limits of philosophy, and the tasks of theology.[3] It is to be seen as both a defence and an exploration of theology as an academically rigorous yet pastorally engaged discipline. The lecture is at times somewhat dense, and would have made considerable demands on its original audience, not least in relation to some of the distinctions Brunner drew in developing his approach.

Brunner opened his analysis by acknowledging the importance of philosophy as a critical tool – a way of asking good questions, of probing the foundations of knowledge. Yet it must be recognized to have limits (*Grenzen*); limits that are defined by human reason – more precisely, human *nature* – itself.

> Philosophy, which fundamentally wishes to call everything into question, because it is only by doing so that it can be a basic discipline, dares not call into question *one* point, *one* certainty – namely, reason itself. It argues that reason is the only drilling tool with which we can work, and that we cannot drill into this tool itself. We cannot use reason to call reason into question.[4]

Yet how can the foundation of a critical discipline also be its object? Is this not tantamount to epistemological circularity? While insisting that theology must welcome the critical questions philosophy raises, Brunner points out that philosophy itself has limits placed upon it by the very nature of its method. In effect, Brunner develops a critique of philosophy which affirms its *critical* role, while denying its *foundational* role. Philosophy is about the refinement of knowledge. But how is such knowledge to be attained in the first place? How can human beings gain access to the truth?

At this point, Brunner introduces the notion of divine revelation. What if truth *comes* to us? What if God chooses to self-disclose in a historical act?

---

[3] "Die Offenbarung als Grund und Gegenstand der Theologie": *Ein offenes Wort*, vol. 1, 98–122.
[4] "Die Offenbarung als Grund und Gegenstand der Theologie": *Ein offenes Wort*, vol. 1, 100.

The Christian faith is the affirmation that this has taken place. It sees this event [*Ereignis*] in Jesus of Nazareth, who we call "Christ". It knows that this point in history is the place at which eternity becomes time, and time eternity. . . . The distinctiveness of Christianity stands or falls with this belief, that in Christ, God himself deals with humanity and speaks to it.[5]

Jesus of Nazareth is thus the revelational and soteriological fulcrum around which everything must turn. In Christ, God speaks to us, and deals with us, bringing both *knowledge* of sin and the possibility of the subsequent *forgiveness* of sin.

So does Brunner's critique of reason mean that revelation is to be deemed irrational? His nuanced response to this question needs careful attention.[6] Faith is a correlative of revelation, Brunner argues. Rational knowledge that is capable of proof is derived within a framework of reasoning that ultimately relies upon the reliability of this framework to secure its outcomes. There is thus an intrinsic circularity to rational argument, which rests on the assumption that reason itself is reliable.[7] Revelation is not irrational, in the sense of necessarily or intrinsically contradicting reason; rather, it originates from outside this limited framework of thought. Reason, for Brunner, is obliged to acknowledge a limit placed on human knowledge; revelation is about this limit being "abolished" or "transcended" from God's side.

Revelation is thus "*anti*-rational" – in the sense that it challenges and overcomes the limits that human reason places upon humanity – while being "at the same time the fulfilment of all rationality, because in it the ground of Reason, the source itself, emerges".[8] This dense, compact statement of Brunner's approach to the relation of theology and reason will be developed further in his later writings, most notably *Revelation and Reason* (1941). It is, however, clearly recognizable as an affirmation of the divine *logos*, incarnate in Christ, being the ultimate foundation of humanity's *logos*.

So what of theology? One of the central tasks of theology is to think through the substance of divine revelation. As the title of Brunner's lecture

---

[5] "Die Offenbarung als Grund und Gegenstand der Theologie": *Ein offenes Wort*, vol. 1, 107.
[6] "Die Offenbarung als Grund und Gegenstand der Theologie": *Ein offenes Wort*, vol. 1, 118.
[7] The broader context of Brunner's reflections should be taken into account here, particularly the criticism of forms of theological "rationalism". Rudolf Otto's emphasis on the "numinous" and "mystery" tended to accentuate the irrational or non-rational aspects of religion, raising questions about whether theological rationality had quite the importance that an earlier generation had assumed: see, for example, Rainer Flasche, "Der Irrationalismus in der Religionswissenschaft und dessen Begründung in der Zeit zwischen den Weltkriegen." In *Religionswissenschaft und Religionskritik*, ed. Hans G. Kippenberg and Brigitte Luchesi, 243–57. Marburg: Diagonal, 1991.
[8] "Die Offenbarung als Grund und Gegenstand der Theologie": *Ein offenes Wort*, vol. 1, 118. For the development of this theme, see Gabriele Lunghini, *Emil Brunner*. Brescia: Editrice Morcelliana, 2009, 39–45.

indicates, revelation is both the "foundation [*Grund*] and object [*Gegenstand*]" of theology.

> Revelation is not merely the content [*Inhalt*], but also the foundation of all theology. There is no fundamental difference between faith and theology, as there is, for instance, between mystical religiosity and theology. Furthermore, theology is thinking further about the thoughts of faith [*das Weiterdenken der Glaubensgedanken*], above all in a situation in which its meaning or validity are threatened by the general outlook of the age [*Zeitbewußtsein*], which also explains the essentially polemical character of all vital theology. Theology is an assault on the sin-distorted intellect; it is the obedience of faith penetrating the realm of thought.[9]

We see here a clear anticipation of Brunner's subsequent recognition of an "eristic" role for theology, in which it acts as the basis for a challenge to and critique of dominant cultural and intellectual ideologies.

Brunner appears to have realized that this inaugural lecture could only be a taster, a sketch map of the intellectual territory he intended to explore. Yet his new position at Zurich allowed him time to think and write. It would only be a matter of time before his emerging approach to theology would be given the fuller exposition that it so clearly needed.

Reason and Theology: An Ecclesial Engagement (1927)

Brunner's first substantial work during his Zurich period took the form of an exploration of a Protestant philosophy of religion. Brunner considered himself as being embedded within the Reformed theological tradition, which assigned a place of honour to both the great Zurich reformer Huldrych Zwingli and his later Genevan counterpart, John Calvin. Yet Brunner's works of the early 1920s show a willingness to engage a broader vision of Protestantism, including the appropriation of some core themes of the theology of Martin Luther, particularly his dialectic between "law" and "gospel", and his notion of the "orders of creation".[10]

---

[9] "Die Offenbarung als Grund und Gegenstand der Theologie": *Ein offenes Wort*, vol. 1, 120–1.

[10] For the Luther-Renaissance, which gained pace after the Great War, see Heinrich Assel, *Der andere Aufbruch: Die Lutherrenaissance – Ursprünge, Aporien und Wege: Karl Holl, Emanuel Hirsch, Rudolf Hermann (1910–1935)*. Göttingen: Vandenhoeck & Ruprecht, 1994, especially 17–22. See also James M. Stayer, *Martin Luther, German Saviour: German Evangelical Theological Factions and the Interpretation of Luther, 1917–1933*. Montreal: McGill-Queen's University Press, 2000, 3–78; Mary Elizabeth Anderson, *Gustaf Wingren and the Swedish Luther Renaissance*. New York: Peter Lang, 2006, 37–72. As Stayer points out (48–78), the rise of dialectical theology led to a new interest in Luther's theology. For Brunner's use of the dialectic between law and gospel as an organizational framework for systematic theology around this time, see David Andrew Gilland, *Law and Gospel in Emil Brunner's Earlier Dialectical Theology*. London: T&T Clark, 2013.

By this time, the movement loosely known as "dialectical theology" was experiencing significant internal tensions along several axes. Nationally, Barth, Brunner, and Thurneysen were Swiss; Bultmann and Gogarten were German. Ecclesially, Barth, Brunner, and Thurneysen were Reformed; Bultmann and Gogarten were Lutheran.[11] Brunner tended to see "dialectical theology" – as he understood the notion – primarily as a Swiss Reformed movement, and regretted the involvement of German Lutherans as diluting the ecclesial distinctiveness of the movement.

So what if Barth were to return to Switzerland? Would not this give the movement a new sense of identity and focus in its proper Swiss Reformed context? The three most important universities in German-speaking Switzerland were Basle (founded 1460), Berne (founded 1834), and Zurich (founded 1833). Each had a reputable faculty of theology, although Basle was widely regarded as pre-eminent among them. By late 1927, as we have seen, Brunner was firmly established as Professor of Theology at Zurich. Thurneysen had moved from St Gallen to Basle, becoming pastor of the city's ancient and prestigious Minster, noted for its monument to Desiderius Erasmus. The Basle Faculty of Theology granted him the status of *Privatdozent* in 1929, and of Professor of Practical Theology in 1941. But what of Berne? And what of Barth, who had moved from Göttingen to Münster in 1925?

In the autumn of 1927, Barth was invited to consider returning from Germany to Switzerland, and take up a chair in dogmatics at the University of Berne. Barth's father had taught at Berne, and Barth himself had begun his studies there in 1904. Barth wrote to Brunner, asking him what he thought of the possibility.[12] Brunner replied immediately and at some length, advising *against* the move. It would, he conceded, be good for Switzerland; indeed, it would be a "disaster" for Berne's Faculty of Theology if he did not accept any such offer. Yet it would damage the Faculty of Theology at Zurich, in that Swiss students would probably rather go to Berne listen to Barth than to Zurich to hear Brunner.[13]

Brunner clearly felt threatened by Barth; primarily, it must be said, at a *reputational* level, yet secondarily in a *theological* manner. Brunner seems

---

[11] For Bultmann's position, see Konrad Hammann, *Rudolf Bultmann: Eine Biographie*. 3rd edn. Tübingen: Mohr Siebeck, 2012, 134–47. Gogarten's role in the emergence of dialectical theology is considered in Matthias Kröger, *Friedrich Gogarten: Leben und Wirken in zeitgeschichtlicher Perspektive*. Stuttgart: Kohlhammer, 1997. For further reflections on his significance, see Friedrich Wilhelm Graf, "Friedrich Gogartens Deutung der Moderne: Ein theologiegeschichtlicher Rückblick." *Zeitschrift für Kirchengeschichte* 100 (1989): 169–230. There is also a significant discussion of Gogarten's changing evaluation of Barth in Stefan Holtmann, *Karl Barth als Theologe der Neuzeit: Studien zur kritischen Deutung seiner Theologie*. Göttingen: Vandenhoeck & Ruprecht, 2007, 159–72.

[12] Barth to Brunner, 30 October 1927: *Karl Barth–Emil Brunner, Briefwechsel*, 159–60. See further Eberhard Busch, *Karl Barth: His Life from Letters and Autobiographical Texts*. London: SCM Press, 1976, 175–6.

[13] Brunner to Barth, 1 November 1927: *Karl Barth–Emil Brunner, Briefwechsel*, 160–3.

to have seen himself as the emerging representative of a distinctive Swiss Reformed theological voice, and realized that he would be swamped if Barth were to return to his homeland. These anxieties would return a decade later, when Barth, forced to leave Germany on account of his opposition to National Socialism, came home to take up a chair of dogmatics at Basle.

Both Barth and Brunner emphasized their Reformed credentials in the years around 1925, seeing their ecclesial identity as shaping their theological vision and its application. Their correspondence of 1923–4 includes reflections on how theology is grounded with a specific confessional community and faith commitment, and how this is to be expressed in a lecture course on dogmatics.[14] Barth's lectures at Göttingen were confessionally rooted, drawing on Heinrich Heppe's standard nineteenth-century compendium of Reformed dogmatics.[15] For his part, Brunner was invited to contribute an essay on Reformed thought to a major reference work on the contemporary state of Protestantism.[16] The essay is revealing in several respects, perhaps most notably on account of Brunner's obvious commitment to a Reformed theological vision. If there is a divergence between Brunner and Barth at this point, it lies in Brunner's tendency to give Calvin a certain degree of priority over the later Reformed tradition, tending to prefer the historically foundational to the more methodologically developed formulations of the tradition.[17]

In 1927 Brunner published *The Philosophy of Religion from the Standpoint of Protestant Theology*. He conceived his task in this work as correcting misunderstandings and false turns within the philosophy of religion, and constructing a positive way forward, specifically within a Protestant theological context. This constructive task demanded an initial clearing of the ground, identifying four influential "half-truths" which had gained traction within Reformed theology, and appropriating what Brunner considered to be valid within them.

The first such "half-truth" is found in Protestant scholasticism's attitude towards the Bible. Brunner argues, on the basis of a somewhat slight and selective engagement with sixteenth-century reformers, that early Protestantism held that "the identity between the Word of Scripture and the Word

---

[14] See, for example, Brunner to Barth, 23 January 1924; *Karl Barth–Emil Brunner, Briefwechsel*, 87–93; Barth to Brunner, 26 January 1924; *Karl Barth–Emil Brunner, Briefwechsel*, 94–6.
[15] Heinrich Heppe, *Die Dogmatik der evangelisch-reformierten Kirche*. Elberfeld: Friderichs, 1861.
[16] Jehle, *Emil Brunner*, 217–23.
[17] Barth's *Christliche Dogmatik* (1927) seemed to some to represent a lapse into seventeenth-century Reformed scholasticism. For comment, see Friedrich Gogarten, "Karl Barths Dogmatik." *Theologische Rundschau* 1 (1929): 60–80; Michael Beintker, *Die Dialektik in der "Dialektischen Theologie" Karl Barths*. Munich: Kaiser Verlag, 1987, 157–79; Bruce L. McCormack, "The End of Reformed Theology: The Voice of Karl Barth in the Doctrinal Chaos of the Moment." In *Reformed Theology: Identity and Ecumenicity*, ed. Wallace M. Alston and Michael Welker, 46–64. Grand Rapids, MI: Eerdmans, 2003.

of God is indirect, not direct".[18] Since there is no such thing as "revelation in itself" (*An-sich-Offenbarung*), the "Word of Scripture is not in itself the Word of God, but the word of human beings". Yet while Orthodoxy has taken a wrong turn, Brunner indicates that it is capable of reformation and redirection.

> For Orthodoxy, the Bible as a book [*das Bibelbuch*] is the divinely revealed truth. It is thus itself something that is revealed [*ein Offenbarungsding*]. For an undistorted Christian faith, Scripture is only revelation when it is joined together with the Spirit of God in the present day.[19]

Citing Luther's famous maxim that "Scripture is the cradle in which Christ is laid",[20] Brunner insists that this cradle is to be distinguished – though not separated from – Jesus Christ. "The Bible is a human witness to God, yet it is also something human through which God reveals himself."[21]

Brunner also identifies the half-truths in rationalism, subjectivism, and historicism, noting how these may be corrected and redirected in the service of a Protestant philosophy of religion. It is, however, the opening chapter of this work, dealing with the place of the critically important notion of revelation within a philosophy of religion, that is perhaps most significant. The question that the philosophy of religion must engage is how to accommodate both the meaning and foundation of religion within the discipline of philosophy, without compromising the specific affirmations of any given religion.[22] In the case of Christianity, this distinctive and essential element is that of revelation. "Its foundation, content and norm is not a human insight, but divine self-disclosure [*Selbstkundgebung*]."[23]

While the contents of divine self-revelation cannot be stipulated in advance by reason, the analysis of that revelation can be regarded as a systematic undertaking. Like philosophy, theology aims to show that there is an "all-embracing context of meaning", by which things may be understood; unlike philosophy, which seeks this context through processes of natural reasoning, theology finds it through the *Logos* of revelation. Theology gives systematic and conceptual (*wissenschaftlich-begrifflichen*) expression to the Christian faith, which in turn arises from the "knowledge and acceptance of God's self-disclosure in Jesus Christ".[24]

Yet Brunner sounds a note of concern at this point, grounded both in his theological vision of the Christian faith and his experience as a pastor.

---

[18] *Religionsphilosophie*, 13; *Philosophy of Religion*, 33.
[19] *Religionsphilosophie*, 77–8; *Philosophy of Religion*, 151.
[20] D. M. *Martin Luthers Werke. Kritische Gesamtausgabe: Deutsche Bibel*. Weimar: Böhlau, 1883–1921, vol. 8, 12. Brunner's references to Luther are generally taken from the older and less reliable Erlangen edition, published in the early nineteenth century.
[21] *Religionsphilosophie*, 79; *Philosophy of Religion*, 155.
[22] *Religionsphilosophie*, 3; *Philosophy of Religion*, 12.
[23] *Religionsphilosophie*, 5; *Philosophy of Religion*, 15.
[24] *Religionsphilosophie*, 5; *Philosophy of Religion*, 15.

While conceding that any attempt to speak about God involves the use of abstract notions, such as those characteristic of theology, Brunner declared that "the primary concern of Christianity is not systematic knowledge [*Wissenschaft*], but the relation of a personal faith to revelation".[25] Since this personal faith aims to overcome such abstract notions as much as possible, the philosophy of religion must lie towards the periphery of faith, rather than at its centre. Although this idea of revelation as personal divine disclosure, eliciting a personal human response and decision, would receive its definitive formulation in 1937 (see pp. 154–72), some of its fundamental themes are evident at this stage.

At this point, Brunner pauses to reflect on the nature of the believing human agent, and how this agent recognizes, accepts, and responds to divine revelation. If human "receptivity" (*Offenheit*) is to be considered as a presupposition for faith, how is it to be understood? Brunner suggests that this takes the form of a human consciousness of "vital need" (*Lebensnot*), which is also a consciousness of guilt. This, he argues, is a negative *Berührungspunkt* – a "point of contact" – for God's self-disclosure. "Revelation is always an answer to a human question."[26] Later in the work, the vocabulary changes, moving from "contact" to "attachment". Brunner locates this "so-called point of attachment [*die sogennante Anknüpfungspunkt*] for revelation" within human nature.[27] For Brunner, the doctrine of revelation must acknowledge that humanity retains an intrinsic "capacity" (*Anlage*) for attachment to God.

Brunner did not explore the implications of this suggestion in any detail at this stage. What is left dangling in the air is the notion of some form of human preparedness for revelation, arising from the divine action of creation. There is something that has been divinely embedded within human nature that prompts and probes, questions and quests, preparing the way for – without actually pre-empting – God's self-revelation in Christ. Over the coming years the vocabulary would change, and the theological notions become clarified. Yet even at this stage, Brunner is clearly mapping out a framework for the discussion of the possibility of divine revelation that is grounded in a doctrine of creation.

In his *Göttingen Dogmatics*, based on his lectures on theology given at Göttingen in 1924, Karl Barth affirmed a cornerstone of his thinking on revelation: human beings are incapable of building bridges to God; yet God has built a bridge to them.[28] While not dissenting from this general principle,

---

[25] *Religionsphilosophie*, 7; *Philosophy of Religion*, 19.
[26] *Religionsphilosophie*, 8; *Philosophy of Religion*, 20.
[27] *Religionsphilosophie*, 49; *Philosophy of Religion*, 98.
[28] Bruce L. McCormack, "Der theologieschichtliche Ort Karl Barths." In *Karl Barth in Deutschland (1921–1935): Widerstand – Bewährung – Orientierung*, ed. Michael Beintker, Christian Link, and Michael Trowitzsch, 15–40. Zurich: Theologischer Verlag, 2005, especially 23–34.

Brunner was clearly forging a theology of revelation grounded in the notion that the divine creation of the world and humanity entailed some form of created correspondence between the structures of the created order – including human consciousness – and God. Revelationally, this would be articulated in terms of the "point of contact"; ethically, it would be expressed in terms of the "orders of creation" (*Schöpfungsordnungen*) – a characteristically Lutheran notion, which Brunner believed ought also to find its expression and application in Reformed dogmatics.

Although the reaffirmation of the importance of the notion of "orders of creation" by Lutheran writers such as Paul Althaus, Werner Elert, Friedrich Gogarten, and Walther Künneth dates from the 1930s,[29] Brunner had clearly come to a recognition of the legitimacy of the notion by the late 1920s. Barth rejected any such idea, reasserting in its place a theology of the one Word of God from which all structures, orders, commandments, and ethical norms for Christian living in the world are to be derived. I shall explore Brunner's development of this notion later in this work.

By this stage, Brunner was clear that his own new approach to theology, as well as that of the wider movement concerned to reaffirm the centrality of divine revelation, needed a manifesto – a work that set out and defended the theological foundations and substance of what Brunner understood by "dialectical theology".

The Mediator: A Manifesto for Dialectical Theology (1927)

In 1927 Brunner published *The Mediator*, still regarded as one of his most original and successful works, on which he had been working for some time.[30] The book did much to establish Brunner's theological reputation in the German-language world, creating the abiding impression that he was a positive and constructive, as well as a prophetic and critical, theological thinker.[31] The work also consolidated his reputation in the English-speaking world as the leading representative of what became known in English – largely, as it happened, through Brunner's influence – as the "theology of

---

[29] See, for example, Paul Althaus, *Theologie der Ordnungen*. 2nd edn. Gütersloh: Evangelischer Verlag, 1935. For Althaus's use of this Lutheran *Leitmotif* see Walter Mann, *Ordnungen der Allmacht: Paul Althaus der Jüngere über die Ordnungen*. Hanover: Lutherisches Verlagshaus 1987; Friedrich Lohmann, "Ein Gott – zwei Regimente: Überlegungen zur 'Zwei-Reiche-Lehre' Martin Luthers im Anschluss an die Debatte zwischen Paul Althaus und Johannes Heckel." *Luther* 74, no. 3 (2003): 112–38.
[30] Jehle, *Emil Brunner*, 230–5.
[31] For analysis, see Yrjö Salakka, *Person und Offenbarung in der Theologie Emil Brunners während der Jahre 1914–1937*. Helsinki: Kirjapaino, 1960; Roman Rössler, *Person und Glaube: Der Personalismus der Gottesbeziehung bei Emil Brunner*. Munich: Kaiser Verlag, 1965; Stephan Scheld, *Die Christologie Emil Brunners*. Wiesbaden: Franz Steinbeck, 1981.

crisis".[32] (In a letter of April 1933, Thurneysen remarked that the phrase "theology of crisis" had "caught on" largely through Brunner's influence.[33]) Brunner's *Mediator* was the first work of substance from this theological perspective to be published in English.

In part, the reputation of this translation – which appeared in 1934 – rested on the theological perceptiveness of its translator, Olive Wyon (1881–1966), who initially studied theology with a view to becoming a missionary. Poor health, however, prevented her from working abroad.[34] While working in Munich in 1899, she discovered that she had a flair for languages. Her theological and linguistic competence was first demonstrated in 1929, when she translated Ernst Troeltsch's massive *Social Teachings of the Christian Churches* into English. Named after the Leicestershire village in which the English reformer John Wycliffe served as rector in the fourteenth century, the Lutterworth Press was a London-based publishing house established in 1932. Over the period 1934 to 1962, Lutterworth published English translations of all of Brunner's major writings in English. In effect, the Lutterworth Press played a role for Brunner in the English-speaking world which paralleled that of Christian Kaiser Verlag in promoting Karl Barth and his circle. Olive Wyon was responsible for the translation of most of Brunner's major works for Lutterworth from 1934 to 1949.[35]

The Mediator can be considered to consist of three dogmatic mini-treatises, connected by the unifying theme of divine revelation. The first major section considers the necessity of revelation; the second the credentials of the mediator; and the third, the work of the mediator in revealing,

---

[32] Barth used this phrase in his Romans commentary; however, its wider adoption appears to date from a later point, and may well have been influenced by an important article by the Catholic theologian Karl Adam (1876–1966), which appeared in 1926: Karl Adam, "Der Theologie der Krisis." *Hochland: Monatsschrift für alle Gebiete des Wissens, der Literatur und Kunst* 23 (1926): 271–86. See further Paul Corset, "Premières rencontres de la théologie catholique avec l'oeuvre de Karl Barth (1922–32)." In *Karl Barth: Genèse et reception de sa théologie*, ed. Pierre Gisel, 151–90. Geneva: Labor et Fides, 1987. German-language theology preferred to designate the movement as "dialectical theology", despite the widespread adoption of the phrase "theology of crisis" in the English-speaking world. Bixler notes the German preference for "theology of dialectic", but retains Brunner's "theology of crisis": Julius Seelye Bixler, "Emil Brunner as a Representative of the Theology of Crisis." *Journal of Religion* 9 (1929): 446–59, especially 446.

[33] Jehle, *Emil Brunner*, 250. This is not to say that the concept of "crisis" is absent from Barth's theology: for reflections on its significance, see Dietrich Korsch, *Dialektische Theologie nach Karl Barth*. Tübingen: Mohr, 1996, 23–39. The issue is the name by which the movement was known.

[34] Wyon's personal papers may be found in the National Library of Scotland, Edinburgh, in collections Acc. 5261 and Acc. 5468.

[35] In the United States, Wyon's translations were initially published by the Macmillan Publishing Company of New York; however, in the longer term, Brunner's works were published by the Westminster Press, Philadelphia.

reconciling, and ruling. In what follows, I shall explore the overall trajectory of Brunner's analysis, and identify its significance.

The work opens with a vigorous insistence upon the necessity of revelation. Brunner's strategy is to demonstrate the inability of humanity to transcend its limits, forcing it to rely upon God bridging the gap between the divine and the human, eternity and time, in an act of self-disclosure. And since God can be known only through God,[36] it must follow that the medium and mode of this self-disclosure are divine. Although Brunner's analysis in this section of *The Mediator* repeats and reworks material already published in his earlier works – most notably, *Die Mystik und das Wort* – his style is here more engaging and less shrill, and his argument framed in a more accessible and less dense manner. Brunner's interest here is not primarily in the possibility of revelation, but in what follows from its actuality.

Revelation, Brunner declares, is *einmalig* – something unique and unrepeatable that takes place at a specific moment in history. He concedes immediately that many regard this emphasis on a historically unrepeatable event of revelation as a "stumbling-block" (*Ärgernis*).[37] The notion that truth ultimately lies beyond the scope of reason calls into question many of the fundamental assumptions of modernity – including the axiom of the omnicompetence of reason, used by Enlightenment writers to call into question the need for revelation in the first place. Brunner rejects the "Scholastic Catholic" idea that there are certain truths about God which can be grasped by reason, and others which lie beyond its scope. Rather, revelation exposes the failure of "all attempts to understand and grasp the divine which derive from reason".[38]

Yet Brunner is emphatic that "dialectical theology" does not entail the rejection of every form of general revelation in either the world of nature or the human consciousness. Human beings continue to bear the "image of God", even if this may be distorted through sin.

> The question is not *whether* there is a general revelation or not; after all, if there were none, nobody would be asking about God. Rather, the question is in what sense this is to be understood – as direct or indirect, or whether the Christian revelation is merely the culmination of this general revelation, or is to be understood as something quite distinct – namely, the actual revelation itself.[39]

Brunner's defence of the necessity of revelation consolidates and, to a limited extent, extends the ideas he developed in earlier works. The second

---

[36] *Der Mittler*, 3; *The Mediator*, 21.
[37] *Der Mittler*, 21; *The Mediator*, 42.
[38] *Der Mittler*, 22–3; *The Mediator*, 43.
[39] *Der Mittler*, 12 n. 2 ; *The Mediator*, 31 n. 2.

major part of the work, however, opens up a new theological vista. Its opening paragraph restates the conclusions of the previous discussion, laying the foundation for an analysis of a Christological approach to God's acts of revelation and reconciliation in what follows.

> God can only be known through God. There is knowledge of God only through revelation. Asserting this is not the distinctive feature of the Christian faith, but of all religion. But the meaning of the Christian faith is, above all things, that only in it – that is, in the revelation of God in Jesus Christ – is this assertion truth and actuality. There is no proof for this faith; those seeking one merely show that they do not understand the statement. For a revelation which could be proved would be no revelation. It would be grounded in some general truth that is independent of it.[40]

Brunner's point is that if A is to prove B, A must be considered to be more reliable or foundational than B. An appeal to any external authority (such as reason) as a potential proof of revelation thus covertly concedes the epistemological primacy and superiority of such an authority – and necessarily relegates revelation to a secondary and subsidiary role. The demand for rational proof of revelation is thus a disguised demand to concede the hegemony of the rationalism of the Enlightenment, or contemporary cultural norms – two theological trends which Brunner had criticized earlier, particularly in his *Philosophy of Religion from the Standpoint of Protestant Theology*.

Brunner's doctrine of revelation is framed in terms of the "Word of God", characterized by the fact that it is *given* in the form of *something that has happened*.[41] It is not something over which humanity has control, or which can be mastered or bypassed. Revelation and salvation, both of which are mediated through the Word of God, lie beyond the limits of humanity. We do not truly know reality; we lack the power to transform ourselves. It is no accident that the New Testament uses the notion of "Word" (Greek: *Logos*) to articulate this notion.

> [The *Logos*] is absolutely necessary for thought; it is the idea that is indispensable for all thought; indeed, we might go so far as to say it is the basic idea of humanity itself – the principle of meaning, of meaningful discourse. . . . Without participation [*Anteil*] in the divine *Logos*, there is no reason, no humanity.[42]

This "principle of ultimate truth" comes to us, not as an abstract immanent idea, but as an event – as a potentially transformative "personal

---

[40] *Der Mittler*, 175; *The Mediator*, 201. The opening sentence repeats an earlier refrain: *Der Mittler*, 3; *The Mediator*, 21.
[41] *Der Mittler*, 178; *The Mediator*, 204.
[42] *Der Mittler*, 181; *The Mediator*, 207.

communication".⁴³ Faith, Brunner argues, comes into being when this Word is taken hold of by the believer – or, to put it more pointedly, when the believer is taken hold of by the Word.⁴⁴

So how is this Word disclosed? Brunner concedes immediately the importance of the prophetic tradition, with its emphasis on a divine word of revelation;⁴⁵ yet Jesus Christ must be considered to transcend this mode of partial divine revelation. Prophets speak words; "Jesus Christ *is* the word that God has to say to us".⁴⁶ Brunner insists that the core of the proclamation of the Christian church lies in the identity and significance of Jesus Christ, who is "true God and true human being [*Mensch*], and is thus also the Mediator".⁴⁷

Although both the divinity and humanity of Christ are essential to a proper understanding of his significance, Brunner observes that the theological debates of the recent past have focused on his divinity. For this reason, Brunner's analysis focuses primarily on defending the divinity of Christ, and considering its implications.⁴⁸ This, particularly when set alongside some unhelpfully phrased statements concerning the humanity of Christ, has led some of his interpreters to suggest that he is Docetic in his Christology.⁴⁹ This seems unfair, failing to take into account the polemical intentions and agendas that underlie Brunner's exposition of Christology in this work, and the context within which its ideas were developed – above all, the lingering influence of liberal Protestant Christologies, which failed to articulate Christ's divinity with any conviction.⁵⁰

For Brunner, incarnation and revelation are locked together. Since "the Word of God comes to us from the far side of the frontier that separates God from humanity",⁵¹ the divine action of revelation cannot be separated – though it can be distinguished – from that of incarnation.

> This Word, which comes to us from the realm beyond all human and historical possibilities, is here, as a person. Jesus Christ is this Word from the other side. ... This event breaks through this frontier. As such, it is revelation, incarnation.⁵²

---

[43] *Der Mittler*, 188; *The Mediator*, 214.
[44] *Der Mittler*, 193; *The Mediator*, 221.
[45] *Der Mittler*, 194–6; *The Mediator*, 222–4.
[46] *Der Mittler*, 204; *The Mediator*, 232.
[47] *Der Mittler*, 206; *The Mediator*, 235.
[48] *Der Mittler*, 206–7; *The Mediator*, 235–6
[49] George Florovsky, "The Last Things and the Last Events." In *The Theology of Emil Brunner*, ed. Charles W., Kegley, 207–26. New York: Macmillan, 1962; Scheld, *Die Christologie Emil Brunners*, 134, 141.
[50] See, for example, the analysis in Hans-Georg Link, *Geschichte Jesu und Bild Christi: Die Entwicklung der Christologie Martin Kählers in Auseinandersetzung mit der Leben-Jesu-Theologie und der Ritschl-Schule*. Neukirchen-Vluyn: Neukirchener Verlag, 1975.
[51] *Der Mittler*, 209; *The Mediator*, 238.
[52] *Der Mittler*, 210; *The Mediator*, 239–40.

Brunner emphasizes the *personal* nature of this divine self-disclosure. This is no communication of mere ideas, but God entering into history. It invites and elicits not merely intellectual acceptance but, more fundamentally, faith and trust.[53] Notions of God based purely on reflection on the world inevitably take the form of an impersonal Demiurge. The "*personal* creator God", however, "makes himself known by disclosing his name, when he reveals himself through his personal Word".[54] Although Brunner had clearly begun to assemble by this stage the elements of a philosophical framework through which he would be able to explore the implications of "personal revelation" in greater detail, a fuller discussion of this aspect of the matter would not emerge until later (see pp. 154–72).

The incarnation is not about a fortuitous alignment or coincidence of medium and message; rather, the Person who enters history *is* "the Word from the other side, from above".[55] Christ is not the bearer of a word which can be detached and considered in isolation. Rather, revelation takes place "*in* him, not merely *through* him".[56] Christ is the revelation, just as Christ is the Word. God does not say "something" though Christ, but enters into history as a Person in "a single fact of history" (*ein einzelnes Geschichtsfaktum*).

Brunner's concept of revelation is strongly Christocentric. Even at this early stage, there is no sense of a Trinitarian foundation for revelation, such as that which can be seen as beginning to emerge within Karl Barth's dogmatics around this time – a point to which I shall return presently (see pp. 50–4).

So what of Christ's humanity? Brunner affirms the humanity of Christ, seeing this as a fundamental and essential element of any orthodox understanding of the identity of Christ. Yet it is clear that Brunner's exposition of Christ's humanity is shaped by a desire to engage and correct the theological tradition stemming from F. D. E. Schleiermacher, A. B. Ritschl, and Adolf von Harnack, which seemed to Brunner to reduce Christ to a religious role model or an inspirational charismatic figure.[57] Both this accentuation of the humanity of Christ and the manner of its theological interpretation represented, for Brunner, a disproportionate and diluting emphasis that unbalanced a delicate Christological equilibrium.

Brunner sought to redress this balance by reasserting the humanity of Jesus Christ within a theological context that decoupled such an affirmation from the inadequate Christological formulations of liberal Protestantism.

---

[53] *Der Mittler*, 233–4; *The Mediator*, 267–8.
[54] *Der Mittler*, 238–9; *The Mediator*, 269–71.
[55] *Der Mittler*, 239; *The Mediator*, 271.
[56] *Der Mittler*, 239; *The Mediator*, 270.
[57] Brunner's analysis of Schleiermacher's Christology is open to question at points: see the analysis of Schleiermacher in Jacqueline Mariña, "Schleiermacher's Christology Revisited: A Reply to His Critics." *Scottish Journal of Theology* 49, no. 2 (1996): 177–200; Lori Pearson, "Schleiermacher and the Christologies behind Chalcedon." *Harvard Theological Review* 96, no. 3 (2003): 349–67.

"Jesus is thoroughly human, as a historical personality and as a subject of history."[58] This has been criticized for failing to achieve a theological balance, in that it lacks any emphasis on a divine aspect or element to the personality of Jesus.[59] While this is true, it fails to meet Brunner's point – namely, that a "personality" is to be understood in terms of a person's historical manifestation and encounter, a "naturally historical human life, to the extent that it can be engaged historically and visibly".[60] In other words, considered as an empirical reality – something which is observed and encountered within the historical process – Jesus is totally natural. Yet, given the framework within which Brunner frames his discussion of Jesus, this does not compromise or contradict the notion that he is also totally divine.

At this point, Brunner makes a theological move which many regarded as precipitate and ill considered. Having emphasized the humanity of Christ, he sought to remove any ideas that might undermine its integrity and authenticity. Seeing the notion of the virgin birth as ultimately subversive of Christ's humanity, Brunner rejected it as a myth. Biblically, Brunner suggested, this doctrine is poorly evidenced. Paul, after all, spoke of Christ simply as being "born of a woman" (Galatians 4:4).[61] Historically, he argued, the concept of the virgin birth of Christ played no part in the Christological debates of the early church.[62] Theologically, he argued, the notion was not necessary to affirm the incarnation of the Son of God.[63] For Brunner, this doctrine was a late and unnecessary development within the church, which arose for dogmatic rather than historical reasons. Why is the "sinlessness of the God-Man" to be made dependent upon a virgin birth?[64] We see here the seeds of Brunner's mature view that the doctrine of the virgin birth actually undermines the humanity of Christ, not least through denying he had a human father.

One of Brunner's purposes in writing *The Mediator* was to provide intellectual substance and elaboration for his own programme of theology, which focused on the primacy of divine revelation, and the role of the divine *Logos* in the revelational process. Brunner's Christological exposition is clearly influenced by this agenda. His concern is to correct and redirect theological trends, including what he regarded as an excessive preoccupation with Christ's humanity, and a failure to articulate its proper theological significance.

Brunner's limited yet focused engagement with the humanity of Christ in *The Mediator* seems to be fundamentally corrective rather than positive. Far from providing a substantial positive exposition of the foundation and

[58] *Der Mittler*, 283; *The Mediator*, 318.
[59] Scheld, *Die Christologie Emil Brunners*, 141.
[60] *Der Mittler*, 283; *The Mediator*, 318.
[61] *Der Mittler*, 323; *The Mediator*, 361–2.
[62] *Der Mittler*, 288; *The Mediator*, 322.
[63] *Der Mittler*, 290; *The Mediator*, 324–5.
[64] *Der Mittler*, 291; *The Mediator*, 325–6.

significance of Christ's human nature, Brunner tends to focus on correcting others, and articulating those aspects of Christ's humanity that are integral to his being the bearer of divine revelation. Indeed, it is possible to read Brunner's *Mediator* in essentially functionalist terms: his argument is that Jesus Christ possesses the necessary credentials in order to function as the channel and bearer of divine revelation.

Brunner's understanding of the role of Christ's humanity is influenced by Luther's concept of the *larvae Dei*. Noting that sinful humanity is unable to "see" God (Exodus 33:20), Luther insisted that there could be no unmediated relationship between God and humanity. God's unaccommodated radiant majesty can never be pursued or perceived directly. In order to shield human beings from the unapproachable light of his glory, Luther argues, God always remains hidden behind a mask (*larva*).[65] God thus envelops and reveals himself under and through created forms – such as in the incarnation, or in the sacraments.

Brunner echoes Luther in suggesting that Christ's humanity is a means of concealing, rather than revealing, God. "This revelation can at the same time be nothing other than a veiling [*Verhüllung*]."[66] God does not speak to us *directly*.

> This revelatory encounter, this divine address and approach, is something very indirect, a revelation through veiling. Precisely at the point at which revelation is complete, it is also a complete veiling . . . because to us there is nothing more ordinary, less impressive, more familiar, than a human person like ourselves.[67]

Like Luther, Brunner insists that God chooses to self-disclose in a manner that conceals as much as reveals. Although Brunner's exposition of this point perhaps lacks the conceptual elaboration found in Luther's writings (especially of the late 1510s), the point he is making is much the same: "God remains a mystery [*Geheimnis*] to us even in revelation."[68]

---

[65] See, for example, Luther's 1535 commentary on Galatians: "Universa autem creatura est facies et larva Dei. Sed hic requiritur sapientia quae discernat Deum a larva. Hanc sapientiam mundus non habet, ideo non potest discernere Deum a larva." D. M. *Luthers Werke. Kritische Gesamtausgabe*. 65 vols. Weimar: Verlag Hermann Böhlaus Nochfolger, 1883–1966, 40 /1.174.12–14. See further Hellmut Bandt, *Luthers Lehre vom verborgenen Gott: Eine Untersuchung zu dem offenbarungsgeschichtlichen Ansatz seiner Theologie*. Berlin: Evangelische Verlagsanstalt, 1958; Klaas Zwanepol, "Zur Diskussion um Gottes Verborgenheit." *Neue Zeitschrift für systematische Theologie und Religionsphilosophie* 48 (2006): 51–9.

[66] *Der Mittler*, 298; *The Mediator*, 333. Scheld is severely critical of Brunner at this point, perhaps failing to appreciate the importance of Brunner's allusions to Luther's *theologia crucis*: Scheld, *Die Christologie Emil Brunners*, 144.

[67] *Der Mittler*, 299; *The Mediator*, 333–4.

[68] *Der Mittler*, 298; *The Mediator*, 334. For a discussion of Luther's views on this point, see Alister E. McGrath, *Luther's Theology of the Cross*. 2nd edn. Oxford: Wiley-Blackwell, 2011, 201–28.

This allows Brunner to clarify the critically important notion of faith, which he interprets in Kierkegaardian terms as a "leap" (*Sprung*), an "act of decision" which entails "crossing over" (*hinübertreten*) from the familiar, and leaving it behind.[69] Faith is a realization that the human figure of Jesus Christ really is "the self-manifestation of God" (*Selbstmitteilung Gottes*), which is known indirectly, not directly.[70] "It is only possible to have a relation of faith towards Christ, a genuine decision, because the divinity of Christ is accompanied by the Incognito of his humanity."[71] A complete disclosure would leave no room for faith. We would see, not believe.

Like Luther before him, Brunner declares faith to be "seeing in the dark".[72] Faith is able to recognize and take hold of the reality in the shadows. As Luther put it in his 1535 commentary on Galatians, here cited by Brunner:

> Christ is the object of faith, or rather not the object but, so to speak, the One who is present in faith itself. Faith is thus a sort of knowledge or darkness that nothing can see. Yet the Christ of whom faith takes hold sits in this darkness as God sat in the midst of shadows on Sinai and in the temple.[73]

Again, like Luther, Brunner sees the "leap" of faith as a divine-grounded and divinely supported insight. "Here is the ultimate risk [*Wagnis*], the ultimate moment of decision – but it is a risk given by God, and a decision created by God."[74]

The final section of *The Mediator* deals with the "work of the Mediator". What does Christ do? Brunner answers this in terms of a classic taxonomy, originally developed by Eusebius of Caesarea in the patristic period, and subsequently reappropriated by Calvin and other Reformed writers – the *munus triplex Christi* ("threefold office of Christ"). Christ is prophet, priest, and king – and as such, reveals God's will, makes sacrifice for the sin of the people, and rules over the community of faith.[75] Barth would also later use this framework in discussing the work of Christ.[76] Yet it is important to

---

[69] *Der Mittler*, 300, 302; *The Mediator*, 335, 339.

[70] *Der Mittler*, 300; *The Mediator*, 336.

[71] *Der Mittler*, 302; *The Mediator*, 337.

[72] *Der Mittler*, 302; *The Mediator*, 338.

[73] *Der Mittler*, 302; *The Mediator*, 338, citing *Luthers Werke*, 40/1.228.34–229.15. I have extended the range of the extract slightly to enable Luther's point to be better appreciated.

[74] *Der Mittler*, 304; *The Mediator*, 339. Note also Brunner's comments about the "mystery of Christ" as a "point of contact" (*Berührungstelle*): *Der Mittler*, 302; *The Mediator*, 337.

[75] For this idea in Ritschl, see Gerald W. McCulloh, *Christ's Person and Life-Work in the Theology of Albrecht Ritschl with Special Attention to Munus Triplex*. Lanham, MD: University Press of America, 1990, 86–145. More generally, see Robert Sherman, *King, Priest and Prophet: A Trinitarian Theology of Atonement*. Edinburgh: T&T Clark, 2004.

[76] Paul Dafydd Jones, *The Humanity of Christ: Christology in Karl Barth's Church Dogmatics*. New York: T&T Clark, 2008, 122–6.

appreciate that this framework is also found in the writings of Luther,[77] and has a long history of use within the Lutheran theological tradition.

Brunner's decision to use this triple Christological taxonomy, though understandable, creates some difficulties for the structuring of his argument. Having already discussed the doctrine of revelation in some detail, including the specific place and function of Jesus Christ as God's primary means of revelation, Brunner is now obliged to discuss the same doctrine still further in the two chapters which constitute the opening section of the "Work of the Mediator".[78] The result is a certain degree of argumentative hiatus, which weakens the force of Brunner's exposition at this point.

Brunner concedes that this focus on revelation might create the impression that he either ignores the soteriological aspects of Christ's work, or relegates them to a role which is subordinate to revelation.[79] Yet while he insists that this is not the intended outcome of his approach, there are many passages in *The Mediator* which assert that the primary role of the Mediator is that of revelation. "The work of the Mediator is, first and foremost, revelation."[80] Yet it is clear that there is a secure theological link between Brunner's views on revelation and redemption. Both affirm the inability of humanity to come to a true knowledge of God or enter into a proper relationship with God by its own innate abilities. The necessity of revelation and redemption alike is predicated on a human deficit, which renders divine intervention necessary. Like Luther before him, Brunner spoke of the humiliation of human pride through the destruction of our illusions of epistemological and soteriological autonomy through the incarnation and cross.[81]

Brunner's discussion of the second office of Christ – redemption – represents a decisive break with the liberal Protestant tradition from about 1890,[82] which tended to regard traditional language about "sin" as outmoded and unhelpful, especially in the light of evolutionary thought.[83] Although Brunner's views on revelation – especially the human inability to know God fully and properly by natural means – reflect his understanding of human sin, his engagement with the theological importance of the notion is at its most intense in dealing with the question of the salvation of humanity.

Brunner argues that liberal theology of the late nineteenth century tried to force a wedge between "primitive Christianity" and the "Pauline doctrine

---

[77] Karin Bornkamm, *Christus: König und Priester. Das Amt Christi bei Luther im Verhältnis zur Vor- und Nachgeschichte.* Tübingen: Mohr Siebeck, 1998.
[78] *Der Mittler,* 359–91; *The Mediator,* 399–434.
[79] *Der Mittler,* 367; *The Mediator,* 407.
[80] *Der Mittler,* 374; *The Mediator,* 416.
[81] *Der Mittler,* 408–9; *The Mediator,* 452–3.
[82] *Der Mittler,* 392–496; *The Mediator,* 435–546.
[83] Rudolf Otto, "Darwinismus von Heute und Theologie." *Theologische Rundschau* 5 (1902): 483–96; 6 (1903): 183–99, 229–36; 7 (1904): 1–15. See more generally Alfred Kelly, *The Descent of Darwin: The Popularization of Darwinism in Germany, 1860–1914.* Chapel Hill, NC: North Carolina University Press, 1981.

of the atonement", seeing the former (but not the latter) as offering a framework for its "rationalist, idealist conception of religion".[84] Protestant liberalism developed a "deeply rooted prejudice" against forensic approaches to atonement, conflating criticism of "objectionable expressions" of the doctrine with a more fundamental rejection of the doctrine itself.[85]

It is clear that Brunner has Anselm of Canterbury's landmark eleventh-century formulation of the doctrine of the atonement in mind at this point. In *Cur Deus homo*, Anselm insisted on the objectivity of human sin, and the necessity of an appropriate satisfaction as the basis for human forgiveness by God.[86] Christ's sacrifice on the cross both reveals the "most profound humiliation" of human guilt, and provides the grounds for its resolution.

> We can perhaps suspect [*ahnen*] the solidarity of guilt [*Schuld*] apart from Christ. However, as history demonstrates, we are unable to grasp it properly. . . . The sacrifice of Christ is the only adequate ground of knowledge for the unconditional solidarity of guilt.[87]

While emphasizing the importance of the sacrifice of Christ (*Christusopfer*) for the redemption of humanity, Brunner also insists that it is the sole basis of a proper knowledge of human guilt. Once more, we see Brunner's characteristic emphasis upon Christ as the only one who discloses our true situation, and has the ability to transform it.

Finally, Brunner touches on a theme that will be worked out in more detail in his later writings: the significance of Christ for the ethics of the Christian community in particular, and for Christian civilization more broadly.[88] Once more, the foundational role of divine self-revelation is made clear from the outset. The revelation of God is the making known of God's will for the world.[89] Again, the theme of an accommodated or veiled revelation comes into play. God's sovereignty is disclosed in a manner that reflects the limitations of humanity. This "merciful veiling of God's glory" takes the form of a "hidden royal power",[90] which exists in tension with the structures and values of the world.

For Brunner, the rule of God is especially to be related to the community of faith – to the Christian church, within which Christ is recognized as king, through faith. In this interim period between his first and second comings, Christ exercises his authority within the church through his Word. "In this

---

[84] *Der Mittler*, 393–4; *The Mediator*, 437–8.
[85] *Der Mittler*, 397; *The Mediator*, 440.
[86] *Der Mittler*, 410–43; *The Mediator*, 455–89.
[87] *Der Mittler*, 458–9; *The Mediator*, 506.
[88] *Der Mittler*, 497–537; *The Mediator*, 548–90.
[89] *Der Mittler*, 497; *The Mediator*, 548.
[90] *Der Mittler*, 501; *The Mediator*, 551.

church, in this faith, Christ is the fundamental principle, through and as the Word . . . Christ wills to rule in no other way than through his Word."[91] While awaiting the final eschatological disclosure of the power and rule of God, the church struggles to be obedient to Christ.

Perhaps some of Brunner's readers may have experienced frustration at his lack of cultural and ethical specificity at this point. Just how is this obedience to be actualized in the present "crisis" of western culture? Perhaps anticipating this criticism, Brunner suggests that there is a danger that Christian ethics becomes formulaic. The task of Christian ethics, he argues, is to return constantly to its ultimate source and foundation, seeing itself as "means of creating space for God" in contemporary cultural and ecclesial concerns.[92] Yet, in fairness to Brunner, we must recognize that *The Mediator* is a theological manifesto rather than the detailed outworking of an ethical system. Brunner would return to these themes at several points in his career (see pp. 78–85, 185–90), implementing the broad approach mapped out so sketchily in this work.

The Trinity: Dogma, not Kerygma

One aspect of Brunner's account of Christian theology set out in *The Mediator* is of particular interest – his understanding of the purpose and place of the doctrine of the Trinity. After a long period of neglect in the eighteenth and nineteenth centuries, reflecting a lack of confidence in both its rational foundations and practical utility,[93] the doctrine of the Trinity enjoyed a resurgence in the twentieth century, particularly through the work of Karl Barth in the late 1920s and early 1930s.[94]

Barth's growing interest in the doctrine of the Trinity is evident in his correspondence of May 1924, in which he explains his conviction that this doctrine provided the necessary presupposition and foundation of his doctrine of the self-revelation of God.[95] The doctrine of the Trinity thus came to be central to grounding and articulating his view of revelation, and was thus located within the prolegomenon to the *Church Dogmatics*, rather than

---

[91] *Der Mittler*, 536; *The Mediator*, 588.
[92] *Der Mittler*, 562; *The Mediator*, 616.
[93] See the analysis in Paul Chang-Ha Lim, *Mystery Unveiled: The Crisis of the Trinity in Early Modern England*. Oxford: Oxford University Press, 2012.
[94] For a general overview, see Roderick T. Leupp, *The Renewal of Trinitarian Theology: Themes, Patterns, & Explorations*. Downers Grove, IL: IVP Academic, 2008. For Barth and Rahner's landmark contributions to this development, see Bernd Oberdorfer, *Filioque: Geschichte und Theologie eines ökumenischen Problems*. Göttingen: Vandenhoeck & Ruprecht, 2001, 350–418.
[95] Bruce L. McCormack, *Karl Barth's Critically Realistic Dialectical Theology: Its Genesis and Development, 1909–1936*. Oxford: Clarendon Press, 1997, 350–8.

its later dogmatic sections.[96] For Barth, the emphasis on God's freedom in revelation – which he considered to be central to the "dialectical theology" programme – was inextricably linked with a Trinitarian understanding of God.

Yet Barth's specific approach to the Trinity was not developed by others associated with the "dialectical theology" movement. This is not to say that they rejected it; they simply did not share his views on the centrality of the doctrine. This is particularly evident in Brunner's discussion of the theological function of the doctrine in *The Mediator*. Brunner's fundamental position is that the doctrine of the Trinity safeguards the mystery of God, warning us that "when we take seriously the knowledge of God in Christ as a revelation of God, we are confronted with the mystery of the revealed God".[97] The doctrine of the Trinity is not itself given in revelation, but results from reflection on revelation – especially the realization that "God was in Christ". As such, the doctrine of the Trinity is to be considered as a dogma, rather than as part of the Christian proclamation itself.

Brunner did not fundamentally alter his position on the doctrine of the Trinity in later years, although he clarified the point at issue between himself and Barth two decades later. For Brunner, the doctrine of the Trinity cannot be considered as an aspect of theological prolegomena; it must be seen as located within a Christian dogmatics in the proper sense of the term. How, Brunner asked, can a doctrine that is itself the outcome of theological reflection be part of a theological prolegomenon? The real problem, he later suggested, is that Barth failed to make a distinction between the "*problem* of the Trinity" and the "*doctrine* of the Trinity".

> [Barth] does not see that the doctrine of the Trinity is the product of reflection, and is not the *kerygma*. The *kerygma* is God revealed in Christ – Christ, the genuine revelation of God. The doctrine of the Trinity, however, is not itself biblical . . . but is the result of theological reflection upon the problem that is necessarily raised by the Christian *kerygma*.[98]

It is not quite clear that Brunner has totally understood Barth at this point. After all, Barth himself was clear that the doctrine of the Trinity was the result of the community of faith's reflection on Scripture, especially its

---

[96] See Barth's discussion of "The Place of the Doctrine of the Trinity in Dogmatics": Karl Barth, *Church Dogmatics*. Edinburgh: T&T Clark, 1975, I/1, 295–304. For further discussion, see Alan Torrance, "The Trinity." In *The Cambridge Companion to Karl Barth*, ed. John Webster, 72–91. Cambridge: Cambridge University Press, 2000; Michael Weinrich, "Theologischer Ansatz und Perspektive der Kirchliche Dogmatik Karl Barths: Trinitärische Hermeneutik und die Bestimmung der Reichweite der Theologie." In *Karl Barth im europäischen Zeitgeschehen (1935–1950): Widerstand – Bewährung – Orientierung*, ed. Michael Beintker, Christian Link, and Michael Trowitzsch, 15–45. Zurich: Theologischer Verlag, 2010.
[97] *Der Mittler*, 243; *The Mediator*, 275.
[98] *Dogmatik I*, 241; *Dogmatics 1*, 236.

attempts to clarify the nature of the God in whom it believed.[99] "The doctrine of the Trinity is what basically distinguishes the Christian doctrine of God as Christian, and therefore what already distinguishes the Christian concept of revelation as Christian, in contrast to all other possible doctrines of God or concepts of revelation."[100]

Yet Brunner's concern remains valid. How can a dogma that is itself the outcome of theological reflection function as the basis of theological reflection? Is there not an intrinsic theological circularity at this point? For example, consider Barth's assertion: "The basis or root of the doctrine of the Trinity, if it has one and is thus legitimate dogma – and it does have one and is thus legitimate dogma – lies in revelation."[101] There is clearly a question about presuppositions and conclusions that needs to be raised here, and Brunner's concerns expressed above can hardly be overlooked. It may be conceded that Barth was not attempting to derive the dogma of the Trinity, but explaining revelation by making explicit its Trinitarian grammar.[102] Yet the question of the *derivation* of that doctrine is nonetheless inevitable, raising the question of whether Barth's own account of the theological validation of the doctrine is historically or theologically defensible.

Brunner affirms the theological legitimacy of the doctrine of the Trinity, but declines to follow Barth in treating it as a positive ground of Christian dogmatics. Indeed, Brunner suggests at several points in *The Mediator* that, whatever positive themes the doctrine of the Trinity may enunciate, the doctrine must be recognized to have a fundamentally *critical* or *negative* role.[103] The doctrine of the Trinity is essentially a "defensive doctrine" (*Schutzlehre*), the development of which was catalysed by controversy within the early church over two fundamental theological statements, whose validity was being called into question: "God alone can help; and Christ alone is this divine help".[104] Had these two axioms remained unchallenged, Brunner suggests, the doctrine of the Trinity would have proved unnecessary.

---

[99] See Barth, *Church Dogmatics*, I/1, 304–13, 332–3, 379–80, especially the excursus on p. 313.
[100] Barth, *Church Dogmatics*, I/1, 301.
[101] Barth, *Church Dogmatics*, I/1, 311.
[102] A point emphasized in George Hunsinger, "Karl Barth's Doctrine of the Trinity, and Some Protestant Doctrines after Barth." In *The Oxford Handbook of the Trinity*, ed. Gilles Emery and Matthew Levering, 294–313. Oxford: Oxford University Press, 2011.
[103] M. A. Schmidt, "Der Ort der Trinitätslehre bei Emil Brunner." *Theologische Zeitschrift* 59, no. 1 (1949): 46–66.
[104] *Der Mittler*, 243–4; *The Mediator*, 276. Wyons's translation unhelpfully assimilates Brunner's formula to the soteriological categories – "God alone can save" – associated with Athanasius during the Arian controversy. While Brunner's text might indeed be taken to imply salvation, its fundamental reference is to divine "help" (*Hilfe*), making a general reference to grace rather than a more specific reference to salvation. Cf. Dietrich Bonhoeffer's famous statement: "Nur der leidende Gott kann helfen!": Dietrich Bonhoeffer, *Widerstand und Ergebung*. Munich: Kaiser Verlag, 1951, 242.

Brunner does not offer any detailed analysis of the development of early Christian theology in support of his contention that the doctrine of the Trinity is, at least to some extent, a historical contingency rather than a theological necessity. Indeed, at this stage, Brunner's published writings show little active interest in early Christian thought in general, or issues of the development of doctrine in particular. His analysis of the factors leading to the development of the doctrine of the Trinity in the early church is somewhat incomplete, and requires considerable expansion – most notably, in relation to the identity and significance of the Holy Spirit, which receives an inadequate and incomplete discussion in *The Mediator*. The historical framework within which Brunner locates the dogmatic significance of the Trinity can only be considered to be a partial account of this development.[105] Yet there is sufficient historical truth in Brunner's assertion to enable it to be taken seriously, not least in the way in which Brunner goes on to distinguish between Christian *dogma* and *kerygma*.

For Brunner, the doctrine of the Trinity is not part of the Christian *kerygma*. It is not itself a "message to be preached", but a theological doctrine whose primary aim is to safeguard the mystery of faith, and preserve it from misunderstandings.[106] The doctrine of the Trinity does not explain anything, Brunner insists, and was never intended to. "Like the New Testament, we can stand still before it, and confess it; but we do not understand it, as it is God's own mystery [*Geheimnis*]."[107]

Brunner is on much safer ground here, and his comments here can easily be defended, historically and theologically.[108] The doctrine of the Trinity can properly be regarded as an attempt to "safeguard a mystery", designed to enclose and enfold something that cannot be fully comprehended,[109] and protect it from reductive rationalizations that impoverish its imaginative appeal and its theological richness.

---

[105] For a fuller discussion of the development of this doctrine, see Lewis Ayres, *Nicaea and Its Legacy: An Approach to Fourth-Century Trinitarian Theology*. New York: Oxford University Press, 2004. Brunner's formulation of the theological dialectic that he believes to lie behind the evolution of Trinitarianism seems to reflect the debate over divine *monarchia* linked with the Arian controversy, particularly the anti-Arian polemical formulations developed by Athanasius. On this, see Christoph Markschies, "Heis Theos – Ein Gott? Der Monotheismus und das antike Christentum." In *Polytheismus und Monotheismus in den Religionen des vorderen Orients*, ed. Manfred Krebernik and Jürgen van Oorschot, 209–34. Münster: Ugarit Verlag, 2002; Alfons Fürst, "Monotheismus und Monarchie: Zum Zusammenhang von Heil und Herrschaft in der Antike." In *Der Monotheismus als theologisches und politisches Problem*, ed. Stefan Stiegler and Uwe Swarat, 61–81. Leipzig: Evangelische Verlagsanstalt, 2006.
[106] *Der Mittler*, 243; *The Mediator*, 275.
[107] *Der Mittler*, 243; *The Mediator*, 276.
[108] See especially Andrew Louth, *Discerning the Mystery: An Essay on the Nature of Theology*. Oxford: Clarendon Press, 1983, 83–6.
[109] Cf. Augustine of Hippo, *Sermo* 117, which focuses on this theme, and includes the famous maxim *si comprehendis non est deus* (*Sermo* 117.3.5). Nello Cipriani, "Le fonti Cristiane della dottrina trinitaria nei primi dialoghi di S. Agostino." *Augustinianum* 34, no. 2 (1994): 253–312.

Brunner is an important – and, it must be said, neglected – contributor to the twentieth-century theological debate over the place and function of the doctrine of the Trinity in a Christian dogmatics. The divergences over the place of the dogmatic location and function of the doctrine of the Trinity within the "dialectical theology" movement of the mid-1920s have not been given due attention, and remain an important point of debate in theology. Brunner's position and voice need to be heard.

The American Reception of the "Theology of Crisis" (1928)

By the late 1920s, the "theology of crisis" was beginning to be taken seriously in Great Britain. The great Scottish theologian Hugh Ross Mackintosh had drawn attention to the movement in a widely read article of 1925.[110] In 1927, John McConnachie (1875–1948) published a generally appreciative account and evaluation of Barth's theology, focusing particularly on Barth's restoration of the category of revelation.[111] Barth's collection of essays *Das Wort Gottes und die Theologie* appeared in an English translation by the noted ecumenist Douglas Horton (1891–1966) as *The Word of God and the Word of Man* in 1928. This helped create new interest in the movement in Great Britain – and, to a lesser extent, in the United States.[112] Some American scholars of substance were taking Barth seriously by this time – most notably, Wilhelm Pauck of the University of Chicago Divinity School.[113] Perhaps more importantly, a sermon of Barth's was translated and published in *The Student World*, the official organ of the World Student Christian Federation.[114] Growing disillusionment with existing religious paradigms within American Protestantism was leading to a willingness on the part of many church and missionary organizations to explore new approaches – such as the "theology of crisis".[115]

[110] H. R. Mackintosh, "The Swiss Group." *Expository Times* 36, no. 2 (1924): 73–5. This journal, aimed particularly at clergy, was not widely read outside Great Britain.
[111] John McConnachie, "The Teaching of Karl Barth: A New Positive Movement in German Theology." *Hibbert Journal* 25 (1926–7): 385–400. For an assessment of McConnachie's role in disseminating Barth's influence, see John McPake, "John McConnachie as the Original Advocate of Karl Barth in Scotland: The Primacy of Revelation." *Scottish Bulletin of Evangelical Theology* 14 (1996): 101–14. The *Hibbert Journal* – which described itself as a "Quarterly Review of Religion, Theology and Philosophy" – was published in London. Although available through the Boston distributor Sherman, French & Co., it was not widely read in the United States.
[112] This work was published by Pilgrim Press, a small publishing house in Boston. In Great Britain, the work was published by Hodder & Stoughton, a mainstream London publisher.
[113] See especially Wilhelm Pauck, "Barth's Religious Criticism of Religion." *Journal of Religion* 8, no. 3 (1928): 453–74.
[114] Karl Barth, "The Inward Man." *The Student World* 21, no. 3 (1928): 309–15.
[115] For the important debates within these circles in the 1920s and 1930s, see Heather A. Warren, "The Theological Discussion Group and Its Impact on American and Ecumenical Theology, 1920–1945." *Church History* 62, no. 4 (1993): 528–43.

In the end, however, it was Brunner, rather than Barth, who would shape and define American understandings of the "theology of crisis". Yet, as Brunner himself later pointed out, this was probably because the English-speaking world initially tended to think of "Barth and Brunner" as "identical twins", with Brunner being simply the "English mouthpiece" of a shared theological position.[116]

Brunner's growing public profile[117] as a representative of the new approach to theology took an important new direction in 1928, when he was invited to return to the United States to deliver the Swander Lectures at Lancaster Theological Seminary in Pennsylvania. He was invited by the president of the seminary, George Warren Richards (1869–1955), who by this stage had developed an interest in the "dialectical school" of theology.[118] Richards offered Brunner a substantial honorarium of $600 for this lecture series, which proved so successful that he was offered a permanent position at the seminary, along with a house and a salary three times that which he was paid at Zurich.[119] Brunner declined this offer, and shortly afterwards received a bonus of 1,000 francs from a grateful Zurich cantonal administration.

Brunner was in the United States for five weeks during September and October 1928. In addition to his five Swander lectures at Lancaster Theological Seminary, he undertook speaking engagements throughout the region, including Hartford Theological Seminary, Harvard Divinity School, Princeton Theological Seminary, and Union Theological Seminary. His profile soared in the region, along with that of the new theological trend he represented. With the publication of his Swander Lectures in 1929, Brunner's version of the "theology of crisis" achieved virtually canonical status in the United States. These lectures, delivered and subsequently published in English, did much to shape English-speaking perceptions of this new theological movement. Although a major review of Brunner's "theology of crisis" appeared in a leading American religious publication in July 1929, this focused on early writings, especially *The Mediator*, rather than on the substance of his Swander Lectures.[120]

Before exploring the ideas developed in this work, two points need to be emphasized. First, Brunner delivered these lectures in the autumn of 1928, when the American economy was booming. As Brunner himself noted in delivering his lectures, there was no "crisis" in America at this time. Americans, he remarked, had little sense of any "impending crisis", on

---

[116] "Reply", 328. Brunner rightly identifies the 1934 debate over natural theology (see pp. 90–127) as ending this misunderstanding of a joint "Barth-Brunner theology".
[117] For some examples of his growing audience, see Jehle, *Emil Brunner*, 238–41.
[118] Dennis Voskuil, "Neo-Orthodoxy." In *Encyclopedia of the American Religious Experience: Studies of Traditions and Movements*, ed. Charles H. Lippy and Peter W. Williams, vol. 2, 1147–57. 3 vols. New York: Charles Scribner's Sons, 1988.
[119] Jehle, *Emil Brunner*, 242–3.
[120] Bixler, "Emil Brunner as a Representative of the Theology of Crisis."

account of their "economic prosperity and political security".[121] Yet shortly after the work finally appeared in print the following year, Wall Street crashed. Brunner's rhetoric of crisis – only now widely available as a published book – suddenly seemed pertinent and prophetic. The "theology of crisis" may have had some limited impact in October 1928; by the end of October 1929, it spoke directly and powerfully to a nation which realized it was in crisis, having lost both its moorings and bearings. Brunner's ideas, in their published form, resonated strongly with a changed cultural mood.

Second, Brunner delivered these lectures in English, drawing on two American colleagues – Karl J. Ernst and George Richards – for help with his translation. The introduction, which was written at a later date, was translated by Douglas Horton, who had developed an interest in the new theology emerging from the circle around Barth and Brunner. Horton's translation is of interest in a number of ways. For example, it uses the English term "ideology" extensively, despite its absence elsewhere in the lectures. It is not clear what German term is being translated here, although it seems likely to be *Weltanschauung*. Perhaps more importantly, the introduction seems more adapted to the vocabulary and style of Barth's version of the "theology of crisis", raising the difficult – and probably unanswerable – question of whether Horton may have unconsciously assimilated Brunner to Barth.

There are, however, more significant and troubling issues related to the main body of the text. Brunner's English is unclear. At point after point, the reader is left unsure of what his sense is meant to be. There is space to note only one such instance, which serves to illustrate the seriousness of the difficulty. In his discussion of revelation, Brunner repeats and extends his basic position in *The Mediator*, this time using simpler language:

> The revelation of God can never be a true revelation without being, at the same time, a disguise, a *kenōsis*. "God incarnate" means that the Mediator, when he appeared in history, was true man. The Son of God *incognito* walked among men. Faith only can pierce the veil.[122]

Consider the final sentence of that extract: "Faith only can pierce the veil." Is this to be understood as "*Only* faith can pierce the veil"? Or as "Faith can *only* pierce the veil" – that is to say, faith has only a limited purchase on reality? Both are perfectly acceptable readings of the English text. When set alongside *The Mediator*, it seems that the first is clearly the intended reading; the second is nevertheless a possibility, hinting at the limited grasp that faith can hope to gain of deeper realities. Access to the (presumed lost) German original would allow this ambiguity to be resolved immediately.

So what are the leading themes of these lectures? Brunner's earlier experiences in the United States had alerted him to the strongly pragmatic nature

---

[121] *The Theology of Crisis*, 1.
[122] *The Theology of Crisis*, 18.

of American intellectual culture.[123] He appears to have realized that abstract theological speculation was unlikely to secure ecclesial and cultural traction on the part of his audience. Brunner therefore pitches his analysis at the practical level. How should we live? The issue is not about "how one may rightly conceive reality, but how one may rightly exist in the midst of that reality".[124] The churches are called upon to engage with the cultural, economic, and social issues of their time. But how are they to do this?

In an implicit critique of pragmatism, Brunner rejects any outlook which declares that it is not necessary to think about beliefs when reflecting on actions.[125] To *exist* rightly, he insists, one must *think* rightly. With the experience of the Great War in mind, Brunner argues that civilization depends on distinguishing between "the consciousness which is a dangerously destructive ideology, and that consciousness that really creates society".[126] The historical situation generates concepts of society and social existence which need to be corrected and challenged. An epoch's "understanding of life" is the root of its social and economic order. What a society believes thus underlies its social, economic, and ethical norms.

This led Brunner to assert that it is impossible to engage practical questions without a "standard of judgement" and an "understanding of life" – whether explicit or implicit.[127] For the Christian, this demonstrates the centrality of theology as a foundation for practical action and social engagement.[128] Theology is called upon to challenge false and deluded ideologies, and ensure that action is grounded on a reliable and trustworthy understanding of life. "True belief is the opposite of the ideology by which man surrenders to an unreal dream of himself."[129] Brunner thus declares his intention to draw a sharp distinction between "the Christian and the idealistic or naturalistic understanding of life",[130] with a view to catalysing debate about the future direction of culture and society.

Brunner's theological positioning of the "theology of crisis" is of considerable significance, and is indicative of his knowledge of the American religious context, acquired in 1919–20, and maintained subsequently. By 1928, American Christianity was gripped by the modernist–fundamentalist controversy, which led to fissure and schism within mainline denominations,

---

[123] A point emphasized by George Cotkin, "Middle-Ground Pragmatists: The Popularization of Philosophy in American Culture." *Journal of the History of Ideas* 55 (1994): 283–302.
[124] *The Theology of Crisis*, xiii.
[125] *The Theology of Crisis*, xxi–xxii.
[126] *The Theology of Crisis*, xvii.
[127] *The Theology of Crisis*, xxi.
[128] Brunner clearly has in mind the American theological tradition which developed around the philosophical corpus of John Dewey around this time: see, for example, Jerome Paul Soneson, *Pragmatism and Pluralism: John Dewey's Significance for Theology*. Minneapolis: Fortress Press, 1993.
[129] *The Theology of Crisis*, xx.
[130] *The Theology of Crisis*, xxiii.

especially Presbyterianism.[131] While these pressures were felt across the denominational divides, they were particularly important to Lancaster Theological Seminary, which had roots in the Reformed tradition. Presbyterianism was being racked by what seemed like two utterly incommensurable – and, to many, equally problematic – ways of conceiving the tasks of theology and the nature of the church. There seemed to be no *tertium quid*, no *via media*.

Although Brunner makes no reference to it, these concerns had been expressed eloquently in an influential article of 1927 by William Adams Brown (1865–1943), Roosevelt Professor of Systematic Theology at Union Theological Seminary, at which Brunner had studied in 1919–20. Brown was highly regarded within the American theological and ecumenical establishment. In the "The Homeless Liberal",[132] he argued that liberalism was in serious trouble, as evidenced by two recent books by Kirsopp Lake (Harvard Divinity School) and J. Gresham Machen (Princeton Theological Seminary). The two works advocated diametrically opposed approaches to theology, showing not the slightest evidence of any common ground or shared approaches. Lake demanded a total break with the theology of the Christian past; Machen demanded its reaffirmation in absolute and uncompromising terms. The only matter on which they were agreed, Brown commented, with evident sadness, was that "there was no place in the church of the future for a middle-of-the-road man", such as himself. Surely, he pleaded, the time had come to "call a halt" to such polemical exaggerations, and rebuild a consensus within mainline Protestantism?

The mood was right for an alternative approach. In a stroke of genius, Brunner presented the "theology of crisis" in precisely those terms – a *via media* between Lake's experiential modernism and Machen's biblicist fundamentalism. While both modernism and fundamentalism were unsatisfactory, if for very different reasons, Brunner insisted that they did not exhaust the theological possibilities open to the churches. "Fundamentalism and orthodoxy in general are a petrification of Christianity; and modernism and all forms of immanence are its dissolution."[133] Both, Brunner insists,

---

[131] See especially Bradley J. Longfield, *The Presbyterian Controversy: Fundamentalists, Modernists and Moderates*. New York: Oxford University Press, 1991.

[132] William Adams Brown, "The Homeless Liberal." *Religious Education* 22, no. 1 (1927): 12–18. The two works referred to were Kirsopp Lake, *The Religion of Yesterday and To-Morrow*. Boston: Houghton Mifflin, 1925; and J. Gresham. Machen, *What Is Faith?* New York: Macmillan, 1925. On Lake – then Winn Professor of Ecclesiastical History at Harvard Divinity School – see A. M. G. Stephenson, *The Rise and Decline of English Modernism*. London: SPCK, 1984, 99–128. Machen left Princeton Seminary in 1929 in protest against what he regarded as its theological liberalism: see George M. Marsden, "Understanding J. Gresham Machen." *Princeton Seminary Bulletin* 11, no. 1 (1990): 46–60.

[133] *The Theology of Crisis*, 14. On specifically American forms of modernism around this time, see William R. Hutchinson, *The Modernist Impulse in American Protestantism*. New York: Oxford University Press, 1976, 288–311. Brunner refers specifically to neither Lake nor Machen; the general positions that they represent, however, are clearly presupposed in his analysis.

represent the same fundamental tendency – a misplaced and uncritical quest for certainty. "Modernism and fundamentalism are born of the same mother, that is, of the fear of sound critical thinking."[134] What does Brunner mean by this?

On the one hand, modernism is "controlled by a non-critical faith in reason", and is thus locked into a limited world, determined by what can be verified. The very possibility of divine revelation is thus excluded as a matter of principle by this dogmatic and uncritical rationalism. Appeals to "experience" – so enthusiastically advocated by Lake – amounted to circular and self-referential accounts of reality.

> What the most modern theology, especially in America, calls *experiencing* God, is in fact *an interpretation* of the world, based on inward spiritual convictions. It is an interpretation of the universe from the point of view of a self-interpreting mind.[135]

On the other hand, fundamentalism – which Brunner tends to equate with a neo-conservative Protestant orthodoxy – is locked into an uncritical "insistence on the rigidity and finality of its form". For Brunner, fundamentalism adopts an uncritical approach to the Bible, which collapses the theologically significant distinction between "the Word of God in the Scriptures" and the "words of the Scriptures".[136] Such an "uncritical interpretation of the Bible" leads inevitably to a legalist (Brunner actually uses the term "pharisaical") understanding of Christianity, which leads to its engagement with the modern world becoming "disfigured and encumbered".[137]

Brunner argued that these two extreme positions on the theological spectrum can be seen as different embodiments of the same fundamental error – uncritical acceptance of flawed theological norms. But there are other viable positions on that theological spectrum, which allow us to maintain both the great themes of the Christian tradition and a commitment to sound thinking. The "theology of crisis" is thus to be seen as a viable, even attractive, possibility for those disillusioned with these opposing formulations of the same basic theological error. Yet Brunner's theological proposal involves the redefinition, rather than the mere reassertion, of the theological middle.

Theology is concerned with "God's movement towards man", which the "Bible calls revelation, reconciliation, redemption, salvation".[138] Brunner here articulates more succinctly a thought which is expressed more diffusely in *The Mediator* – namely, that the movement of God towards humanity has many aspects or layers. Revelation is not a "miraculous theophany" – that

---

[134] *The Theology of Crisis*, 21.
[135] *The Theology of Crisis*, 28–9.
[136] *The Theology of Crisis*, 18–19.
[137] *The Theology of Crisis*, 21.
[138] *The Theology of Crisis*, 13.

is, a "direct appearance of the Deity".[139] True revelation is indirect and veiled, communicated through the Word, which can only be grasped and understood by faith. Yet this same divine movement towards humanity offers transformation, as much as illumination.

> It pleased God in his mercy to throw a bridge across the chasm between himself and man and to blaze a trail where man himself could not go. It pleased God to visit man who cannot come to God. This approach of God to man, this divine condescension, this entering into a world of sin and sinners burdened with their sense of contradiction to him, just this constitutes the mystery of divine revelation and reconciliation in the incarnate and crucified Christ.[140]

Brunner stresses that it is God who "removes the contradiction by bearing it himself" on the cross. In every respect, God takes the initiative – in coming to us, in resolving the human contradiction, and in making reconciliation. "Faith is real faith only when man has given himself up and relinquished his trust in his religion and rests on God alone."[141]

Later in the work, Brunner explores issues of ethics and politics, in particular criticising the "fatal error" of identifying the biblical notion of the "Kingdom of God" with optimistic theories of progress deriving from the Enlightenment.[142] It is not difficult to see the ideas so powerfully developed in the 1930s in an emergent form in these chapters. Yet it is clear that many in the United States saw the appeal of Brunner's theological vision lying chiefly in its capacity to clear the ground, and allow a fresh and positive approach to theology to emerge in the aftermath of the damaging fundamentalist controversies of the 1920s. The positive reception to Brunner's approach, especially within American organizations concerned with missionary work and student ministry,[143] clearly suggested a resonance between his approach and the needs of the age.

Brunner's star was now rising in the English-speaking world.[144] But what of his own European context? What of his relation to Barth? And how was his new theological programme being received amongst his peers?

---

[139] *The Theology of Crisis*, 34.
[140] *The Theology of Crisis*, 60.
[141] *The Theology of Crisis*, 61.
[142] *The Theology of Crisis*, 111. It is possible that Brunner was criticizing certain aspects of the "social gospel", then prevalent within American Protestantism. For the American context of this movement, see William R. Hutchison "The Americanness of the Social Gospel: An Inquiry in Comparative History." *Church History* 44, no. 3 (1975): 367–81. For a more critical approach, see Susan Curtis, *A Consuming Faith: The Social Gospel and Modern American Culture*. Columbia, MO: University of Missouri Press, 2001.
[143] See, for example, J. H. Oldham, "Review of Books." *International Review of Missions* 19, no. 74 (1930): 280; Jesse R. Wilson, "Reviews." *Far Horizons* 11, no. 7 (1931): 31. *Far Horizons* was the successor to the *Student Volunteer Movement Bulletin*.
[144] For reasons that are not understood, *The Theology of Crisis* was never published in German: Jehle, *Emil Brunner*, 250.

3
Reflections on the Tasks of Theology, 1929–1933

Brunner returned to Switzerland from his triumphant lecture tour of the north-eastern United States at the end of October 1928.[1] He rejoined his wife in Basle, where they spent a few days with Eduard Thurneysen before returning to Zurich in time for the winter semester. Brunner's contacts with the English-speaking world would continue in the next few years. In March 1931, he travelled to Great Britain, and delivered five lectures at King's College London. He then journeyed to Scotland, and gave what appear to have been truncated versions of these lectures at Trinity College Glasgow, and New College, Edinburgh.[2] In June 1930, he went again to Edinburgh to receive an honorary doctorate in theology.

I shall consider some of the themes developed in these 1931 lectures presently, as they remain of landmark importance, and have yet to be fully appreciated in the German-language theological world. They include the statement for which Brunner is now best known in the English-speaking world: "The Church exists by mission, just as a fire exists by burning."[3]

Yet my initial focus is on Brunner's reflections on the role of theology in connecting with culture, particularly his concern that the churches should have a rigorously theological foundation for their critique of the ideologies that were coming to play such a significant role in European intellectual life. By 1930 Brunner had given clear expression to a major theme in his understanding of theology, already implicit in many of his writings of the early 1920s – namely, that one of the main tasks of theology is *critical*, in that it is called upon to challenge and counter the ideologies of its age. I shall consider this theme and its cultural background in what follows.

---

[1] Frank Jehle, *Emil Brunner: Theologe im 20. Jahrhundert*. Zurich: Theologischer Verlag, 2006, 244.
[2] Jehle, *Emil Brunner*, 250.
[3] *The Word and the World*, 108.

Emil Brunner: A Reappraisal, First Edition. Alister E. McGrath.
© 2014 John Wiley & Sons, Ltd. Published 2016 by John Wiley & Sons, Ltd.

Crisis: The Rise of Ideology in Western Europe, 1920–1935

The Great War (1914–18) traumatized many intellectuals in western Europe, raising deep and troubling questions concerning the adequacy of settled ways of thinking, especially optimistic views on human nature and the stabilizing influence of culture.[4] The war shook the cultural and intellectual tectonic plates of western Europe, causing many to lose their faith in civilization and the inevitability of human progress.[5] Oswald Spengler's *Decline of the West* (1918) and J. B. Bury's *Idea of Progress* (1920) called into question the idea of a continuous upward development of human culture and civilization.[6] The conditions were ripe for social and political instability, as old authority structures were toppled or discredited.[7]

The most significant of these radical shifts was the 1917 Bolshevik Revolution in Russia,[8] which took place in two stages. There was an initial uprising against the tsarist regime early in 1917 in St Petersburg, then the Russian capital. This "February Revolution" (which actually happened in March 1917, according to the western calendar) took place against the background of massive Russian losses in the Great War, and increasing disillusionment with the social and economic policies of the tsar. In the chaos of the situation, members of the Duma – the Russian imperial parliament – seized power, and declared themselves to be the provisional government of the nation. The tsar and his family were placed under house arrest. At this stage, the intention of the revolutionaries was to bring about a liberal democracy within the collapsed Russian empire. Negotiations with Germany led to the humiliating Treaty of Brest-Litovsk, which brought the war to an end by conceding massive tracts of territory.

Yet a more radical group, led by Vladimir Ilich Lenin (1870–1924) and informed by Karl Marx's political ideas, was in the process of consolidating its influence. The Bolshevik faction seized its opportunity in the "October Revolution" (which took place in November 1917, according to the western

---

[4] See the general analysis of Belinda Davies, "Experience, Identity, and Memory: The Legacy of World War I." *Journal of Modern History* 75 (2003): 111–31. The aftermath of the Great War was especially troublesome for German liberal Protestantism, which tended to posit a close relationship between church and state: see especially Thomas Nipperdey, *Religion im Umbruch: Deutschland 1870–1918*. Munich: C. H. Beck, 1988, 92–106.

[5] See, for example, Paul Fussell, *The Great War and Modern Memory*. Oxford: Oxford University Press, 1975; Modris Eksteins, *Rites of Spring: The Great War and the Birth of the Modern Age*. Boston: Houghton Mifflin, 1989.

[6] Robert A. Nisbet, *The History of the Idea of Progress*. New York: Basic Books, 1980, 321–2.

[7] Charles S. Maier, "The Two Postwar Eras and the Conditions for Stability in Twentieth-Century Western Europe." *American Historical Review* 86, no. 2 (1981): 327–52.

[8] See Mark Steinberg, *Voices of Revolution, 1917*. New Haven, CT: Yale University Press, 2001; Rex A. Wade, *The Russian Revolution, 1917*. Cambridge: Cambridge University Press, 2005.

calendar), establishing a workers' state. Civil war broke out, in which the Bolshevik "Red Army" fought the "White Army" of foreign troops and internal opponents of the Bolsheviks. By 1924, the tsar and his family had been executed and any credible opposition to the Bolsheviks eliminated. The Soviet Union became a state governed by an ideology, with state organs directed towards its propagation in neighbouring states – above all, Germany.[9] The unsuccessful "November Revolution" of 1918–19 led German revolutionaries such as Rosa Luxemburg (1871–1919) to agitate for a Soviet-style workers' state.[10] Marxism-Leninism, whether in popularized or more academic forms, became a significant influence in the Weimar Republic during the 1920s.

In one sense, the Weimar Republic (1919–33) can be seen as a democratic polity imposed on imperial Germany by the victorious allies in the aftermath of the Great War.[11] The failed Soviet-style revolution of 1918–19 highlighted the need for stability and security within the former German empire. Yet the Weimar Republic attracted little support from Christian theologians. Adolf von Harnack, Martin Rade, and Ernst Troeltsch were the most prominent among its few religious supporters.[12] Most – including Karl Barth – were critical.[13] Yet this must not be taken as representing any endorsement of anti-democratic tendencies by Barth;[14] it was simply a consistent application of his principles, which led him to refuse to acknowledge any political system as ultimately Christian. Weimar was not the Kingdom of God; Christians had to work out how best to live out their lives in this situation.[15] Brunner took a similar position in the 1920s, particularly in his 1928 lectures *The Theology of Crisis*.[16]

---

[9] Adam Bruno Ulam, *The Bolsheviks: The Intellectual and Political History of the Triumph of Communism in Russia*. Cambridge, MA: Harvard University Press, 1965.
[10] On which see Alexander Gallus, ed., *Die vergessene Revolution von 1918/19*. Göttingen: Vandenhoeck & Ruprecht, 2010.
[11] Eric D. Weitz, *Weimar Germany: Promise and Tragedy*. Princeton, NJ: Princeton University Press, 2007.
[12] As argued by Trutz Rendtorff, *Christentum zwischen Revolution und Restauration: Politische Wirkungen neuzeitlische Theologie*. Munich: Claudius Verlag, 1970.
[13] Klaus Tanner, "Protestantische Demokratiekritik in der Weimarer Republik." In *Die Kirche und die Weimarer Republik*, ed. Richard Ziegert, 23–35. Neukirchen: Neukirchen-Vluyn, 1994; Christophe Chalamet, "Karl Barth and the Weimar Republic." In *The Weimar Moment: Liberalism, Political Theology, and Law*, ed. Leonard V. Kaplan and Rudy Koshar, 241–68. Lanham, MD: Lexington, 2012.
[14] The view somewhat improbably propounded by Falk Wagner, "Theologische Gleichschaltung: Zur Christologie bei Karl Barth." In *Die Realisierung der Freiheit: Beiträge zur Kritik der Theologie Karl Barths*, ed. Trutz Rendtorff, 10–43. Gütersloh: Gütersloher Verlagshaus Mohn, 1975.
[15] As pointed out by Timothy R. Gorringe, *Karl Barth: Against Hegemony*. Oxford: Oxford University Press, 1999, 91.
[16] *The Theology of Crisis*, 92–113, especially 108–10. Brunner does not specifically mention the Weimar Republic, but the general principles he enunciates are easily transposed to this context.

In part, the appeal of this ideology reflected the financial crisis which gripped Germany during the 1920s.[17] The failure of a democratic government to come to grips with the crisis created space for ideologically driven alternatives – Communism and National Socialism.[18]

In Italy, Benito Mussolini came to power in 1922, propounding a Fascist ideology, loosely modelled on forms of Social Darwinism, which repudiated democratic rule, arguing that it led to weak government. Although this ideology was malleable and open to local adaptations,[19] its appeal in the face of the failure of democratic governments to take decisive action in the face of economic and political difficulties could hardly be ignored.

On the other side of the Atlantic, things looked rather different. There was no "crisis" in the United States in the aftermath of the Great War, as there had been in western Europe. The United States was a late and somewhat reluctant entrant to the war. Its territories were never under threat, and its economic and military commitment to the war was modest.[20] After a brief recession in 1920–1, the American economy began to expand, leading to a rising stock market and rising standards living and social expectations.[21] Brunner's visit in 1919–20 brought home to him the radical difference in the economic and social situations faced by the churches in western Europe and the United States.

Yet despite this cultural divergence, Brunner proclaimed his "theology of crisis" from a number of significant ecclesial platforms in the United States in 1928 (see pp. 54–60), publishing *The Theology of Crisis* in 1929. He faced a double challenge in using this theological terminology. First, Americans tended not to be particularly concerned about any kind of theory, whether theological or economic. The mindset was pragmatic, rather than theoretical. And secondly, few in America thought that they faced a crisis of any kind. If there was a religious crisis, it concerned how Protestant denominations coped with internal tensions over the challenges of modernity in a rapidly changing social context.

Then everything changed. In October 1929, Wall Street crashed. The signs of economic overheating were perhaps more easily seen with

---

[17] The best is Gerald D. Feldman, *The Great Disorder: Politics, Economics, and Society in the German Inflation, 1914–1924*. New York: Oxford University Press, 1993.
[18] Richard J. Evans, *The Coming of the Third Reich*. London: Allen Lane, 2003, 77–230.
[19] Zeev Sternhell, Mario Sznajder, and Maia Ashéri, *The Birth of Fascist Ideology: From Cultural Rebellion to Political Revolution*. Princeton, NJ: Princeton University Press, 1994. For its appeal in France, see Mark Antliff, *Avant-garde Fascism: The Mobilization of Myth, Art, and Culture in France, 1909–1939*. Durham, NC: Duke University Press, 2007.
[20] Robert H. Zieger, *America's Great War: World War I and the American Experience*. Lanham, MD: Rowman & Littlefield, 2000.
[21] Gene Smiley, "A Note on New Estimates of the Distribution of Income in the 1920s." *Journal of Economic History* 60, no. 4 (2000): 1120–8. For the background, see Gene Smiley, *Rethinking the Great Depression*. Chicago: I. R. Dee, 2002, 1–30.

hindsight;[22] at the time, they do not seem to have been fully appreciated, nor their implications grasped. The Great Depression began in the United States. There was now a real crisis of confidence within America's easy-going pragmatic outlook. Brunner's *Theology of Crisis*, which had appeared only months earlier, now seemed prophetic. Its moment had come.

The Wall Street crash of October 1929 marked the beginning of a worldwide slump of unprecedented severity, which proved fatal for the political stability of the Weimar Republic in Germany.[23] A chain of events was unleashed which led to the political triumph of Adolf Hitler's National Socialist German Workers' Party, widely known as the "Nazis". Hitler was installed as the German chancellor in 1933. Joseph Goebbels translated the ideology of National Socialism into a popular movement, replete with a quasi-religious symbolism and mythology.[24] Nazi ideology began to exercise influence in Switzerland during the 1930s, with Wilhelm Gustloff (1895–1936) playing a significant role in advancing its agendas in German-speaking Switzerland.[25]

Where older European conflicts involved national interests, the new continental fault-lines were increasingly ideological. National issues and identities might be brought into these conflicts; nevertheless, their roots lay in ideologies rather than nationalism. As ideology became an increasingly powerful force in Europe from the late 1920s, it became increasingly significant for Christian churches to be able to develop a theological response to this new phenomenon. The rise of National Socialism and Marxism-Leninism reflects the rise of ideologically driven movements and agendas in western Europe, which remained important until the 1950s, when support for them began to diminish.[26]

In 1929 Brunner published an essay which laid the foundation for a theological engagement with the new ideologies. With the benefit of hindsight, this can be seen as one of his most important theological achievements. It has not received the attention it merited, either at the time or in

---

[22] Peter Rappoport and Eugene N. White, "Was the Crash of 1929 Expected?" *American Economic Review* 84 (1994): 271–81.
[23] Harold James, "Economic Reasons for the Collapse of the Weimar Republic." In *Weimar: Why Did German Democracy Fail?*, ed. Ian Kershaw, 30–57. London: Weidenfeld & Nicolson, 1990. More generally, see Patricia Clavin, *The Great Depression in Europe, 1929–1939*. London: Palgrave Macmillan, 2000.
[24] For the early forms of this ideology, see Thomas Klepsch, *Nationalsozialistische Ideologie: Eine Beschreibung ihrer Struktur vor 1933*. Münster: LIT Verlag, 1990.
[25] Matthieu Gillabert, *La propagande nazie en Suisse: L'affaire Gustloff 1936*. Lausanne: Presses Polytechniques et Universitaires Romandes, 2008.
[26] For classic accounts of the reasons for the rise and fall of the importance of ideologies in western Europe from about 1950, see Raymond Aron, "Fin de l'âge idéologique?" In *Sociologica*, ed. T. W. Adorno and W. Dirks, 219–33. Frankfurt: Europäische Verlaganstalt, 1955; Otto Brunner, "Der Zeitalter der Ideologien." In *Neue Wege der Sozialgeschichte: Vorträge und Aufsätze*, 194–219. Göttingen: Vandenhoek & Ruprecht, 1956.

subsequent historical and theological reflection. For this reason, I shall consider it closely in what follows.

Brunner's Challenge to Ideology: The "Other Task of Theology" (1929)

In 1929, a short paper by Brunner entitled "Die andere Aufgabe der Theologie" ("The Other Task of Theology") appeared in *Zwischen den Zeiten*, the journal founded in 1922 by Barth, Gogarten, and Thurneysen as an organ for the emerging dialectical theology movement.[27] The "first task of theology", Brunner declares, is to call the church to reflect on the Word of God. Such a theology is necessarily biblical and systematic, rather than historical or philosophical.[28] It is essentially *biblical* in so far as the Bible is the primary witness to the event of revelation. It is essentially *systematic* in so far as it explores the conceptual connections (*sachliche Zusammenhängen*) of the Word witnessed to in the Bible.

Yet while such "contemplative representation" of the Word is the primary task of theology, it cannot be separated from a second – the critique of existing human ways of thinking and believing. Brunner had already made this point in *The Theology of Crisis*, where he emphasized the importance of theological engagement with "ideologies" and "understandings of life". He now gave this theological critique a name: theology, he declared, necessarily had an "eristic" (from the Greek *erizein*, "to debate") role. Brunner found himself forced to invent this term, having misgivings about others – such as the softer "apologetic" and the harsher "polemic".[29] This task of theology concerned engaging, challenging, and subverting the ideologies of the world, especially naturalism and idealism.[30] Yet the term "eristic" never really caught on, perhaps contributing to the gradual marginalization of Brunner's important insight.

Three fundamental points – all of which are explored in his writings up to this point – underlie Brunner's insistence that the "eristic" aspects of Christian theology be recognized, alongside the traditional understanding of dogmatics as the systematic explication of divine revelation.

---

[27] "Die andere Aufgabe der Theologie": *Ein offenes Wort*, vol. 1, 171–93. For this theme in the Barth–Brunner correspondence, see Werner Kramer, "'Die andere Aufgabe der Theologie': Ein bleibendes Anliegen Emil Brunners im Briefwechsel mit Karl Barth." *Theologische Zeitschrift* 57 (2001): 363–79.
[28] "Die andere Aufgabe der Theologie": *Ein offenes Wort*, vol. 1, 171.
[29] "Die andere Aufgabe der Theologie": *Ein offenes Wort*, vol. 1, 176.
[30] The best assessment of Brunner's eristic approach is Michael Roth, *Gott im Widerspruch? Möglichkeiten und Grenzen der theologischen Apologetik*. Berlin: de Gruyter, 2002, 464–563. See also Paul G. Schrotenboer, *A New Apologetics: An Analysis and Appraisal of the Eristic Theology of Emil Brunner*. Kampen: Kok, 1955; Gabriele Lunghini, *Emil Brunner*. Brescia: Editrice Morcelliana, 2009, 59–88.

1   The church faced ideological challenges – such as the rise of Bolshevism in the 1910s and, although Brunner could not have known this in 1929, the rise of National Socialism in the 1930s – and was under an obligation to engage with these. The church could not ignore the fact that it exists in a world shaped by a variety of "understandings of life", some of which were benign, and others dangerous. Theology must provide the churches with a platform for intellectual engagement with the surrounding culture, by allowing it to discriminate between the benign and the pathological.
2   The church must engage with the world in which it is located, where existential questions dominate, learning the language of its cultural context. Dogmatics is an activity in which the church explores and articulates its own resources; eristics is an activity in which the church enters into dialogue with its cultural context on the basis of its dogmatic foundations.[31]
3   Christian history indicates that Christian theology often developed in polemical or confrontational situations, especially during the period of the early church. Recognizing the eristic dimension of theology is about realizing that the church is often called to debate issues of the day, offering responses to situations and questions that are specific to a given situation.[32] Where some argue that dogmatics is a "timeless" restatement of Christian truth, Brunner prefers to think of theology as being "born of the need of the hour, and burdened with that need".[33] As he later put it, there is "an *evangelium perennis* but not a *theologia perennis* . . . The gospel remains the same, but our understanding of the gospel must ever be won anew."[34]

None of these insights were new to Brunner, in that all had been explored in his earlier writings. Brunner's essay "The Other Task of Theology" is best seen as a consolidation of these points, framed in a pointed manner, designed to challenge an approach which he believed failed to do justice to the nature of theology, or to engage adequately with the situational needs and opportunities of the church. Not surprisingly, one of the positions Brunner critiques – though in an understated manner – is the position adopted by Barth in the second edition of his commentary on Romans.

---

[31] At this point, Otto Ritschl's somewhat critical review of Barth's *Dogmatik im Entwurf* should be noted, especially his concern that preachers must be grounded in the cultural context of their audience before they can communicate effectively and gain a hearing for the gospel in the secular world: Otto Ritschl, "Rezension über Barths *Christliche Dogmatik im Entwurf.*" *Theologische Literaturzeitung* 53 (1928): 217–28.
[32] For a detailed analysis of the importance of this point for Brunner, see Heinrich Leipold, *Missionarische Theologie: Emil Brunners Weg zur theologischen Anthropologie*. Göttingen: Vandenhoeck & Ruprecht, 1974, 151–290.
[33] *The Theology of Crisis*, xiii.
[34] "Toward a Missionary Theology", 816.

Brunner had clearly enunciated this "eristic" theme in his earlier work *The Theology of Crisis*. He there argued that theology provides the Christian community with a platform from which it can critique the dominant ideas of its culture – the "generative thoughts" that can lead to dangerous ideologies, on the one hand, or to wisdom on the other.[35] Theology offers the church a means by which it can discriminate between false ideologies and realistic understandings of human existence.[36]

Brunner sharpens this approach in "The Other Task of Theology". Theology is about challenging the self-positing and self-justifying *Vernunftaxiom* ("axiom of reason").[37] An essential aspect of every conflict in which theology becomes involved, through serving the Word of God, is the calling into question of this axiom of reason. Theological polemic is directed above all against the axiom of reason.

This "axiom of reason", Brunner suggests, is generally framed using a "non-existential concept of truth",[38] which is inattentive to the subjective side of human existence, and thus fails to do justice to the Christian understanding of truth, or to the apologetic possibilities within culture. Theology is able to recover an authentic approach to reason from the exaggerated conceptions of reason that had gained influence since the time of the Enlightenment.

It is by exposing the pretensions of reason that its proper use is to be discerned. By allowing the "delusion of reason" (*Vernunftwahn*) to be grasped and recognized, theology allows the theologically legitimate use of reason to be discovered and applied. For Brunner, true belief is *right* belief. Faith is not "blind"; rather, it is about seeing things properly, as they really are.[39]

Brunner's exposition of the "other task of theology" implies that human reason is at least partly capable of grasping the inner rationality of faith, and realizing the limitations of a purely rational outlook on life. Theology does not aim at the "violation" (*Vergewaltigung*) of human reason, but at "overpowering" (*Überwältigung*) its hegemony. Brunner's imagery points to theology aiming at reasoned consensus, rather than at intellectual coercion. Theology is able to open doors to faith without recourse to the famous *sacrificium intellectus*.[40] It aims to abolish rational delusions, correct false turns, and fulfil the deepest – and, Brunner would add, God-given – intentions of human reason.

Yet this understanding of the eristic role of theology is laden with presuppositions about the nature of the divine–human nexus in revelation, especially the extent of human reason to be able to grasp something of the

---

[35] *The Theology of Crisis*, xvii.
[36] *The Theology of Crisis*, xxi.
[37] "Die andere Aufgabe der Theologie": *Ein offenes Wort*, vol. 1, 172.
[38] "Die andere Aufgabe der Theologie": *Ein offenes Wort*, vol. 1, 187.
[39] "Die andere Aufgabe der Theologie": *Ein offenes Wort*, vol. 1, 173.
[40] "Die andere Aufgabe der Theologie": *Ein offenes Wort*, vol. 1, 173.

reality that is conveyed in divine revelation. It is perhaps at this point that Brunner's divergence from Barth around this time is to be seen at its clearest. Consider the following succinct and pointed statement of this "other" task of theology.

> It is the most fundamental task of eristic theology to show that humanity can only understand itself correctly through faith, and that it can only achieve what it longs for inwardly through the Word of God; that only through the Christian faith can it become what it is meant to be, and which it has tried to become itself, in various ways.[41]

Now if theology is able to "show" (*zeigen*) humanity that it can only understand itself properly through faith, and achieve its proper destiny in and through the Christian faith, does this not presuppose a certain human ability to reason in order to reach such insights? Is not an ability to connect up with humanity presupposed in any attempt to "show" humanity where it has gone wrong?

Brunner's anthropology now begins to play a critically important role. Some of his critics at this point suggest that his doctrine of revelation is determined by his anthropology; this is a somewhat unsatisfactory criticism, in that Brunner's anthropology is actually determined by his understanding of revelation. This becomes clear in his emphatic insistence that it is the "unanimous witness of experience, the Bible, and all classical Christian theology" that there is a "human knowledge of God" that is "not a saving knowledge".[42] This fundamental datum shapes Brunner's reflections on human nature. Any authentically Christian understanding of humanity must come to terms with the biblical and theological insistence that humanity has an innate idea of God, even if this amounts to a "not-knowing", or a "not-knowing-rightly". Humanity bears God's image, and is thus capable of some "knowledge" of God, no matter how distorted this may be. Human questioning about God is itself indicative that there is in fact a "point of connection [*Anknüpfungspunkt*] within humanity for the divine proclamation".[43]

---

[41] "Die andere Aufgabe der Theologie": *Ein offenes Wort*, vol. 1, 177.
[42] "Die andere Aufgabe der Theologie": *Ein offenes Wort*, vol. 1, 178. Brunner does not elaborate on this, but it is highly likely that he has the Reformed tradition in mind. His phrasing echoes Calvin's understanding of the scope and limits of a natural knowledge of God: see, for example, Edward A. Dowey, *The Knowledge of God in Calvin's Theology*. New York: Columbia University Press, 1952; David Reiter, "Calvin's 'Sense of Divinity' and Externalist Knowledge of God." *Faith and Philosophy* 15 (1998): 253–70; Barbara Pitkin, *What Pure Eyes Could See: Calvin's Doctrine of Faith in Its Exegetical Context*. New York: Oxford University Press, 1999, 159–63. On the later Reformed tradition, see Martin Klauber, "Jean-Alphonse Turrettini (1671–1737) on Natural Theology: The Triumph of Reason over Revelation at the Academy of Geneva." *Scottish Journal of Theology* 47 (1994): 301–25.
[43] "Die andere Aufgabe der Theologie": *Ein offenes Wort*, vol. 1, 178. ". . . der in der Tat der *Anknüpfungspunkt* der göttlichen Botschaft im Menschen ist".

Brunner rejects any suggestion that this notion of a "point of connection" represents some kind of Pelagianism. The basic point is that the Christian proclamation "does not address a human being who knows and possesses absolutely nothing from God". The notion of being *ansprechbar* – in everyday German, "approachable", but in Brunner's more technical sense, "addressable" – now begins to emerge as a core theme in Brunner's understanding of human nature. Although Brunner derived the notion of "addressability" (*Ansprechbarkeit*) from the personalist philosopher Ferdinand Ebner (see p. 26), Brunner's use of the notion is best seen as reflecting a conviction of its theological utility than a commitment to its philosophical correctness.

Such a natural "knowledge" of God is inadequate as any kind of foundation for Christian theology, and is not to be understood or interpreted as such. Nevertheless, it remains true that the human questioning about God points to some inner "knowledge of a God", however unreliable and inadequate this may be. "The proper task of Christian eristics is thus to teach human beings to understand their own question about God."[44]

Yet this "questioning" must not be understood in purely cognitive terms. It can be framed in terms of anxiety, or an inner sense of contradiction. Brunner's language in many parts of this essay is existential, concerned with the inner experiential world of human nature. His reading of Kierkegaard alerted him to the deficiency of purely cognitive approaches to theology, which offered an "objectivity" which failed to encapsulate and communicate the subjective aspects of faith. Where Barth valued Kierkegaard around this time for his critical perspectives,[45] Brunner was more interested in the way in which Kierkegaard illuminated the subjectivity of faith, allowing theology to connect up with existential concerns.

An eristic theology, Brunner argues, recognizes that it is impossible to expose and explore the fundamental internal contradictions of humanity without engaging with fundamentally existential questions. There is a danger, he suggests, that theology may become preoccupied with "objective theoretical reasoning" (*objektiver theoretischer Beweisführung*) and thus betray its own subject-matter (*Sache*). In order to show humanity that "it is not what it wants to be; that it is in contradiction with itself, without any prospects, unable to help itself out", it is necessary to engage at a subjective level with the existential domain, after the manner of Pascal and Kierkegaard.[46]

The marked divergence from Barth here and at other points was obvious, even if Brunner sometimes chose to understate it. Perhaps the most significant remark in the essay is to be found in Brunner's suggestion that a "false

---

[44] "Die andere Aufgabe der Theologie": *Ein offenes Wort*, vol. 1, 179.

[45] As noted by Lee C. Barrett, "Karl Barth: The Dialectic of Attraction and Repulsion." In *Kierkegaard's Influence on Theology: 1 – German Protestant Theology*, ed. Jon Stewart, 1–41. Aldershot: Ashgate, 2012.

[46] "Die andere Aufgabe der Theologie": *Ein offenes Wort*, vol. 1, 178.

enthusiasm for the honour of God" has led some theologians to demolish the "bridge which God has left sinful humanity towards faith".[47] This, he argued, was without warrant, either from the New Testament or from the Reformation tradition. "The rejection of a *theologia naturalis* from the outset and in every sense of the term is neither Pauline nor faithful to the Reformation."[48]

Barth could hardly overlook this challenge, which led to what seems to have been a somewhat tense confrontation on 6 June 1929 between the two at the "Bergli", the home of Rudolf and Gerty Pestalozzi in the mountains overlooking Lake Zurich, which served as Barth's summer retreat. This was followed by what appears to have been a more conciliatory meeting a month later. In an article of 1930,[49] Barth was critical of Brunner's eristic approach, suggesting that it amounted to trying to limit or control divine self-revelation, ultimately making theology dependent on anthropology. "Incredibly good theology loses its way over one small point: it no longer says that human thought engages with the Word of God only through faith."[50]

For his part, Brunner made it clear that he could not see why Barth should find difficulty with a theologically grounded anthropology, or a *theologia naturalis* that rested on rigorously theological foundations.[51] Both seemed to him to safeguard central dogmatic concerns, while allowing a theologically rigorous engagement with cultural and intellectual concerns across a broader front. Barth and Brunner would publicly disagree on this issue in 1934; this, however, was simply the open manifestation of differences that were already firmly established and mutually acknowledged by 1929.

Furthermore, Brunner argued, preaching had both "eristic" and "dogmatic" elements – something he believed that Barth had either failed to see at all, or had at least failed to see *clearly*. "Preaching proclaims the word – certainly! But it speaks it to *people*."[52] Failing to grasp the eristic dimension of theology means that preaching does not connect up with contemporary people; it simply *declaims* "pure doctrine" to them, failing to make contact at the existential level.

If theology is to engage with the contemporary concerns of humanity, challenging people's illusions and helping them realize that their true concerns are not what they believe them to be, Brunner argues that it must

---

[47] "Die andere Aufgabe der Theologie": *Ein offenes Wort*, vol. 1, 190.
[48] "Die andere Aufgabe der Theologie": *Ein offenes Wort*, vol. 1, 191.
[49] Karl Barth, "Die Theologie und der heutige Mensch." *Zwischen den Zeiten* 8 (1930): 374–96.
[50] Karl Barth, "Die Theologie und der heutige Mensch", 394–5. Barth's essay criticizes Brunner, Bultmann, and Gogarten, indicating Barth's growing impatience with his colleagues.
[51] See especially Brunner's long and pained letter to Barth of 8 June 1929: *Karl Barth–Emil Brunner, Briefwechsel*, 174–81.
[52] "Die andere Aufgabe der Theologie": *Ein offenes Wort*, vol. 1, 192.

address the current situation of its audience, in both church and society at large. His approach to theology is marked by his explicit recognition of the historically and culturally situated character of both theological reflection and preaching. Theological reflection "does not take place in a vacuum," but in a context that is already populated with spiritual ideas and values – like a house that is already occupied, to which theology seeks access.[53]

Yet perhaps the most significant point to be made concerning Brunner's insistence upon the explicit recognition of an eristic dimension to theology – whether this term is used or not – concerns the readiness of the churches to challenge and subvert ideologies. Theology is about struggle (*Kampf*) and service (*Dienst*), enabling the church to be heard and understood in the world, and challenging the validity and reliability of alternative worldviews.[54] For Brunner, understanding the proper identity and function of Christian theology is about enhancing the theological readiness of the Christian communities to deal with cultural contexts which cannot comprehend, or are deliberately opposed to, the Christian proclamation.

Although some suggest that it was Barth's theology that enabled and empowered the German churches as they struggled to cope with the rise of the ideology of National Socialism, it is important to appreciate that Brunner offered those same churches a ready-made theological template for the assessment and subversion of such ideologies. Its core elements were in place by 1929, even though Brunner continued to develop their foundations and extend their reach over the next decade.[55] Brunner's insistence upon the "eristic" task of Christian theology had the potential to enable the churches to engage its cultural alternatives, both by forewarning of the possibility of hostile ideologies, and by providing theological resources in order that they might be engaged and neutralized.

The approach that was adopted, defended, and commended by Brunner can be traced back to debates within the early church about attitudes to secular culture, and especially Roman imperial culture. Where some (such as Justin Martyr) seemed to offer a somewhat uncritical "Yes", and others (such as Tertullian) an equally uncritical "No", to secular ideas, Augustine argued for their *critical appropriation*.[56] Brunner regarded Barth as offering a simplistic negation of the human sciences; a more appropriate response was their critical engagement, filtering out what could be used with profit, and discarding what could not. Brunner saw one of the central tasks of theology as providing such a filter, enabling the theologian to engage in

---

[53] "Die andere Aufgabe der Theologie": *Ein offenes Wort*, vol. 1, 171.
[54] "Die andere Aufgabe der Theologie": *Ein offenes Wort*, vol. 1, 189.
[55] See, for example, his paper "Secularism as a Problem for the Churches." *International Review of Missions* 19 (1930): 495–511.
[56] For further discussion, see Robert L. Wilken, *The Spirit of Early Christian Thought: Seeking the Face of God*. New Haven, CT: Yale University Press, 2003; Carol Harrrison, *Rethinking Augustine's Early Theology*. Oxford: Oxford University Press, 2006.

critical dialogue with the broader world of culture, appropriating what was valuable or useful.

This is especially clear in Brunner's assessment of how a theologian might engage with contemporary psychology, perhaps seen at its clearest in a lecture he delivered at a conference in Spandau – a western district of Berlin – in March 1930.[57] As noted earlier (pp. 18–20), Brunner was aware of the importance of psychology, and had given thought to its potential implications for theology. In this lecture, he noted that the fundamental characteristic of any "science" is its "absence of presuppositions" and its "purely empirical character".[58] Yet he urged caution on any who advocated an uncritical use of empirical psychology for theological purposes. Psychology takes a "definite worldview" (*bestimmte Weltanschauung*) – which Brunner goes on to identify as a form of naturalism – as its "axiomatic presupposition".[59]

By identifying such ideological precommitments within the discipline, Brunner argued, the Christian is in a position to criticize its overstatements, and sift out what can be of value to the ideas and ministry of the churches. Noting the multiplicity of approaches to psychology, Brunner insists that they are open to theological critique, evaluation, and hence partial appropriation. The Christian faith provides a normative or regulative standpoint, from which their value and utility may be judged.[60]

None of them is in a position to recognize the limits and provisionality of their perspectives, unless these standpoints are understood as mere working methods, whose grounds and limits are both rooted in the Christian faith.

Brunner thus argued for the legitimacy and utility of a specifically "Christian or biblical psychology", understood as an aspect of a theological anthropology.[61] Such a Christian psychology would be "regulative" rather than "constitutive" – in other words, rather than providing its own distinct research programmes, a Christian psychology is to be conceived as offering a framework of interpretation and evaluation by which the critical appropriation of secular psychological theories and methods might be undertaken.[62] In particular, Brunner noted how the fundamental theological notions of humanity as created in the image of God, on the one hand, and being fallen and sinful on the other, provided a framework for understanding the tensions observed within human nature,[63] including the "contradiction" which he was coming to regard as constitutive of humanity.

---

[57] Jehle, *Emil Brunner*, 239–40. For the text of the lecture, see *Gott und Mensch*, 70–100; *God and Man*, 136–78.
[58] *Gott und Mensch*, 71; *God and Man*, 137.
[59] *Gott und Mensch*, 71; *God and Man*, 138.
[60] *Gott und Mensch*, 97; *God and Man*, 174.
[61] *Gott und Mensch*, 79 n. 1; *God and Man*, 150 n. 1.
[62] *Gott und Mensch*, 81; *God and Man*, 152.
[63] *Gott und Mensch*, 81–6; *God and Man*, 152–9.

Some portray Brunner as offering an unconditional or uncritical affirmation of secular viewpoints and methods. It is impossible to maintain this position. Brunner's opposition to what he regarded as Barth's monolithic "No" was not its polemical inversion – an equally uncritical "Yes" – but a theologically constructed and grounded framework of evaluation, which enabled discerning judgements to be made concerning what was to be affirmed, and what to be rejected. Brunner's vision of "eristic theology" – whether it is to be referred to by that clumsy term or not – allows the Christian community to engage in critical dialogue with culture, rather than withdrawing into its own linguistic and theological ghetto.

Presenting Dialectical Theology in Britain: *The Word and the World* (1931)

The positive reception of his ideas in the United States in 1928 led Brunner to accept invitations to speak on his theological vision at King's College London in March 1931. He went on from London later that month to give a shortened version of the lectures at Edinburgh and Glasgow. His lectures set out to clarify the nature and scope of "dialectical theology".[64] Brunner's choice of this term merits further reflection, given his preference for a "theology of crisis" in 1928. He continued to value the phrase "theology of crisis". It highlighted the internal contradictions of human experience, and the fact that humanity was placed in the "critical position" of having to make an "existential decision" about its true identity and purpose.[65] Yet Brunner's clear preference is now for "dialectical theology". Why?

Brunner's response demonstrates once more the growing importance of the eristic dimension of his vision of theology. "For Christianity, the conflict with modern thinking is a fight for its very existence."[66] Theology enables the church to challenge this "type of modern thought which, although wearing a Christian disguise, is really in antagonism to the thought of Scripture". For Brunner, this "fight with modern thinking is the task, supremely, of theology".[67] The five London lectures, Brunner declared, were "an active part of this struggle". They contain much of his mature insights on theology *in nuce*, stated with clarity and concision.

These lectures have not been given their due weight in assessing the nature and scope of Brunner's theological vision, despite his clear statement of their programmatic significance. Yet he makes it clear that these lectures have a double role: engaging the modern world, and clarifying the nature

---

[64] The published version of these lectures – *The Word and the World* – reproduces the text of the London lectures. No German edition of this work was ever produced.
[65] *The Word and the World*, 7.
[66] *The Word and the World*, 5.
[67] *The Word and the World*, 6.

of "dialectical theology". Even from the terse statements which preface these lectures, it is clear that Brunner's understanding of this approach to theology is not Barth's. Yet it is historically impossible to define "dialectical theology" in terms of Barth's (changing) framework, when it is clearly a contested notion, with others – such as Gogarten and Brunner – offering accounts of its fundamental themes and methods which indicate its diversity. "Neither Barth not I nor any other member of our group has conferred on it this title."[68]

So where does Brunner begin his theological exposition? Paradigmatically, with the prologue to the fourth gospel, parts of which serve as a motto to the first lecture, entitled "The Word of God and Reason".[69] The word became flesh – that is, "truth has come, or more accurately, has *become*, in an historical event" – in "the absolutely unique event which by its very nature could happen only once, or never at all".[70] When modernity speaks of "truth", it means "timeless truths" or "eternal truths" – all truth which human beings, to the extent that they are human, know or could know.[71] But Christianity is different. The Christian faith deals with

> a knowledge of God which in no way is founded in man, which by no means is obtainable by man through his religious or metaphysical faculties or through his religious experience. It is knowledge of God from beyond all human possibilities – truth which is given in the event which constitutes revelation, in the unique decisive occurrence of history, in the Word of God.[72]

In his earlier writings, Brunner tended to emphasize the "limits" (*Grenzen*) of humanity, which prevented it from gaining access to the vantage point of the "far side". His understanding of the human predicament has now expanded, leading him to suggest a qualititative, not merely quantitative, difference between truths of human knowledge and of revelation. Brunner's point now is that divine revelation takes a form and discloses a content which is fundamentally different from everything that humanity itself can know on the basis of its own resources. In terms of both its "source as well as its content",[73] it stands over and above notions of truth arrived at by human endeavour.

Brunner asserts that concepts of truth arising from ethics, religion, and metaphysics have three general characteristics: they are *universal, timeless,*

---

[68] *The Word and the World*, 6. It is not clear how Brunner's London audience would have understood his reference to "our group", which suggests a degree of collaboration and collusion that does not actually seem to have existed. By this time, Barth had largely washed his hands of his former theological partners Brunner, Bultmann, and Gogarten, maintaining theological intimacy only with Thurnseysen.
[69] *The Word and the World*, 11.
[70] *The Word and the World*, 11–12.
[71] *The Word and the World*, 12.
[72] *The Word and the World*, 16.
[73] *The Word and the World*, 18.

and *impersonal*. In marked contrast, the "Christian faith asserts that the Word of God is not general, that it is historical, and that it is personal."[74] Revelation is thus not about the *amplification* of human knowledge; it is about the *disclosure of a different kind* of knowledge. God does not extend our natural grasp of truth, which conceives God "only as an object, not as subject". Rather, God "interrupts the monologue of our thought about God", and addresses us as a "Thou".[75]

Revelation is thus about the interruption of the individual's "monologue". We might believe – or tell ourselves – that we are the "master of the world", and that God is "somehow localized in it", as an object to be found or discovered at our convenience and discretion. Divine self-disclosure, Brunner argues, is tantamount to divine *self-assertion*, in which we are forced to realize that we are no longer masters of our own world. Faith is an existential decision; it is my "relation towards the God who speaks to me from outside myself"; it is a recognition that this God is Lord of my world. As Brunner deftly remarked, "A thought-of God is never Lord."[76] The limits and scope of reason must be acknowledged: "Where reason pretends to know God, it creates a reason-God, and that always is an idol."[77]

Brunner here develops ideas he had set out earlier in a lecture delivered in the autumn of 1929 to a vacation conference in Stuttgart, in which he compared philosophical notions of God with the "creator God of faith".[78] The human situation is such that we need to be told something that we are incapable of telling ourselves. We need to recognize our intrinsic tendency to yearn to master what we experience by forcing everything into a system. Yet God simply cannot be tamed and constrained in this manner.[79] Divine revelation challenges human notions of autonomy, exposing our philosophical notions of God as idols of our own making, and demanding that we listen and respond to God's self-disclosure.

> God's communication represents an assertion of mastery [*Herrschaftsanspruch*] over me.... The revelation of God represents the shattering of my narcissistic thinking, in which I am always at the centre; the event in which God displaces me from this central position, so that I cease to be my own master, and acknowledge another as master.[80]

Using Ebner's dialogical categories, Brunner insists that God refuses to be treated as an object, but remains a "subject over against me", so that "I

---

[74] *The Word and the World*, 18.
[75] *The Word and the World*, 22–3.
[76] *The Word and the World*, 25.
[77] *The Word and the World*, 33.
[78] Jehle, *Emil Brunner*, 239–40. For the text of the lecture, see *Gott und Mensch*, 1–23; *God and Man*, 38–69.
[79] *Gott und Mensch*, 15–16; *God and Man*, 58–9.
[80] *Gott und Mensch*, 15–16; *God and Man*, 59–60.

become an object", in effect surrendering the autonomy of my world and ideas to God.[81]

Such ideas are explored further in Brunner's London lectures. In revelation, God addresses humanity, asking to be heard, and allowed to enter. Revelation is about the shattering of preconceived mental worlds, and human preconceptions and constructions of who God is, and what God wants. God "is knowable only by the act of His self-impartation in His Word, in which He Himself tells us His will, in the double sense – His demand and his Gift, His commandment, and His Word of grace".[82] In being addressed by God, human beings are enabled to become "truly personal". That God is "personal" is indicated in many ways, yet perhaps most importantly in that God chooses to become known "by His telling us His own name".[83] God "is the self-speaking, not the thought-of or the looked-at God".[84] The initiative in self-disclosure thus lies with God.

For Brunner, the idea of revelation entails a recognition that, since the Word originates beyond human reason, it cannot be judged by that reason. "God gives the world something absolutely new and at the same time final from outside of all that is historical, ideal, and human; something that cannot be verified, pronounced upon, or pigeonholed, but only believed."[85] Brunner here draws attention to the *subjectivity* of faith. Faith is to be sharply distinguished from "all objective knowledge", whether orthodoxy or rationalism. It is "subjective in the sense that here all cool disinterestedness, all scientific objectivity, is banished".[86]

Yet perhaps the most distinctive feature of these lectures is Brunner's accentuation of the missionary tasks of Christian believers and the church. In his final lecture, dealing with "the church and society", Brunner emphasizes the obligations laid upon believers by faith. "Everyone who receives this Word, and by it salvation, receives along with it the duty of passing this Word on."[87] Mission is thus an integral aspect of the lives of believers and the Christian community:

> The Church exists by mission, just as a fire exists by burning. Where there is no mission there is no Church; and where there is neither Church nor mission, there is no faith.[88]

There is a danger, Brunner warns, that the church can lose its identity and its distinct function by becoming "thoroughly poisoned by modern

---

[81] *Gott und Mensch*, 16; *God and Man*, 59–60.
[82] *The Word and the World*, 30.
[83] *The Word and the World*, 30.
[84] *The Word and the World*, 64.
[85] *The Word and the World*, 45.
[86] *The Word and the World*, 75.
[87] *The Word and the World*, 108.
[88] *The Word and the World*, 108.

thought".[89] If the church simply proclaims "social ethics applied to public life", it is writing its own death certificate. The gospel begins by *giving*, not *demanding*. "It gives to the world what the world neither has nor knows; it discloses the secret of God's loving purposes, the message of reconciliation; thus laying a foundation for community."[90]

Brunner would return to his reflections on the nature of the church later in his career (see pp. 182–3, 199–204). Given his later concerns, it is important to note how he accentuates the ability of the Word of God to generate community. Confronted with a "fundamental individualism which makes community impossible",[91] he argues that God's word creates and sustains both truth and community. Although he does not give a full explanation of what he has in mind, the hints are clear enough to allow us to follow them through. "The truth of the divine Word is no impersonal truth; it consists in love."[92] Brunner's basic point is that God addresses humanity, to call people out of their solitude and individuality into a community of truth and love.

A Theological Ethics: *The Divine Imperative* (1932)

Brunner's emphasis upon theology's place in the life of the Christian individual and community is expressed particularly in his concern to establish a theological ethics – that is to say, an ethic that is authentically Christian, reflecting and expressing core theological principles.[93] The Word of God generates, sustains, and informs the Christian community. For Brunner, the core theological issue that must be addressed is that which so troubled Paul and Luther: if we are justified by faith, what is the basis of ethics? Surely the proclamation of the central Reformation doctrine of justification by faith leads to moral paralysis, in that there is no obvious motivation for good works?

Brunner considered this concern in a lecture delivered in the autumn of 1929 at various universities in the Netherlands, dealing with the relation of justification and ethics,[94] a theme which was foundational to his later ethical reflections. The lecture is important in terms of confirming Brunner's embeddedness within the theological tradition of the Reformation, particularly in relation to Martin Luther.[95] For Brunner, it is essential that Christian

---

[89] *The Word and the World*, 124.
[90] *The Word and the World*, 125.
[91] *The Word and the World*, 126.
[92] *The Word and the World*, 127.
[93] Svend Andersen, *Einführung in die Ethik*. 2nd edn. Berlin: de Gruyter, 2005, 286–91; Matthias Zeindler, "Emil Brunner (1889–1966)." In *Schweizer Ethiker im 20. Jahrhundert: Der Beitrag theologischer Denker*, ed. Wolfgang Lienemann and Frank Mathwig, 85–104. Zurich: Theologischer Verlag, 2005.
[94] "Der Rechtfertigungsglaube und das Problem der Ethik." In *Gott und Mensch*, 24–46; *God and Man*, 70–102.

morality should have its own distinct and defensible foundation, and that it should not be reduced to the generalized rational ethics of a "religion of the Enlightenment".[96] The utility of an ethical system is an indication neither of its truth nor of its Christian character.

Brunner argues that a properly Christian ethics rests on two fundamentally theological convictions: first, that humanity is unable to attain the good without grace; and second, that a secular ethic is essentially that of self-realization, reflecting a form of egoism. For Brunner, the doctrine of justification functions as a critic of such approaches, insisting in the first place that we are to be judged against a criterion that is not of our own creation – namely, the law of God – and in the second that we are not capable of achieving its goals in our own strength.[97] This second point plays such an important role in Brunner's ethical thought that it needs further comment.

For Brunner, any ethical system constructed and articulated outside the Christian revelation rests upon the deeply problematic notion of the "goodness of humanity", and the attendant belief that, once a moral obligation is recognized, it can be achieved. Such an ethics is ultimately Pelagian, reflecting a "works-righteousness" that is grounded in the view that humanity is able to establish a correct relationship with God unaided, thus discerning and performing good. On this view, "humanity is God's equal [ebenbürtiger] partner."[98]

The self-revelation of God in Christ abolishes this "legalistic relationship with God". God's gracious acts of self-revelation and the bestowal of grace allow us to see things in a new way, and to act differently as a result.[99] The "glorious freedom of the children of God" consists in being liberated from the delusion that we are called upon, or expected, to achieve goodness. God's self-disclosure leads to a reorientation and de-centring of human existence, in that our lives are no longer egocentric, concerned with self-actualization. The Christian life is not about "human striving", but about "God's giving".[100] Christian ethics is about a divinely ordained and divinely

---

[95] For the theological issues raised by Luther's *articulus iustificationis*, see Ernst Wolf, "Die Rechtfertigungslehre als Mitte und Grenze reformatorischer Theologie." *Evangelische Theologie* 9 (1949): 298–308. Barth's disinclination to accept Wolf's analysis is a significant indication of his ambivalence towards Luther's articulation of this doctrine: see Alister E. McGrath, "Karl Barth and the *Articulus Iustificationis*: The Significance of His Critique of Ernst Wolf within the Context of His Theological Method." *Theologische Zeitschrift* 39 (1983): 349–61. Barth and Brunner differed over their interpretations of Wolf's important study *Martin Luther: Das Evangelium und die Religion* (1934) – which Brunner considered to support the notion of an *Anknüpfungspunkt*: Jehle, *Emil Brunner*, 302.
[96] *Gott und Mensch*, 24–5; *God and Man*, 70–1.
[97] *Gott und Mensch*, 28–9; *God and Man*, 76–7.
[98] *Gott und Mensch*, 28; *God and Man*, 75.
[99] *Gott und Mensch*, 32; *God and Man*, 82.
[100] *Gott und Mensch*, 33; *God and Man*, 82. "[Der Mensch] hat seinem Leben nicht mehr in eigenen Streiben, sondern in Gottes Geben."

enabled response to God's self-disclosure, which discloses God's will *for us* – and hence what God desires *from us*.[101]

These fundamental themes, set out in Brunner's 1929 Dutch lectures, are developed and expanded in *The Divine Imperative* (1932). It is important to consider the full original German title of this work: *Das Gebot und die Ordnungen: Entwurf einer protestantisch-theologischen Ethik* ("The Command and the Orders: An Outline of a Protestant Theological Ethics"). The title of the later English translation of this work – *The Divine Imperative* – must be regarded as somewhat unhelpful, even if it was well-meaning (and was actually sanctioned by Brunner himself). The German title conveys precisely both the substance and the context of Brunner's landmark text. It is an attempt to develop an approach to Christian ethics, located within the Protestant ecclesial and theological tradition, based on an appeal to the dual concepts of the "[divine] command" and the "orders [of creation]".

The use of the phrase "orders of creation" might seem to imply a static situation, in which some social structures have permanent ethical validity. As we shall see, Brunner did not take the view that any specific "order" is "willed" by God, or has some absolute divine authorization. Rather, his point was that God's command to us is addressed to a specific situation. We are called to respond to God within the "actual social environment" in which we are placed, rather than some abstract location, disconnected from history and culture.[102]

Brunner explicitly embeds himself within a theological tradition he believes to have emerged within the formative period of Protestant theology in the sixteenth century. His reading of both Luther and Calvin persuaded him of the importance of the notions of *lex naturalis* and *cognito Dei naturalis* for ethics and apologetics. While this judgement was contested at the time, particularly in the case of Luther, recent scholarship has strongly affirmed Brunner's fundamental theological insights.[103] Modern Luther scholarship has created conceptual space for a recalibration of theological ethics grounded in Luther's approach, giving a new lease of life to that of Brunner. The revival of interest in the natural law tradition on the part of Protestants and evangelicals in the late 1990s and

---

[101] *Gott und Mensch*, 39; *God and Man*, 91.

[102] See especially *Das Gebot und die Ordnungen*, 332–3; *The Divine Imperative*, 339.

[103] See, for example, Antti Raunio, "Natural Law and Faith: The Forgotten Foundations of Ethics in Luther's Theology." In *Union with Christ: The New Finnish Interpretation of Luther*, ed. Carl E. Braaten and Robert W. Jenson, 96–124. Grand Rapids, MI: Eerdman, 1998; David Yeago, "Martin Luther on Grace, Law and Moral Life: Prolegomena to an Ecumenical Discussion of *Veritatis Splendor*." *The Thomist* 62 (1998): 163–91; Bernd Wannenwetsch, "Luther's Moral Theology." In *The Cambridge Companion to Martin Luther*, ed. Donald K. McKim, 120–35. Cambridge: Cambridge University Press, 2003. See also the older study of John T. McNeill, "Natural Law in the Thought of Luther." *Church History* 10 (1941): 211–27.

beyond clearly points to Brunner as a theological dialogue partner in the further development of this agenda.[104]

The Divine Imperative was widely recognized as a landmark proposal for a theological ethics embedded within the Protestant tradition, and taking its distinctive theological tenets with the utmost seriousness. The work opens with what could be regarded as a set piece of "eristic theology", in the form of a sustained theological critique of any "natural morality" (*natürliche Sittlichkeit*).[105] This extended eristic discussion echoes points made in the opening chapters of *The Mediator* and the Dutch lecture on ethics of the autumn of 1929. Brunner opens by asserting, and subsequently demonstrating, that there is no self-evidently correct notion of "the Good"; indeed, such is the diversity of opinion on the issue that many have declared the question to lie beyond meaningful resolution. The question of the nature of "the Good" is both unavoidable (*unvermeidlich*) and incapable of resolution by secular means. As a result of his historical and theological critique of "natural morality", Brunner concludes that it has collapsed into a "field of rubble", lacking any firm foundation or sense of coherence. Such theories are based on abstract moral "principles" and the elimination of any notion of "guilt". In his sustained theological critique of such naturalist theories of ethics, Brunner argues that they are ultimately intellectually unsustainable.[106]

Yet Brunner is emphatic that these difficulties with prevailing secular ethical theories do not demand the rejection of the deepest moral intuitions of humanity. Despite its obvious failures, naturalism has "preserved something of the truth". Brunner's ethical vision does not entail the negation of human moral instincts, but corrects their distortion by secular ethical systems. A Christian ethic, like the Christian faith itself, is not based on any "idea" or "principle" which can function as some kind of "synthesis". Rather, it is based on God's self-revelation, which discloses the true state of things, and the "action of divine restoration" which is proclaimed in God's justification by grace alone. The failure of secular ethics thus puts us in a position in which we are receptive to a hearing of the "divine command" – a "law without legalism", which creates the possibility of responding to God's address in love and obedience.[107] God summons believers, initially to a personal relationship of faith, and subsequently to a faithful obedience through which that faith is appropriately expressed.

---

[104] See J. Budziszewski, *Written on the Heart: The Case for Natural Law*. Downers Grove, IL: InterVarsity Press, 1997; Michael Cromartie, ed., *A Preserving Grace: Protestants, Catholics, and Natural Law*. Grand Rapids, MI: Eerdmans, 1997. Brunner's reflections on human contradiction can be usefully related to J. Budziszewski, *The Line Through the Heart: Natural Law as Fact, Theory, and Sign of Contradiction*. Wilmington, DL: Intercollegiate Studies Institute, 2009.
[105] *Das Gebot und die Ordnungen*, 1–94; *The Divine Imperative*, 17–107.
[106] *Das Gebot und die Ordnungen*, 58; *The Divine Imperative*, 67.
[107] *Das Gebot und die Ordnungen*, 54–68; *The Divine Imperative*, 68–81. This section recapitulates many of the points made in the Dutch lecture of 1929 (see pp. 78–9).

For Brunner, Christian ethics is not about enforced conformity to a rulebook. Rather, the believer is called upon, individually and personally, to live out the Christian life in a manner which embodies and expresses the love of God which God commands. "The Christian never has to act according to general principles, but always according to the concrete command of love."[108] At times, Brunner treats "the Divine Command" (*das Gottes Gebot*) as notionally equivalent to "the love which God commands" (*die von Gott gebotene Liebe*).

As Brunner himself acknowledges, this essentially relational approach to ethics makes it impossible to envisage God's intentions in a given situation in advance. The predictability and generality of "Law" gives way to the individual and situational specificity of "Command". We therefore have to receive the divine command "afresh each time through the words [*Reden*] of the Spirit".[109] Brunner counterbalances this potentially individualist understanding of Christian ethics – "I do what I believe God wants me to do" – with the notion of the "orders of creation", which impose structure and limits on our actions.[110] Brunner interprets these "created orders" (*Schöpfungsordnungen*) as "the existing realities of human social life, which underlie all historical existence as unalterable presuppositions [*unveränderliche Voraussetzungen*]".[111] Such "orders of creation" – such as the state and family – enable humanity to restrict the impact of sin, and impose limits on the scope of human actions. There is thus a sense in which Christian ethics is essentially conservative, aiming to preserve what is already in existence.

Yet Brunner qualifies this approach in an important manner. These "orders" must ultimately be recognized as distorted and flawed through sin. "What is given [*das Gegebene*] is not what has been created by God [*das Gottesgeschaffene*], but what has been created by God in its distorted form as a result of sin."[112] This is an insight of revelation, which prohibits us from passively endorsing and accepting the structures of the world as if they were automatically to be considered as divine. We do not have access to *das Gottesgeschaffene*; we therefore are in danger of confusing this primordially good created order with what we observe around us – what

---

[108] *Das Gebot und die Ordnungen*, 182; *The Divine Imperative*, 197. Note that the English translation tends to translate the German term *das Gebot* as both "command" and "commandment", apparently according to context. Although this is entirely understandable, it could lead to confusion at points.

[109] *Das Gebot und die Ordnungen*, 97; *The Divine Imperative*, 111.

[110] For good accounts of the ethical limits of such a "theology of orders", see Hans-Richard Reuter, *Rechtsethik in theologischer Perspektive: Studien zur Grundlegung und Konkretion*. Gütersloh: Kaiser Verlag, 1996, 94–101; Martin Honecker, *Einführung in die theologische Ethik: Grundlagen und Grundbegriffe*. Berlin: de Gruyter, 2002, 291–303.

[111] *Das Gebot und die Ordnungen*, 194; *The Divine Imperative*, 210. See further Howard Douglas Lee, *The Orders of Creation in the Ethical Theory of Emil Brunner*. Dubuque, IA: University of Iowa Press, 1972.

[112] *Das Gebot und die Ordnungen*, 199; *The Divine Imperative*, 214–15.

Brunner terms *das Gegebene*. Furthermore, human sinfulness means that something that is essentially good can be subverted, and become idolatrous. What was intended to help people live together collectively could degenerate into an instrument of tyranny assuming absolute significance, and thus assuming the role of an idol.

God's work as creator must therefore be set alongside and seen in the light of God's work as redeemer, with the latter providing us with a theological lens which enables us to recognize the penultimacy of the given order.

> Adaptation [*Einfügung*] to the existing order, in that it has been created by God, is thus the *first* word of Christian ethics; but it is never its *last*. What God wills as Creator is always the first; but – even when seen completely apart from our sin – it is not the last. For God wills to draw out the creation beyond itself, into the *perfection* of all things. God does not preserve the world in order to preserve it, but in order to perfect it.[113]

Brunner's point is that there is a tension between the orders of creation and redemption. The present order of things is not to be identified with the "created order" *tout simple*; rather, it is a refracted or distorted version of this order, which requires transformation. Christian ethics is not about accepting things as they are, but about being willing to be agents of transformation and renewal. The divine "command" therefore demands discernment in any given situation, and cannot be reduced simply to an impetus to conserve. Although Brunner is often designated as a representative of the "divine command" school of ethics,[114] this judgement needs to be treated with some caution. Brunner's ethics is somewhat more complex than this reductionist assessment implies.

Brunner's explicit appeal to the "orders of creation" further alienated him from Barth, who regarded this as a deplorable lapse into a theologically indefensible account of natural law.[115] What defence could be offered against the possibility that such "orders" were simply human constructions, lacking any revelational foundation? Yet we need to recall that none of the confessional documents of the Reformation – whether Lutheran or Reformed – rejected

---

[113] *Das Gebot und die Ordnungen*, 198–9; *The Divine Imperative*, 214.

[114] See, for example, Dale E. Burrington, "The Command and the Orders in Brunner's Ethic." *Scottish Journal of Theology* 20 (1967): 149–64; David Andrew Gilland, *Law and Gospel in Emil Brunner's Earlier Dialectical Theology*. London: T&T Clark, 2013. For significant recent defences of the "Divine Command" approach to ethics, see Robert Merrihew Adams, *Finite and Infinite Goods: A Framework for Ethics*. New York: Oxford University Press, 1999; David Baggett and Jerry L. Walls, *Good God: The Theistic Foundations of Morality*. New York: Oxford University Press, 2011.

[115] See Barth's rather glacial letter to Brunner of 10 January 1933: *Karl Barth–Emil Brunner, Briefwechsel*, 213–17. For an excellent account of Barth's approach, see David VanDrunen, *Natural Law and the Two Kingdoms: A Study in the Development of Reformed Social Thought*. Grand Rapids, MI: Eerdmans, 2010, 316–47.

the notion of natural law. Furthermore, Brunner's development of the dialectic between creation and redemption, and his insistence that the socially phenomenological must not be equated with the theologically legitimate, place him at some distance from the position that Barth actually critiqued.

Brunner's *Divine Imperative* consolidated his reputation as a substantial thinker, willing to provide a rigorous theological foundation for the life and witness of Christians, individually and corporately. There is, he declared, an "indissoluble connection" between dogmatics and ethics.

> Every theme of dogmatics is necessarily also a theme of ethics. There is no "dogmatics" as such, just as there is no "ethics" as such; rather, dogmatic knowledge as such always aims at existential – and therefore ethical – thought, just as ethical knowledge is grounded in a knowledge of dogmatics.[116]

It is not difficult to appreciate that the field of dogmatics that Brunner considers to be especially important for ethics is anthropology. A Christian understanding of human nature, developed in the light of God's self-revelation in Christ, subverts the forms of ethical reasoning favoured by the Enlightenment and Romanticism, not least because of their failure to engage the fundamental problem of human sin and guilt. Brunner is not given to citing English poets; nevertheless, Robert Browning's lines from *Gold Hair* seem peculiarly appropriate in reflecting on Brunner's significance as a Christian ethicist:

> 'Tis the faith that launched point-blank its dart
> At the head of a lie – taught Original Sin,
> The corruption of man's heart.[117]

Yet Brunner's ethics reflect other core themes of his anthropology – perhaps most obviously his emphasis on human identity as shaped by a relationship with God, which provides the context for ethical reflection and action.[118] Brunner's emphasis on the individual's relationship with God through faith never leads him into the utopian notion of the self-sufficient moral thinker, divorced from society and tradition. Human beings exist individually and socially; that is part of the order of creation. "The truly personal self and the community arise and disappear in the same act."[119] Yet it is not unfair to suggest that certain aspects of his anthropology still require a little further fleshing out, partly to give added plausibility to his

---

[116] *Das Gebot und die Ordnungen*, 71; *The Divine Imperative*, 84.
[117] *The Poems of Robert Browning*. Ware, Herts.: Wordsworth Editions, 1993, 474. Brunner would, of course, have preferred to speak of "guilt" rather than "original sin".
[118] See Sara Stöcklin, *Grundlagen der Ethik bei Emil Brunner*. Munich: Grin Verlag, 2008, 14–22.
[119] *Das Gebot und die Ordnungen*, 277–92; quote at p. 288; *The Divine Imperative*, 293–307; quote at p. 303.

ethical vision, but more fundamentally to give stability to his theology of human nature. I shall return to explore this further when I consider his remarkable *Man in Revolt* (1937).

The range of Brunner's ethical vision – which can only be hinted at in this brief account – is impressive, showing both mastery of theological detail and attentiveness to the complexity of human existence and experience. If doubts remained about Brunner's commitment to connecting theology with the life of the church and society, this substantial volume provided grounds to dispel them. Yet his commitment to the life of the churches led him to develop a relationship with a group of Christians that proved to be somewhat ambivalent. In what follows, I shall explore how Brunner came to be associated with the "Oxford Group".

A Problematic Liaison: Brunner and the Oxford Group

One of Brunner's most characteristic traits was his concern for denominational diplomacy and dialogue, especially with the churches of the English-speaking world. His trips to Great Britain and the United States were well received, and raised his profile considerably. If American or British theologians had been asked during the 1930s to name a prominent Swiss theologian, most would have responded by naming Brunner.

Yet Brunner's ecumenical instincts occasionally led him to make what might now be seen as misjudgements, particularly when he stood at some cultural distance from the movements he chose to favour. One such movement was the Oxford Group, founded by the American Lutheran pastor Frank Buchman (1878–1961).[120] Buchman's first pastoral ministry was based in a suburb of Philadelphia in 1902. Yet problems developed, and Buchman seems to have had some kind of breakdown. He took an extended holiday to Europe to recuperate, and ended up visiting the Keswick Convention in 1908.

The Keswick Convention, located in England's Lake District, had by that time established itself as a centre of personal spiritual renewal within the evangelical tradition.[121] Founded in 1875, the Convention was mainly

---

[120] Many German sources refer to this as *die Oxforder Gruppenbewegung* – "the Oxford Group Movement". This addition of the term "movement," which is absent from English references to the Group, risks confusing it with the "Oxford Movement" (German: *die Oxforder Bewegung*) – the high church revival movement within the Church of England during the nineteenth century, initially led by John Keble (1792–1866), John Henry Newman (1801–90), and Edward Bouverie Pusey (1800–82). For an early reference to this movement in German, see F. Reiff and J. Hesse, *Die Oxforder Bewegung und ihre Bedeutung für unsere Zeit*. Basle: Bahnmeier, 1875.

[121] See the contemporary account of its aims and character provided in Charles F. Harford, ed., *The Keswick Convention: Its Message, Its Method and Its Men*. London: Marshall Brothers, 1907.

concerned with the development of the "higher life",[122] and attracted many leading evangelical preachers from Great Britain and the United States. Buchman had probably hoped to hear one of the keynote preachers. Instead, he found himself listening to the Welsh preacher Jessie Penn-Lewis (1861–1927) in a half-empty chapel. Her revivalist preaching evoked an "experience of the cross" within him, and proved to be a life-changing event. Buchman began to work for the YMCA, and came into contact with leading figures such as John R. Mott. In 1921, he founded the First Century Christian Fellowship, preaching mainly to student audiences on personal renewal and revival.[123]

During the 1920s Buchman established a base at Oxford. Perhaps because of this, the growing movement based on his ideas came to be known as the Oxford Group from 1929. Buchman's emphasis on seeking God's will through quietness and listening, linked with sharing stories of encouragement and transformation, attracted attention. Opinion polarized at Oxford;[124] nevertheless, it was seen as a spiritually significant phenomenon by many senior bishops in the Church of England.

The movement enjoyed international success – including in Switzerland, where Theophil Spoerri (1890–1974), Professor of Romance Philology at Zurich, became one of Buchman's closest supporters.[125] Although Brunner first came across the Oxford Group in 1928 during a visit to Princeton, his growing commitment to the movement from the summer of 1932 was a result of its activities in Switerland.[126] During this time, its influence in Switzerland became a matter of national comment, and its conferences attracted large audiences: 10,000 attended a rally in Lausanne in the spring of 1937. Buchman and his team were greeted personally by the Swiss president, Rudolf Minger, in 1935. Brunner attended an Oxford Group house party at Ermatingen, which led him to develop an admiration for its ability to reach cultural elites outside the church, and gain a hearing for the Christian faith. One of Brunner's most popular works – *Our Faith* (1935), a thoughtful introduction to the leading themes of the Apostles' Creed –

---

[122] For attempts to broaden the scope of the movement, see Ian M. Randall, "Spiritual Renewal and Social Reform: Attempts to Develop Social Awareness in the Early Keswick Movement." *Vox Evangelica* 23 (1993): 67–86.

[123] The best study is Daniel Sack, "Men Want Something Real: Frank Buchman and Anglo-American College Religion in the 1920s." *Journal of Religious History* 28, no. 3 (2004): 260–75.

[124] The case of the Oxford New Testament scholar B. H. Streeter (1874–1937) is especially important: see Philip Boobbyer, "B. H. Streeter and the Oxford Group." *Journal of Ecclesiastical History* 61, no. 3 (2010): 541–67. Barth was concerned that the Oxford Group appeared to suggest that numerical growth or the quality of religious or moral experience could be viewed as reflecting the truth of divine revelation. Streeter responded to Karl Barth's critique of the Oxford Group in 1937: B. H. Streeter, "Professor Barth vs. the Oxford Group." *London Quarterly and Holborn Review* 6 (April 1937): 145–9.

[125] See the excellent account in Jehle, *Emil Brunner*, 274–81.

[126] See Brunner's personal account of his involvement in his 1932 essay "Meine Begegnung mit der Oxforder Gruppenbewegung": *Ein offenes Wort*, vol. 1, 268–88.

arose from his increasing involvement in the training of the Group's local leadership in Switzerland.

Brunner's interest in the doctrine of the church had been modest, perhaps even minimal, before his involvement with the Oxford Group. His *Divine Imperative* devoted its final section to a reflection on the nature of the church. This, however, shows no sign of a coherent ecclesiology; its purpose was rather to explicate the place of ethics within the life of the Christian community, as distinguished from other communities – such as the state, or the cultural community. Brunner sketches some leading themes and motifs that must be part of any viable ecclesiology, yet merely colligates them, where a more rigorous process of integration is clearly required.

Brunner's growing involvement with the Oxford Group appears to have kindled his interest in developing the idea of the church as a fellowship. In a late reminiscence, dating from 1955, he commented that the Oxford Group alerted him "for the first time" to the "close connection between spiritual reality and fellowship or communion".[127]

Why did Brunner find this movement so attractive? In a somewhat defensive letter to Barth, partly arising out of their growing disagreement over the merits of the Oxford Group, Brunner indicated that his sympathy with the movement had nothing to do with systematic theology;[128] rather, it reflected his appreciation of the Group's pastoral and spiritual impact in Zurich, which compared favourably with Brunner's experience of traditional Swiss Protestant congregations. Brunner's growing appreciation of the Group's success in developing communities of faith led him to believe its approaches might be instrumental in countering institutional traditionalism within the Swiss Reformed church. Part of the answer may also lie in his familiarity with and openness towards the forms of Protestantism of the English-speaking world, within which the Group had its origins.

Brunner came increasingly to emphasize the church's role in creating and sustaining fellowship and community, and suggested that traditional ecclesiologies were losing sight of this concern on account of institutional preoccupations. For Brunner, voluntary associations – such as the Oxford Group – could enable churches to rediscover this neglected aspect of Christian identity and existence. I shall return to consider this point later (pp. 199–204), in dealing with Brunner's later work *The Misunderstanding of the Church*.

The Work of the Holy Spirit: The Copenhagen Lectures (1934)

Yet there are excellent reasons for thinking that Brunner found the Oxford Group to be a significant stimulus to one specific aspect of his theology –

---

[127] "Intellectual Autobiography", 243.
[128] Letter to Karl Barth, 16 January 1933: *Karl Barth–Emil Brunner, Briefwechsel*, 217–22, especially 220–1.

namely, his understanding of the role of the Holy Spirit, which he came to frame in increasingly experiential and personal terms from late 1934. In September of that year Brunner delivered three lectures on the work of the Holy Spirit at the University of Copenhagen. These lectures, published in 1935, have not received the attention that they deserve, partly because they have been overshadowed by other theological debates in which Brunner became involved during 1934.

In the 1930s, German-speaking Reformed pneumatology tended to link the Holy Spirit particularly with the inspiration and interpretation of Scripture, generally seeing pneumatology as an extension of Christology.[129] Brunner broke with this pattern, emphasizing the role of the Holy Spirit in popular revivals, which were generally treated with disdain by academic theologians. Noting that such events as "glossolalia, prophecy, and the working of all kinds of wonders" were characteristic of the early Christian experience,[130] Brunner suggested that the theologically normative notion of "sacred objectivity" in effect excluded such experiences from serious consideration.[131] There was, he suggested, a need both to recalibrate the place of experience in the Christian life and to provide a theological interpretation of such experiences in terms of the person and work of the Holy Spirit, who stands at the "centre of Christian doctrine and the Christian life".[132] For Brunner, the Spirit "converts divine truth into human actuality".

In case his readers missed the obvious implication of this point, Brunner spells out its significance for his own approach to theology. "Precisely the best thing about this theological theme is that it establishes a point of contact [*Berührungspunkt*] between divine revelation and a personal experience of faith."[133] With this move, Brunner consolidates his notion of the "point of contact": it is not simply something that is embedded in the order of creation; it is something that is actualized in human experience through the Holy Spirit – and therefore cannot be dismissed as an idolatrous human assertion of autonomy, or an attempt on the part of humanity to determine the place and time of divine revelation.

This renewed interest in experience on Brunner's part clearly raises the question of whether he has reverted to the type of neo-Protestant subjectivism that he had earlier criticized, particularly in the forms which this took in the works of Schleiermacher.[134] Yet Brunner avoided this by insisting that

---

[129] A point often made concerning Barth's pneumatology: see, for example, Robert W. Jenson, "You Wonder Where the Spirit Went." *Pro Ecclesia* 2 (1993): 296–304; Daniel I. Migliore, "*Vinculum Pacis*: Karl Barths Theologie des Heiligen Geistes." *Evangelische Theologie* 60, no. 2 (2000): 131–52.
[130] *Vom Werk des Heiligen Geistes*, 6.
[131] *Vom Werk des Heiligen Geistes*, 7.
[132] *Vom Werk des Heiligen Geistes*, 3.
[133] *Vom Werk des Heiligen Geistes*, 8.
[134] Gerhard Ebeling, *Wort und Glaube: Beiträge zur Fundamentaltheologie, Soteriologie und Ekklesiologie*. Tübingen: Mohr, 1975, 392–3. See also Hans-Jürgen Goertz, *Geist und Wirklichkeit: Eine Studie zur Pneumatologie Erich Schaeders*. Göttingen: Vandenhoek & Ruprecht, 1980, 44–9.

such experience is to be seen as God-wrought, through the Holy Spirit.[135] A right understanding of the Holy Spirit undergirds the fundamental belief that God encounters us in an utterly transformative (*grundverändernden*) manner, reordering human existence so that we are fundamentally changed in consequence.[136]

In the light of Brunner's encounter with the Oxford Group, perhaps the most interesting of the three lectures is the second, dealing with the Christian life, including reflections on ecclesiology. Traditional Reformed ecclesiologies had emphasized the role of the Word in constituting and maintaining ecclesial identity, often subsuming the person and work under the concept of the "Word of God".[137] Brunner, while not yet breaking from such traditional approaches, raised questions about emphasis and centrality.

> Church order, church legislation, offices, preaching, catechesis, pastoral care, and the sacraments have a firm place within a church that is grounded on the Word and Spirit of God. They are the necessary means of the church; nothing less – but nothing more. Yet the *reality* of the church is based on the efficacy of the Holy Spirit. It is not merely a Reformed doctrine, but incontestably that of the New Testament as well, that it is not the *opus operatum* of church functions but only and alone the efficacy of the Holy Spirit that brings forth a real church and a real faith.[138]

As we shall see, Brunner would give added substance to his emerging views on ecclesiology in later years (see pp. 199–204).

Yet it seems to have been his comments on the failings of "the theological renewal of the last two decades" – for which we should read "dialectical theology" – which particularly riled Karl Barth.[139] Brunner declared that this movement has found the Holy Spirit to be an "embarrassment [*Verlegenheit*] or a challenge", preferring to follow the conventional pathway of Reformed Orthodoxy through the "identification of the Word and the Spirit". For Brunner, its doctrine of the Holy Spirit is the criterion by which theological reflection can be judged against the reality of faith. No attempt to hide behind an "objectivist falsification of the witness of the New Testament" can conceal this "poverty of the Spirit" (*Geistarmut*).

Barth's irritation over this treatise is to be set against a much more significant controversy of this period. We must now examine a controversy of 1934 that is widely regarded as a landmark in the career of Brunner – the debate with Karl Barth over natural theology.

---

[135] *Vom Werk des Heiligen Geistes*, 40. Note also the comments about "mysticism" at 15.
[136] *Vom Werk des Heiligen Geistes*, 10–11.
[137] See, for example, Christopher L. Elwood, "Calvin's Ecclesial Theology and Human Salvation." In *John Calvin's Impact on Church and Society*, ed. Martin Ernst Hirzel and Martin Sallmann, 90–104. Grand Rapids, MI: Eerdmans, 2009.
[138] *Vom Werk des Heiligen Geistes*, 50.
[139] *Vom Werk des Heiligen Geistes*, 8.

4
Natural Theology? The Barth–Brunner Debate of 1934

The discussion of major intellectual or cultural questions is often catalysed by landmark debates that sometimes achieve iconic status – such as the 1975 debate on "language and learning" between Jean Piaget and Noam Chomsky at Royaumont Abbey, which was generally regarded as marking a victory for Chomsky.[1] Such debates serve to focus attention on key points of interpretation, raising their profile within the broader intellectual constituency, and allowing at least a provisional assessment of the merits of the leading options within the field.

Many suggest that the 1934 debate between Karl Barth and Emil Brunner represents a landmark in the discussion of the legitimacy, nature, and scope of natural theology.[2] Indeed, many would argue that this is now the only

---

[1] Massimo Piattelli-Palmarini, ed., *Language and Learning: The Debate between Jean Piaget and Noam Chomsky*. Cambridge, MA: Harvard University Press, 1980. See further Massimo Piattelli-Palmarini, "Ever Since Language and Learning: Afterthoughts on the Piaget-Chomsky Debate." *Cognition* 50 (1994): 315–46.

[2] The best historical account of the origins and development of the debate is found in Frank Jehle, *Emil Brunner: Theologe im 20. Jahrhundert*. Zurich: Theologischer Verlag, 2006, 293–321. For theological reflections on the issues, see Gerhard Sauter, "Theologisch miteinander streiten: Karl Barths Auseinandersetzung mit Emil Brunner." In *Karl Barth in Deutschland (1921–1935): Aufbruch – Klärung –Widerstand*, ed. Michael Beintker, Christian Link, and Michael Trowitzsch, 267–84. Zurich: Theologischer Verlag, 2005; Gabriele Lunghini, *Emil Brunner*. Brescia: Editrice Morcelliana, 2009, 76–88. For the wider dispute about natural theology, see especially Hans-Joachim Birkner, "Natürliche Theologie und Offenbarungstheologie: Ein theologiegeschichtlicher Überblick." *Neue Zeitschrift für systematische Theologie und Religionsphilosophie* 3, no. 3 (1961): 279–95; Christof Gestrich, *Neuzeitliches Denken und die Spaltung der dialektischen Theologie: Zur Frage der natürlichen Theologie*. Tübingen: Mohr, 1977; Christoph Kock, *Natürliche Theologie: Ein evangelischer Streitbegriff*. Neukirchen-Vluyn: Neukirchener, 2001, 23–102; Eberhard Jüngel, "Gelegentliche Thesen zum Problem der natürlichen Theologie." In *Entsprechungen: Gott – Wahrheit – Mensch*, 198–201. Tübingen: Mohr Siebeck, 2002.

Emil Brunner: A Reappraisal, First Edition. Alister E. McGrath.
© 2014 John Wiley & Sons, Ltd. Published 2016 by John Wiley & Sons, Ltd.

"debate" for which Brunner is remembered. So was this really a defining moment in the discussion of natural theology? No. As we shall see, this debate is interesting, and serves as an important window onto tensions, concerns, and disagreements within German-language Reformed theology in the 1930s. Yet it cannot be regarded as a landmark discussion of the issues attending a Christian natural theology.

In the first place, this was not really a debate about natural theology at all. The issues under consideration primarily concerned the implications of the doctrine of creation, the nature of revelation, and the capacity of humanity to discern and respond to that revelation. As a result of the 1934 debate, Brunner came to realize that he needed to extend and defend his approach by writing a work of theological anthropology rather than of natural theology.

Secondly, the "debate" did not involve a meeting of persons, still less a meeting of minds. It focused on two hastily written tracts, neither of which can be said to have fairly represented the opposing position, nor even to have given an adequate account of the author's position. Both writers are open to the criticism of having produced slapdash tracts rather than serious pieces of respectful theological engagement. The debate unquestionably polarized opinion; it did not, however, significantly clarify or resolve many of the points at issue.

Third, the controversy did not involve leading representatives of the Christian theological constituency as a whole, but was limited to two Swiss Reformed theologians, each already associated with the "dialectical" approach to theology.[3] Both had severe misgivings about existing approaches to natural theology, one regarding it as beyond redemption, the other arguing for its reformulation on the basis of its present state of dereliction and incoherence. As Brunner later protested, he was not an advocate of natural theology, as this is traditionally understood.[4] Barth always regarded Brunner's sympathy towards some form of natural theology to be a direct outcome of his unhealthy preoccupation with the "other" task of theology.

Fourth, the 1934 debate did not arise from, or reflect, anything that was fundamentally new in the theological positions of the two participants. The publication of the correspondence between Karl Barth and Emil Brunner in

---

[3] For their interaction in this debate, see John W. Hart, *Karl Barth vs. Emil Brunner: The Formation and Dissolution of a Theological Alliance, 1916–1936*. New York: Peter Lang, 2001, 149–76; Klaus-Peter Blaser, "Communiquer l'incommunicable révélation: Le conflit Barth-Brunner revisité à la lumière de leur correspondance." *Etudes théologiques et religieuses* 78 (2003): 59–67.

[4] *Der Mensch im Widerspruch*, 509; *Man in Revolt*, 527. Brunner here remarks that, due to some unfortunate turns of phrase in *Nature and Grace*, he is now "seen by many as a representative of a 'natural theology' in the usual sense of the term". This, Brunner insists, was not his intention. Unfortunately, this perception has become the reality, despite its obvious shortcomings.

2000 made it clear that Barth and Brunner had already debated some core topics of relevance to natural theology – such as the *imago Dei*, the orders of nature, the point of contact, and the relation of nature and grace – in their earlier correspondence.[5] The tensions between them thus did not come into being in 1934, but can be traced back to the beginning of their relationship. This was not a "new" controversy, but a public manifestation of tensions and differences that had been building up for some time.

It itself, this public controversy must be seen as an important development in the wider perception of the Barth–Brunner relationship, highlighting the lack of clear identity of a "dialectical" approach to theology. Not everyone was aware of the tensions within the "theology of crisis" in the late 1920s or early 1930s – such as the emerging differences between Barth and Gogarten over theological anthropology, dating from 1928–9.[6] The tensions within the movement were revealed and discussed in private correspondence between its core members; they had not, however, been openly debated in public. There is no question of the dialectical theology movement being "shattered" or "torn apart" by this controversy of 1934; there was never sufficient agreement within the group to allow it to have had a "unity" in the first place. The tensions and divergences had always been there; the difference was that a wider audience now became aware of them.

In the English-language world, which then knew Brunner better than Barth and supposed the two to represent a similar viewpoint, the intensity and acrimony of the debate over such a fundamental revelational theme caused much surprise.[7] In his speaking engagements in the United States and Great Britain, Brunner tended to represent the "theology of crisis" as a coherent movement, whose chief members were Barth and himself.[8] In

---

[5] For the best study of this tense relationship in the period leading up to, and immediately after, the 1934 controversy on natural theology, see Hart, *Karl Barth vs. Emil Brunner*. Hart rightly traces the tensions in their relationship back to 1918, when Brunner was already concerned about the "one-sidedness" of Barth's conception of revelation (16–17). See also the analysis in this volume: pp. 9–12, 14–16, 35–6, 39–40, 41–2.

[6] See the important paper by Friedrich Gogarten, "Das Problem einer theologischen Anthropologie." *Zwischen den Zeiten* 7 (1929): 493–511. For discussion of this significant divergence, see Peter Lange, *Konkrete Theologie? Karl Barth und Friedrich Gogarten "Zwischen den Zeiten" (1922–1933). Eine Theologiegeschichtlich-systematische Untersuchung im Blick auf die Praxis theologischen Verhaltens.* Zurich: Theologischer Verlag, 1972, 248–54.

[7] This point is often missed by those who retroject today's familiarity within the English-language theological world with Barth and an awareness of his differences with Brunner onto the very different situation of the 1930s. John Baillie's 1946 introduction to the debate is a fascinating period piece for this reason: John Baillie, ed., *Natural Theology, comprising "Nature and Grace" by Professor Dr. Emil Brunner and the reply "No!" by Dr. Karl Barth.* London: Geoffrey Bless, 1946, 5–12. For comments on English-language Barth reception, with particular reference to the work of Thomas F. Torrance, see Alister E. McGrath, *T. F. Torrance: An Intellectual Biography*. Edinburgh: T&T Clark, 1999, 113–45. For earlier attitudes, see especially John McPake, "John McConnachie as the Original Advocate of Karl Barth in Scotland: The Primacy of Revelation." *Scottish Bulletin of Evangelical Theology* 14 (1996): 101–14.

[8] For example, *The Word and the World*, 6.

North America, the debate proved to be something of a setback for Barth,⁹ and it would be more than a decade before his reputation recovered. Reinhold Niebuhr, for example, was more impressed negatively by Barth's rudeness and arrogance than positively by his theological acumen, criticizing his "peculiar quality of personal arrogance and disrespect for the opponent".¹⁰

In this chapter I shall consider this important debate in detail, giving proper attention to its cultural and theological contexts. As will become clear, the Barth–Brunner debate is actually of somewhat limited value in advancing serious discussion of the purpose and place of natural theology, partly as a result of the brevity and superficiality of its content and its generally polemical tone. It is difficult to judge these two competing visions of natural theology on the basis of such an inadequate presentation of their fundamental themes. Nevertheless, it is impossible to discuss the proper dogmatic significance of natural theology for modern Protestant theology without reference to this debate.

To begin with, we need to set the context. How was the notion of "natural theology" understood at the time? In one sense, the debate between Barth and Brunner concerns what is to be understood by natural theology – a question which takes analytical precedence over the question of whether it is to be judged as legitimate or useful.¹¹ As Eberhard Jüngel pointed out in 1975, German-language Protestant theology has been distinctively "nervous" about natural theology, which was at the heart of some of its most contentious disputes during the twentieth century.¹² Natural theology came to function as a *Streitbegriff* – a boundary marker, a defining criterion of authenticity, a touchstone of orthodoxy – within German-speaking Protestant theology from about 1950 to 2000. It was impossible to discuss

---

⁹ As John Webster rightly points out, the stridency of Barth's "No!" caused his supporters in North America some embarrassment: it "sealed the fate of the former dialectical theology group, but also provided evidence to generation of North American readers that Barth was at heart a polemicist (and a rude one at that) rather than a constructive church theologian". John Webster, *Barth*. London: Continuum, 2000, 7.

¹⁰ Reinhold Niebuhr, *The Nature and Destiny of Man: A Christian Interpretation*. 2 vols. London: Nisbet, 1941, vol. 1, 215 n. 1. It is illuminating to set Niebuhr's comment alongside the themes explored and dialogical virtues affirmed by David Fergusson in his "The Reformed Tradition and the Virtue of Tolerance." In *Public Theology for the 21st Century: Essays in Honour of Duncan B. Forrester*, ed. William Storrar and Andrew Morton, 107–21. London: T&T Clark, 2004.

¹¹ For an early exploration of the centrality of the importance of this question for "dialectical theology", see Johannes Ries, *Die natürliche Gotteserkenntnis in der Theologie der Krisis im Zusammenhang mit dem Imagobegriff bei Calvin: Aufweis der Grundlagen und Versuch einer Kritik*. Bonn: Hanstein, 1939.

¹² Eberhard Jüngel, "Das Dilemma der natürlichen Theologie und die Wahrheit ihres Problems: Überlegungen für ein Gespräch mit Wolfhart Pannenberg." In *Entsprechungen: Gott – Wahrheit – Mensch*, 158–77. Tübingen: Mohr Siebeck, 2002. Richebächer declares natural theology to be a problem for Protestant theology; his analysis, however, is limited to German-speaking theology: Wilhelm Richebächer, *Die Wandlung der natürlichen Theologie in der Neuzeit*. Frankfurt am Main: Peter Lang, 1989.

the notion seriously without standing in the shadow of previous debates.[13] For Karl Barth, an interest in natural theology was fundamentally un-Protestant – an expression of a "Catholic heart" that had no place in a properly Protestant dogmatics.[14] These tensions are peculiar to German-language Protestantism, and have not been characteristic of discussions of natural theology in other Protestant contexts – above all, within the English-speaking world – or within Catholicism. The Barth–Brunner debate was of seminal importance in causing these theological fault-lines to develop, even if we must leave open the question of whether the debate *created* or merely *exposed* these tensions.

An appropriate point at which to begin our discussion is to reflect on the origins and development of the theological category of "natural theology", noting its underlying complexity and ambivalence.

Natural Theology: A Contested Notion

The origins of the phrase "natural theology" lie in classical antiquity. Marcus Terentius Varro (116–27 BC) set out a threefold taxonomy of approaches to theology:[15] "mythical theology" (*theologia fabulosa*), "civil theology" (*theologia civilis*), and "natural theology" (*theologia naturalis*).[16] Underlying the term *theologia naturalis* is a fundamental human intuition: that, in some way and to some extent, the natural world possesses a capacity to point through and beyond itself to something greater – a transcendent reality, such as God.[17]

Marcus Tullius Cicero (106–43 BC) developed such points in his *De natura deorum*, arguing that nature's providential care for both animals and

---

[13] The best study of how natural theology emerged as a defining concept within German-speaking Protestantism is Kock, *Natürliche Theologie: Ein evangelischer Streitbegriff*.

[14] See Karl Barth, "Die Theologie und die heutige Mensch." *Zwischen den Zeiten* 8 (1930): 375–96, especially 393–5. Barth's concern is that a disillusionment with both atheism and liberalism leads to a regrettable and unnecessary renewal of interest in natural theology. Barth's tendency to associate "natural theology" specifically with Catholicism appears to have developed during the 1920s as a result of conversations with Erich Przywara S.J.: see Amy Marga, *Karl Barth's Dialogue with Catholicism in Göttingen and Münster*. Tübingen: Mohr Siebeck, 2010, 47–50.

[15] See Yves Lehmann, *Varron théologien et philosophe romain*. Brussels: Latomus, 1997, 193–225.

[16] See the important studies of Godo Lieberg, "Die 'Theologia Tripartita' in Forschung und Bezeugung." *Aufstieg und Niedergang der römischen Welt* 4 (1973): 63–115; idem, "Die 'Theologia Tripartita' als Formprinzip antiken Denkens." *Rheinisches Museum für Philologie* 125 (1982): 25–53.

[17] See my exposition of these themes in the 2008 Richardson Lectures at the University of Newcastle, the 2009 Gifford Lectures at the University of Aberdeen, and the 2009 Hulsean Lectures at the University of Cambridge: Alister E. McGrath, *The Open Secret: A New Vision for Natural Theology*. Oxford: Blackwell, 2008; idem, *A Fine-Tuned Universe: The Quest for God in Science and Theology*. Louisville, KY: Westminster John Knox Press, 2009; idem, *Darwinism and the Divine: Evolutionary Thought and Natural Theology*. Oxford: Wiley-Blackwell, 2011.

human beings, the complex design of the human and animal bodies, and the intricate interdependency of all parts of nature pointed to the existence of some artificer or designer.[18] Cicero himself suggested that analogies might be drawn with certain mechanisms – such as water-clocks or sundials – to point towards the conclusion of apparent design entailing the existence of a designer.[19]

A similar approach was developed by Dio Chrysostom (c.40–c.120) in his *Olympic Oration*, probably dating from around the year 107.[20] Chrysostom here asserts that humanity developed its idea of divinity through reflection on the wonders of the natural world. Awe-inspiring or wonder-evoking sights in the heavens (such as the sun, moon, and stars) and on earth (such as the winds and woods, rivers and forests) pointed to the existence of the divine powers who brought them into being, and which could be known through them.[21] Chrysostom saw the power of natural forces, as much as the beauty and ordering of nature, as indicators of their divine origination and signification.

Yet other classical writers were more cautious, noting the ambiguity of the natural world. Although Virgil's *Georgics* (written in 29 BC) exult in the beauty of the natural world, finding great pleasure in its richness and diversity, his nascent natural theology confronts without mastering the darker side of nature – such as the constant threat of attack by wild animals, or fear of the untameable forces of nature which could destroy life and render agriculture impossible.[22]

The imperial physician Galen of Pergamum (129–c.200) saw the configuration of human muscles as offering strong evidence of design, and constructed a teleological account of the created order on the basis of his physiological insights. Christian apologists were quick to use substantially the same argument, but attributing such teleological dimensions of the human body to God, perhaps most notably in the case of Lactantius's *De opificio Dei* (written around 303).[23] Augustine of Hippo developed his own natural theology, clearly based on Varro's formulation of the concept,[24] seeing this as an important means of allowing the church to engage with secular Roman thought.

---

[18] Cicero, *De natura deorum*, II.34. "An, cum machinatione quadam moveri aliquid vedemus, ut sphaeram ut horas ut alia permulta, non dubitamus quin illa opera sint rationis."
[19] Lloyd P. Gerson, *God and Greek Philosophy: Studies in the Early History of Natural Theology*. London: Routledge, 1994, 155–60.
[20] Hans-Josef Klauck, "Nature, Art, and Thought: Dio Chrysostom and the *Theologia Tripertita*." *Journal of Religion* 87 (2007): 333–54, especially 341–50.
[21] Hans Dieter Betz, "God Concept and Cultic Image: The Argument in Dio Chrysostom's Oratio 12 (Olympikos)." *Illinois Classical Studies* 29 (2004): 131–42.
[22] Pierre Boyancé, "La religion des 'Géorgiques' à la lumière des travaux récents." *Aufstieg und Niedergang der Römischen Welt* II.31.1 (1980): 549–73.
[23] Lactantius, *De opificio Dei*, 2–13. Lactantius here seems to make indirect use of Galen.
[24] Albrecht Dihle, "Die *Theologia Tripertita* bei Augustin." In *Geschichte – Tradition – Reflexion: Festschrift für Martin Hengel zum 70. Geburtstag*, ed. Hubert Cancik, 183–202. Tübingen: Mohr Siebeck, 1996.

The term developed new associations in the eighteenth century. A new form of "natural theology" began to emerge in England, reflecting the ideas of the Newtonian "scientific revolution".[25] In part, this development reflected the perception that a natural theology might open new conceptual possibilities, allowing a synthesis of social and natural order at a time when religious and social tensions seriously undermined the construction of any form of social consensus on traditional appeals to the Bible or previous political consensus.[26] The new interest in natural theology was a result of growing intellectual unease about traditional understandings of religious authority, partly reflecting an increasing awareness of difficulties in interpreting the Bible, and some aspects of its status as a source of knowledge.[27] The term "natural theology" increasingly came to designate a means of demonstrating the rationality of belief in God at a time when this was under serious challenge.

Barth tends to present the emergence of natural theology in the modern period as an expression of the characteristic tendency of sinful humanity to affirm its epistemic and soteriological independence. Humanity could discover and relate to God under terms of its own choosing, rather than those mandated by the Christian proclamation. If knowledge of God can be achieved independently of God's self-revelation in Christ, then it follows that humanity can dictate the terms and conditions, not to mention the substance, of its knowledge of God.

The background to the emergence of this style of natural theology is, however, rather more complex than Barth allows. Barth's linguistic and geographical horizons may have prevented him from fully appreciating the cultural factors that led to the emergence of natural theologies as apologetic tools in England in the late seventeenth and early eighteenth centuries. It is undoubtedly true that the "autonomy" motif was significant for Deists and others in England at this time wishing to promote a certain style of natural theology. Yet it is not difficult to discern another motif – growing anxiety concerning the reliability of the Christian revelation, and especially specific concerns about the authority of the Bible, reflecting changes in the English cultural scene at this time. The primary motivation for undertaking natural theology within English Christianity during the late seventeenth and the eighteenth centuries was not *dogmatic*, but *apologetic*. The church itself did not reject revelation; it realized that it needed to relate the gospel to a culture which no longer felt inclined to accept this notion. Natural theology

---

[25] For a detailed study of this development, see McGrath, *Darwinism and the Divine*, 49–84.

[26] Scott Mandelbrote, "The Uses of Natural Theology in Seventeenth-Century England." *Science in Context* 20 (2007): 451–80.

[27] One of the best studies of this development remains Henning Reventlow, *Bibelautorität und Geist der Moderne: Die Bedeutung des Bibelverstandnisses für die Geistesgeschichtliche und politische Entwicklung in England von der Reformation bis zur Aufklärung.* Göttingen: Vandenhoeck & Ruprecht, 1980, 161–469.

rapidly became an apologetic tool of no small importance.[28] Although some believed it was designed to affirm religion in an increasingly scientific age, it also served to affirm the natural sciences in a persistently religious age.[29]

These distinctively English forms of natural theology proved to be of defining importance for the German *Aufklärung*. Thus Johann August Eberhard's influential *Vorbereitung zur natürlichen Theologie* (1781), which served as an important source for Immanuel Kant's views on natural theology,[30] explicitly notes and affirms a series of English writers as major influences on the reshaping of German natural theology in response to the new intellectual currents of the eighteenth century.[31] The supposedly self-evident meaning of "natural theology" as "a human attempt to gain knowledge of God apart from revelation" reflects a specific set of historical circumstances in the early Enlightenment. Other understandings of the notion remain legitimate possibilities for discussion and exploration.

On the basis of this brief historical analysis, it is clear that the understanding of natural theology as a means of attaining knowledge of God without recourse to divine revelation emerged during the modern period, in response to certain distinctly modern concerns. If Karl Barth is regarded as an "anti-modern theologian",[32] his decision to focus on this specifically modern notion of natural theology is entirely understandable. Yet it needs to be noted that there are other historical forms of natural theology with a significant historical pedigree, which are not embedded within or moulded by a modernist worldview.

Furthermore, the English situation was dominated by Protestant concerns and voices. There were no significant contributions to the English

---

[28] This development was not limited to England; it can also be seen clearly in shifting attitudes in Geneva towards natural theology, as a result of the growing influence of Enlightenment rationalism: Michael Heyd, "Un rôle nouveau pour la science: Jean Alphonse Turrettini et les débuts de la théologie naturelle à Genève." *Revue de théologie et philosophie* 112 (1982): 25–42; Martin I. Klauber, "Reason, Revelation, and Cartesianism: Louis Tronchin and Enlightened Orthodoxy in Late Seventeenth-Century Geneva." *Church History* 59 (1990): 326–39; Maria-Cristina Pitassi, "L'apologétique raisonnable de Jean-Alphonse Turrettini." In *Apologétique 1680–1740: Sauvetage ou naufrage de la théologie?*, ed. Maria-Cristina Pitassi, 99–118. Geneva: Labor et Fides, 1991.

[29] Stephen Gaukroger, "Science, Religion and Modernity." *Critical Quarterly* 47, no. 4 (2005): 1–31.

[30] Kant's pre-critical essay "Untersuchungen über die Deutlichkeit der Grundsätze der natürlichen Theologie und der Moral" should be noted here. This lecture, delivered in 1762 and published in 1764, primarily concerns itself with the relation of mathematical and metaphysical truth. For comment, see Hans-Jürgen Engfer, "Zur Bedeutung Wolffs für die Methodendiskussion der deutschen Aufklärungsphilosophie: Analytische und Syntetische Methode bei Wolff und beim vorkritischen Kant." In *Christian Wolff, 1697–1754: Interpretationen zu seiner Philosophie und deren Wirkung*, ed. Werner Schneiders, 48–65. Hamburg: Meiner, 1986.

[31] For Kant's annotations on this work, see Immanuel Kant, *Gesammelte Schriften*. 30 vols. Berlin: Reimer, 1902, vol. 28, 491–606.

[32] For an assessment of this way of thinking about Barth, see Dietrich Korsch, *Dialektische Theologie nach Karl Barth*. Tübingen: Mohr, 1996, 78–81.

debate of the eighteenth century from Catholic voices. These were excluded by the dominant Protestant establishment, which remained suspicious of Catholicism as a result of the political chaos of the 1690s, when James II sought to reconvert England to Catholicism.[33]

Historically, there are very good reasons for suggesting that Karl Barth's critique of the generic notion of "natural theology" is actually an *indirect* critique of a specifically English approach to the subject, which arose during the early modern period in response to a specific cultural situation. Barth's unhelpful universalization and essentialization of the category of "natural theology" fails to take account of the fact that it designates multiple approaches to the relation of God and nature, and is open to recalibration and redirection in response to criticism.[34]

The Barth–Brunner debate, then, concerns a specific approach – or perhaps a range of approaches – to natural theology that achieved hegemony in western Europe in the modern period. Yet this specificity is not restricted to the concept of natural theology under consideration. We must understand from the outset that the Barth–Brunner debate over natural theology also possesses an *ecclesial* specificity that tends to detach it from the wider discussion of the theme – for example, in the writings of Thomas Aquinas[35] – and thus limit its historical significance. Barth and Brunner both saw themselves as representing and working within a Reformed theological tradition, with a particular concern to engage its later development in response to intellectual and cultural modernity. The Barth–Brunner debate is best seen as an "in-house" discussion, reflecting the norms, tensions, and history of the Reformed tradition on the one hand, and the specific agendas and concerns of the "dialectical theology" movement on the other. For both writers, this ecclesial grounding gave a peculiar importance to the views of leading representatives of the Reformed theological tradition, especially during its formative phase.

Inevitably, this led both Barth and Brunner to place considerable emphasis on classic Reformed writers and confessional documents of the sixteenth century, such as John Calvin (1509–64), Theodore Beza (1519–1605), and the "Gallic Confession" (1559). Since Barth and Brunner both regarded themselves as standing within this tradition, it is important to evaluate their relationship to it at this point.

Yet the specificity of the debate goes beyond its Reformed roots. The debate reflects cultural, social, political, and historical themes specific to the

---

[33] For details of the socio-political context of the "Augustan Age" in England, see McGrath, *Darwinism and the Divine*, 49–84.

[34] For the multiple conceptions of natural theology, see McGrath, *Darwinism and the Divine*, 15–18. A different typology can be found in David Fergusson, "Types of Natural Theology." In *The Evolution of Rationality: Interdisciplinary Essays in Honor of J. Wentzel Van Huyssteen*, ed. F. Le Ron Shults, 380–93. Grand Rapids, MI: Eerdmans, 2006.

[35] For the conceptual richness of Aquinas's natural theology, see Norman Kretzmann, *The Metaphysics of Theism: Aquina's Natural Theology in Summa Contra Gentiles I*. Oxford: Clarendon Press, 1997; idem, *The Metaphysics of Creation: Aquinas's Natural Theology in Summa Contra Gentiles II*. Oxford: Clarendon Press, 1999.

German-language world in the decades between the two world wars – above all, the collapse of the Weimer Republic and the triumph of National Socialism in Germany. The Barth–Brunner debate of 1934 was culturally embedded, and its theological judgements were clearly influenced by non-theological factors. It is essential that any wider theological debate today about the nature and scope of natural theology be detached from the ecclesially restricted and culturally shaped clash between Barth and Brunner.

Furthermore, we must note that the Barth–Brunner debate has had the most unfortunate consequence of poisoning serious historico-theological study of the early Reformed tradition *by Reformed theologians*.[36] The disturbing tendency to read Calvin through Barthian spectacles on the question of natural theology or the knowledge of God has led to theological prejudices compromising historical scholarship. Both Barth and Brunner interpret the early Reformed tradition in the light of their own theological presuppositions, offering highly selective readings of Calvin and other Reformed sources. The force of Barth's rhetoric solidified the view that natural theology was off-limits for responsible Protestant theologians.[37] It is only since 1990 that serious historical study of theology of this period has broken free from the constraints of the Barth–Brunner debate, with important implications for the renewal of interest on the part of Reformed theologians in natural law and wider associated issues.[38]

The first book of the 1559 edition of Calvin's *Institutes* opens with discussion of one of the fundamental problems of Christian theology: how do we know anything about God? Even before turning to discuss this question, however, Calvin stresses that knowledge of God cannot be detached from, nor allowed to merge with, knowledge of human nature or of the world.[39] Calvin's delicately balanced interplay between God and the world, the creator and the creation, is grounded in the notion of a non-saving knowledge

---

[36] The most obvious example of this can be found in Günter Gloede, *Theologia naturalis bei Calvin*. Stuttgart: Kohlhammer, 1935. Gloede was one of Brunner's students, and his analysis reflects Brunner's standpoint somewhat uncritically. See Jehle, *Emil Brunner*, 308. For two more recent discussions of Calvin's views that are similarly tainted by the Barth–Brunner debate, see Edward A. Dowey, *The Knowledge of God in Calvin's Theology*. New York: Columbia University Press, 1952; T. H. L. Parker, *Calvin's Doctrine of the Knowledge of God*. Edinburgh: Oliver & Boyd, 1969. Dowey is sympathetic to Brunner's reading of Calvin, Parker to Barth's. The historical value of both studies is significantly reduced by this theological bias. For a careful study of the relation of Barth and Calvin on the issue of the knowledge of God (which would have been improved by considering a wider range of Barth's writings), see Cornelis van der Kooi, *As in a Mirror: John Calvin and Karl Barth on Knowing God: A Diptych*. Leiden: Brill, 2005, especially 417–54.

[37] This point underlies Kock's observation that one's attitude towards "natural theology" became a criterion of personal orthodoxy within Protestantism after the Second World War: Christoph Kock, *Natürliche Theologie: Ein evangelischer Streitbegriff*. Neukirchen-Vluyn: Neukirchener, 2001.

[38] A point stressed by Stephen John Grabill, *Rediscovering the Natural Law in Reformed Theological Ethics*. Grand Rapids, MI: Eerdmans, 2006, 21–53.

[39] Eberhard Busch, *Gotteserkenntnis und Menschlichkeit: Einsichten in die Theologie Johannes Calvins*. Zurich: Theologischer Verlag, 2005.

of God, which can act as a gateway to the fuller, saving knowledge of God characteristic of the Christian tradition. Locating his discussion of a natural knowledge of God within the greater framework of the rationality of faith,[40] Calvin affirms that a general knowledge of God may be discerned throughout the creation – in humanity, in the natural order, and in the historical process itself. Two main grounds of such knowledge are identified.

In the first place, Calvin argues that God has implanted a "sense of divinity" (*sensus divinitatis*) or a "seed of religion" (*semen religionis*) within every human being.[41] God has endowed human beings with some inbuilt sense or presentiment of God's existence. In the second, Calvin holds that reflection on the created order points to the conclusion that a God exists and that this God is the creator of the world. "God has revealed himself in such a beautiful and elegant construction of heaven and earth, showing and presenting himself there every day, that human beings cannot open their eyes without having to notice him."[42]

Calvin makes no suggestion that this knowledge of God based on the created order is peculiar to, or restricted to, Christian believers. There is a way of discerning God which is common to those inside and outside the Christian community (*exteris et domesticis communem*). Anyone, by intelligent and rational reflection upon the created order, should be able to arrive at the idea of God. Drawing on the rich imagery used to depict nature at this stage in intellectual history, Calvin declares that the created order is a "theatre" or "mirror" for displaying the divine presence, nature, and attributes.[43] Although God is invisible and incomprehensible, God is made known under and through the form of created and visible things. Calvin thus draws a distinction between a *cognitio Dei creatoris* as a general human knowledge of God as creator and a specifically Christian *cognitio Dei redemptoris*, which focuses on God's work of redemption in Christ.[44] Calvin formulates this distinction in terms of an *informing* knowledge of God the creator (accessible through nature and revelation) and a *converting* knowledge of God the redeemer (accessible only through revelation). It is only through Scripture that the believer has access to knowledge of the redeeming actions of God in history, culminating in the life, death, and

---

[40] Günter Frank, "Gläubige Vernunft – vernünftigen Glaube: Luther, Melanchthon und Calvin und die Frage nach einem vernünftigen Glaube." In *Calvinus Clarissimus Theologus*, ed. Herman J. Selderhuis, 141–57. Göttingen: Vandenhoeck & Ruprecht, 2012.

[41] Calvin, *Institutio Religionis Christianae*, I.iii.1, I.v.1. For further analysis, see Susan Elizabeth Schreiner, *The Theater of His Glory: Nature and the Natural Order in the Thought of John Calvin*. Durham, NC: Labyrinth Press, 1991.

[42] Calvin, *Institutio Religionis Christianae*, I.v.1.

[43] Diana Butler, "God's Visible Glory: The Beauty of Nature in the Thought of John Calvin and Jonathan Edwards." *Westminster Theological Journal* 52 (1990): 13–26.

[44] The way in which Calvin holds these two notions together has been the subject of considerable debate: see, for example, the influential account in Edward David Willis, *Calvin's Catholic Christology: The Function of the So-Called Extra Calvinisticum in Calvin's Theology*. Leiden: Brill, 1966, 120–4.

resurrection of Jesus Christ. This doctrine of a "twofold knowledge of God", which plays a significant thematic role in Calvin's exposition of Christian theology in the final edition of his *Institutes*,[45] is problematic at points; for our purposes here, we may note that Barth and Brunner tend to pick up on different aspects of Calvin's analysis, and adapt them to their own ends.

Karl Barth's Views on Natural Theology, 1918–1933

In his early writings during the period 1916–22, Barth mounts a protest against human constructions which masquerade as divine revelation. Characteristic of this early period is the emphasis that he places upon the "otherness" of God, which is reflected in his "theology of crisis", and especially his insistence upon the chasm separating God and humanity which prevents the latter from discovering or knowing God on its own terms and on its own grounds.[46]

Barth was not on his own here. This growing sense of the need to see God as an "other", distinct from culture, is reflected in Karl Holl's famous wartime lecture of 31 October 1917, delivered before the University of Berlin, widely regarded as having inaugurated the Luther renaissance by demonstrating how radically Luther's concept of God differed from the culturally accommodated deity of liberal Protestantism.[47]

Barth's articulation of the otherness of God is primarily linked with his critique of religion, on the one hand, and his emphasis on the total sovereignty of God in revelation on the other. Although this emphasis on the "otherness" of God is traditionally associated with his *Romans* commentary, it can be found in many works of this era, such as his lecture of 16 January 1916 in the Aarau Stadtkirche on the theme of "the righteousness [*Gerechtigkeit*] of God".[48] Here, as so often in his writings of this period, the catastrophe of the Great War is prominent in his thought, not least on account of its implications for the moral and theological competency of humanity.[49] At this stage, Barth's polemic against human constructions

---

[45] Brian G. Armstrong, "*Duplex Cognitio Dei*, or the Problem and Relation of Structure, Form, and Purpose in Calvin's Theology." In *Probing the Reformed Tradition: Historical Studies in Honor of Edward A. Dowey*, ed. Elsie Anne McKee and Brian G. Armstrong, 135–51. Louisville, KY: Westminster John Knox Press, 1989.

[46] See especially the discussion in Karl Barth, *Der Römerbrief*. 2nd edn. Munich: Kaiser Verlag, 1922, 213–55.

[47] Karl Holl, "Was verstand Luther unter Religion?" In *Gesammelte Aufsätze zur Kirchengeschichte*, 1–110. Tübingen: J. C. B. Mohr, 1928. For similar issues in relation to the development of the theology of Dietrich Bonhoeffer, see Wolf Krötke, "Dietrich Bonhoeffer and Martin Luther." In *Bonhoeffer's Intellectual Formation: Theology and Philosophy in His Thought*, ed. Peter Frick, 53–82. Tübingen: Mohr Siebeck, 2008.

[48] Karl Barth, "Die Gerechtigkeit Gottes." In *Das Wort Gottes und die Theologie*, 5–17. Munich: Kaiser, 1925.

[49] The political context of much theology of this era is stressed by Jan Rohls, *Protestantische Theologie der Neuzeit*. 2 vols. Tübingen: Mohr Siebeck, 1997, vol. 2, 186–348.

of divinity, erected in the face of God like some new tower of Babel, is focused primarily on the notion of *religion*.[50]

While it is entirely possible to argue that some form of critique of natural theology is implicit in Barth's earlier writings, his *explicit* engagement with this issue dates from the mid-1920s. Barth did not engage the specific concept of "natural theology" in his *Romans* commentary or earlier writings, tending to use the category of "religion" to designate human self-assertion and self-justification in the face of God. In the second edition of his *Romans* commentary, Barth critiques the idea of "religion" as a human construction erected in opposition to God – a criticism that would later be directed against natural theology.[51] In 1927 he identified the primary target of his criticisms as "Schleiermacher's conversion of theology into anthropology".[52] Yet natural theology is still not identified as the enemy of Barth's theological programme; nor is it in any case clear that Schleiermacher can legitimately be considered to be an exponent of a natural theology.

It is certainly possible to argue that various forms of natural theology were implicit – and occasionally explicit – within sections of German Romanticism,[53] with which Schleiermacher has a clear affinity. Yet Schleiermacher himself does not accentuate the notion of natural theology, nor treat it as emblematic for his theological approach.[54] If "Barth's battle against natural theology was in respect of content a conflict with the theology of the nineteenth century",[55] it is important to note that Barth did not initially frame this "conflict" in terms of natural theology.

By 1923 Barth was in the process of beginning to identify the theologically subversive expression of human autonomy with "natural theology",[56] laying the groundwork for establishing a historical and theological link

---

[50] As correctly pointed out by Attila Szekeres, "Karl Barth und die natürliche Theologie." *Evangelische Theologie* 24 (1964): 229–42.
[51] Barth, *Der Römerbrief*, 213–55.
[52] Karl Barth, *Die christliche Theologie im Entwurf*. Munich: Kaiser Verlag, 1927, 82–7.
[53] See Johann Kreuzer, "'Die Sphäre die höher ist, als die des Menschen: Diese ist der Gott.' Hölderlin und die natürliche Theologie." In *Idealismus und Natürliche Theologie*, ed. Margit Wasmaier-Sailer and Benedikt Paul Göcke, 238–57. Freiburg im Breisgau: Verlag Karl Alber, 2011.
[54] For the central themes of Schleiermacher's approach, see the excellent study of Jacqueline Mariña, *Transformation of the Self in the Thought of Friedrich Schleiermacher*. New York: Oxford University Press, 2008. For some aspects of its development, see Maureen Junker, *Das Urbild des Gottesbewusstseins: Zur Entwicklung der Religionstheorie und Christologie Schleiermachers von der ersten zur zweiten Auflage der Glaubenslehre*. Berlin: Walter de Gruyter, 1990.
[55] Hans-Joachim Kraus and H. Berkhof, *Karl Barths Lichterlehre*. Zurich: Theologischer Verlag, 1978, 39.
[56] For an excellent analysis, see Christoph Kock, *Natürliche Theologie: Ein evangelischer Streitbegriff*. Neukirchen-Vluyn: Neukirchener Verlag, 2001, 23–86. One of the many merits of this important study is its emphasis on the interconnections between the theological reception of Schleiermacher and the formulation of a natural theology (103–50).

between "neo-Protestantism" and "natural theology".[57] He seems to have begun to conceive natural theology as a framing device for a cluster of theological methodologies and attitudes that he considered to subvert the primacy of God's self-revelation.[58] He may have been influenced here by Ernst Troeltsch's formulation of the theological tasks of modernity in terms of a natural theology;[59] this, however, is not a sufficient explanation of his growing tendency in the later 1920s to use the category of "natural theology" to articulate and colligate his concerns about theological tendencies which denied, subverted, or marginalized God's sovereignty in revelation.

Barth now tends to group the various theological (or, perhaps we should say, *anti*-theological) trends he discerns within nineteenth-century theology under the aegis of a "natural theology" which – as Barth chooses to define it – is to be understood as a theology "which comes to humanity from nature" (*von der Mensch von Natur herkommt*), articulating humanity's "self-preservation and self-affirmation" (*Selbstbewahrung und Selbstbehauptung*) in the face of God. Natural theology is portrayed as the paradigmatic instantiation of the sinful human longing for self-justification, the negative side of a controlling dialectic between a true theology based upon revelation, on the one hand, and a human self-justification based upon anthropology on the other.[60]

Barth's hostility towards "natural theology" is thus an expression of his hostility towards any theological doctrine or method which undermines the necessity, actuality, and uniqueness of God's self-revelation. If knowledge of God can be achieved independently of God's self-revelation in Christ, then it follows that humanity can dictate the place, time, means, and ultimately *content* of its knowledge of God.[61] Natural theology, for Barth, represents an attempt on the part of humanity to understand itself apart from and in isolation from revelation, representing a deliberate refusal to accept the necessity and consequences of revelation. One of Barth's central concerns is to expose the myth of human autonomy, and identify its consequences for theology and ethics.[62] Theology seeks to respect and safeguard the

---

[57] For a good overview of the development of Barth's focus on this theological concept as a marker of human refusal to accept divine revelation, see Szekeres, "Karl Barth und die natürliche Theologie."

[58] See especially his letter to Eduard Thurnseysen, dated 20 December 1923: *Karl Barth–Eduard Thurneysen Briefwechsel*. 3 vols. Zurich: Theologischer Verlag, 1974, vol. 2, 205–12.

[59] As noted by Uwe Stenglein-Hektor, *Religion im Bürgerleben: Eine Frömmigkeitsgeschichtliche Studie zur rationalitätskrise liberaler Theologie um 1900 am Beispiel Wilhelm Herrmann*. Münster: LIT Verlag, 1997, 187–93.

[60] See Karl Barth, "Schicksal und Idee in der Theologie." In *Theologische Fragen und Antworten*. Zollikon: Evangelischer Verlag, 1957, 54–92, especially 85–7.

[61] On this general point, see Regin Prenter, "Das Problem der natürlichen Theologie bei Karl Barth." *Theologische Literaturzeitung* 77 (1952): 607–11.

[62] On the theme of autonomy in Barth's writings, see John Macken, *The Autonomy Theme in the Church Dogmatics: Karl Barth and His Critics*. Cambridge: Cambridge University Press, 1990, 69–80; Thies Gundlach, *Selbstbegrenzung Gottes und die Autonomie des Menschen: Karl Barths Kirchliche Dogmatik als Modernisierungsschrift evangelischer Theologie*. Frankfurt am Main: Peter Lang, 1992.

autonomy of God, as expressed in revelation.[63] The human desire to assert itself and take control over things is seen by Barth as one of the most fundamental sources of error in theology, leading to the erection of theological towers of Babel – purely human constructions, erected in the face of God.[64]

For Barth, there is a close link between natural theology and the theme of human autonomy. As he understands the concept, natural theology concerns the human desire to find God on humanity's own terms. Natural theology thus appears to posit a second source of revelation alongside Jesus Christ, as he is attested in Scripture. The affirmation of a natural theology appears to contradict the fundamental principle that God reveals himself in Christ, implying that God reveals himself in nature independent of his self-revelation in Christ. For Barth, revelation is only to be had through the revelation of God, as a consequence of God's gracious decision that he is to be known. There is no manner in which God can be known outside and apart from God's self-revelation.[65] Barth's view that natural theology was tantamount to an assertion of human autonomy in theology led him to express serious concerns about certain statements found in earlier Reformed confessional documents, especially the Gallic and Belgic Confessions.[66]

Barth's trenchant hostility towards natural theology was solidified still further as a result of developments within the Weimar Republic in 1933, which eventually led to its collapse. It must be appreciated that the Barth–Brunner debate on natural theology took place against a political and ideological backdrop which made any serious theological discussion of the issues associated with natural theology virtually impossible. From the outset, the political presuppositions and consequences of natural theology became an integral part of the debate. Although many interpreters of Barth present his hardening attitudes towards natural theology as an issue of theological method,[67] it is clear that this cannot be discussed in isolation from the cultural, social, and political debates of the age in which he became involved.[68] The shifting political situation in Germany as a result of Hitler's triumph of 1933 led Barth to assess the political consequences of "natural

---

[63] As emphasized by Trutz Rendtorff, "Radikale Autonomie Gottes: Zum Verständnis der Theologie Karl Barths und ihrer Folger." In *Theorie des Christentums*, 161–81. Gütersloh: Mohn, 1972.

[64] Bruce L. McCormack, *Karl Barth's Critically Realistic Dialectical Theology: Its Genesis and Development 1909–1936*. Oxford: Clarendon Press, 1995, 167.

[65] This is stressed at point after point: see, for example, *Church Dogmatics*. Edinburgh: T&T Clark, 1975, II/1, 3–4, 69, 206–7. The general point at issue can be studied in Ingrid Spieckermann, *Gotteserkenntnis: Ein Beitrag zur Grundfrage der neuen Theologie Karl Barths*. Munich: Kaiser, 1985; McCormack, *Barth's Critically Realistic Dialectical Theology*, 241–88.

[66] *Church Dogmatics*, II/1, 127.

[67] For example, Spieckermann, *Gotteserkenntnis*; McCormack, *Barth's Critically Realistic Dialectical Theology*.

[68] For an early statement of this point, see Friedrich-Wilhelm Marquardt, *Theologie und Sozialismus: Das Beispiel Karl Barths*. 3rd edn. Munich: Kaiser, 1985.

theology". What Barth regarded as the unacceptable political outcomes of natural theology now became an indication of its inauthenticity. This use of an implicit political criterion for theological adjudication hovers over the Barth–Brunner debate of 1934, and cannot be ignored. In certain ways, the controversy of 1934 cannot be dissociated from the Nazification of German society and culture.

Given the importance of these developments, we must turn to assess their implications for Barth's perception of Brunner's understanding of natural theology, and the wider debate about the place of an appeal to nature in Reformed dogmatics.

A Game-Changer: The Nazi Power Grab of 1933

In January 1933, National Socialism triumphed in Germany. Adolf Hitler was sworn in as chancellor of Germany by President Paul von Hindenburg.[69] This remarkable "power grab" (*Machtergreifung*) prepared the ground for the sweeping away of traditional balances and checks on power, with the result that, by the middle of 1933, Hitler was in a position of total authority within Germany. The Nazification of German culture began. To understand the relevance of this development for any debate about natural theology, we need to understand the impact of the Nazi "power grab" for two institutions: the German churches, and the faculties of theology of German universities.

The Weimar Republic, Germany's first democracy, inherited a dire financial situation as a result of the Treaty of Versailles (28 June 1919), which brought the Great War to an end. Not only did Germany need to pay its substantial war debts; it was also liable for massive reparation costs. The fledgling democratic state struggled to survive economically. It was only by early 1929 that some degree of stability began to emerge. But in October 1929 the American stock market crashed, causing leading American banks to call in their loans to Germany. A fresh economic crisis began, leading to increased disillusionment with the main political parties of the Weimar Republic. Support for extreme parties of the left and right surged. By 1932 it was obvious that the Republic's supporters could no longer command a parliamentary majority. Adolf Hitler was the only political leader capable of commanding a legislative majority. It became inevitable that he would be invited to form a government.

German Protestantism faced major difficulties during the period of the Weimar Republic. The unification of Germany in 1870 had seen Protestantism

---

[69] See especially Richard J. Evans, *The Coming of the Third Reich*, London: Allen Lane, 2003, 77–307. Older studies of importance include Norbert Frei, "Machtergreifung: Anmerkungen zu einem historischen Begriff." *Vierteljahrshefte für Zeitgeschichte* 31 (1983): 136–45; Gotthard Jasper, *Die gescheiterte Zähmung: Wege zur Machtergreifung Hitlers 1930–1934*. Frankfurt am Main: Suhrkamp, 1986, 126–52.

secure a privileged status in the newly established German empire.[70] In the Wilhelmine state, Protestant churches had, in effect, become the religious establishment. The open and somewhat uncritical support given to the Kaiser's war policies by Protestant church leaders and theologians led to something of a backlash after the end of the Great War.[71]

A new national mood began to develop, critical of the Protestant establishment and its links with the war, characterized by growing secularism, religious indifference, and rising anti-clericalism.[72] The close ties between church and state were cut, and church schools were placed under threat. Many German Protestants were disturbed by these developments, in which major decisions were taken by a left-of-centre government, in which Catholics were represented, and Protestants were not. Most Protestant church leaders hoped for a change in the political order as a way of reversing their declining influence, and safeguarding both religion and religious education in what many considered to be an increasingly secularized state, with growing sympathy for non-Christian religious groupings. Hitler was seen by many Protestants as someone who would reverse such trends, and restore at least something of the pre-war situation.[73]

The challenges to Protestant hegemony during the period of the Weimar Republic were not limited to the reduction of its status in relation to Catholicism. Alternative belief systems began to emerge. Public interest in neo-paganism had risen substantially, with forms of German nature religion gaining popular support.[74] The German Faith Movement (Deutsche

---

[70] A point emphasized by John S. Conway, "The Political Role of German Protestantism, 1870–1990." *Journal of Church and State* 34 (1992): 819–42; Marjorie Lamberti, "Religious Conflicts and German National Identity in Prussia, 1866–1914." In *Modern Prussian History: 1830–1947*, ed. Philip G. Dwyer, 169–87. London: Longman, 2001.

[71] The role of Adolf von Harnack in this development was of particular importance: J. C. O'Neill, "Adolf von Harnack and the Entry of the German State into War, July–August 1914." *Scottish Journal of Theology* 55, no. 1 (2002): 1–18. For the impact of Harnack's support for the Kaiser's war policies on the young Karl Barth, see Wilfried Härle, "Der Aufruf der 93 Intellektuellen und Karl Barths Bruch mit der liberalen Theologie." *Zeitschrift für Theologie und Kirche* 72 (1975): 207–24. See further Karl Barth, *Evangelische Theologie im 19. Jahrhundert*. Zurich: Zollikon, 1957, 6.

[72] Jochen Jacke, *Kirche zwischen Monarchie und Republik: Der preussische Protestantismus nach dem Zusammenbruch von 1918*. Hamburg: Hans Christians Verlag, 1976; Daniel R. Borg, *The Old Prussian Church and the Weimar Republic: A Study in Political Adjustment, 1917–1927*. Hanover, NH: University Press of New England, 1984.

[73] Klaus Scholder, *Die Kirchen und das Dritte Reich: Vorgeschichte und Zeit der Illusion 1918–1934*. Munich: Econ Ullstein, 2000. The role of Catholicism is of historical importance, but not central to our purposes in this analysis. Something of the complexity of Catholicism's attitude towards National Socialism in the 1920s can be seen from Heinz Hürten, "Kardinal Faulhaber und die Juden: Eine frühe Stellungnahme der katholischen Kirche zum Nationalsozialismus." *Zeitschrift für bayerische Landesgeschichte* 68 (2005): 1029–34.

[74] For discussion of this and related movements in the early 1930s, see Horst Junginger, "Die Deutsche Glaubensbewegung als ideologisches Zentrum der völkisch-religiösen Bewegungen." In *Die völkisch-religiöse Bewegung im Nationalsozialismus: Eine Beziehungs- und Konfliktgeschichte*, ed. Uwe Puschner and Clemens Vollnhals, 65–101. Göttingen: Vandenhoeck & Ruprecht, 2012.

Glaubensbewegung), initiated by Jakob Wilhelm Hauer (1881–1962), was modelled partly on Hinduism and partly on *völkische* ideas.[75] Hauer had hopes that its Aryan pedigree would lead to it becoming the state religion of Nazi Germany – a hope that was never in fact fulfilled.[76] Ernst Bergmann's *Confessio Germanica* (1933) also set out a neo-pagan creed, clearly devised as the antithesis of a classic Christian Trinitarian faith: "I believe in the God of German religion who works in nature, in the exalted human spirit, and in the strength of his people. . . . And in the helper in need, Krist [*der Nothelfer Krist*] who fights for the nobility of the human soul. And in Germany, the land for the cultivation of a new humanity."[77]

The Faith Movement of German Christians (Glaubensbewegung deutsche Christen), which emerged in 1932 and rapidly became known simply as the German Christians, sought to retain a more orthodox Christian belief system, while accommodating itself to the new political situation, believing it was possible to affirm National Socialism *politically*, and Christianity *ecclesially*.

> We German Christians believe in our saviour Jesus Christ, in the power of his cross and resurrection. Jesus' life and death teach us that the way of struggle is also the way of love and the way of life. . . . As for every people, the eternal God has implanted as creator in our people a law that is distinct to it. This law assumed historical form in the leader Adolf Hitler and in the National Socialist state fashioned by him. This law speaks in the history of our people that has grown out of blood and soil. Fidelity to this law demands of us the fight for honour and freedom.[78]

Initially, the German Christian movement was essentially a National Socialist faction group within German Protestantism, affirming the "leadership principle" (*Führerprinzip*) that had become typical of fascist organizations throughout Europe around this time.[79]

On 23 July 1933, Hitler established a unified German Protestant Church (Deutsche evangelische Kirche). This retained the federal structure, based on twenty-eight territorially defined Protestant churches (*Landeskirchen*), developed in 1922 during the period of the Weimar Republic. The German

---

[75] Schaul Baumann, *Die Deutsche Glaubensbewegung und ihr Gründer Jakob Wilhelm Hauer (1821–1962)*. Marburg: Diagonal, 2005. On the Aryan dimension, see Ulrich Hufnagel, "Religionswissenschaft und indische Religionsgeschichte in den Arbeiten Jakob Wilhelm Hauers: Wissenschaftskonzept und politische Orientierung." In *Indienforschung im Zeitenwandel: Analysen und Dokumente zur Indologie und Religionswissenschaft in Tübingen*, ed. Heidrun Brückner, 145–74. Tübingen: Attempto, 2003.

[76] Karla O. Poewe, *New Religions and the Nazis*. New York: Routledge, 2006, 18–127.

[77] Junginger, "Die Deutsche Glaubensbewegung als ideologisches Zentrum der völkisch-religiösen Bewegungen," 80.

[78] Kurt Dietrich Schmidt, *Die Bekenntnisse und grundsätzlichen Äusserungen zur Kirchenfrage des Jahres 1933*. Göttingen: Vandenhoeck & Ruprecht, 1934, 102. For the background, see Carsten Nicolaisen, *Der Weg nach Barmen: Die Entstehungsgeschichte der Theologischen Erklärung von 1934*. Neukirchen-Vluyn: Neukirchener Verlag, 1985; Eberhard Busch, *Die Barmer Thesen 1934–2004*. Göttingen: Vandenhoeck & Ruprecht, 2004.

[79] Bruce F. Pauley, "Fascism and the *Führerprinzip*: The Austrian Example." *Central European History* 12, no. 3 (1979): 272–96.

Christian faction won the elections to the new church's most important ecclesiastical offices, and moved to align the church with National Socialist doctrines and institutions. This development within the churches was part of the wider process of *Gleichschaltung* – an enforced process of assimilation in which German social, political, and cultural institutions were brought into line with Nazi ideology during the period 1933–7. Churches were decorated with swastikas, and a series of new symbols and rituals introduced to demonstrate the unity between the church and the Nazi state.[80]

This process of "bringing into line" was especially significant within German university faculties of theology. It became clear at a very early stage that the Nazi administration regarded educational institutions as central to its quest for ideological hegemony within Germany. Leading German universities were persuaded by various means to fall in line with the ethos and outlook of National Socialism.[81] The overall picture is complex: some academics openly advocated Nazism; others declined to oppose it; many were sacked on racial or political grounds. Within this overall Nazification of the German higher education system, faculties of theology were singled out for particular attention.[82] In part, this reflected a realization that today's theology students were tomorrow's pastors and bishops. Gaining control of university theology faculties was seen as part of the Nazi regime's larger strategy of gaining control of the churches.

The process of *Gleichschaltung* alarmed many within the German Protestant churches at this time, including Dietrich Bonhoeffer and Karl Barth. The German churches were being railroaded into an ideological corral, in which they were deprived of any intellectual foundation on the basis of which to reassert their identity and mission.[83] One of the major

---

[80] For the tensions that resulted, see Kurt Meier, *Kreuz und Hakenkreuz: Die evangelische Kirche im Dritten Reich*. Munich: Deutscher Taschenbuch Verlag, 1992, 32–124.

[81] Major recent studies include Eckhart Krause et al., eds., *Hochschulalltag im Dritten Reich: Die Hamburger Universität 1933–1945*. 3 vols. Berlin: Reimer, 1991; Christian Jansen, *Professoren und Politik: Politisches Denken und Handeln der Heidelberger Hochschullehrer 1914–1935*. Göttingen: Vandenhoeck & Ruprecht, 1992; Dieter Langewiesche, "Die Universität Tübingen in der Zeit des Nationalsozialismus: Formen der Selbstgleichschaltung und Selbstbehauptung." *Geschichte und Gesellschaft* 23 (1997): 618–46; Heinrich Becker et al., eds., *Die Universität Göttingen unter dem Nationalsozialismus*. 2nd edn. Munich: Saur, 1998; Anne Christine Nagel, ed., *Die Philipps-Universität Marburg im Nationalsozialismus: Dokumente zu ihrer Geschichte*. Stuttgart: Franz Steiner, 2000; Steven P. Remy, *The Heidelberg Myth: The Nazification and Denazification of a German University*. Cambridge, MA: Harvard University Press, 2002; Henrik Eberle, *Die Martin-Luther-Universität Halle in der Zeit des Nationalsozialismus 1933–1945*. Halle: Mitteldeutscher Verlag, 2002.

[82] See the substantial analysis in Fritz Heinrich, *Die deutsche Religionswissenschaft und der Nationalsozialismus: Eine ideologiekritische und wissenschaftsgeschichtliche Untersuchung*. Petersberg: Imhof Verlag, 2002.

[83] For an excellent study of the tensions of this period, see Gerhard Besier, "Hans Asmussen, Karl Barth und Martin Niemöller im 'Kirchenkampf': Theologie und Kirchenpolitik in 'Schülerschaft', Partnerschaft und Gegnerschaft." In *Hans Asmussen im Kontext heutiger ökumenischer Theologie*, ed. Josef Außenmair, 46–78. Münster: LIT Verlag, 2001.

concerns was the emergence of a theology of creation that lent credibility to the National Socialist ideology. The noted Lutheran theologian Paul Althaus developed concepts of the "orders of creation" or "primordial revelation" which were easily assimilated to Nazi themes.[84] On the basis of his *Schöpfungsglaube*, Althaus developed a political theology based on the "orders" of the people (*Volk*), the family, and the state.[85] Although Althaus developed his notion of the "orders of creation" in the 1920s, before Hitler's rise to power, his apologia for National Socialism is partly based on its respect for, and reinforcement of, these orders.[86]

My own reading of Althaus's theological and political writings from about 1925 to 1935 suggests that an essentially benign theological concept (the "orders of creation"), which Althaus appears to have regarded as being, in the first place, well grounded in the writings of Luther, and in the second, of value in achieving a degree of theological and social stability in the era following the Great War, became seen as toxic because of a changing political and ideological context, which allowed such a theological concept to be deployed in the service of National Socialism. This regrettable development is to be seen as a matter of historical contingency, rather than theological necessity. Barth, however, both asserted the intrinsic theological unacceptability and denounced the compromised social and political outcomes of Althaus's theology of the orders of creation.[87]

On 10 March 1933 Barth delivered a lecture in Copenhagen which identified the themes that he regarded as central to the emerging conflict within the German churches in the light of the Nazi *Machtergreifung*. He declared that the construction of a viable theological alternative to the German Christian movement rested on the unequivocal rejection of natural theology.

> The inevitable controversy about natural theology is a controversy about a right obedience in theology [*der . . . unvermeidliche Streit gegen die natürliche Theologie ist ein Streit um den rechten Gehorsam in der Theologie*] . . . It must abandon each and every natural theology and dare, in that narrow

---

[84] Paul Knitter, "Die Uroffenbarungslehre von Paul Althaus – Anknüpfungspunkt für den Nationalsozialismus? Eine Studie zum Verhältnis von Theologie und Ideologie." *Evangelische Theologie* 33, no. 2 (1973): 138–64. For a general survey of Althaus's theology, see Hans Grass, "Die Theologie von Paul Althaus." *Neue Zeitschrift für Systematische Theologie* 8 (1966): 213–41.

[85] See especially Paul Althaus, *Evangelium und Leben: Gesammelte Vorträge*. Gütersloh: Bertelsmann, 1927; idem, *Kirche und Volkstum*. Gütersloh: Bertelsmann, 1928. More generally, see Robert P. Ericksen, "The Political Theology of Paul Althaus." *German Studies Review* 9, no. 3 (1986): 547–67.

[86] For this notion in Nazi ideology, see Lutz Raphael, "Radikales Ordnungsdenken und die Organisationtotalitärer Herrschaft: Weltanschauungseliten und Humanwissenschaftler im NS-Regime." *Geschichte und Gesellschaft* 27 (2001): 5–40.

[87] For Brunner's approach to this notion, see Howard Douglas Lee, *The Orders of Creation in the Ethical Theory of Emil Brunner*. Dubuque, IA: University of Iowa Press, 1972.

isolation, to cling alone to the God who has revealed himself in Jesus Christ.[88]

All other approaches to theology, Barth declared, led away from that God. That was the inevitable outcome of certain indefensible approaches to theology – such as those of Hirsch and Althaus within the German Christian movement, but also those of Gogarten and Brunner.

It is clear that Barth's heightened concerns about the concept of "natural theology", as he defined this notion, reflected his views on the social and political situation within Germany resulting from the Nazi takeover. In that – as Barth understood things – natural theology played an important role in providing theological legitimation for the German Christian movement around this time, especially as represented by Althaus, Barth appears to have seen the theological subversion and neutralization of this dangerous notion as being of decisive ecclesial significance. The "German church crisis" thus provided the context in which Barth made certain judgements about the *political* implications and consequences of natural theology.

The essential point to appreciate is this: by 1934, Barth regarded any theology grounded in an appeal to "nature" or "creation" to be indefensible, partly because of its inability to offer a theological firewall against ideological *Gleichschaltung*, which both assimilated Christian ideas to a National Socialist master-narrative, and claimed them as supportive of its *völkische* policies. In a letter to Brunner of October 1933, Barth made clear that the German context made certain ways of theologizing deeply problematic. Somewhat caustically, Barth suggested that since Brunner did not actually live in Germany, he was not well placed to understand how critical the situation had become there.[89] Things became much worse a month later. At a rally in the Sports Palace in Berlin on 13 November 1933, Reinhold Krause (1893–1980), a schoolteacher who had risen to prominence within Nazi circles in Berlin, demanded a radical Nazification of Christianity, including the rejection of the Old Testament as a Jewish – and hence non-Aryan – book.

By this time, the elimination of any trace of Jewish influence in the public sphere had become a central theme of *Gleichschaltung*. It was inevitable that churches and their educational institutions would be forced into line with this aspect of the Nazification of German academic culture. In the case of faculties of theology, this manifested itself particularly in two developments. The first was an attempt to at least neutralize the Jewishness of Jesus

---

[88] Karl Barth, "Das Erste Gebot als theologisches Axiom." *Zwischen den Zeiten* 13 (1933): 127–43; quote at p. 142. For comment, see Gestrich, *Neuzeitliches Denken und die Spaltung der dialektischen Theologie*, 158–9; André Demut, *Evangelium und Gesetz: Eine systematisch-theologische Reflexion zu Karl Barths Predigtwerk*. Berlin: de Gruyter, 2008, 281–4.
[89] Barth to Brunner, 22 October 1933: *Karl Barth–Emil Brunner, Briefwechsel*, 237–40. Barth raised these concerns partly in response to Brunner's involvement with the Oxford Group, which he considered unacceptable.

of Nazareth;[90] the second was a drive to marginalize the Old Testament, in that it was seen as a Jewish document. The impact of these policies was particularly important at the University of Jena, which became a Nazi stronghold in 1934.[91]

In an indication of things to come, Walter Grundmann (1906–76) was appointed to the chair of New Testament at Jena, despite lacking what most would have regarded as credible academic credentials. His strongly pro-Nazi views were welcomed by the university administration, and found their expression in a tract advocating the elimination of Jewish symbols, ideas, and history from German church life and theological reflection.[92] Jesus of Nazareth was reinterpreted as an Aryan figure,[93] his Jewish roots being denied or overlooked. This growing Nazi influence was evident in developments within the so-called "Quest for the Historical Jesus" during the later 1930s, which increasingly advocated a disengagement from history as a means of marginalizing the Jewish origins and roots of Jesus of Nazareth. The impact of National Socialism on the prevailing assumptions of German biblical criticism and interpretation remains a topic of importance, not least because some of its assumptions appear to have remained embedded within these disciplines until relatively recently.[94]

The Old Testament was quickly marginalized from the theological curriculum. Jena became the first theological faculty in Germany to abolish the requirement for theology students to study Hebrew. In announcing this, the faculty explained that it was not necessary to know anything about the Old Testament in the study of Jesus of Nazareth. This posed a particular problem for the Old Testament scholar Gerhard von Rad (1901–71), a member of the theology faculty at Jena from 1934 to 1945,[95] who considered the Old Testament essential to an understanding of Jesus of Nazareth in particular, and the New Testament in general. His views led to his being marginalized within the faculty. Not one of the forty-five doctoral dissertations submitted

---

[90] Susannah Heschel, *The Aryan Jesus: Christian Theologians and the Bible in Nazi Germany*. Princeton, NJ: Princeton University Press, 2008.

[91] Uwe Hoßfeld, Jürgen John, Oliver Lehmuth, and Rüdiger Stutz, eds., *"Kämpferische Wissenschaft": Studien zur Universität Jena im Nationalsozialismus*. Cologne: Böhlau, 2003.

[92] Walter Grundmann, *Die Entjudung des religiösen Lebens als Aufgabe deutscher Theologie und Kirche*. Weimar: Verlag Deutsche Christen, 1939. For comment, see Heschel, *The Aryan Jesus*, 67–165. For the most extensive study of his career, see Roland Deines, Volker Leppin, and Karl-Wilhelm Niebuhr, eds., *Walter Grundmann: Ein Neutestamentler im Dritten Reich*. Leipzig: Evangelische Verlagsanstalt, 2007.

[93] Heschel, *The Aryan Jesus*, 26–66.

[94] For reflections on this contentious issue, see Martin J. Buss, *Biblical Form Criticism in Its Context*. Sheffield: Sheffield Academic Press, 1999, 327–33; Wayne Meeks, "A Nazi New Testament Professor Reads His Bible: The Strange Case of Gerhard Kittel." In *The Idea of Biblical Interpretation: Essays in Honor of James L. Kugel*, ed. Hindy Najman and Judith H. Newman, 513–44. Leiden: Brill, 2004.

[95] Bernard M. Levinson, "Reading the Bible in Nazi Germany: Gerhard von Rad's Attempt to Reclaim the Old Testament for the Church." *Interpretation* 62 (2008): 238–54; Heschel, *The Aryan Jesus*, 201–40.

to the Faculty of Theology during the period 1934–45 was supervised by von Rad.

Theological faculty and students who refused to conform to either of these norms were dismissed from their employment, or failed in their examinations. One research student at Jena who argued that the ideas of Jesus of Nazareth had to be understood against their background in the Old Testament was failed on political grounds. The student, it was argued, had failed to grasp the National Socialist doctrine that "the question of race is the fundamental question".[96]

By the beginning of 1934, it was clear to many that German Christianity was in the process of being Nazified. The Confessing Church (Bekennende Kirche) was formed in response to the deteriorating ecclesial situation, prompted initially by the so-called "Aryan Clause",[97] which prohibited clergy with Jewish ancestry from holding any position within the churches. The Confessing Church rapidly extended its agenda beyond this single issue, seeing itself as the last defence of authentic Christianity in the face of relentless pressure to assimilate it to Nazism. Karl Barth became a leading figure within the movement, contributing significantly to the theological articulation of its strategy and public statements.[98] It was inevitable that, as a Swiss national, he would now be expelled from Germany.[99]

In May 1934 the "Barmen Theological Declaration" (*Barmer Theologische Erklärung*) was published.[100] This document reasserted the independence of the church from the state, and emphatically declared that the roots of the Christian church lay not in German culture, but in Jesus Christ.

> Jesus Christ, as he is attested for us in Holy Scripture, is the one Word of God which we have to hear and which we have to trust and obey in life and in death. We reject the false teaching, that the church could and should

---

[96] Susannah Heschel, "The Theological Faculty at the University of Jena as 'a Stronghold of National Socialism'." In *"Kämpferische Wissenschaft"*, ed. Hoßfeld et al., 452–71; quote at 460.

[97] The so-called *Arierparagraph* of April 1933 can be seen as an extension of earlier limitations on the role of Jews in German public life during the Wilhelmine period: Stephan Malinowski, *Vom König zum Führer: Sozialer Niedergang und politische Radikalisierung im deutschen Adel zwischen Kaiserreich und NS-Staat*. 3rd edn. Berlin: Akademie-Verlag, 2004, 336–57.

[98] For the theological concerns, see Jan Rohls, *Protestantische Theologie der Neuzeit*. 2 vols. Tübingen: Mohr Siebeck, 1997, vol. 2, 404–11.

[99] For the process leading to this development, see Hans Prolingheuer, *Der Fall Karl Barth, 1934–1935: Chronographie einer Vertreibung*. 2nd edn. Neukirchen-Vluyn: Neukirchener Verlag, 1984.

[100] For analysis, see Carsten Nicolaisen, *Der Weg nach Barmen: Die Entstehungsgeschichte der Theologischen Erklärung von 1934*. Neukirchen-Vluyn: Neukirchener Verlag, 1985; Eberhard Busch, *Die Barmer Thesen, 1934–2004*; Petra Bahr, Martin Dutzmann, Heino Falcke, Johanna Haberer, Wolfgang Huber, Margot Käßmann, and Michael Welker, *Begründete Freiheit: Die Aktualität der Barmer Theologischen Erklärung*. Neukirchen-Vluyn: Neukirchener Verlag, 2009.

acknowledge any other events and powers, figures and truths, as God's revelation, or as a source of its proclamation, apart from or in addition to this one Word of God. . . . We reject the false teaching, that the church is free to abandon the form of its proclamation and order in favour of anything it pleases, or in response to prevailing ideological or political beliefs [*der jeweils herrschenden weltanschaulichen und politischen Überzeugungen*].[101]

It was a moment of crisis, in which Barth and others took their stand against a *gleichgeschaltete* pseudo-church.

Yet the Barmen Theological Declaration was not a full-frontal assault against Nazism, as some have suggested. It is significant that the declaration contains no quotations from the Old Testament; that it makes no attempt to connect the church with Israel; and that it fails to reassert the Jewishness of Jesus of Nazareth. Barmen is best seen, not as a rejection of Nazi ideology, but as a declaration of ideological independence on the part of the churches, with the potential for further development. Revelation is Christologically concentrated, and set at some distance from such notions as the "orders of creation" or some "primal revelation". For Barth, some such Christological foundation was essential to the preservation of ecclesial identity and freedom.

Yet in May 1934, at this moment of crisis, Barth found himself having to respond to a public assault on his views of natural theology from someone who was – however incorrectly – seen as one of his immediate theological circle. In that very month, Emil Brunner published *Natur und Gnade* ("Nature and Grace"). Brunner's unexpected public intervention seemed to Barth to represent the reassertion of precisely the kind of theology which had so compromised the German church in the previous year, and the undermining of a theology which offered the only hope for its preservation. It was hardly a propitious start to what would prove to be an ill-tempered and poorly formulated debate.

Brunner's Public Criticism of Barth: *Nature and Grace* (1934)

It is important to note that Brunner's 1934 discussion of the limits and scope of a legitimate natural theology was framed without reference to the rise of National Socialism in Germany. Brunner saw no reason to acknowledge or create a link between the theological question of whether God might choose to use the created order as a means of revelation and the ecclesial question of the authority of the state and its claims to influence the life of the church.

Isolated from the ideological firestorm that was having such an impact on Germany, Brunner found himself baffled by Barth's theological misgivings

---

[101] Wilhelm Niesel, ed., *Bekenntnisschriften und Kirchenordnungen der nach Gottes Wort reformierten Kirche*. Zurich: Evangelischer Verlag, 1938, 335–6.

about natural theology. Lacking any experience of the political crisis now growing in Germany, and its implications for Christianity in Germany, Brunner seems to have failed to comprehend the manner and extent of the politicization of theology in Germany. His inability to grasp the political consequences of an appeal to the "orders of creation" within a Nazi context prevented him from understanding how theological debates no longer concerned purely dogmatic issues. The game had changed.

Brunner's failure to grasp Barth's concerns reflected a deeper shortcoming, which partly arose from his isolation from the German context. Although Barth's caustic remark about Brunner's distance from the German situation appears harsh, there is an uncomfortable truth in his observation. Brunner wanted to discuss a series of themes at the detached level of academic theology. Barth was of the view that, at least for the time being, this was no longer possible.

Despite his own reservations about the notion of natural theology, Brunner believed Barth's negative attitude towards his emerging approach was not justified by either the concept itself or his own cautious and limited explorations of its themes. When Barth's Copenhagen lecture of January 1933 was published in the summer of that year, Brunner felt that the only explanation for Barth's criticism was that he had not properly understood Brunner's position. This impression was consolidated when Ernst Wolf published a short treatise on Martin Luther's theology, which touched on the question of natural theology.[102] Brunner found himself strongly in agreement with Wolf's analysis of Luther's concept of the natural knowledge of God, and was thus puzzled why Barth considered them to be so fundamentally opposed on this matter. He wrote to Barth in February 1934, expressing his bewilderment over the issue. Perhaps he had expressed himself imperfectly in his writings. Yet it seemed to Brunner that he, Luther (as interpreted by Wolf), and Barth were fundamentally at one on the issue of the natural knowledge of God.[103]

Yet Barth declined to acknowledge any such agreement between them, however limited. They were, Barth declared, set on totally different theological courses. Barth suggested that Brunner's theological approach inverted the Exodus, leading to a return to captivity amidst the fleshpots of Egypt.[104] Brunner was clearly pained by Barth's attitude towards him, which seemed to him to be incomprehensible, a refusal to take him seriously as a theological thinker, perhaps even amounting to a pointed personal snub. It is possible that this unhealthy mingling of frustration and anxiety may echo Brunner's

---

[102] Ernst Wolf, *Martin Luther, das Evangelium und die Religion*. Munich: Kaiser, 1934, especially 9–13. This short treatise was published as a special issue of the journal *Theologische Existenz Heute*, which had been founded by Barth and Gogarten in 1933.

[103] Brunner to Barth, 26 February 1934: *Karl Barth–Emil Brunner, Briefwechsel*, 244–8, especially 245.

[104] Jehle, *Emil Brunner*, 300.

"deeply rooted inferiority complex" in relation to Barth, which their mutual friend Eduard Thurneysen had perceptively noted some years earlier.[105]

Brunner's sharper criticisms of Barth had hitherto been confined largely to his correspondence, and had not been expressed publicly. Perhaps riled by Barth's openly stated criticisms of himself and other "dialectical theologians", Brunner felt the time had come to resolve matters more openly. Early in May 1934, Brunner wrote somewhat curtly to Barth to advise him that he would shortly publish a booklet (*Büchlein*) aiming to "understand what unites and separates us", set within a shared framework of biblical and Reformational assumptions.[106] It is important to appreciate that Brunner remained convinced that he and Barth shared a common theological programme – a "theology of the Word of God" which gives due weight to both the biblical witness and to the way in which this was given specific formulation during the period of the Reformation.[107]

Nature and Grace, a mere forty-four pages in length, was published by the Tübingen publisher J. C. B. Mohr at the beginning of May 1934,[108] and quickly sold out. A second edition followed in 1935. Despite Brunner's somewhat feeble protests to the contrary, it is clear that this is a polemical work, directed against what Brunner regards as wrong turns in Barth's thought, and precipitated partly by Barth's personal hostility towards him. Barth, he suggests, had presented him as "a thoroughly unreliable theologian who showed treacherous inclinations both towards Thomism and Neo-Protestantism".[109] In his "great purge", Barth had disowned his former friends – including Brunner himself. Things need to be sorted out, Brunner suggests. And what better way than to try and clarify Barth's ideas, and challenge his "false antitheses" and "one-sidedness", which merely lead to the "petrification" of serious theological discussion?

---

[105] Thurnseysen to Barth, 21 October 1930: *Karl Barth–Eduard Thurneysen Briefwechsel*, vol. 3, 56.
[106] Brunner to Barth, 8 May 1934: *Karl Barth–Emil Brunner, Briefwechsel*, 249–50.
[107] Both Barth and Brunner resisted any attempt to merge the theological notion of the "Word of God" with the "words of the Bible": for comment on this general issue, see Graf-Franz Stuhlhofer, "Worte Gottes in der Bibel: Gegen eine undifferenzierte Gleichsetzung von Bibel und Wort Gottes." *Zeitschrift für Theologie und Gemeinde* 16 (2011): 66–89.
[108] "Natur und Gnade: Zum Gespräch mit Karl Barth," in *Ein offenes Wort*, vol. 1, 333–66; "Nature and Grace", in *Natural Theology*, 15–64. The original 1934 German text of Brunner's booklet is also available in Walter Fürst, ed., *"Dialektische Theologie" in Scheidung und Bewährung 1933–1936*. Munich: Kaiser Verlag, 1966, 169–207. References here are to the German edition in *Ein offenes Wort*. Barth's "Nein!" is cited from the 1934 edition of the text provided in Fürst, ed, *"Dialektische Theologie" in Scheidung und Bewährung 1933–1936*, 208–58. For an English translation of Barth's response to Brunner, see "No!", *Natural Theology*, 67–128.
[109] "Natur und Gnade", 333; "Nature and Grace", 15. Barth used the term "neo-Protestantism" to refer to the defective form of Protestantism as a form of "pietistic and rationalistic Modernism", which he regarded as emerging from the tradition of Schleiermacher, Ritschl, and Harnack. See the analysis in Kimlyn J. Bender, *Karl Barth's Christological Ecclesiology*. Aldershot: Ashgate, 2005, 95–8.

It is incorrect to suggest that Brunner's booklet *Nature and Grace* represents an explicit manifesto for natural theology. He does not even mention the notion of natural theology in the work's title or preface. It emerges in the course of discussion as a theological notion which provides Brunner with a framework for an engagement with Barth's ideas, in effect coordinating a number of concerns that Brunner identifies with Barth's approach. However, the work is clearly written in the full knowledge of Barth's unequivocal rejection of natural theology, particularly the trenchant statements of the Copenhagen lecture of January 1933.[110]

Even a casual reading of the work makes it clear that Brunner has severe misgivings over the concept of "natural theology". What is needed, he insists, is a *new form* of natural theology. He explicitly excludes any notion of *theologia naturalis* as "a self-sufficient rational system of natural knowledge of God".[111] This, for Brunner, represents an abuse and distortion of the idea, to which others might easily be added. Yet he insists that the rejection of natural theology is as unacceptable as its abuse; the critical question concerns how his theological generation "may find the way back to a proper *theologia naturalis*" – a task which Brunner believes will be assisted more by the affirmations of John Calvin than by the negations of Karl Barth.[112] In seeking to renew or reformulate a proper natural theology, Brunner is obliged to combat its inadequate or dysfunctional formulations, as much as to set forward his own alternative. His use of the term "proper" (*recht*) is of critical importance: he is aware of inadequate versions of such a theology, and believes it is important to identify and adopt an approach that is rooted in the Bible and the theology of the Reformation.

So what form should such a "proper natural theology" take? Brunner argues that, since God "leaves the imprint of his nature [*den Stempel seines Wesens*] upon what he does", it follows that it is a fundamentally Christian belief that "the creation of the world is at the same time a revelation, a self-communication of God".[113] While sin diminishes the human capacity to recognize and respond to such a self-communication of God, there is no biblical warrant for suggesting that sin destroys the "perceptibility of God in his works". Therefore the question emerges: how are these two kinds of revelation – that is, revelation in creation and revelation in Jesus Christ – related to one another?[114] Brunner is adamant that, from a Christian perspective, the answer lies in the latter clarifying and perfecting the former.

---

[110] Brunner notes this lecture specifically as a matter of concern: "Natur und Gnade", 333 n. 1; "Nature and Grace", 61 n. 1.
[111] "Natur und Gnade", 374; "Nature and Grace", 58.
[112] "Natur und Gnade", 374–5; "Nature and Grace", 59–60: "Es ist die Aufgabe unserer theologischen Generation, sich zur rechten theologia naturalis zurückzufinden."
[113] "Natur und Gnade", 343; "Nature and Grace", 25.
[114] "Natur und Gnade", 343; "Nature and Grace", 26.

> In faith, on the basis of revelation in Jesus Christ, we shall not be able to avoid speaking of a double revelation – of a first in his creation, which can only be recognized in all its greatness by those whose blindness has been healed by Christ [*dem durch Christus der Star gestochen ist*]; and of a second in Jesus Christ, in the full light of which they can clearly see the first, which far surpasses whatever the first was able to show him.[115]

Brunner takes his stand on Romans 1, whose "double statement" he regards to be unassailable and unavoidable: namely, "that God did not leave himself without witness [*unbezeugt*] to the heathen, but that nevertheless they did not know him in such a way that it became their salvation".[116] Only the Christian – that is, someone "who stands within the revelation in Christ" can be said to possess a "true natural knowledge of God".

Brunner returned to this point in his popular *Our Faith*, a short catechetical work which emerged from his activities with the Oxford Group in Switzerland.[117] This work, published in 1935 but written a year earlier, used readily accessible language to convey theological points to a lay readership. His comments on the possibility of a natural knowledge of God merit close attention, in the light of his more extended discussions in *Nature and Grace* and *Revelation and Reason*. For Brunner, human beings in God's creation are like dogs in an art gallery: they "see" the paintings in one sense, yet totally fail to appreciate them in another.

> Human beings have never known God correctly. The book of nature is not enough to reveal God to such uneducated and unperceptive students as ourselves! The Creator has therefore given us another, even more clearly written book, through which to know him – the Bible. In it, he has shown us, as it were, his own picture [*sein eigenes Bild gezeigt*], so that everyone has to see that it is him, the Creator. This picture is called "Jesus Christ". In him, we know the Creator for the first time, as he really is. For in him, we know for the first time, what God intends for the creation.[118]

Brunner here reproduces the basic consensus of the Reformed tradition of the sixteenth and seventeenth centuries, to the effect that there are two modes of knowing God, one through the natural order, and the second through Scripture, with the second mode being clearer and fuller than the first.[119] As noted earlier (pp. 99–101), this is essentially the substance of

---

[115] "Natur und Gnade", 344; "Nature and Grace", 26–7.
[116] "Natur und Gnade", 345; "Nature and Grace", 27.
[117] Jehle, *Emil Brunner*, 323–4.
[118] *Unser Glaube*, 23–4; *Our Faith*, 25.
[119] See, for example, *Confessio Gallicana*, 1559, article 2; *Confessio Belgica*, 1561, article 2. For comment, see Kenneth J. Howell, *God's Two Books: Copernican Cosmology and Biblical Interpretation in Early Modern Science*. Notre Dame, IN: University of Notre Dame Press, 2002. Barth's critical comments on these two Reformed confessions should be noted: Barth, *Church Dogmatics*, II/1, 127.

Calvin's doctrine of the *cognitio Dei creatoris* and *cognitio Dei redemptoris*. It should be recalled that both Barth and Brunner regarded the heritage of the Reformation to be an important resource in contemporary theological debates, with the question of the theological reappropriation of Calvin of particular importance.[120] Brunner is certainly able to demonstrate that Calvin believes that a natural knowledge of God can be had *extra muros ecclesiae*.[121] The question, however, is how such a notion can function as the basis of a constructive natural theology.

In attempting to clarify his options, Brunner turns to discuss how the critical term "nature" is to be interpreted. "In the phrase 'natural revelation', the word 'natural' is to be understood in a double sense, one objective-divine, and one subjective-human."[122] We see here Brunner's expression of his frustration with what he regards as the "one-sidedness" of Barth's approach to revelation, which, in his view, fails to engage seriously with the human subject as the recipient of revelation. The term "nature" can thus be applied in one sense to "such permanent capacity for revelation [*dauernde Offenbarungsmächtigkeit*] as God has bestowed upon his works, to the traces of God's own nature which he has expressed and made known in them".[123]

Brunner therefore turns to consider the "subjective-human" aspects of natural theology. What notion of human nature is disclosed in and through Jesus Christ, and subsequently authenticated by Scripture as a whole? The question, of course, is not simply one about human *nature*; it is more fundamentally about human *capacities*. Famously, Brunner insisted that a distinctive aspect of human identity was *Wortmächtigkeit* ("a capacity for words").[124]

Brunner develops his account of human capacities using the biblical notion of the *imago Dei* as a controlling image. Humanity is created in the "image of God". What does this imply about human identity and capacities? For Brunner, the proclamation of the church depends upon "the creaturely relation between the Word of God and human words".[125] This relation is grounded in humanity bearing the *imago Dei*.

[120] For a study of Barth's ambivalent attitude towards Calvin, see Sung Wook Chung, *Admiration and Challenge: Karl Barth's Theological Relationship with John Calvin*. New York: Peter Lang, 2002.
[121] See his analysis at "Natur und Gnade", 352–67; "Nature and Grace", 35–50, drawing on his pupil Günter Gloede's study of Calvin, which was published the following year.
[122] "Natur und Gnade", 345; "Nature and Grace", 27.
[123] "Natur und Gnade", 345; "Nature and Grace", 27.
[124] Barth appears to have misread this anthropological capacity as *Offenbarungsmächtigkeit* – "a capacity for revelation" – which is clearly not what Brunner intended. For a debate over this issue, see Trevor Hart, "A Capacity for Ambiguity? The Barth-Brunner Debate revisited." *Tyndale Bulletin* 44 (1993): 289–305; Stephen Andrews, "The Ambiguity of Capacity: A Rejoinder to Trevor Hart." *Tyndale Bulletin* 45 (1994): 169–79.
[125] "Natur und Gnade", 372; "Nature and Grace", 56: "Nie kann die Kirche anders verkündigen als vermöge der schöpfungsmäßigen Beziehung zwischen Gotteswort und Menschenwort." For the use of such Old Testament passages in the controversy of 1934, see Claus Westermann, "Karl Barths Nein: Eine Kontroverse um die theologia naturalis. Emil Brunner–Karl Barth (1934) in perspektiven des Alten Testaments." *Evangelische Theologie* 47 (1987): 386–95.

On the basis of a brief and somewhat questionable biblical exegesis, Brunner draws a distinction between two aspects of this "image of God". In its formal sense, the *imago Dei* designates the fundamental distinction between humanity and the remainder of the created order. It undergirds the fundamental theological insight that humanity is "the centre and apex of creation" (*der Mittel- und Höhepunkt der Schöpfung*).[126] In its material sense, the "image of God" designates the capacity of humanity to enter into a relationship with God, which is lost, and requires restoration through grace.

For Brunner, humanity thus retains the "image of God" in its formal sense, in that it is characterized by its "capacity for words" (*Wortmächtigkeit*) and "capacity to respond" (*Verantwortlichkeit*).[127] Although the German term *Verantwortlichkeit* is traditionally translated as "responsibility" at this point, this somewhat mechanical translation fails to express Brunner's fundamental anthropological belief, essential to a right understanding of his natural theology at this juncture – namely, that humanity has a created capacity to respond to the Word of God. To use Brunner's vocabulary: *Ansprechbarkeit* presupposes *Verantwortlichkeit*: the capacity to be addressed by God presupposes the capacity to respond to God.[128]

Aware of the possibility of being misunderstood at this point, Brunner stresses that he does *not* mean that humanity naturally *possesses* revelation; the point at issue is that humanity alone possesses the "purely formal possibility" of being addressed by God (*Ansprechbarkeit*). To hear God's word is one thing; to believe it is quite another. Humanity is responsible because it is capable of being addressed in this way. There thus exists "a point of attachment for the divine grace of redemption" (*Anknüpfungspunkt für die göttliche Erlösungsgnade*).[129]

Developing this point, Brunner argues that "the Word of God does not, first of all, have to create the human capacity for words".[130] Despite the Fall, humanity has never lost its distinctive capacity for words, which is the precondition of any capacity to hear and respond to the Word of God.[131] Yet this formal human capacity for words does not imply a material capacity to believe the Word of God. To hear is one thing; to believe is another. "The Word of God itself creates the human ability to believe the Word of God – and thus the ability to hear it in *such a way* that can only be heard through believing."[132] Humanity possesses, by nature, a knowledge of God,

---

[126] "Natur und Gnade", 340; "Nature and Grace", 23.
[127] Brunner's concept of responsibility should be viewed alongside that of Dietrich Bonhoeffer: see Berndt Wannenwetsch, "'Responsible Living' or 'Responsible Self'? Bonhoefferian Reflections on a Vexed Moral Notion." *Studies in Christian Ethics* 18 (2005): 125–40.
[128] "Natur und Gnade", 348; "Nature and Grace", 31: "Diese Ansprechbarkeit ist denn auch die Voraussetzung für die Verantwortlichkeit. Nur das überhaupt ansprechbare Wesen ist verantwortlich, nur bei ihm kann man von Entscheidung reden."
[129] "Natur und Gnade", 348; "Nature and Grace", 31.
[130] "Natur und Gnade", 349; "Nature and Grace", 32.
[131] "Natur und Gnade", 340; "Nature and Grace", 23.
[132] "Natur und Gnade", 349; "Nature and Grace", 32 (emphasis added).

of the law, and of its own nature which "may be very confused and distorted"; this is, however, a "necessary, indispensable point of contact for divine grace".[133]

This point – which Brunner, it must be said, does not articulate as clearly as his purposes require – lies at the heart of Brunner's analysis. There are indeed points of contact for the Word of God within human nature, even *fallen* human nature. The Word of God does not need to create its own points of entry, for they are already in place. So, given that humanity already has a created capacity for words, and a capacity to hear the Word of God, what is the point of revelation? What does it achieve? Brunner's discussion of this point is terse, succinct, and frustratingly brief. We may summarize his ideas like this.

What the Word of God *does* create is the human ability to *believe*. Anyone can hear God's word; the question, however, is *how we hear it in a particular way*. The point that Brunner is trying to make is that, if revelation is not *recognized as* revelation, it cannot *be* revelation. "The Word of God itself creates the human capability [*Fähigkeit*] to believe the Word of God, and thus the capability to hear it in such a way that is only possible as a believer."[134] This, for Brunner, is a matter of divine grace, not natural human achievement. Brunner thus argues that faith is a God-wrought response to the hearing of the Word of God – a response which lies beyond sinful humanity's innate capacities. For this reason, Brunner insists that "the doctrine of *sola gratia* is not in the least compromised" by his idea of a "point of contact".[135]

Brunner further argues that the ability of the church to proclaim the gospel to secular culture rests upon a created correlation (*eine schöpfungsmäßige Beziehung*) between human words and the Word of God.[136] This raises the question of the church's responsibility to reflect upon its proclamation, and take care to ensure that it is adequately adapted to the contexts being engaged. "Wherever the church proclaims the Word of God through human words, she must choose from amongst human words those that somehow correspond to the Word of God."[137] For Brunner, the proclamation of the Word of God needs to be intelligible. While conceding the role of the Holy Spirit in the interpretation and application of revelation to the human heart, Brunner insists that this does not absolve theology from the task of reflecting on how best to communicate it. "The church must proclaim in an intelligible [*verständlichen*] way, otherwise even the best proclamation, in terms of its contents, will be useless."[138]

Brunner introduced an important clarification in the second edition of his booklet. Having declared that it is the task of his theological generation

---

[133] "Natur und Gnade", 349–50; "Nature and Grace", 32–3.
[134] "Natur und Gnade", 349; "Nature and Grace", 32.
[135] "Natur und Gnade", 349; "Nature and Grace", 32.
[136] "Natur und Gnade", 372; "Nature and Grace", 56.
[137] "Natur und Gnade", 372; "Nature and Grace", 56.
[138] "Natur und Gnade", 372; "Nature and Grace", 56.

to "find the way back to a proper *theologia naturalis*",[139] Brunner added a note insisting that he did not mean to imply that a rediscovery of a proper natural theology is "the most important or the only task of theology". A Christian natural theology is "only a part – yet, on account of its missionary and practical significance, an *important* part – of the task of reflecting on the Word of God incarnate in Jesus Christ, given to us in Scripture alone".[140]

A natural theology cannot hope to prove God's existence; nevertheless, it can identify and address the eristic possibilities that exist for the church as it seeks to proclaim the gospel.[141] This theme is, for Brunner, the "other task of dogmatics".[142] Alongside the dogmatic project, theology must see itself as an agent of apologetics and evangelism, being able to engage with – while at the same time speaking in terms that can be understood by – the human and natural sciences.[143] As Brunner understood this task, this involved critiquing non-Christian worldviews with a view to demonstrating their inner incoherence.[144]

Brunner's Later Views on Natural Theology: *Revelation and Reason* (1941)

It will be clear that Brunner's booklet of 1934 was written in some haste, with polemical rather than constructive intentions. It is therefore appropriate to consider his more mature views on natural theology, as these are set out in some detail in his 1941 work *Revelation and Reason*. Although Brunner interacts with Barth at points in this analysis, his intellectual trajectory is not determined by this interaction, nor does it cause him to deviate from his intended goal. Brunner's views on natural theology are probably better determined on the basis of this later work, rather than his 1934 formulations.

Brunner's doctrine of revelation, as set out in this work, can be summarized as follows.[145] Negatively, he emphasizes the limits of human knowledge.

---

[139] "Natur und Gnade", 372; "Nature and Grace", 56.
[140] *Natur und Gnade*, 2nd edn., 59–60.
[141] For this concept and the use that Brunner makes of it, see Paul G. Schrotenboer, *A New Apologetics: An Analysis and Appraisal of the Eristic Theology of Emil Brunner*. Kampen: Kok, 1955, especially 10–59; Michael Roth, *Gott im Widerspruch? Möglichkeiten und Grenzen der theologischen Apologetik*. Berlin: de Gruyter, 2002, 464–563.
[142] See the critically important essay of 1929, discussed earlier: "Die andere Aufgabe der Theologie": *Ein offenes Wort*, vol. 1, 171–93.
[143] Werner Kramer, "'Die andere Aufgabe der Theologie': Ein bleibendes Anliegen Emil Brunners im Briefwechsel mit Karl Barth." *Theologische Zeitschrift* 57 (2001): 363–79.
[144] This aspect of Brunner's writings of the late 1920s and 1930s has often been noted – for example, see Hart, *Karl Barth vs. Emil Brunner*, 201 "Although Brunner spent more time [than Barth] in conversation with non-Christian (or Neo-Protestant) philosophers, he engaged them to defeat them, not to learn from them."
[145] Brunner himself offers such a summary in 1946: see *Dogmatik I*, 24–31; *Dogmatics 1*, 14–21.

Human beings, using unaided reason, are limited to a knowledge of the world. God, however, stands outside this domain of knowledge. A proper knowledge of God can only arise when there is a "self-disclosure, a self-manifestation of God – that is, when there is revelation". For Brunner, the core of this divine revelation is "the Word become flesh".[146] Although there are many "forms of revelation", these all converge on Jesus Christ, the decisive self-communication of God. Revelation is thus inseparable from historical facts, and can be understood only in and through them. So where does a natural knowledge of God fit into this scheme?

For Brunner, the starting point for any discussion of "natural theology" or a "natural knowledge of God" is clear – it can only begin from the biblical material.

> Holy Scripture teaches a "general" or "creation-revelation [*Schöpfungsoffenbarung*]", but not a "natural theology". It does not teach that this creation-revelation, which is given to *all*, corresponds to an actual, self-effecting knowledge of God, so that humanity may know God in spite of and in sin. Rather, it belongs to the very nature of human sin that the developing knowledge of God which results from through God's revelation is suppressed by it, so that the revelation which God gives humanity in order to bring about knowledge of Himself becomes instead the source of an empty idolatry.[147]

This leads Brunner to formulate what, for him, is the central paradox of revelation, which we may summarize as follows: humanity only knows it is sinful because of God's revelation; yet it is because humanity is sinful that this revelation cannot lead to the knowledge of God.[148]

Brunner clearly distances himself from any notion of natural theology, construed as the possibility of a general, self-authenticating knowledge of God, which may be had outside the Christian revelation. God's revelation in creation brings about a knowledge of sin, but cannot liberate humanity from that sin. Brunner therefore insists that any concept of revelation of God in nature must be conceived as an integral, inseparable element of God's special, historical revelation. "The doctrine of general revelation is included within the doctrine of salvation in Jesus Christ as its presupposition."[149]

Brunner's hostility to the specific term "natural theology" is clearly a matter of vocabulary, rather theological substance. He rejects the idea that humanity can attain a full knowledge of God through the autonomous exercise of its reason, apart from divine revelation, while simultaneously insisting that such a full knowledge of God embraces and enfolds the notion that creation is able to bear witness to the creator, in a form that is acces-

---

[146] *Offenbarung und Vernunft*, 95–117; *Revelation and Reason*, 95–118.
[147] *Offenbarung und Vernunft*, 66; *Revelation and Reason*, 65 (emphasis original).
[148] *Offenbarung und Vernunft*, 66; *Revelation and Reason*, 65.
[149] *Offenbarung und Vernunft*, 66; *Revelation and Reason*, 65. The discussion here echoes the basic themes of the 1934 essay "Nature and Grace".

sible to humanity. This does not mean, Brunner insists, that there is any theological basis for "a *theologia naturalis* which serves as the basis for a supplementary *theologia revelata*".[150]

Brunner clearly holds that the doctrine of creation lays the foundation for the fundamental theological affirmation that God is disclosed in the created order. A proper *theologia naturalis* is embraced by a *theologia revelata*, which both provides its foundation and defines its proper scope and limits. "That which is created bears the stamp of its creator."[151] Brunner therefore rejects Barth's doctrine of the *analogia fidei*, arguing that the doctrine of the *analogia entis*, far from being a theological distinctive of Roman Catholicism, is simply "part of the common Christian inheritance of belief from the earliest days of the church", and is attested in the writings of the Reformers, especially Calvin.[152]

The importance of the "point of contact" became a recurrent theme in Brunner's writings around this time, particularly as he emphasized the importance of the apologetic and missionary tasks of the Christian church. Identifying the appropriate "point of contact" was, he argued, integral to the ministry of the church. As he put it in 1936: "The discovery of the right point of contact is absolutely decisive for all missionary and pastoral work."[153]

It is clear that Brunner's anthropology is central to his approach to natural theology. "Humanity has been made in the image of God, and the law is written in the heart of humanity."[154] For Brunner, these both point to the created human capacity to discern God within the created order. "There is a correspondence between the self-manifestation [*Selbstmanifestation*] of God in the works of creation, which surround humanity like a theatre (to use a common expression of Calvin's) and the self-manifestation of God upon and within humanity, which enables it to recognize that external revelation as such."[155] Yet that process of discerning God within creation itself depends upon the grace of God, and cannot be thought of as a purely human activity.

Brunner here distances himself from those who suggest that nature is "fallen". It is not nature that is fallen, but humanity. Brunner's statements here merit close analysis:

> Holy Scripture knows nothing about the revelation through creation [*Schöpfungsoffenbarung*], whether in humanity itself or in other spheres of existence, having been destroyed by sin. The phrase "fallen nature" is alien

---

[150] *Offenbarung und Vernunft*, 68; *Revelation and Reason*, 66.
[151] *Offenbarung und Vernunft*, 68; *Revelation and Reason*, 67.
[152] *Offenbarung und Vernunft*, 68; *Revelation and Reason*, 67.
[153] *Die Kirchen, die Gruppenbewegung und die Kirche Jesu Christi*, 14. See also the points made in his earlier essay "Die Frage nach dem 'Anknüpfungspunkt' als Problem der Theologie": *Ein offenes Wort*, vol. 1, 239–67.
[154] *Offenbarung und Vernunft*, 70; *Revelation and Reason*, 68.
[155] *Offenbarung und Vernunft*, 74; *Revelation and Reason*, 73.

to the Bible. It is not the creation, but humanity which is fallen. It is not that the creation-revelation has been destroyed, but that through sin humanity perverts what God has given into idolatry.[156]

Developing themes he finds stated in Paul's letter to the Romans,[157] Brunner argues that there remains a self-revelation of God within creation, which renders humanity without excuse, in that it is confronted with the actuality of God.[158] Working within the traditional Reformed notion of the "double knowledge of God", as creator and redeemer (see pp. 100–1), Brunner argues that such a natural knowledge of God "has no saving significance", but prepares the way for the fuller, saving knowledge of God. But once that fuller, saving knowledge of God has come, it transforms the way in which we see the created order. It is seen, read, interpreted, and approached from the standpoint of faith.

The essential point is that a "natural theology" is an impossibility from the standpoint of unbelief. On account of sin, humanity is blinded; it is only when our "eyes have been opened" that we are "able to see what God shows us through his revelation in creation". That self-revelation of God is there for all to see; yet sin blinds the created, natural human capacity, as one created in the image of God, to discern the creator in the creation. "Due to the sin of humanity, this meaning has been concealed from them; either they do not see this obvious [*augenfällige*] revelation of God, or they seriously misunderstand it."[159]

Brunner's use of ocular imagery at this point has a long history of use in the western literary and theological tradition, and gives iconic depth to his argument.[160] Nature bears the permanent imprint of the divine nature; we, however, are unable to see this. One of the effects of sin is to dim our vision, to prevent us from seeing what really is there. Our eyes need to be healed by grace; we need to be *told* about something that we are unable to discover for ourselves – but which, once discovered, is found to make sense. For Brunner, God's self-disclosure in Christ enables us to understand and appreciate more fully what is already present, latent, within the created order.

As Brunner has so often been misunderstood and misrepresented at this point, he must be allowed to make these points on his own terms and in his own words. The core concept is that natural theology is only possible through grace, from the standpoint of faith. "Natural theology" is an aspect

---

[156] *Offenbarung und Vernunft*, 73–4; *Revelation and Reason*, 72–3.
[157] *Der Römerbrief*, 18–22; *Romans*, 21–4.
[158] *Offenbarung und Vernunft*, 73–8; *Revelation and Reason*, 72–80.
[159] *Offenbarung und Vernunft*, 77; *Revelation and Reason*, 76. The use of the term *augenfällig* (which I have translated as "obvious") should be noted: the word literally means "available to the eyes". The point is that God's revelation is there to be seen – for those who can see.
[160] For this tradition, and its deployment in the writings of C. S. Lewis (1898–1963), see Alister E. McGrath, "The Privileging of Vision: Lewis's Metaphors of Light, Sun, and Sight." In *The Intellectual World of C. S. Lewis*. Oxford: Wiley-Blackwell, 2013, 83–104.

of "Christian theology", in that it presupposes the fundamental beliefs of the Christian faith, which ultimately lie beyond human reason, even though they are not inconsistent with it.[161] As Brunner summarizes his own approach:

> It is not on the basis of our own reason, but on the basis of the saving revelation of God, that we teach about revelation through creation [*Schöpfungsoffenbarung*]. We do not pursue "natural theology", but, in the context of Christian theology, we teach about this specific form of revelation, which is bestowed on all humanity, yet is not correctly received by all, because all are sinners. Since it is Jesus Christ alone who reopens to us the buried entrance to this source of the knowledge of God that has been given to us, there is no question of minimizing the status of Christ, or diminishing the *sola gratia*, which some have feared from the affirmation of this teaching.[162]

We can set out Brunner's argument more formally as a series of propositions, as follows:

1. God reveals himself within the created order. This self-revelation of God in creation is universally available – yet requires to be "seen".
2. Sinful humanity is blinded to this revelation. Creation is not "fallen"; humanity, however, is. As a result, it does not "see" God within nature, and consequently either ignores or distorts this natural, non-saving knowledge of God.
3. Since natural theology involves the proper discernment of God within nature, this must therefore be recognized as lying beyond the capacity of sinful humanity.
4. Faith in Christ heals human blindness, allowing redeemed humanity to "see" God's self-disclosure within creation. From the standpoint of reception of God's self-revelation in history, culminating in Christ, God's self-revelation in nature can be discerned.
5. Natural theology is thus indeed a genuine intellectual possibility – but only *from within the standpoint of faith*.

So what of Brunner's critique of Barth, set out with some force – but rather less clarity – in 1934? In his more reflective and considered analysis of 1941, Brunner identified what now seemed to him to be the chief difficulties in Barth's approach.[163] Brunner welcomed what he saw as Barth's attempt to distinguish between what many would call a "natural theology" and a "*Christian* natural theology", which Brunner glosses as "a doctrine

---

[161] For Brunner's discussion of this particular point, see *Offenbarung und Vernunft*, 408–17; *Revelation and Reason*, 412–22.
[162] *Offenbarung und Vernunft*, 78; *Revelation and Reason*, 77.
[163] Brunner's 1941 analysis is based on *Church Dogmatics*, II/1, rather than on Barth's earlier writings. For Brunner's somewhat unsatisfactory account of Barth's earlier views, see "Natur und Gnade", 334–9; "Nature and Grace", 17–22.

of revelation through creation grounded in Scripture".[164] Such a natural revelation could not be considered to be "saving", in that, being impersonal, it lacked the capacity to transform individuals.[165]

This represents a clarification of Brunner's earlier view about the relation between *Schöpfungsoffenbarung* and *Heilsoffenbarung* – which are clearly recognizable variants of the *duplex cognitio Domini* of the earlier Reformed tradition. In 1934, Brunner tended to explain this relationship is terms of the degrees of clarity and illumination which they offered.[166] In 1941, having subsequently developed his notion of "truth as encounter", he now characterizes this distinction in terms of an impersonal experience of revelation through the creation, and a personal encounter with revelation in Jesus Christ (pp. 154–72).

Barth, Brunner argued, treated natural theology as a "timeless abstract truth of a natural relationship with God".[167] His point here is that Barth understood natural theology, not as something that is legitimated by revelation itself, but as a natural human activity, conducted without reference to, or dependence upon, the self-disclosure of God. But what if God's self-disclosure includes a mandate for natural theology? Brunner notes, with a certain degree of satisfaction, that even Barth himself "has to acknowledge that the Scriptures bear witness to such a revelation through creation".[168] Yet Barth nevertheless insisted, to Brunner's irritation, of speaking of a "natural *knowledge* of God", when Brunner clearly believed that the biblical witness demanded that he ought to speak of "*revelation* through creation".

Brunner, writing in 1941, expresses irritation that a core theme of his 1934 controversy with Barth has not been properly understood. A radical distinction must be drawn between two quite different approaches to a "theology of nature" (*Naturtheologie*) – Brunner's own "biblical-objective", and the "rational or Catholic-subjective". The former affirms a doctrine of "*revelation* through the creation"; the latter, a doctrine of "a natural *knowledge* of God".[169] If Barth had recognized this distinction, Brunner declares, the controversy between them would have been at an end.

So why does Barth refuse to use the term "revelation" to refer to God's disclosure through creation, preferring to speak of "a natural knowledge of God" instead? For Brunner, the point at issue is Barth's fundamental and axiomatic refusal to accept that God might choose to use the created order as a means of revelation, despite the biblical witness to the contrary. In referring to this as "knowledge", Barth implies that these are insights derived through human reflection, rather than disclosed through a divine initiative.

---

[164] *Offenbarung und Vernunft*, 78–9; *Revelation and Reason*, 77–8. Barth's formulation of the point at issue, it should be noted, is somewhat different.
[165] Brunner's point here is based on his analysis set out in *Truth as Encounter* (1937): see pp. 154–72.
[166] "Natur und Gnade", 344; "Nature and Grace", 26–7.
[167] *Offenbarung und Vernunft*, 79; *Revelation and Reason*, 78.
[168] *Offenbarung und Vernunft*, 79; *Revelation and Reason*, 78.
[169] *Offenbarung und Vernunft*, 80; *Revelation and Reason*, 79.

Barth's language is a reflection of his theology: God does not disclose through the creation; rather, human beings actively and autonomously seek God though creation, and thus find a God of their own inventing. Brunner charges Barth with departing from the biblical witness, especially as interpreted during the Reformation.

> Barth continues to think that any recognition of a revelation through creation must imply the recognition of a natural knowledge of God. He is unwilling to let go of the axiom that there is only one revelation. Barth thus takes the true statement "Only through the historical revelation of the old and new covenant does sinful humanity find itself in a situation in which it can recognize the original revelation of creation, which is concealed from it by sin" and states this falsely, as "There is only one – the historical revelation in Christ [*die geschichtliche Christusoffenbarung*]."[170]

Finally, Brunner considers Barth's critique of the *analogia entis*, which he sees as an integral element of his rejection of natural theology. Barth is, Brunner insists, quite right to affirm that the *analogia entis* does not provide an adequate foundation for the construction of a natural theology. "These created analogies [*Analogien der Schöpfung*] are not a way to a legitimate theological knowledge for sinful humanity." Rather, they are a "false turn" (*Irrweg*), which leads sinful humanity to interpret them in a pantheistic manner. The analogies are there, embedded within the created order; the problem is that, without the "historical revelation in Christ", human beings are unable to interpret them correctly. Only from the standpoint of divine revelation in Christ are these analogies seen correctly, and grasped for what they really are.

> Created things already bear this imprint [*Stempel*] within themselves; they do not need to acquire it through the historical revelation in Christ. . . . These analogies do not exist because of faith, but they are only rightly seen through faith.[171]

Barth's Response: *No!* (1934)

Having published *Nature and Grace* in early May 1934, Brunner waited anxiously to hear from Barth. How would he respond? By the end of September, Brunner had become alarmed at the stony silence. Unable to contain his anxiety, he finally wrote to Barth, expressing concern that he had not heard from him.[172] Surely Barth and he were still in fellowship, despite their differences?

---

[170] *Offenbarung und Vernunft*, 80; *Revelation and Reason*, 79.
[171] *Offenbarung und Vernunft*, 81; *Revelation and Reason*, 80.
[172] Brunner to Barth, 30 September 1934: *Karl Barth–Emil Brunner, Briefwechsel*, 252–6. There were some issues about non-delivery of Brunner's letters that may have fuelled Brunner's concerns: see *Briefwechsel*, 252 n. 1.

Barth's irritated and rather disdainful reply came, like a thunderbolt, by return of post.[173] On 1 October 1934, he declared that their fellowship was at an end. The warm reception given by theologians within the German Christian movement to Brunner's booklet[174] had convinced Barth that Brunner was on the wrong side of a critically important argument. Brunner had undermined Barth's theologically constructed platform of resistance against the German Christians. Brunner was appalled by this argument of "guilt by association", and wrote immediately to Barth, protesting against such a judgement. So what if German Christian writers such as Paul Althaus or Karl Fezer liked his booklet? That didn't make his arguments false or evil! What, Brunner wondered, was left of theological scholarship if the reactions of other people were allowed to become a criterion of truth or falsity?[175] (The same issue emerged around the same time when Barth reacted against Brunner's pamphlet *Vom Werk des Heiligen Geistes* (1935), partly because he believed it showed the influence of the Oxford Group, which he cordially disliked.)[176]

Brunner concluded that Barth had lapsed into a sectarian mentality, smearing everyone who failed to agree with him with the label "heretic". Once more, Brunner reiterated his belief that he and Barth were essentially agreed on fundamentals; their differences arose primarily through misunderstanding or miscommunication – for which Brunner was fully prepared to take responsibility. Yet Brunner's correspondence betrays a palpable sense of intellectual isolation. He was on his own.

Brunner's sense of theological isolation was alleviated significantly in October 1934, when Peter Brunner published a study of Calvin's ideas of general and special revelation, with a short "Afterword" by Ernst Wolf, focusing on Brunner's *Nature and Grace*.[177] Brunner was relieved as much as delighted. He wrote to Ernst Wolf, on or around 2 October, expressing his sense of relief on reading both essays. "When I read P. Brunner's essay, my first thought was: Thank God! I am no longer on my own!" Brunner "agreed with every word" of the article.[178]

---

[173] Barth to Brunner, 1 October 1934: *Karl Barth–Emil Brunner, Briefwechsel*, 256–61.
[174] See, for example, the very positive review of Brunner's work in *Deutsches Pfarrerblatt* 1934, which drew Barth's ire: see Barth, "Nein!", 212; "No!", 72.
[175] Brunner to Barth, 2 October 1934: *Karl Barth–Emil Brunner, Briefwechsel*, 261–6, especially 262.
[176] See the exchange of letters over the text of this document in Barth's letter to Brunner, 1 October 1934: Barth to Brunner, 1 October 1934; *Karl Barth–Emil Brunner, Briefwechsel*, 256–61, especially 256; and Brunner's response of 2 October: Barth to Brunner, 1 October 1934; *Karl Barth–Emil Brunner, Briefwechsel*, 261–6, especially 263. This booklet was based on three lectures given at the University of Copenhagen in September 1934.
[177] Peter Brunner, "Allgemeine und besondere Offenbarung in Calvins Institutio." *Evangelische Theologie* 1 (1934–5): 189–215; Ernst Wolf, "Anmerkungen zu Emil Brunner, Natur und Gnade." *Evangelische Theologie* 1 (1934–5): 215–16.
[178] Letter to Ernst Wolf, circa 2 October 1934: *Karl Barth–Emil Brunner, Briefwechsel*, 434–8.

Peter Brunner's remarks might have reassured Brunner. But what did Karl Barth, the object of Brunner's explicit public criticism, have to say in response? Brunner had no doubt of Barth's intense hostility towards his approach. But what would he say *publicly* in response?

Barth's formal and public response to Brunner was set out in October 1934 in the booklet *Nein! Antwort an Emil Brunner* ("No! A Reply to Emil Brunner"). Most Barth scholars agree that Barth's rather condescending tone in this somewhat hastily written work limits its value as a piece of serious theological analysis. In fairness to Barth, we must recall that 1934 was a year of crisis for him, as he saw the rejection of natural theology as central to his programme of theological resistance to National Socialism and its allies in ecclesial encroachment, the German Christian movement. In fairness to Brunner, however, we must note that Barth's reasons for treating natural theology in this manner seemed unpersuasive and implausible.

So what is the theological substance of Barth's response to Brunner? The following points seem to be of particular importance. First, Barth emphasized that this theological disagreement had assumed particular urgency and importance on account of the German church crisis. Brunner's approach represented a "precursor" of a "future theology of compromise", which must be resisted.[179] Brunner had failed to realize how the political situation in Germany impacted on theological discussion.

Barth linked Brunner's interest in natural theology – even at those points at which Brunner was critical of the notion – with a more fundamental error on his part, namely, his core belief that there was "another" task of theology. For Barth, Brunner's incorrect belief that theology has an intrinsically eristic role inexorably leads into the quagmire of natural theology.[180] Barth insists that he himself has no interest in any such natural theology, which he alleges to be deficient and unacceptable in two respects – its object and its method. In terms of its object (*Gegenstand*), natural theology is fundamentally different from the "revelation of God in Jesus Christ"; and for that reason, its "method [*Weg*] is fundamentally different from the exposition of Holy Scripture".[181] At points, Barth seems to imply that Brunner is not doing theology at all.[182] There are hints that Brunner's natural "theology" is little more than anthropology.

Setting aside any personal distress at the forceful manner in which Barth expressed himself, it is not difficult to understand Brunner's exasperation at Barth's response. Brunner's approach was grounded in his belief that Holy Scripture *authorizes* the enterprise of acknowledging that God is revealed in some manner, and to some extent, in the natural world, even if we require

---

[179] Barth, "Nein!", 212; "No!", 69.
[180] Barth, "Nein!", 212, 216; "No!", 69, 77.
[181] Barth, "Nein!", 214; "No!", 75.
[182] As suggested by John C. McDowell, "Karl Barth, Emil Brunner and the Subjectivity of the Object of Christian Hope." *International Journal of Systematic Theology* 8 (2006): 25–41, especially 33–4.

divine grace in order to be able to discern this, and can only grasp it properly from the standpoint of revelation in Christ. Barth seemed to negate the notion of any revelation of God *extra Christo* as a matter of principle.

It is tempting to dismiss this 1934 debate as a dialogue of the deaf, in which each participant was so enmeshed in his own working assumptions and conceptual definitions that he could only see his opponent's positions through the stipulative and evaluative framework afforded by his own. Yet there are some points at which Barth makes fair and important points of substance, which must be taken with seriousness. One of the most important of these is his critique of Brunner's notion of the *imago Dei*, which plays a significant role in providing a rationale for his approach to natural theology. The particular point of issue concerns Brunner's distinction between the "formal" and "material" aspects of the image, which Barth regards as intellectually unsustainable, and theologically valueless.[183]

As we saw earlier (pp. 118–20), Brunner distinguishes two aspects of the "image of God" in humanity.[184] The "formal" aspect of this image concerns what distinguishes humanity from the remainder of creation, irrespective of whether humanity is sinful or not. Brunner insists that this aspect of the "image of God" embraces two fundamental human capacities which distinguish humanity from the remainder of creation: the ability to reason, and a capacity for words. The "material" aspect of the image of God concerns the capacity of humanity to enter into a relationship with God. Brunner insists that the formal aspect of the image of God remains untouched by sin; the material aspect, however, is lost, and requires restoration.

Barth was clearly baffled by this distinction, which he considered to be deeply problematic. He concurred with Brunner's insistence that humanity remains humanity, despite sin. So what? After all, Barth pointed out, even as sinners, human beings remain human, instead of becoming tortoises.[185] But what, Barth demands, has this to do with the question of any natural receptivity towards the Word of God? The condition of being human is simply not in itself sufficient to undergird the theological affirmations that Brunner wishes to make. In any case, the distinction between the "formal" and material" aspects of the image of God is unsustainable. After pointing out some of the difficulties, Barth comments that he can only conclude that Brunner's "distinction between the 'formal' and 'material' *imago Dei*, which at first sight was so impressive, was not meant all that seriously".[186]

Barth notes in particular Brunner's ambivalence over just what humanity can naturally know about God from the world. There is, Barth remarks, some confusion here. What does it mean to say that the world is "somehow

---

[183] See Joan O'Donovan, "Man in the Image of God: The Disagreement between Barth and Brunner Reconsidered." *Scottish Journal of Theology* 39 (1986): 433–59.
[184] See the brief discussion in "Natur und Gnade", 340–2; "Nature and Grace", 23–5.
[185] Barth, "Nein!" 218; "No!", 79.
[186] Barth, "Nein!", 226–7; "No!", 89–90.

recognizable" as God's creation? Barth points to Brunner's inconsistencies in his analysis of this point, where at certain points he appears to suggest that such knowledge is impossible for sinful humanity, and at others that such knowledge is indeed possible, but in a blurred or distorted manner.[187] Barth immediately concedes that God is indeed able to reveal himself to sinful humanity – but sees no reason to concede Brunner's points in doing so. The fact that God reaches humanity through his Word does not actually depend upon, or even necessitate the notion of, the formal possibility of humanity being addressed by God.[188]

Barth's chief concern was with Brunner's notion of *Offenbarungsmächtigkeit*, which he incorrectly interpreted as a human "capacity for revelation". Brunner only used this term once in *Nature and Grace*, and applied it specifically to the God-given capacity of the created order to disclose God – that is, "such permanent capacity for revelation [*dauernde Offenbarungsmächtigkeit*] as God has bestowed upon his works".[189] In *No!*, Barth tended to frame Brunner's notion as *Offenbarungsmächtigkeit des Menschen* ("the human capacity for revelation") as if this were representative of Brunner's position as a whole. It is clearly nothing of the sort. Brunner was outraged at what he regarded as a blatant misrepresentation. "Some twenty times or so Karl Barth quotes from my writing the expression *Offenbarungsmächtigkeit des Menschen* which I not only have never employed at all, but which I heartily detest as heretical as much as he does."[190] While Brunner unquestionably used the term *Offenbarungsmächtigkeit* in his pamphlet, he interpreted this *objectively* as an aspect of the created order, not *subjectively* as a capacity on the part of the human interpreter.

This misunderstanding – possibly amounting to a misrepresentation – of Brunner's approach on Barth's part is a pity, as Barth makes some important points which are too easily overlooked by those who, disturbed by his exaggerations and misrepresentations, are inclined to dismiss *Nein!* as a piece of lightweight polemic. One of these valid points relates to Brunner's concern to distinguish – yet correlate – *Schöpfungsoffenbarung* and *Heilsoffenbarung*. Barth rightly challenges Brunner on this point on whether he has actually managed to achieve this. "For what reason can Brunner maintain that a real knowledge of the true God, however imperfect it may be (and what knowledge of God is not imperfect?) does not bring salvation?"[191] If a real knowledge of God is mediated through creation, is that not in itself a *saving* knowledge, in that it is a *real* knowledge? Or, Barth mischievously asked, is Brunner somehow suggesting that idolatry is some kind of preparation for the gospel?

[187] Barth, "Nein!", 219–21; "No!", 80–3.
[188] Barth, "Nein!", 226; "No!", 89.
[189] "Natur und Gnade", 345; "Nature and Grace", 27.
[190] *Der Mensch im Widerspruch*, 509; *Man in Revolt*, 527.
[191] Barth, "Nein!", 220; "No!", 82.

Two themes – one explicit and the other implicit – are of critical importance in the Barth–Brunner controversy of 1934. The explicit theme concerns a Christian understanding of human nature. One aspect of this theme is the purpose and place of natural theology – yet this is clearly subordinated to, and framed within the context of, a theological account of human nature. The implicit theme – as Oliver O'Donovan pointed out some time ago – was the place of theology in shaping Christian moral knowledge, which was given added intensity during the 1930s on account of the urgent need for the church's theologically grounded response to the political situation of the day.[192]

In reflecting on Barth's response to his approach in 1934, Brunner seems to have realized that the approach developed in *Nature and Grace* was ultimately shaped by his anthropological beliefs, which clearly required further development and clarification, not least in the light of the criticisms directed against them by Barth. In the foreword to the second edition of *Nature and Grace*, Brunner declared that the best response to Barth would take the form of a rigorous and thoroughly *theological* anthropology, emphasizing in particular the concept of human responsibility. Such a theological anthropology would be set out in some detail in his 1937 work *Man in Revolt*, regarded by some as one of his most significant theological writings. At several points during this later work,[193] Brunner makes it clear that it is to be seen as his definitive response to Barth's *No!*

In the next chapter I shall consider this work in more detail, noting its significance for Brunner's overall theological vision.

---

[192] Oliver O'Donovan, *Resurrection and Moral Order: An Outline for Evangelical Ethics*. Grand Rapids, MI: Eerdmans, 1986, 90–1.
[193] *Der Mensch im Widerspruch*, 18–19; *Man in Revolt*, 11.

5
Brunner's Theological Anthropology: *Man in Revolt* (1937)

Who are we? What is this mysterious creature that we call "humanity"? Many would argue that some such questions have been at the heart of philosophical and religious reflection since the beginning of civilization. Nevertheless, their importance must be regarded as having been accentuated with the rise of modernity, and its increasing emphasis upon human autonomy and rationality. The Presocratic philosopher Protagoras's declaration that "humanity [*anthrōpos*] is the measure of all things" has perhaps been misunderstood;[1] yet the sentiment, appropriately interpreted, lies at the heart of the Enlightenment project.[2]

In developing a theological anthropology in the intellectual climate of the 1930s, Brunner faced challenges on two opposing fronts. On the one hand, some theologians regarded any such attempt as improper, representing a potentially destabilizing threat to theology by making it critically dependent on secular assumptions and norms that lay beyond its control. Perhaps the most significant representative of such a position at this time was Karl Barth. On the other hand, natural and social scientists regarded anthropology as an essentially objective discipline, grounded on an empirical method, which precluded theology as a matter of principle. What conceivable role could there be for transcendent notions in what was essentially an empirical discipline?

---

[1] For the translation issues attending this fragment, see Lazlo Versényi, "Protagoras' Man-Measure Fragment." *American Journal of Philology* 83, no. 2 (1962): 178–64. For its philosophical interpretation, see Edward Schiappa, *Protagoras and Logos*. Columbia, SC: University of South Carolina Press, 2003, 117–40.

[2] See Isaiah Berlin, *The Proper Study of Mankind*. New York: Farrar, Straus & Giroux, 1997; B. W. Young, *Religion and Enlightenment in Eighteenth-Century England: Theological Debate from Locke to Burke*. Oxford: Clarendon Press, 1998; Louis Dupré, *The Enlightenment and the Intellectual Foundations of Modern Culture*. New Haven, CT: Yale University Press, 2004.

Emil Brunner: A Reappraisal, First Edition. Alister E. McGrath.
© 2014 John Wiley & Sons, Ltd. Published 2016 by John Wiley & Sons, Ltd.

Brunner's task was to develop a theological anthropology which met both these concerns, in a manner that was not merely intellectually opportunistic. *Man in Revolt* is rightly regarded as one of the finest attempts to develop such a distinctively Christian understanding of human nature in the twentieth century.[3] In what follows, I shall explore the contours of Brunner's approach. I shall begin by reflecting on the factors that made the development of a Christian account of human nature and identity of such pressing importance in the 1930s, before moving on to consider how Brunner developed an approach which he believed resolved the two methodological difficulties just noted. Finally, I shall consider the overall shape of Brunner's theological anthropology, and sketch its implications for his theology in general.

The Need for a Theological Anthropology

The anthropocentrism of the Enlightenment posed a significant challenge to Christian theology, necessitating an appropriate response. This became especially obvious during the 1830s, as interest developed in the theory that religion and its attendant ideas were essentially human constructions, reflecting fundamentally psychological and cultural factors, rather than divine revelation.[4] How was theology to respond to these developments? One answer was to take further the approach pioneered by Schleiermacher, which recognized the new importance of human feeling, and sought to use this as a starting point for theological reflection. Others, however, regarded this anthropological turn with scepticism, seeing it as representing the reduction of theology to anthropology, or at best, the incorporation of a modern self-understanding into theology.

By the end of the Great War, a sense of "displacement" had become firmly embedded in western culture. In 1917 Sigmund Freud argued that the medieval worldview had suffered three fatal blows: Copernicanism had displaced any notion that the earth stood at the centre of the universe; Darwinism had displaced any notion that humanity had any intrinsic or ordained special place in the natural world; and Freud himself displaced any notion that humanity had total control over its own thoughts and actions.[5] The significance of

---

[3] The best assessment to date is the substantial critical account in Uwe Lüdemann, *Denken – Glauben – Predigen: Eine kritische Auseinandersetzung mit Emil Brunners Lehre vom Menschen im Widerspruch*. Frankfurt am Main: Peter Lang, 1998.

[4] See Charles Wackenheim, *La faillité de la religion d'après Karl Marx*. Paris: Presses Universitaires de France, 1963; Heinz Hüsser, *Natur ohne Gott: Aspekte und Probleme von Ludwig Feuerbachs Naturverständnis*. Würzburg: Konigshausen & Neumann, 1993.

[5] Sigmund Freud, "Eine Schwierigkeit der Psychoanalyse." *Zeitschrift für Anwendung der Psychoanalyse auf die Geisteswissenschaften* 5 (1917), 1–7. For an expanded discussion of these themes, see Mirko Lüttke, *Die Kränkung des Menschen: Die Naturwissenschaften und das Ende des antik-mittelalterlichen Weltbildes*. Würzburg: Königshausen und Neumann, 2012.

humanity was increasingly seen as a human construction, rather than a divine endowment.[6] It was clear that the formulation of some kind of theological anthropology was required in the aftermath of the Great War, if only to avoid a total disconnection between Christian discourse and the wider culture.

It proved to be a particular difficulty for the "dialectical theology" movement in the late 1920s, as tensions within the movement over this and related issues came to the fore. Friedrich Gogarten's 1929 paper on the problem of a theological anthropology argued that cultural shifts since the Middle Ages had propelled questions about the place of humanity to the centre of cultural and theological debate.[7] The cultural context had changed, and theology had to engage this changed situation. Gogarten was critical of Schleiermacher's theological response to this anthropological turn. Yet in one sense, he suggested, Schleiermacher was fundamentally right: theology had to engage with this development. "It is no longer possible to do real theology", Gogarten declared, "other than by placing the problem of anthropology at the centre of reflection."[8]

Yet for Barth, this threatened to compromise the unique status of theology and its contents. Might not theology be reduced to an anthropological theory, developed independently of divine revelation?[9] In the early 1930s, Barth struggled to develop his own approach to a theological understanding of human nature which safeguarded the priority of revelation. He would later develop such an anthropology on the basis of his decision to understand every doctrine from a Christological standpoint, in which God's self-revelation in Christ disclosed a proper understanding of human nature.[10]

But what about Brunner? We have already seen how anthropological issues came to play a leading role in the 1934 debate between Barth and Brunner (see pp. 113–21), even though this debate is traditionally held to have concerned natural theology. Admittedly, Barth exaggerated the extent of such anthropological investment on Brunner's part, partly through his inaccurate and misleading interpretation of the term *Offenbarungsmächtigkeit*. As noted above (pp. 131–2), Brunner interpreted this telling term *objectively*,

---

[6] There is much useful material on these themes in Uwe Hoßfeld, *Geschichte der biologischen Anthropologie in Deutschland: Von den Anfängen bis in die Nachkriegszeit*. Stuttgart: Franz Steiner Verlag, 2005.

[7] Friedrich Gogarten, "Das Problem einer theologischen Anthropologie." *Zwischen den Zeiten* 7 (1929): 493–511.

[8] Gogarten, "Das Problem einer theologischen Anthropologie," 505. For the debate between Barth and Gogarten over a theological anthropology, see Peter Lange, *Konkrete Theologie? Karl Barth und Friedrich Gogarten "Zwischen den Zeiten" (1922–1933). Eine Theologiegeschichtlich-systematische Untersuchung im Blick auf die Praxis theologischen Verhaltens*. Zurich: Theologischer Verlag, 1972, 248–54.

[9] For Barth's concerns at this point, see especially the older study of Dale Snyder, *Karl Barth's Struggle with Anthropocentric Theology*. The Hague: Wazzez, 1969.

[10] Stuart D. McLean, *Humanity in the Thought of Karl Barth*. Edinburgh: T&T Clark, 1981; Daniel Price, *Karl Barth's Anthropology in Light of Modern Thought*. Grand Rapids, MI: Eerdmans, 2002, 97–164.

as referring to the created order, which was marked by "such permanent capacity for revelation [*dauernde Offenbarungsmächtigkeit*] as God has bestowed upon his works". Barth chose to interpret it *subjectively*, referring to some alleged capacity for revelation that was intrinsic to humanity. Barth's persistent attribution of the phrase *Offenbarungsmächtigkeit des Menschen* to Brunner – despite the fact that Brunner did not use it, and disavowed it – seriously weakened the credibility of Barth's analysis at this point.

Nevertheless, it is clear that anthropological issues played a significant role in Brunner's thought during the controversy of 1934. The difficulty was that these anthropological insights – such as the nature of the *imago Dei*, and the impact of sin on humanity – often seemed to be only loosely coordinated within his thought. In effect, Brunner had placed these ideas in parallel columns, without achieving their theological colligation and systematization. His decision to write a major work of theological anthropology must be seen as arising from his debate with Barth, and as intended to place his own position on a firmer intellectual footing.

The result of this was *Man in Revolt*. (Unfortunately, the English title fails to bring out the importance of "contradiction" for Brunner's understanding of human nature.) In this work, Brunner developed what he considered to be an authentically Christian understanding of human nature, and explored its implications for the life and thought of the church.[11] It is perhaps the most rewarding of his works to study, not least because of its comprehensive vision of the foundations and scope of a Christian anthropology. Moreover, Brunner shows himself able and willing to engage with recent challenges to a Christian anthropology – such as those developed by Marx, Darwin, Nietzsche, and Freud.[12]

I begin my reflections with one of the most difficult questions underlying any attempt to develop a Christian anthropology. What is – or can be – distinctively *Christian* about what many would regard as an intrinsically empirical discipline?

The Impossibility of an "Objective" Anthropology

In setting out to construct a theological anthropology, Brunner had to provide a coherent answer to those who suggested that it was impossible to do this without falling into the trap that Barth believed awaited any unwise enough to undertake such a venture. How could theology avoid making itself dependent upon an "independent" theory of human nature, which would ultimately compromise the autonomy and integrity of divine revela-

---

[11] Frank Jehle, *Emil Brunner: Theologe im 20. Jahrhundert*. Zurich: Theologischer Verlag, 2006, 334–9.
[12] See his preliminary comments in *Der Mensch im Widerspruch*, 39–43; *Man in Revolt*, 24–8.

tion?[13] To explore this point, we need to look at a framing strategy which was hinted at – though not in a developed form – in *The Divine Imperative*, but was articulated more fully subsequently. Brunner terms this the "law of the closeness of relation" (*Gesetz der Beziehungsnähe*).[14]

While discussing the concept of the "invisible church" in *The Divine Imperative*, Brunner pointed out the need to recognize some form of correlation – but not identity – between the human and the divine.

> Pure doctrine, the proclamation of "nothing but the gospel", is not the Word of God. God may speak through less pure doctrine, and might not speak through the purest doctrine. Yet it is clear that there is the closest and most intimate connection [*die höchste, engste Beziehungsnähe*] between the human and divine acts.[15]

Brunner does not develop this point further, and leaves his readers somewhat unsure of the full significance of his point. It was only subsequently that he clarified his meaning properly, and showed how it is theologically useful.

In his later work *Revelation and Reason* (1941), Brunner invited his readers to imagine two quite distinct disciplines: Christian mathematics and Christian anthropology. Nobody, Brunner suggests, would dream of speaking of a specifically *Christian* mathematics – or Christian formal logic, for that matter. But why not? Sin darkens reason[16] – but it does so to different extents in different domains of knowledge. So what determines the differing impact of sin on different disciplines and domains of knowledge?

Brunner's answer is fundamental to his understanding of how Christian theology is to be brought into discussion with other disciplines.

> The nearer anything lies to that centre of existence in which we are concerned with its totality [*das Ganze*] – that is, our relation to God, and our personal existence – the greater the disruption of rational knowledge [*Störung der Vernunfterkenntnis*] through sin. The further that something lies from this centre, the less the impact of this disrupting factor, with a corresponding reduction in the difference between the knowledge of the believer and the unbeliever.[17]

---

[13] For these themes in Barth's debate with Heinrich Scholz in the early 1930s, see Alister E. McGrath, "Theologie als Mathesis Universalis? Heinrich Scholz, Karl Barth, und der wissenschaftliche Status der christlichen Theologie." *Theologische Zeitschrift* 62 (2007): 44–57.

[14] For the phrase, see *Offenbarung und Vernunft*, 379; *Reason and Revelation*, 383.

[15] *Das Gebot und die Ordnungen*, 514; *The Divine Imperative*, 528. Olive Wyon's English translation misses the point Brunner is trying to make. For discussion of Brunner's point, see Martin Abraham, *Evangelium und Kirchengestalt: Reformatorisches Kirchenverständnis heute*. Berlin: de Gruyter, 2007, 106–7.

[16] *Offenbarung und Vernunft*, 378; *Reason and Revelation*, 382: "... den von Sünde und der durch sie geschehenen Verdunkelung der Vernunft". For a good account of this approach, see Stephen K. Moroney, *The Noetic Effects of Sin: A Historical and Contemporary Exploration of How Sin Affects Our Thinking*. Lanham, MD: Lexington Books, 2000, 31–4.

[17] *Offenbarung und Vernunft*, 378; *Reason and Revelation*, 383. Brunner may use the German term *Störung* at this point to mean "interference" (as in a radio transmission), which makes good sense in this context.

Logic and mathematics are conceptually dislocated from any fundamental understanding of our relation to God and nature as persons. For this reason, Brunner argued that a Christian and non-Christian would take more or less the same approach to these disciplines, making it meaningless to qualify either as "Christian". Similar comments applied to physics and chemistry.

But in other domains of knowledge, things were different. This disruption through sin is "maximal in theology, minimal in the exact sciences, and zero in the formal sciences". On the basis of this analysis, anthropology would be the domain of thought in which this disruption through sin would be at its greatest. Here, any attempt on the part of sinful humanity to give an account of itself would be prone to delusion and distortion.

Brunner's point was perhaps developed less clearly than many would like. His point is that any account of humanity *developed by human beings* is dogged by self-referentiality, and is hence incapable of any objectivity of judgement. From a Christian perspective, humanity's capacity for judgement is distorted and darkened through sin; this distortion is seen at its greatest at those points at which human vested interests are called into question – such as our ideas about God, or ourselves.[18] The greater the degree of vested interest we have in a given domain of knowledge, the more likely we are to distort it for our own ends. It is, Brunner argues, therefore impossible to have a neutral, presuppositionless, or objective anthropology, precisely because of the "closeness of relation" between the anthropological *knower* and what is anthropologically *known*.

Brunner's approach allowed him to defend the notion of a "Christian anthropology" in the face of the objection that this is as meaningless as "Christian mathematics".[19] He conceded that in many areas of human knowledge – for example, as we have seen, logic and chemistry – it is not meaningful to speak of a specifically Christian approach to the theme. Yet his use of the "closeness of relation" principle allowed him to identify various domains in which it is not merely appropriate, but *necessary*, to adopt a specifically Christian perspective. Anthropology is perhaps the most luminous example of such a domain.

Furthermore, the use of a theological theoretical framework to "view" human nature is not inconsistent with an empirical approach to anthropology. Brunner's anthropology anticipates the recognition in the later twentieth century of the "theory-laden" nature of observation.[20] We do not view nature

---

[18] The interconnectedness of "knowledge of God" and "knowledge of ourselves" in Reformed theology can be traced back to Calvin – see, for example, *Institutio Religionis Christianae*, 1.i.1: wisdom "consists almost entirely of two parts: the knowledge of God and of ourselves. But as these are connected together by multiple links, it is not easy to determine which of the two precedes and gives rise to the other." For Brunner's exploration of this point, see especially *Der Mensch im Widerspruch*, 75–6; *Man in Revolt*, 72–3.

[19] See the extended discussion at *Der Mensch im Widerspruch*, 64–7; *Man in Revolt*, 60–3.

[20] See his extended criticism of the notion of "presuppositionless knowledge": *Der Mensch im Widerspruch*, 61–4; *Man in Revolt*, 57–60.

"objectively", but through a set of theoretical spectacles.[21] We may assume that we are seeing things as they really are; in fact, our observations are covertly shaped by implicit theoretical expectations as to what we are seeing. Scientific progress takes place partly through identifying existing theoretical commitments, and discovering whether these can be supplanted by others. Brunner anticipated this point in *Man in Revolt*, and identified its theological significance:

> The question is not whether it is problematic for human beings to draw on what lies beyond the realm of the given in trying to understand themselves; it concerns what this standpoint should be. The understanding of human nature always leads us – in whatever way we please – either into the region of metaphysics, or into that of religious faith.[22]

A purely "empirical" anthropology is thus an impossibility. Any attempt by human beings to make sense of themselves will involve going beyond the realm of the empirically given, ultimately resting on transcendent presuppositions of one sort or another, whether these are explicitly recognized or not. "The presupposition of all anthropologies is that humanity must be seen from a standpoint [*Standort*] which is 'above' humanity."[23] This, Brunner suggests, helps explain the remarkable diversity of views of humanity found throughout history, up to the present day, despite its allegedly "empirical" foundations. Yet it also provides a basis for insisting upon the legitimacy of a *theological* anthropology, which similarly offers a perspective on human nature and identity which is grounded "in a standpoint which is 'above' humanity".[24]

Brunner therefore argues for both the necessity and intellectual legitimacy of a Christian anthropology. Human nature is seen and interpreted from within the context of divine revelation.

> The Christian doctrine of humanity maintains that, while it understands humanity from the truths of revelation, which are not accessible to experience, it does not in any way contradict what can be known about humanity through experience; on the contrary, it places this knowledge gained by experience into its proper context.[25]

---

[21] William F. Brewer and Bruce L. Lamber, "The Theory-Ladenness of Observation and the Theory-Ladenness of the Rest of the Scientific Process." *Philosophy of Science* 68 (2001): S176–86; Matthias Adam, *Theoriebeladenheit und Objektivität: Zur Rolle von Beobachtungen in den Naturwissenschafte*. Frankfurt am Main: Ontos Verlag, 2002. For the original statement of this approach, see N. R. Hanson, *Patterns of Discovery: An Inquiry into the Conceptual Foundations of Science*. Cambridge: Cambridge University Press, 1961.

[22] *Der Mensch im Widerspruch*, 64; *Man in Revolt*, 60.

[23] *Der Mensch im Widerspruch*, 67; *Man in Revolt*, 63–4.

[24] *Der Mensch im Widerspruch*, 67; *Man in Revolt*, 63–4.

[25] *Der Mensch im Widerspruch*, 65; *Man in Revolt*, 61. It is interesting to conjecture how Brunner's approach could be correlated with the stratified anthropological model first set out in 1938 by Erich Rothacker, *Die Schichten der Persönlichkeit*. 4th edn. Bonn: Bouvier, 1948. Rothacker's model allows different "levels of explanation" to be proposed, creating conceptual space for revelational perspectives.

Brunner's point here is that the use of such a specifically and explicitly *theological* perspective fits into a broader pattern of seeing and evaluating human nature from a standpoint which is "beyond" or "above" humanity – in other words, something which transcends the limits of the empirical.

Before we move on to consider the leading themes of Brunner's anthropology in more detail, we must pause and note the implications of his "law of closeness of relation" for the interaction of Christian theology and the natural sciences. Barth's approach does little to encourage any positive engagement of these disciplines;[26] Brunner's, however, provides a platform for a critical theological engagement with the natural sciences, allowing a calibrated appropriation of scientific insights based on a theological foundation.

Having cleared the ground for his theological anthropology, Brunner now began to lay out its fundamental themes. In what follows, we shall consider these themes, correlating them with their cultural context, and exploring their broader theological significance.

The Dependence of Humanity on God

Brunner's reflections on human identity involve affirmation, differentiation, and negation. His task is not merely to develop a theologically grounded vision of human nature; it is to distinguish this from its alternatives, and indicate his reasons for rejecting them. He locates two quite distinct elements to this process of distinguishing a Christian anthropology from its secular rivals: the *method* by which it is derived, and the *substance* of the resulting anthropology. For Brunner, these are the two sides of the same coin. To give an example: because humanity is incapable of knowing God unaided, an authentic anthropology rests upon divine revelation.

It is clear that Brunner's main concern was to place clear blue water between a distinctively Christian understanding of human nature and a family of alternative conceptions, each shaped to varying extents by the core ideas of the Enlightenment. So what are these core ideas? A recent study identifies the themes that are relevant to our reflections on Brunner:

> Enlightenment was a desire for human affairs to be guided by rationality rather than by faith, superstition, or revelation; a belief in the power of human

---

[26] Harold P. Nebelsick, "Karl Barth's Understanding of Science." In *Theology Beyond Christendom: Essays on the Centenary of the Birth of Karl Barth*, ed. John Thompson, 165–214. Allison Park, PA: Pickwick Publications, 1986. Thomas F. Torrance is one of the most significant theologians to engage in this dialogue, adopting a modified Barthian stance. For a general assessment, see Alister E. McGrath, *Thomas F. Torrance: An Intellectual Biography*. Edinburgh: T&T Clark, 1999, 195–235; more specifically, see Tapio Luoma, *Incarnation and Physics: Natural Science in the Theology of Thomas F. Torrance*. Oxford: Oxford University Press, 2002.

reason to change society and liberate the individual from the restraints of custom or arbitrary authority; all backed up by a world view increasingly validated by science rather than by religion or tradition.[27]

At each of these three points, Brunner's Christian anthropology is sharply distinguished from the family of rival visions of humanity, inspired by the Age of Reason.

1. Brunner insists that human reason has only a limited purchase on reality, and is unable to deliver reliable knowledge of God. If we are to know what God is like, we need God to tell us.
2. Brunner regards human beings as limited in their agency and competency, partly on account of the debilitating impact of sin. At points, he anticipates later criticisms of Enlightenment rationalism – such as those of the Frankfurt School – which challenged the instrumental rationality of the Enlightenment for its complicity in authoritarianism.[28]
3. Brunner refuses to accept that "science" is able to offer an adequate objective account of human nature.

I have already touched on all of these themes; in what follows, I shall focus particularly on Brunner's notion of human dependence on God, and its implications for our self-understanding.

"Humanity can only understand itself in God, more precisely, in the Word of God. It can only understand itself in terms of the one who established it."[29] Brunner articulates the absence of human autonomy at two levels: we are incapable of discovering for ourselves what God is like – and hence also of discovering who and what we really are; and we are equally incapable of saving ourselves. The doctrines of creation and redemption alike affirm our ultimate dependence on God. Humanity must recognize that it is not an autonomous being.[30]

Brunner's argument at this point would probably have been theologically uncontroversial in Reformed theological circles at the time; the real debate concerned the extent to which humanity is dependent, and how this is articulated in terms of a doctrine of election or sin. Yet the wider context against which Brunner affirms the dependence of humanity on God must be appreciated. The rejection of human autonomy is implicitly a rejection of the worldview of the Enlightenment – a positioning of the Christian understanding of human nature against its secular alternatives, which had gained cultural traction in the aftermath of the Great War. Brunner thus

---

[27] Dorinda Outram, *The Enlightenment*. Cambridge: Cambridge University Press, 1995, 3.
[28] See, for example, Herbert Marcuse, *One-Dimensional Man: Studies in the Ideology of Advanced Industrial Society*. Boston: Beacon Press, 1964; John Gray, *Enlightenment's Wake: Politics and Culture at the Close of the Modern Age*. London: Routledge, 1995.
[29] *Der Mensch im Widerspruch*, 75; *Man in Revolt*, 72.
[30] *Der Mensch im Widerspruch*, 75; *Man in Revolt*, 79.

articulates what he regards as a realistic and chastened vision of human nature, implicitly contrasting this with the utopian and optimistic understandings of human nature prevalent in the era immediately preceding the Great War. There is clearly an "eristic" element to Brunner's anthropology, which challenges secular visions of human nature as much as it affirms a Christian alternative – above all, by questioning the adequacy of its conceptual foundations.

The "Contradiction" within Humanity

What is distinctive about human nature? For Brunner, the answer lies partly in a fundamental contradiction (*Widerspruch*) within human nature. This theme is clearly stated in the German title *Der Mensch im Widerspruch*, and is obscured by the English *Man in Revolt*. So what does Brunner mean by this? The great English essayist William Hazlitt (1778–1830) expressed this contradiction in one way: "Man is the only animal that laughs and weeps; for he is the only animal that is struck with the difference between what things are and what they ought to be."[31] The notion of a contradiction within humanity is perhaps the most fundamental theme in Brunner's anthropology, and it is important to establish precisely what he means by this. Unfortunately, Olive Wyon's translation of *Der Mensch im Widerspruch* makes Brunner difficult to understand at points, by failing to render consistently the German terms *Widerspruch* ("contradiction") and *Gegensatz* ("opposition" or "conflict").[32]

Brunner's notion of the "contradiction" can be summarized as follows. Humanity is created in the image of God, yet has decided (*bestimmt*) to exist in opposition (*Gegensatz*) to its God-given destiny. This conflict between the true and the actual nature of humanity gives rise to the contradiction (*Widerspruch*) within human nature. For Brunner, the true nature of things is also disclosed through revelation, which allows us to "understand and explain humanity correctly" in terms of the conflict between the truth and actual reality (*Wirklichkeit*) of humanity.[33]

Brunner argues that this essentially *theological* insight chimes with human experience. "Just as everyone knows something about the higher and distinctive aspects of humanity", he declares, "so everyone also knows

---

[31] William Hazlitt, *Essays*. London: Walter Scott, 1889, 269.
[32] There are many examples of this – most notably, the translation of the title of chapter 6. Brunner here intends us to focus on the "conflict" between ideal and empirical humanity, which underlies the "contradiction" within human nature. The German title of the chapter is "Der Gegensatz: Die Zerstörung des Gottesbildes"; Wyon translates this as "The Contradiction: The Destruction of the Image of God". The structure of the chapter makes it clear that this is better translated as "The Conflict: The Destruction of the Image of God". See *Der Mensch im Widerspruch*, 116; *Man in Revolt*, 114.
[33] *Der Mensch im Widerspruch*, 116; *Man in Revolt*, 114.

something about the contradiction within humanity." Yet while "common sense" – Brunner uses the English phrase, for which there is no exact German equivalent – is aware of this contradiction within humanity – for example, in the problem of human evil – it has no explanation for it.[34] Brunner warns against thinking of this simply as "something contradictory" within human nature. Rather, it is to be seen as a fundamental conflict or division (*Spaltung*) within a human being.[35]

There are strong echoes of Luther's *totus homo* anthropology here,[36] which refused to treat sin and righteousness as aspects of human nature. Sin is not merely something within human nature that is corrupt; rather, it is the corruption of human nature in its totality. Sin cuts through the whole of human existence, and cannot be isolated in some hermetically sealed compartment. It is not one part of human nature which is sinful, and requires redemption. Humanity, as a totality, is sinful, and stands in need of radical transformation through Christ. Brunner perhaps articulates this point most clearly in his 1948 Robertson Lectures at the University of Glasgow: "It is not a part of a human being which is guilty of sin but the whole human being. ... We could express it like this: we not only commit sins, but we are sinners." [37]

So what exactly is sin? Brunner indicated his strong sympathy with a classical doctrine of sin, while at the same time raising concerns about its traditional modes of formulation and conceptualization – above all, Augustine of Hippo's notion of a physically transmitted "original sin" – more specifically, the "doctrine of the Fall of Adam [*Sündenfall Adams*] and of the original sin handed down by him to subsequent generations".[38] There is a tension, a "conflict", within humanity arising from the tension between what was meant to be, and what has actually happened.

> The traditional ecclesiastical doctrine deals with this conflict [*Gegensatz*] under the double concept of the Fall and original sin. The first of these suggests that the conflict consists in defection [*Abwendung*] from our origin; the second that it is a fateful determination of reality [*schicksalsmäßige Bestimmtheit der Wirklichkeit*].[39]

Brunner has no fundamental objection to this way of thinking, pointing out that it articulates points which remain valid and important. Yet the traditional approach has, in Brunner's view, a significant weakness, which is that

---

[34] *Der Mensch im Widerspruch*, 117; *Man in Revolt*, 115.
[35] *Der Mensch im Widerspruch*, 120; *Man in Revolt*, 118.
[36] See Erdmann Schott, *Fleisch und Geist nach Luthers Lehre unter besonderer Berücksichtigung des Begriffs totus homo*. Darmstadt: Wissenschaftliche Buchgesellschaft, 1969.
[37] *Das Ärgernis des Christentums*, 62; *The Scandal of Christianity*, 65. For comment on the relation of the English and German texts of this work, see p. 214 n. 33.
[38] *Der Mensch im Widerspruch*, 121; *Man in Revolt*, 119.
[39] *Der Mensch im Widerspruch*, 120; *Man in Revolt*, 118.

it fails to integrate necessity and responsibility on the one hand, and totality and individuality on the other.

What Brunner was getting at here is the link between the Fall of Adam, and human sin. There are two concerns. First, how can human beings today be held responsible for something which happened of necessity through biological transmission? Augustine's approach holds that original sin is something that is transmitted biologically, over which we have no control – and therefore represents something for which we cannot really be held accountable. Second, how can an individual's actions in the past be said to be constitutive for humanity today? How does the sin of Adam affect humanity as a whole? For Brunner, the "traditional ecclesiastical doctrine" – by which he really means Augustine's doctrine of the Fall and original sin – fails to establish a credible connection between necessity and responsibility on the one hand, and totality and individuality on the other. And what of the related notion of the "fallenness of creation"? How does this fit into the overall picture?

Brunner's reformulation of the notions of Fall and original sin involves drawing a distinction between what the "traditional" doctrine *means*, and what it *says*.[40] Brunner locates the problem in what the doctrine *says*, not what it *means*. For Brunner the doctrine declares that it is

> the responsible act of an individual, whose guilt is attributed to us on incomprehensible grounds, and whose sin is transferred to us in a manner that contradicts the proper nature of sin – namely, through natural inheritance.[41]

For Brunner, there is indeed a "scandal" attached to the idea of sin. Yet this should not be the arbitrary and unnecessary scandal of the traditional ecclesiastical doctrine, which asks us to accept that "we are made responsible for a sin that someone else committed". Rather, the church should focus on the properly biblical scandal, namely that humanity tries to evade responsibility in the sight of God, or to deny total dependence upon God.[42]

The proper meaning of the doctrine of original sin is that sin is not simply a *possibility*; it is an *actuality*. In one sense, Brunner argues, Christian theology is not concerned to offer an explanation for the universality of human sin; its primary role is to affirm that this is indeed, the case, and explore its implications for Christian life and thought. Sin is a corporate, as much as an individual, matter. Arguing against a literal or historical reading of the Genesis narrative of the origins of sin, Brunner insists that "each one of us is 'Adam'". To say that we are "sinners" or "fallen creatures" does not tell us anything about the cause of our situation; it simply asserts that each of

---

[40] *Der Mensch im Widerspruch*, 143–6; *Man in Revolt*, 142–5.
[41] *Der Mensch im Widerspruch*, 144; *Man in Revolt*, 143.
[42] Brunner also develops this point in *Das Ärgernis des Christentums*, 49–70; *The Scandal of Christianity*, 51–72.

us in our totality "is involved in this act of turning away from God".[43] As Brunner put this in 1948:

> The picture of humanity that we gain in our own life and in the history of humanity is thoroughly puzzling and contradictory. It reflects the contradiction that Pascal set out in that famous double concept of the "grandeur et misère de l'homme," and which he elaborated in an incomparably realistic and psychologically sharp picture of real humanity.[44]

So what of the more positive side of Brunner's anthropology? How does he incorporate the idea of the *imago Dei* into his vision of human nature? I shall explore this in the following section.

The Image of God and Human Identity

I have already noted (pp. 118–20, 130–1) how Brunner appealed to the idea of the "image of God" at several critical points in his 1934 debate with Karl Barth.[45] One of the chief achievements of *Man in Revolt* was to give order and structure to Brunner's hitherto somewhat disconnected thoughts on human nature and identity. For Brunner, the idea that we are created in the image of God is a "figurative expression" (*Gleichniswort*) which both describes human origins and clarifies the distinctive features of human identity.[46] It is an integral aspect of his understanding of the *humanum*, defined as that which distinguishes human beings from the non-human creation.[47] So what does this phrase mean?[48]

While Brunner explores the history of the idea, his fundamental concern is to insist that it is to be interpreted Christologically. The "image of God" is fully and definitively revealed in Christ, and is therefore to be viewed and interpreted through a Christological lens. Through the application of this hermeneutical tool, "the concept of the *imago* is torn out of its Old Testament structural or morphological rigidity, and the dynamic understanding of the *imago* is established, as being-in-the-word-of-God through faith".[49]

---

[43] *Der Mensch im Widerspruch*, 150; *Man in Revolt*, 149.
[44] *Das Ärgernis des Christentums*, 65; *The Scandal of Christianity*, 68. Pascal's French phrase means "the greatness and misery of humanity".
[45] Joan O'Donovan, "Man in the Image of God: The Disagreement between Barth and Brunner Reconsidered." *Scottish Journal of Theology* 39 (1986): 433–59.
[46] *Der Mensch im Widerspruch*, 86; *Man in Revolt*, 83.
[47] *Der Mensch im Widerspruch*, 95; *Man in Revolt*, 93.
[48] For a survey of recent interpretations, see A. Jónsson Gunnlaugur and S. Cheney Michael, *The Image of God: Genesis 1:26–28 in a Century of Old Testament Research*. Stockholm: Almqvist & Wiksell International, 1988; Otto Kaiser, "Der Mensch, Gottes Ebenbild und Statthalter auf Erden." *Neue Zeitschrift für systematische Theologie und Religionsphilosophie* 33 (1991): 99–111.
[49] *Der Mensch im Widerspruch*, 491; *Man in Revolt*, 501.

In 1934, Brunner argued that it was necessary to distinguish two distinct aspects or understandings of the *imago Dei*: the formal and the material (see pp. 118–20). This distinction was, it must be said, a little artificial and forced, suggesting that Brunner may have overloaded the notion with a theological burden that it was not capable of bearing. However, he insisted that some such distinction was necessary, not so much on account of the way in which the theme of the "image of God" is used in the Old Testament, but on account of the manner in which it is developed in the New. Brunner's basic point is that there are ontological and relational dimensions to the *imago Dei*. Sin brings about no ontological change in human nature; yet our relationship to God is fundamentally altered from that of obedience to disobedience. The ontological reality (Brunner's "formal" image of God) is thus actualized and becomes observable in the realm of relationships (the "material" image of God).

In its formal sense, the image of God designates the *humanum*, defined as that which distinguishes human beings from the non-human creation, such as a capacity for words, and responsibility. This has not been lost as a result of sin, and, indeed, cannot be lost in principle. Sin does not affect the ontology of humanity; its impact is experienced and observed at the level of relationships. Human beings are indeed sinful; they nevertheless remain human beings. The "formal" image defines and sustains the *humanum*, the special status of humanity within the created order, which is not only not abolished by sin, but is actually the presupposition of the human ability to sin.

Tellingly, Brunner insists that the formal aspect of the image is fully present in all people, and is "the starting-point for a 'natural' knowledge of God". He had already made this point in *Nature and Grace* (1934):

> Nobody can deny that there is such a thing as a point of attachment [*Anknüpfungspunkt*] for the divine grace of redemption, if they recognize that only human beings (and not sticks and stones) are able to receive the Word of God and the Holy Spirit. This point of attachment is the formal *imago Dei*, which not even the sinner has lost – the fact that a human being is a human being, the *humanitas* defined earlier as a capacity for words and responsibility [*Wortmächtigkeit und Verantwortlichkeit*].[50]

This point is developed and amplified in *Man in Revolt*, with one significant alternation. Brunner appears to have appreciated the force of Barth's 1934 criticism of his categories of the "formal" and "material" aspects of the image of God. Brunner now abandoned this terminology, while insisting that this did not lead to any theological changes in his position. The language might have changed; the ideas remained the same.[51] Although some

---

[50] "Natur und Gnade", 348; "Nature and Grace", 31.
[51] *Der Mensch im Widerspruch*, 498–9; *Man in Revolt*, 512–13.

would suggest that Brunner's original terms were simply confusing, he shifted the blame for any misunderstanding to his readers, who were "lacking in the logical education needed to allow for an understanding of the idea". He declared that he had now "renounced the expression 'formal *imago*'", without changing his mind on the two different notions of *imago Dei* which he found in Scripture. Instead, he now began to speak of the "humanity-of-the-sinner" (*Humanität-des-Sünders*) in its "dialectical relation" to the "*Imago*-origin" (*Imago-Ursprung*). Brunner emphasizes the essential unity of the relational and structural understandings of "*Imago*-origin", with the former understanding taking priority over the latter.

Brunner argues that the New Testament focuses on what he had earlier called the "material" realization of this God-given quality and capacity. Although there are points at which the New Testament reflects the notion of the image of God, found in the Old Testament,[52] there is a fundamentally new dimension given to the notion through Jesus Christ, as the Word of God incarnate. It is by being "in the Word of God" that the true *imago Dei* is restored, and humanity is transformed.

> The presupposition of this new, New Testament doctrine of the *Imago* – in contrast to that of the Old Testament – is that humanity's quality of being created in the image of God [*Gottesbildlichkeit*] has been lost, that humanity must for this reason be renewed, so that the whole work of Jesus Christ in reconciliation and redemption can be summed up in this central concept of the renewal and consummation of the Divine Image in humanity.[53]

Responsible being is thus about initially *being called* and *being addressed* by God, and subsequently *being determined and posited* by God in such a way that it is ultimately self-determining and self-positing. Declaring that humanity is created in the image of God is to acknowledge that we receive our existence *from* the divine Word and *according to* the divine Word which became flesh in Jesus Christ. It is to be "called" *into being* and sustained *in being* by God's gracious Word of election, made known in Jesus Christ.

Brunner therefore argued that God's work of creating humanity is incomplete until the image of God has been renewed. "The being of humanity, in contrast to other forms of creaturely being, is not something that is completed." Whereas God produces other aspects of the created order "as they ought to be", humanity is different. "God retains humanity in his workshop." The creation of humanity is only completed "as an answer to a call".[54]

---

[52] Brunner suggests that 1 Corinthians 11:7 and James 3:9 belong in this category. The "new" – i.e. *material* – sense of the term *imago Dei* is to be found at Romans 8:29; 2 Corinthians 3:18; Ephesians 4:24; and Colossians 3:10. *Der Mensch im Widerspruch*, 491; *Man in Revolt*, 500–1.
[53] *Der Mensch im Widerspruch*, 491; *Man in Revolt*, 501.
[54] *Der Mensch im Widerspruch*, 99–101; *Man in Revolt*, 97–9.

Brunner's comments at this point raise two important questions. First, in what way does God "call" humanity? From 1937, Brunner increasingly answered this question in a dialogical manner, a matter which I shall explore further in the following chapter (pp. 161–72). Second, if God leaves humanity "unfinished", does Brunner intend us to expand this narrative of divine completion in evolutionary terms? Given the importance of Darwinism within the intellectual culture of the 1930s, we must consider the question of Brunner's relation to Darwinism at this point.

Humanity and Evolution: The Limits of Darwinism

One of the more attractive features of Brunner's theological project is his willingness to engage alternative worldviews. This does not involve accommodation to such alternative readings of reality; rather, it is about developing a theological platform from which alternative positions may be examined and criticized. Brunner's idea of "eristic" theology embraces and expresses a theological manifesto – namely, to engage ideologies, whether classical or contemporary.

Yet a question must be raised here about the status of Darwin's approach. Is Brunner's eristic theology really capable of engaging with the scientific method? It is a moot point. On my reading of Brunner, he held that there is a somewhat limited potential for theology to engage meaningfully with what Brunner himself referred to as the "formal" sciences of logic and mathematics, or the "exact" sciences of physics, chemistry, or biology.

Two points must be made immediately, which help us understand why Brunner felt it was appropriate to engage Darwinism. First, Brunner had concerns that certain traditional approaches to theology – such as the Augustinian narrative of the fall of humanity – included what he held to be unwarranted historical claims. Where some theologians might see the Darwinian narrative as a threat to traditional ideas of the Fall and original sin, Brunner held that it liberated theology from an improper historicization of what was essentially a theological truth. This point was, of course, made earlier, particularly within English theological circles in the late nineteenth century, perhaps most memorably by Aubrey Moore (1848–90). According to Moore, though appearing "under the guise of a foe" Darwin had done "Christianity the work of a friend". How? By liberating it from a defective vision of God.[55] For Moore, Darwin posed a challenge to the somewhat impoverished vision of God found in the writings of William Paley; for Brunner, Darwin liberated theology from what he considered to be crudely historical accounts of creation and fall.

Second, Darwin's evolutionary theory is notoriously prone to metaphysical inflation, thus ceasing to be a provisional scientific theory and becoming

---

[55] See Richard England, "Natural Selection, Teleology, and the *Logos*: From Darwin to the Oxford Neo-Darwinists, 1859–1909." *Osiris* 16 (2001): 270–87.

instead a worldview.[56] Brunner's approach to theology was well adapted to engaging Darwinism in this more developed sense, exposing its metaphysical pretensions and philosophical underpinnings. As forms of Social Darwinism gained cultural traction within the German-speaking world in the 1930s,[57] it was clearly appropriate for Brunner to offer a theological challenge and counter-proposal to this development.

It is not unreasonable to suggest that Brunner's theological project had to engage Darwinism at some point, and that the most appropriate point at which to do so was in his exposition of the Christian doctrine of human nature. Yet it is important to emphasize that Brunner's theology is not articulated as a conscious and specific response to Darwinism. A careful reading of his works, particularly *Man in Revolt*, suggests that he considered it important in general to engage with alternative worldviews and their understandings of human nature, and identified Darwinism as one of the most significant specific intellectual challenges to the Christian faith in the 1930s.[58]

Brunner's discussion of the doctrine of evolution in *Man in Revolt* singles out the pervasive cultural influence of evolutionary theory as a major impediment to a right understanding of the Christian doctrine of human nature. Why? Because it leads us to believe that "everything that exists is best understood from the point of view of its development".[59] This "genetic postulate" has become both an axiom and a dogma for modern humanity. Brunner argues that this is true for all three understandings of evolution which were dominant in the 1930s – the naturalist, idealist, and romantic.[60]

---

[56] For this critically important distinction, see Alister E. McGrath, *Darwinism and the Divine: Evolutionary Thought and Natural Theology*. Oxford: Wiley-Blackwell, 2011, 32–40.
[57] The best study is Hans-Günter Zmarzlik, "Der Sozialdarwinismus in Deutschland: Ein Beispiel für die gesellschafts-politischen Mißbrauch naturwissenschaftlicher Erkenntise." In In *Kreatur Mensch: Moderne Wissenschaft auf der Suche nach dem Humanum*, ed. Günter Altner and Gerhard Heberer, 289–311. Munich: Moos, 1969. For the intellectual roots of this development, see Gregory Claeys, "The 'Survival of the Fittest' and the Origins of Social Darwinism." *Journal of the History of Ideas* 61 (2000): 223–40.
[58] See his preliminary comments in *Der Mensch im Widerspruch*, 39–43; *Man in Revolt*, 24–8. The increasingly significant role that Social Darwinism played in western European culture justified Brunner's assertion. For example, it is relatively easy to argue that the *Führerprinzip* was a Social Darwinist construct. For the influence of Darwinism in Germany at this time, see Richard Weikart, *From Darwin to Hitler: Evolutionary Ethics, Eugenics, and Racism in Germany*. New York: Palgrave Macmillan, 2004.
[59] *Der Mensch im Widerspruch*, 382; *Man in Revolt*, 390.
[60] Brunner here refers to the understandings of evolution found in the Kantian tradition, and in the writings of Henri Bergson, especially his notion of *évolution créatrice*. These have generally receded into the background in more recent discussions. For comment, see Frederick Burwick and Paul Douglass, eds., *The Crisis in Modernism: Bergson and the Vitalist Controversy*. Cambridge: Cambridge University Press, 1992; John Zammito, "Teleology Then and Now: The Question of Kant's Relevance for Contemporary Controversies over Function in Biology." *Studies in History and Philosophy of Science* C 37 (2006): 748–70. It is important to recall Brunner's earlier engagement with the writings of Bergson (p. 17), which clearly influenced his perception of his significance in this regard.

150 Brunner's Theological Anthropology: Man in Revolt *(1937)*

Brunner locates the specific challenge of Darwinism to traditional Christian theology as lying particularly in the difficulties that it raises concerning the doctrines of the "primitive state" (*Urstand*) and "Fall" (*Sündenfall*).[61] Traditional theological narratives of human development, framed in terms of a historical paradise and fall, were increasingly seen as implausible in the light of geological and biological theories. Brunner considered that traditional forms of theological anthropology were called into question both by the suggestion that the emergence of humanity was a more protracted and extended process than had earlier been appreciated, and by the Darwinian insistence that the ontological gap between humanity and animals was much narrower than had once been assumed.

Brunner, however, argues that Darwinism is vulnerable to the "metaphysical prejudice" (*Voreingenommenheit*) of most of its advocates.[62] It needed to be interpreted as a provisional scientific hypothesis, rather than being elevated into a totalizing, permanently valid account of reality. Furthermore, Brunner remained unpersuaded that a purely "genetic" account of things was adequate. An account of something's origins is not adequate as an understanding of its significance. Brunner illustrated this by considering a work of art – Michelangelo's *Moses*.[63]

It is relatively easy, Brunner suggests, to give a "causal-genetic" account of the origins of this work, examining its physical origins and the artistic process which led to a block of marble being transformed into the work of art. Yet the physical account of the origins of the work is incomplete. It omits the "inner picture", the "idea of the artist", which ultimately found its expression in *Moses*. To understand the meaning of the work, we need access to the mind of its creator, to the idea that inspired the masterpiece. A scientific account of human origins is necessarily incomplete. We must weave into our account the "mysterious 'something' that coordinates the parts into a coherent whole, and assigns a place and function to each of its parts".

Brunner's argument echoes themes found in the critical ontology of Nicolai Hartmann (1882–1950).[64] Hartmann argued that the complex, variegated nature of reality had to be reflected in multi-layered accounts of nature, including humanity. A total account of humanity would embrace multiple levels of explanation, each of which is adequate in its own way, but which required supplementation if the overall significance of humanity was to be appreciated. Brunner's argument is that a historical, chemical, or physical account of human origins and nature is

---

[61] *Der Mensch im Widerspruch*, 385; *Man in Revolt*, 393.
[62] *Der Mensch im Widerspruch*, 387; *Man in Revolt*, 395.
[63] *Der Mensch im Widerspruch*, 387–8; *Man in Revolt*, 395–6.
[64] See, for example, Nicolai Hartmann, *Zum Problem der Realitätsgegebenheit*. Berlin: Pan-Verlagsgesellschaft, 1931; idem, *Zur Grundlegung der Ontologie*. 3rd edn. Meisenheim am Glan: Anton Hain, 1948. For the best study in English, see W. H. Werkmeister, *Nicolai Hartmann's New Ontology*. Tallahassee: Florida State University Press, 1990.

only part of the picture. It requires supplementation if the full picture is to be disclosed. A theological anthropology supplements such scientific perspectives, and occasionally challenges them – although Brunner's examples tend to suggest that such challenges primarily relate to misunderstandings of the natural sciences, or their improper metaphysical inflation.

So what are the implications of evolutionary theory for Christian theology, especially a theological anthropology? An obvious starting point concerns the interpretation of the Bible, particularly its statements on origins. Like his Marburg colleague Rudolf Bultmann, who famously called for the "demythologization of the New Testament", Brunner believed that the "biblical worldview" was linked with an archaic understanding of the universe, which was now hopelessly outdated. Yet for Brunner this worldview was the vehicle for, and did not represent or contain the substance of, divine revelation. He uses an analogy to make this point clearer.

> The ancient worldview is *only the alphabet* in which biblical people, who had no other, had to write down the God-revealed Word. We no longer use the alphabet of the ancient cosmogony; we now have a new alphabet, with Copernican, Newtonian, and Einsteinian letters. But only a fool would conclude that when the old alphabet was destroyed, divine revelation itself was destroyed with it! We need to take the trouble to use the new alphabet to proclaim the old truths of revelation in a new way![65]

Having established this general principle, Brunner then argues that too many "theologians, preachers, and believers" are wedded to "the historical picture of the creation of the world and the Fall of humanity". Yet it is no longer possible to believe that the "history of humanity" and "cosmic history" are fundamentally the same.[66] However, when the Christian account of reality is properly understood, and not framed in terms of some obsolete cosmology or view of history, there is no fundamental impediment to its proper understanding and proclamation. Irrespective of whether the world is measured by the relatively limited comprehension of the ancient world, or the more expanded understanding of time and space associated with our own age, the fundamental Christian affirmation remains the same – namely, that humanity has been created "in and for the Word of God", which has been revealed in our world of time and space.[67]

For Brunner, the Copernican revolution and its modern cosmological developments do not raise any fundamental issues of concern for Christian theology. They expand the canvas on which the history of salvation is portrayed; but they do not force revision of its fundamental theological trajectory. But what of more specifically Darwinian concerns? What, for example, of Darwin's contraction of the gap between humanity and the

---

[65] *Der Mensch im Widerspruch*, 414–15; *Man in Revolt*, 423.
[66] *Der Mensch im Widerspruch*, 415; *Man in Revolt*, 423–4.
[67] *Der Mensch im Widerspruch*, 417; *Man in Revolt*, 425–6.

animals, widely seen as one of his more significant challenges to traditional Christian doctrines of human nature?[68]

Brunner's anthropology is surprisingly resistant to Darwinian trauma. To begin with, Brunner refuses to define or characterize humanity in any other terms than "a capacity for words and responsibility" (*Wortmächtigkeit und Verantwortlichkeit*). Others might attempt to distinguish humanity from animals by pointing to the use of tools; Brunner, however, sees this as a flawed distinction, and insists on a properly theological account of human distinctiveness.[69] For Brunner, the line of demarcation between human beings and animals is to be placed "where the Bible sees it" – that is, in the quality of having being created in the image of God, and in the "spiritual-responsible personal being of humans" (*geistig-verantwortlichen Personsein des Menschen*).[70]

These characteristics – which Brunner repeatedly asserts in terms of "a capacity for words and responsibility" – do not derive their legitimacy from a Darwinian or an anti-Darwinian narrative; they are, Brunner insists, the proper outcome of a theologically serious, yet historically realistic, reading of the biblical texts. Brunner declares that, despite a Darwinian narrative of biological descent, human beings must be regarded as empirically distinct from the animals. Theology offers an additional layer of interpretation of this empirical distinction, grounded in the fundamental notion that humanity alone has been created in the image of God.[71]

Brunner's concept of the image of God is not linked to either a biological or historical notion of a "fall" that robs humanity of a primordial God-given quality, originally present in the gift of creation. The Old Testament uses the term *imago Dei* as "an accolade [*Auszeichnung*] for humanity as it presently exists"; it is "never applied to a way of human existence [*Seinsweise*] that is lost through the Fall".[72] Brunner's approach thus insulates theological reflection about human identity and capacity from any precise chronological account of human origins or development.

Brunner's account of the distinctiveness of human nature is not dependent on innate human achievements (such as the ability to develop tools), but is based on an essentially theological account of the nature of God's call and a human response. This framework is reflected in Brunner's characteristic emphasis on the human capacity for words, and capacity to respond. Yet although both these notions are embedded in Brunner's notion of revelation, it has to be asked whether this genuinely engages the issues. For example, Brunner's anthropology, however theological in its orienta-

---

[68] For the issue, see McGrath, *Darwinism and the Divine*, 169–71.
[69] See further Daniel K. Miller, "Responsible Relationship: *Imago Dei* and the Moral Distinction between Humans and Other Animals." *International Journal of Systematic Theology* 13, no. 3 (2011): 329–39.
[70] *Der Mensch im Widerspruch*, 410; *Man in Revolt*, 418–19.
[71] *Der Mensch im Widerspruch*, 411–12; *Man in Revolt*, 420–1.
[72] *Der Mensch im Widerspruch*, 489; *Man in Revolt*, 500.

tion, ultimately requires the affirmation of certain human capacities or abilities, which mark them off from other animals.

Perhaps this point is best appreciated by considering Brunner's doctrine of the innate capacity of the created order to bear witness to its creator – the objective notion of a "a permanent capacity for revelation" (*dauernde Offenbarungsmächtigkeit*) which God has bestowed on creation.[73] Do the birds of the air recognize God's revelation in the natural world they inhabit? Or the fish of the sea? These are not idle, pointless questions. Brunner's anthropology, no matter how theological it may be, ultimately involves essentially empirical judgements about capacities for observation and interpretation, which inevitably become attached to or associated with such theological notions as the *imago Dei*.

Brunner argues that the issue distinguishing animals from humanity is not "intellect", but "spirit" – that is, the "seeking of truth for truth's sake".[74] Animals know nothing "beyond" their immediate sphere of existence. Human beings bear the *imago Dei*; animals do not. One is, however, left with a sense of unease about a potentially arbitrary interpretation of the notion of the "image of God", and its correlation with a human capacity held to be essential to divine self-disclosure. If God cannot self-disclose to animals, it is because God has created them in such a manner that they cannot recognize or respond to that revelation.

Man in Revolt made clear Brunner's preoccupation with theological anthropology, and his conviction that the cultural and political situation of the late 1930s demanded a recovery and reassertion of Christian insights. He would develop his anthropology further in a series of lectures given in Uppsala in 1937, to which we now turn.

---

[73] "Natur und Gnade", 345; "Nature and Grace", 27.
[74] *Der Mensch im Widerspruch*, 410; *Man in Revolt*, 418–19.

6
Objectivity and Subjectivity in Theology: *Truth as Encounter* (1937)

In the autumn of 1937, Brunner delivered six lectures on the Olaus Petri Foundation at the University of Uppsala in Sweden. Brunner had been invited to lecture by Arvid Runestam (1887–1962), president of the Petri Foundation, when he met Brunner at a conference in Paris in the spring of 1934.[1] In their subsequent correspondence, they explored several possible titles for the lecture series, such as "The Problem of Truth in Christian Theology" (Brunner), "The Objective and the Subjective in Christianity" (Runestam), and "Certainty and Truth in the Christian Faith" (Brunner). Finally, they agreed on the title "Truth as Encounter", at the suggestion of Brunner's friend Gottlob Spörri (1899–1990), pastor of the eastern Swiss city of St Gallen.

Brunner used these Swedish lectures to explore the relationship between "subjective" and "objective" in the Christian faith. They are now primarily remembered for his famous development of the theme of "truth as encounter [*Begegnung*]"; nevertheless, they give us a remarkably clear perspective on what must be considered to be Brunner's mature understanding of the nature of faith, truth, and revelation.[2]

In an autobiographical reflection of 1949, Brunner explained how the ideas developed in these lectures were fundamental to his theological development. His exploration of the theological consequences of personalism, he declared, was "perhaps the most important of my new insights". This laid the foundations for some major themes of his writings during the 1940s,

---

[1] For the details, see Frank Jehle, *Emil Brunner: Theologe im 20. Jahrhundert*. Zurich: Theologischer Verlag, 2006, 346–7.
[2] The best study of this aspect of Brunner's thought up to 1937 remains Yrjö Salakka, *Person und Offenbarung in der Theologie Emil Brunners während der Jahre 1914–1937*. Helsinki: Kirjapaino, 1960.

especially his conceptualization of "personalism in revelation and faith as the divine-human encounter" and his adoption of "personalism as the basis of the Christian ethic".[3]

Given the importance that Brunner attributed to them, I shall therefore consider these lectures in some detail, setting them against the context of their intellectual background.

Object and Subject in Theology: The Context to Brunner's Thought

How do human subjects experience and interpret the external world? This general question, widely debated within philosophy since the time of Descartes, is of obvious theological importance. In its simplest form, the debate concerns how human observers ("subjects") perceive an external world of entities ("objects"). Traditionally, it is often formulated in three questions:

What is the knower?
What is the known?
What is the relationship between the knower and the known?

Although classical debates tend to focus on human knowledge of the empirical world, the discussion can clearly be extended to include knowledge of "other minds". Theologically, it embraces the question of the nature and limits of human knowledge of God, and the forms that divine self-disclosure might take.[4]

Although the subject-object distinction was a frequent subject of discussion within British empiricism, Brunner's reflections on this issue are located within a long-standing German-language discussion of the theme, which framed it in a quite different manner. Developing Kant's formulation of the issue in his *Critique of Pure Reason*, Karl Leonhard Reinhold (1757–1823) argued that cognition was to be understood as the conscious representation of an object by a subject and that such "representations" involved both the subject and object of cognition.[5] Johann Gottlieb Fichte (1762–1814) gave this approach a more radical twist, arguing that cognition generated the distinction between subject and object by positing a distinction between the "I" and "not-I".[6] Yet many remained persuaded of the inevitability and

---

[3] "Toward a Missionary Theology", 817.
[4] See the discussion in James Brown, *Subject and Object in Modern Theology*. London: SCM Press, 1955.
[5] For these ideas, see Wayne Martin, *Idealism and Objectivity: Understanding Fichte's Jena Project*. Stanford, CA: Stanford University Press, 1997, 81–99.
[6] Martin, *Idealism and Objectivity*, 100–41. On Fichte's approach in general, see Frederick Neuhauser, *Fichte's Theory of Subjectivity*. Cambridge: Cambridge University Press, 1990.

universal scope of the subject-object dichotomy, seeing this as fundamental to any viable theory of knowledge.[7]

By the end of the Great War, the German-language discussion of the issue had reached something of an impasse. The two most widely adopted solutions lay in assimilating the object to the subject, on the one hand, or assimilating the subject to the object on the other. The widely used image of knowledge as "seeing things" presupposed a passive object being properly seen by an active subject.[8] Yet with the translation of the works of the Danish philosopher Søren Kierkegaard (1813–55) into German, another solution began to emerge.[9]

While Kierkegaard was not unknown in German-speaking academic circles prior to the Great War, it is fair to say that he had limited impact on both theology and philosophy. Theodor Haecker's study of Kierkegaard's approach to the "Subject-Object Problem" appeared in 1913, on the eve of the Great War.[10] In part, this late development reflected difficulties in translating some of Kierkegaard's terms into German.[11] By the late 1920s, however, Kierkegaard had secured significant philosophical and theological traction,[12] not least on account of his criticisms of the limitations of Enlightenment rationalism.

In the *Concluding Unscientific Postscript* (1846) to his *Philosophical Fragments*, Kierkegaard set out his idea of "truth as subjectivity", partly in reaction against what he regarded as the excessive objectivist rationalism of German idealism. What does Kierkegaard mean by this phrase? Considered objectively, truth merely seeks attachment to the right object, correspondence with an independent reality. Considered subjectively, however, truth seeks achievement of the right attitude, an appropriate relation between object and knower. "Knowledge has a relationship to the knower, who is essentially an existing individual, and ... for this reason all essential knowledge is essentially related to existence. Only ethical and ethico-religious knowledge

---

[7] For the importance of this point in understanding the rise of postmodernity's emphasis on "alterity", see Michael Theunissen, *The Other: Studies in the Social Ontology of Husserl, Heidegger, Sartre, and Buber*. Cambridge, MA: MIT Press, 1984.

[8] See the seminal essay by Hans Blumenberg, "Licht als Metapher der Wahrheit." *Studium Generale* 10 (1957): 432–47. For an assessment of this model, see Philipp Stoellger, *Metapher und Lebenswelt: Hans Blumenbergs Metaphorologie als Lebensweltthermeneutik und ihr religionsphänomenologischer Horizont*. Tübingen: Mohr Siebeck, 2000, 70–80.

[9] For a general overview, see Samuel Hugo Bergman, *Dialogical Philosophy from Kierkegaard to Buber*. Albany, NY: State University of New York Press, 1991.

[10] Theodor Haecker, *Sören Kierkegaards Philosophie der Innerlichkeit*. Munich: Schreiber, 1913. Theologians found Kierkegaard to be a particularly significant resource in the aftermath of the Great War: see Werner Elert's analysis of this "Kierkegaard Renaissance" in *Der Kampf um das Christentum*. Munich: Beck, 1921, 430–4.

[11] Heiko Schulz, "Rezeptionsgeschichtliche Brocken oder die *Brocken* in der deutschen Rezeption." *Kierkegaard Study Yearbook* (2004): 375–451.

[12] Heiko Schulz, "Germany and Austria: A Modest Head Start. The German Reception of Kierkegaard." In *Kierkegaard's International Reception: Northern and Western Europe*, ed. Jon Stewart, 307–420. Aldershot: Ashgate, 2009.

has an essential relationship to the existence of the knower."[13] This leads Kierkegaard to define "truth" in terms that explicitly include the engagement of the knower with the known: "*An objective uncertainty held fast in an appropriation-process of the most passionate inwardness is the truth*, the highest truth attainable for an *existing* individual."[14]

Kierkegaard's dialogical approach is primarily a protest against earlier ways of conceptualizing the subject-object relationship, and only secondarily a solution to its problems. For Kierkegaard, human individuality was too easily lost; its preservation demanded a reconceptualization of existing ways of thinking. Philosophers such as Martin Heidegger (1889–1976) and Karl Jaspers (1883–1969) developed existential philosophies based on this approach during the 1930s. Yet many came to see Kierkegaard's approach as offering a way of resolving difficulties in conceptualizing the nature of Christian faith and revelation in the light of the agenda of the Enlightenment, especially within the "dialectical theology" movement.[15] Brunner was no exception. In his Uppsala lectures, he declared that Kierkegaard was the "greatest theologian of the modern period".[16]

Yet where Barth saw Kierkegaard as an exponent of the "infinite qualitative distinction" between time and eternity on the one hand, and God and humanity on the other, Brunner appreciated the potential of Kierkegaard to offer solutions to the "Subject-Object Problem." He was not the first to notice this. Others had seen how Kierkegaard's approach might provide a way of dealing with – if not a solution to – the problem. Two German-language writers stand out as being particularly important in the immediate post-war era: the Austrian philosopher Ferdinand Ebner (1882–1931) and the German Jewish philosopher and mystic Martin Buber (1878–1965).

Ebner's *Das Wort und die geistigen Realitäten* ("The Word and Spiritual Realities") was written in the winter of 1918–19, and appeared in 1921.[17] This somewhat inchoate work makes significant demands of its readers; however, it repays study. After an initial atheist phase, Ebner began to return to his Christian roots in the late 1910s. His theological reflections were mainly stimulated by Kierkegaard, Dostoevsky, Johann Georg Hamann, and Wilhelm von Humboldt, and focused on the existential overcoming of

---

[13] Søren Kierkegaard, *Concluding Unscientific Postscript*. Princeton, NJ: Princeton University Press, 1974, 107. See further Stephen N. Dunning, *Kierkegaard's Dialectic of Inwardness: A Structural Analysis of the Theory of Stages*. Princeton, NJ: Princeton University Press, 1985.
[14] Kierkegaard, *Concluding Unscientific Postscript*, 182 (emphasis in original). See further C. Steven Evans, *Subjectivity and Religious Belief: An Historical, Critical Study*. Grand Rapids, MI: Eerdmans, 1978.
[15] Schulz, "Germany and Austria: A Modest Head Start", 334–41.
[16] *Wahrheit als Begegnung*, 60; *The Divine-Human Encounter*, 57.
[17] Ferdinand Ebner, *Das Wort und die geistigen Realitäten: Pneumatologische Fragmente*. Innsbruck: Brenner Verlag, 1921. For comment, see Augustinus Karl Wucherer-Huldenfeld, *Personales Sein und Wort: Einführung in den Grundgedanken Ferdinand Ebners*. Vienna: Böhlau, 1985; Bernhard Casper, *Das dialogische Denken: Franz Rosenzweig, Ferdinand Ebner und Martin Buber*. 2nd edn. Freiburg: Alber, 2002.

"self-loneliness" (*Icheinsamkeit*).[18] Ebner regarded the human capacity for language as being of decisive importance, seeing this as an indication of the need for interpersonal relationships.

In the preface to *Das Wort und die geistigen Realitäten*, Ebner presents the core thesis of his work. Assuming that human existence has a "spiritual significance", and that it is reasonable to speak of a "spiritual nature" within humanity, Ebner declares that this "spiritual entity" is related to "something *outside* itself, *through* which and *in* which it exists".[19] He framed this in terms of an "I-Thou"[20] relationship, which gives content and stability to the spiritual life of humanity.

A related approach was developed by Martin Buber. Although the early Buber was influenced by the Kantian tradition, by the early 1920s he was moving towards a form of "dialogical personalism", informed by both Kierkegaard's notion of "truth as subjectivity" and by the mysticism of Hasidism, which emphasized a direct human relationship with God.[21] His ideas were set out in *Ich und Du* ("I and Thou") in 1922. Buber's fundamental distinction is between two possible modes of relationship between human beings and the world, including God and other human beings. Buber designates these attitudes as "I-Thou" and "I-It".

> The attitude [*Haltung*] of humanity is twofold in accordance with the two basic words [*Grundworte*] it can speak. The basic words are not single words but word-pairs. One basic word is the word-pair "I-Thou". The other basic word is the word-pair "I-It."[22]

The basic difference is that an "I-It relationship" (*Ich-Es-Beziehung*) refers to relating to an object which is observed, and an "I-Thou relationship" (*Ich-Du-Beziehung*) to a person that addresses us, and to whom we respond. For Buber, an "I-Thou relationship" is to be characterized as an "encounter" (*Begegnung*), which is personal and immediate; an "I-It relationship" takes the form of "experience" (*Erfahrung*), which is objective and impersonal. It is possible – but improper – to treat a "Thou" in impersonal and objective ways, so that the "Thou" becomes an "It". In effect, Buber distinguished

---

[18] The best study of Ebner's reflections on the "Pascalian *moi*" and its *Icheinsamkeit* is Richard Hörmann, "'Subjektivität' in den *Fragmenten*." In *Pneumatologie als Grammatik der Subjectivität: Ferdinand Ebner*, ed. Ermenegildo Bidese, Richard Hörmann, and Silvano Zucal, 133–42. Münster: LIT Verlag, 2012.

[19] Ebner, *Das Wort und die geistigen Realitäten*, 12.

[20] Ebner, like most German-speaking personalist philosophers, uses the word-pair "Ich-Du", which cannot be adequately translated into English as "I-You", since *Du* is both *familiar* and *singular*. Translators have generally found that the use of the older English "Thou" is the only adequate way of conveying the sense of the word-pair into English, despite its obvious drawbacks (most notably, the introduction of an "archaic" voice).

[21] For the difficulty many felt in locating Buber's work on an epistemological map, see the classic study of Maurice S. Friedman, "Martin Buber's Theory of Knowledge." *Review of Metaphysics* 8, no. 2 (1954): 264–80.

[22] Martin Buber, *Ich und Du*. Stuttgart: Reclam, 2008, 3.

two quite different possible attitudes and world-relations, based on the phenomenological distinction between being as being and being as entity.[23]

Buber was clear regarding the religious foundations and implications of his approach. There is one "Thou", he argues, who can never become an "It". It is resistant to any attempt to relocate it to an objectified world. According to Buber, much theology goes astray by reducing God to an "It" – in effect, treating God as something to be experienced, rather than someone who addresses us and is to be encountered. For Buber, the most important thing that Israel knew about its God had little to do with the technicalities of theology: it was that God could be addressed as a "Thou".

Whereas some forms of mysticism attempt to overwhelm the gulf between the self and the "Absolute" through a mystical union, Buber holds that the essence of religion is a dialogue between humanity and God. He contrasts the Jewish concept of *emunah* and the Greek concept of *pistis*; the former, he suggests, is faith in the sense of trust in God, while the latter is faith in the sense of belief in the truth of propositional statements. Every I-Thou relationship is to be seen as a relationship of grace. The "eternal Thou" is to be discerned in and through human relationships. "The extended lines of relationships intersect in the 'eternal Thou' [*im ewigen Du*]."[24]

Ebner and Buber both set out ways of understanding humanity's relationship with God which were theologically fertile, developing Kierkegaard's ideas in ways that opened up important angles of exploration for systematic theology. We should not be surprised that Brunner realized their importance. His 1937 Uppsala lectures gave him the opportunity to develop his ideas on faith and revelation in greater detail.

Although Brunner does not mention this in his Uppsala lectures, the contours of such an approach had been sketched at the same university four years earlier by the young philosopher of religion John Olof Cullberg (1895–1983), who later became bishop of Västerås.[25] In his *Das Du und die Wirklichkeit* ("The Thou and Reality"), published in 1933, Cullberg affirmed the theological importance of the new forms of personalism that had gained momentum in the last decade. The individual subject – the "I" – is to be placed in a "concrete context – the life of fellowship [*das Gemeinschaftsleben*], the I-Thou relationship". Cullberg thus argues that "the 'I' as an individual is an abstraction; only the 'I' that stands in a relationship with *a 'Thou'* has any concrete content".[26] Cullberg noted how dialectical theology had wrestled with such issues, giving a brief account of

---

[23] For the development of this idea in Levinas, see Stephan Strasser, "Buber and Levinas: Philosophical Reflections on an Opposition." In *Levinas & Buber: Dialogue & Difference*, ed. Peter Atterton, Matthew Calarco, and Maurice S. Friedman, 37–48. Pittsburgh: Duquesne University Press, 2004.
[24] Buber, *Ich und Du*, 71.
[25] John Cullberg, *Das Du und die Wirklichkeit: Zum ontologischen Hintergrund der Gemeinschaftskategorie*. Uppsala: Uppsala Universitetes Arsskrift, 1933.
[26] Cullberg, *Das Du und die Wirklichkeit*, 17 (emphasis in original).

the positions of both Barth and Brunner, hinting that Brunner's approach in *Die Mystik und das Wort* (1924) – which had made appreciative reference to Ebner – was capable of further development.

One further point must be made before going further. Brunner, Buber, and Ebner can all be regarded as critics of depersonalizing trends in the aftermath of the Great War, which became particularly significant in the 1930s. Growing anxiety began to emerge in western European circles about the impact of the collectivist philosophy then emerging in the Soviet Union, which seemed to eliminate personal identity to serve the needs of the state.[27] The forms of individualism that had gained ground in Russia during the period before the Great War were overwhelmed by a collectivist ideology.[28] Yet recent scholarship has emphasized the collectivist dimensions of Nazi ideology, noting how this marked a break with the individualism that was more characteristic of other forms of modernism.[29] Brunner in particular came to see the rise of the totalitarian state – whether Marxist-Leninist or Nazi – as entailing a loss of personal identity. So how might human individuality be recovered and safeguarded?

Brunner's response to this question in the later 1930s must not be seen as theologically opportunistic, a precipitate response to extreme and unrepresentative political situations. It is easily argued that some form of depersonalization is implicit within the modernist project *as a whole*.[30] The commodification of humanity as a result of capitalism is only one of a number of ways in which the significance and value of the human individual was being called into question and eroded.[31] Brunner's carefully considered theological response to this specific set of situations has the potential to engage questions about human identity and individuality arising from the modernist project as a whole.

So what theological platform, secure from ideological manipulation, might be developed for safeguarding personal identity? Brunner's Uppsala

---

[27] See Lynne Viola, *Peasant Rebels Under Stalin: Collectivization and the Culture of Peasant Resistance*. Oxford: Oxford University Press, 1996, 13–44.

[28] For example, see Mark D. Steinberg, *Proletarian Imagination: Self, Modernity, and the Sacred in Russia, 1910–1925*. Ithaca, NY: Cornell University Press, 2002.

[29] See the important studies of Mark Roseman, "National Socialism and Modernisation." In *Fascist Italy and Nazi Germany: Comparisons and Contrasts*, ed. Richard Bessel, 197–229. Cambridge: Cambridge University Press, 1996; and especially the nuanced account in Moritz Föllmer, "Was Nazism Collectivistic? Redefining the Individual in Berlin, 1930–1945." *Journal of Modern History* 82, no. 1 (2010): 61–100.

[30] See especially Markus Schroer, *Das Individuum der Gesellschaft: Synchrone und diachrone Theorieperspektiven*. Frankfurt: Suhrkamp Verlag, 2000, 15–283. For a broader cultural analysis of the issues, see Charles Taylor, *Sources of the Self: The Making of the Modern Identity*. Cambridge: Cambridge University Press, 1989; Jerrold Seigel, *The Idea of the Self: Thought and Experience in Western Europe since the Seventeenth Century*. Cambridge: Cambridge University Press, 2005.

[31] Richard Sennett, *The Corrosion of Character: The Personal Consequences of Work in the New Capitalism*. New York: Norton, 1998.

lectures of 1937 represent one of the most significant attempts to develop a theological understanding of the relation of revelation and faith which avoids the problematic notions of "subject" and "object" arising from the Enlightenment, particularly in relation to the Kantian tradition.[32] Yet they also provide an understanding of human identity as a "Thou" – rather than an "It" – which resists commodificationist and collectivist reductions of human individuality.[33] In what follows, I shall consider Brunner's exposition of these notions in detail, and clarify their significance.

Objectivity and Subjectivity: Brunner's Criticism of Existing Paradigms

Brunner opens his lectures with a reflection on the nature of theology itself. The task of theology, he declares, is to "achieve clarity over what the church is to proclaim, what the Christian is to believe, and what the practical consequences of this proclamation and faith are for the church and its individual members".[34] He then distinguishes three separate "roots".[35]

1 The *exegetical*. Theology concerns the proper interpretation and application of the Bible. Brunner here notes that the Christian community needs to be helped to use the Bible properly – not simply in understanding individual passages, but in the perhaps greater task of "grasping their correlation", so that "individual concepts can be related to revelation in its totality".

2 The *didactic*. Brunner insists that there is a pedagogical role to theology, in that the church needs to be instructed "in the main contents of the history of revelation". Yet while affirming the importance of a "short compendium or catechism" as such a means of instruction, Brunner notes that some Christians will need more than this – especially those who are "alert to the thinking and problems of their time". It must be remembered that Brunner's *Unser Glaube* ("Our Faith") – in effect a brief compendium of Christian doctrine, based on the Apostles' Creed – had been published two years earlier in 1935, indicating Brunner's own commitment to this fundamental pedagogical ministry.

3 The *polemical*. Brunner insists that, as a matter of historical fact and theological necessity, the tasks of theology must include "critical reflection

---

[32] Cynthia Bennett Brown, "The Personal Imperative of Revelation: Emil Brunner, Dogmatics and Theological Existence." *Scottish Journal of Theology* 65, no. 4 (2012): 421–34.
[33] Barth's use of personalist approaches is of interest: Mark J. McInroy, "Karl Barth and Personalist Philosophy: A Critical Appropriation." *Scottish Journal of Theology* 64, no. 1 (2011): 45–63. Curiously, this article fails to consider Brunner's approach, and the possibilities that it opened up.
[34] *Wahrheit als Begegnung*, 10; *The Divine-Human Encounter*, 10.
[35] *Wahrheit als Begegnung*, 10–13; *The Divine-Human Encounter*, 10–12.

and controversy". Ideas arise within the community of faith which are not well grounded in divine revelation. These, Brunner declares, must be identified and eliminated.

This third category is particularly important, as it overlaps with what Brunner had earlier termed an "eristic" approach to theology.[36] He had avoided the term "polemical" to refer to this task of theology, feeling that this was too strident. Yet in these 1937 lectures, he appears to have reverted to this alternative mode of expression. However, it seems that the "critical reflection and controversy" that he wishes to encourage is understood primarily to take place within the community of faith, and to focus on the correct formulation of Christian theology. The polemical aspect of theology concerns primarily the identification of malformed, destructive, or inadequate manners of articulation of fundamental theological truths.

So what sort of theological errors or false turns does Brunner have in mind? It soon becomes clear that his lectures are concerned with the identification and correction of one fundamental error – an excessive reliance on the "Subject-Object antithesis". Brunner holds that the origin of this maladapted development is to be traced back to the period of the early church.

> Early in the history of the church, under the influence of Greek philosophy, the understanding emerged that the divine revelation in the Bible was about the communication of those doctrinal truths that were inaccessible to human reason, so that faith consisted of accepting such supernaturally revealed doctrines as true.[37]

The idea that Christian theology had been contaminated by Greek metaphysical ideas was familiar at the time of Brunner's lectures. Writers such as Adolf von Harnack had argued that ideas such as "dogma" or the incarnation were essentially Hellenistic in origin, and thus to be rejected.[38] Brunner acknowledges such a potentially distorting effect of Greek philosophy on early Christian thought, but locates its impact elsewhere – on the concepts of faith and truth. He argues that such a misunderstanding is not to be compared to some localized defect – such as an abscess in the human body – but is rather to be thought of as a systemic error, to be compared to blood poisoning, which ultimately ends up corrupting every organ in the body.

---

[36] Salakka, *Person und Offenbarung in der Theologie Emil Brunners*, 137–45.
[37] *Wahrheit als Begegnung*, 12; *The Divine-Human Encounter*, 12.
[38] E. J. Meijering, *Die Hellenisierung des Christentums im Urteil Adolf von Harnack*. Amsterdam: Kampen, 1985. For more recent evaluations of the issue, see Matthias Lutz-Bachmann, "Hellenisierung des Christentums?" In *Spätantike und Christentum: Beiträge zur Religions- und Geistesgeschichte der griechisch-römischen Kultur und Zivilisation der Kaiserzeit*, ed. Carsten Colpe, Ludger Honnefelder, and Matthias Lutz-Bachmann, 77–98. Berlin: Akademie Verlag, 1992.

So how did this misunderstanding arise? Brunner argues that this interpretation of both "truth" and "faith" rests on the inappropriate use of an "Object-Subject Antithesis". His basic thesis, set out in uncompromisingly clear terms, is that the use of this antithesis "in understanding the truth of faith [*Glaubenswahrheit*]" is in reality a "disastrous misunderstanding" which damages both Christian life and thought. "The biblical understanding of faith cannot be grasped through the Subject-Object antithesis, but is falsified through it."[39]

What does Brunner understand by the phrase "Object-Subject antithesis", on which he places so much weight? What does this "pair of conceptions" (*Begriffspaar*) designate? Brunner clarifies both concepts as follows. "Objectivism" designates the human tendency to wish to master something that is ultimately not under human control – to "manipulate it, as if it were an object".[40] Brunner suggests that this objectifying tendency is found in medieval sacramental theology. The priest, he suggests, is here understood to take control of a process by which the bread becomes the body of Christ. What was once conceived as an act of divine grace now becomes an instance of human institutional control.[41]

Brunner also discerns this process of "objectification as control" at work in the church's discussion of divine revelation. He is emphatic that "revelation remains God's right and God's deed";[42] it is only through the power of the Holy Spirit that revelation takes place. "The Word of God is *kein verfügbares Objekt*" – a German phrase, literally meaning "no available object", yet which suggests an object that is open to human manipulation or control – but is "a free gift of grace".

Brunner's point is that the Word of God is not a concrete reality that is "available", presented to our senses for our controlled consideration, but is rather something that is dependent upon the "free intervention" of God. The church found this inconvenient, Brunner suggested, and thus sought to master God's revelation. The church required certainty and control, and thus developed institutional systems by which God's revelation could be codified, confirmed, and above all *regulated*.

> The Church built up a powerful apparatus, a system of ecclesiastical safeguards, by means of which it could have authority over divine revelation. . . . The authority of the divine word was delegated to the legal apparatus of the Church.[43]

---

[39] *Wahrheit als Begegnung*, 14; *The Divine-Human Encounter*, 13.
[40] *Wahrheit als Begegnung*, 16; *The Divine-Human Encounter*, 15.
[41] Brunner justifies his concerns by appealing to a statement found in Friedrich Heiler, *Der Katholizismus: Seine Idee und seine Erscheinung*. Munich: Reinhardt, 1923, 224: "the transformation of the elements" comes about "by means of the formula of consecration spoken by the priest, who is endowed with divine power".
[42] *Wahrheit als Begegnung*, 17; *The Divine-Human Encounter*, 16.
[43] *Wahrheit als Begegnung*, 18; *The Divine-Human Encounter*, 17.

Brunner saw this process of objectification in terms of an ecclesiastical *codification* – the "development of systems of authority and safeguards" – which was intended to secure ecclesiastical *control* over divine revelation. Revelation was entrusted to the church; the church now controls what has been entrusted to it.

Brunner's caustic assessment of Objectivism up to this point focused primarily on Catholicism. In a move that may have unsettled some in his audience, he suggested that certain forms of Protestantism were prone to the same problem. Protestant Orthodoxy demonstrated the same desire to control divine revelation by "freezing" it, treating the Bible was a "collection of divine pronouncements" containing the "essence of divinely revealed doctrine".[44]

Brunner thus argued that Protestant confessional dogmas – especially the doctrine of the verbal inspiration of the Bible, and the idea that the Bible was essentially a textbook of revealed doctrines – distorted the Reformation's understanding of the disclosure and proclamation of the Word of God. "A position of dependence upon the Word of God is usurped by an appeal to pure doctrine, which is treated as equivalent to the Word of God."[45] Although Brunner locates the origins of this development in the generations after the Reformation,[46] he hints that its origins can be seen even in the Augsburg Confession itself – the 1530 document that Lutherans regard as being one of their foundational documents. Brunner insisted that Holy Scripture is not the *object* of faith, but the *means* by which God creates faith – not a faith in the Bible, but a faith in the God who is revealed in the Bible.

What, then, of "Subjectivism"? Brunner made clear from the outset his misgivings about any subjective approach to theology grounded in "individualist enthusiasm", which refuses to recognize that there is anything "fixed or divinely given", eschewing rules and the notion of authority. Brunner's description of "Subjectivism" reflects his fear of spiritual anarchy, the principled refusal to acknowledge or accept any principles, save that of the unfettered right of individuals to do and think as they please – a tendency given spurious theological justification through an appeal to the spontaneity and unpredictability of the Holy Spirit.[47]

Once more, Brunner finds Protestantism to have been at fault. He argues that Pietism represented an excessively subjectivist reaction against the formal and objective understanding of faith that was characteristic of

---

[44] *Wahrheit als Begegnung*, 23; *The Divine-Human Encounter*, 22.
[45] *Wahrheit als Begegnung*, 23; *The Divine-Human Encounter*, 22.
[46] Brunner does not defend such historical judgements in these lectures; however, his basic points are echoed in most recent studies of the emergence of confessionalism: see, for example, Bodo Nischan, *Lutherans and Calvinists in the Age of Confessionalism*. Aldershot: Ashgate, 1999; John M. Headley, Hans Joachim Hillerbrand, and Anthony J. Papalas, eds., *Confessionalization in Europe, 1555–1700: Essays in Honor and Memory of Bodo Nischan*. Aldershot: Ashgate, 2004.
[47] *Wahrheit als Begegnung*, 18–19; *The Divine-Human Encounter*, 18–19.

Protestant Orthodoxy. Pietism, Brunner suggests, was a renewal movement that expressed legitimate concerns in the face of the excessive objectivism of Orthodoxy. This outstanding episode in church history led to the regeneration of a desiccated church and individual faith, and fostered a renewal of church life and witness.[48] Nevertheless, this turn to the subjective was freighted with dangers, not least the threat of a retreat into an inner world of experience, disconnected from any objective dimension of faith.[49] Brunner finds the implementation of this trend, not so much within Pietism itself, but in the synthesis of Pietism and rationalism encountered in the theological project of F. D. E. Schleiermacher, which tends to evacuate the faith of the church of its content. "The Word is no longer a divinely revealed authority or the foundation of faith, but merely a means of expressing faith."[50]

Having noted that Pietism was essentially a subjectivist reaction against the over-intellectualization of faith within Protestant Orthodoxy, Brunner argues that the theological aftermath of the Great War of 1914–18 was characterized by a reaction against the subjectivism of Schleiermacher's legacy. Brunner does not mention the name of Karl Barth; it would, however, have been quite obvious to his audience who he had in mind here. A "new objectivism" emerged, emphasizing that the church was the "recipient and proclaimer of the Word of God". Its retrospective reconstruction of the theological history of the immediate pre-war period led to the lionization of writers such as Martin Kähler (1835–1912) and Adolf Schlatter (1852–1938), who exercised little influence in their own time, but were now regarded as prophets of more recent trends.[51]

Yet while welcoming this trend towards theological rebalancing and recalibration, Brunner indicates his disquiet about some of its outcomes. Instead of achieving a proper balance between objectivity and subjectivity, "dialectical theology" has degenerated into a "theological and ecclesial objectivism", which merely repeats some of the fundamental failings of classical Protestant Orthodoxy – such as a "one-sided assertion of doctrine; an identification of doctrine and the Word of God; an excessive valuation of confessional formulations and dogma; and a one-sided emphasis on the objective in preaching".[52]

Brunner presents this as an unfortunate and quite unnecessary distortion of the intentions of the "group of 'dialectical theologians'" to which he

---

[48] *Wahrheit als Begegnung*, 24; *The Divine-Human Encounter*, 23. Brunner does not concern himself with the historical difficulties of defining "Pietism" as a social phenomenon, such as those noted in Johannes Wallmann, "Was ist Pietismus?" *Pietismus und Neuzeit* 20 (1994): 11–27.
[49] A similar criticism of Pietism was made by Karl Barth: Eberhard Busch, *Karl Barth und die Pietisten: Die Pietismuskritik des jüngeren Barth und ihre Erwiderung*. Munich: Kaiser, 1978.
[50] *Wahrheit als Begegnung*, 26; *The Divine-Human Encounter*, 25.
[51] *Wahrheit als Begegnung*, 27–8; *The Divine-Human Encounter*, 26–7.
[52] *Wahrheit als Begegnung*, 28; *The Divine-Human Encounter*, 27.

himself belonged, and who had until recently enjoyed a degree of consensus in terms of the theological trends they wished to oppose. Surely dialectical theology needed to reclaim its Pietist roots? Did it not owe a substantial intellectual debt to such giants as Kierkegaard and Christoph Blumhardt (1842–1919)?[53] Pietism unquestionably had its "dubious aspects"; nevertheless, its recovery of the subjectivity of faith had to be taken seriously. For Brunner, dialectical theology ought to be characterized by the slogan: "Beyond Orthodoxy and Pietism – biblical faith!"[54]

Overcoming the Object-Subject Impasse: Brunner's Strategy

So how is this false antithesis of the Objective and Subjective to be overcome? How can a viable theological trajectory be navigated between the Scylla of a "resurgent Orthodoxy" on the one hand, and the Charybdis of a "neo-Pietism" on the other?[55] Brunner had begun to appreciate one possible approach in 1919–20 during his time at Union Theological Seminary, New York (see pp. 12–13). While studying the psychology of religion under George Albert Coe (pp. 18–20), Brunner had reflected on the notion of the "self-finding of the 'I' in the 'Thou'" (*das Sichfinden des Ich im Du*).[56] Although this idea was not explored in any depth in Brunner's writings immediately following his American period, it is clear that his brief engagement with American psychology of religion had opened up for him a way of thinking that transcended the somewhat barren "spectator" theory of knowledge, which regarded knowledge as the correct apprehension of a passive object by an active subject. In part, this development reflects the influence of the great American psychologist William James who insisted that the knower was changed by knowledge.[57] Knowledge is thus never independent of the knower.

Brunner brings this kind of framework – whether derived directly from Coe or not – to his discussion of the "Objective-Subjective" antithesis in theology, especially in relation to the question of the knowledge of God. However, it does not feature explicitly in his analysis.[58] Instead, he moves on, in his second Uppsala lecture, to focus on the "biblical understanding of truth". Although he here proposes his own positive approach to the bibli-

---

[53] For Blumhardt's influence on Brunner's father, see Jehle, *Emil Brunner*, 22–4.
[54] *Wahrheit als Begegnung*, 30; *The Divine-Human Encounter*, 28.
[55] *Wahrheit als Begegnung*, 30; *The Divine-Human Encounter*, 28.
[56] George Albert Coe, *The Psychology of Religion*. Chicago: University of Chicago Press, 1916, 246–62. See Brunner's remarks at *Erlebnis, Erkenntnis und Glaube*, 53.
[57] William James, *Essays in Radical Empiricism*. Cambridge, MA: Harvard University Press, 1976, 21.
[58] Brunner's comments about the impact of the psychology of religion on American "theology" – he uses the citation marks to indicate a certain scepticism about its credentials – suggests that he regards its application, especially within the Chicago school, to be fraught with a risk of anthropological reductionism: *Wahrheit als Begegnung*, 27; *The Divine-Human Encounter*, 25.

cal understanding of truth, this chapter is better seen as a critique of an implicit (and unacknowledged) tendency to read the Bible from the perspective of the Enlightenment's normative framing of the "subject-object" dichotomy, which has been assumed to be a self-evident or normative manner of interpreting the Bible's views on human knowledge of God.

A further point of interest about Brunner's analysis of the biblical notion of truth is the absence of any serious engagement on his part with biblical texts or biblical scholarship. If his reflections on the concept of truth found in the Bible are grounded on biblical exegesis, this is carefully concealed from his readers. The overall impression is that Brunner's articulation of this theme is imposed upon the biblical text, rather than based upon a detailed study of biblical passages or terms.[59] His rejection of a prevailing interpretative framework is loosely correlated with biblical texts, yet fails to undertake anything even approaching a systematic account of what the Bible understands by "truth".

The critical point that Brunner articulates is that the Bible's notion of truth is not framed in a purely cognitive or propositional manner; rather, it is fundamentally *relational*. Theology is not concerned with the formal articulation of a biblical "doctrine of truth" (*Lehre von der Wahrheit*), but rather with attempting to grasp the "hidden presuppositions" or "structure" of the biblical revelation.[60] Like Calvin before him, Brunner questions whether it is possible to have a purely disinterested or "objective" knowledge of God. The intellectual possibility of such a knowledge is safeguarded by the "Object-Subject" antithesis. But what if this cannot be sustained? What if the believer steps outside this framework through an act of faith in God?

For Brunner, the focus of biblical revelation concerns the relationship (*Beziehung*) of God to humanity, and humanity to God.[61] Kant argued that we can never know a thing as it really is in itself (*Ding-an-sich*); we can only know observable manifestations of this thing, as an object of perception.[62] Brunner declares that there is no biblical doctrine of *Gott-an-sich* or *Menschen-an-sich*, as if these were abstract concepts. God and humanity are to be grasped relationally. The Bible "always sees God as *Gott-zum-Menschen-hin* and humanity as *Menschen-von-Gott-her*"[63] – in other words,

---

[59] See Thomas Böhm, "Das Wahrheitsverständnis in Bibel und Früher Kirche." In *Die Geschichte des philosophischen Wahrheitsbegriffes*, ed. Markus Enders and Jan Szaif, 49–64. Berlin: de Gruyter, 2006. Note Böhm's references to Brunner's concerns (49–50).
[60] *Wahrheit als Begegnung*, 32; *The Divine-Human Encounter*, 30.
[61] *Wahrheit als Begegnung*, 33; *The Divine-Human Encounter*, 31.
[62] See, for example, John W. Yolton, *Realism and Appearances: An Essay in Ontology*. Cambridge: Cambridge University Press, 2000. Although Kant's approach was highly influential from the late 1860s, as a result of Otto Liebmann's call for a return to Kant in *Kant und die Epigonen* (1865), it was criticized by Nietzsche: see Kurt Mosser, "Nietzsche, Kant and the Thing in Itself." *International Studies in Philosophy* 25 (1993): 67–77.
[63] *Wahrheit als Begegnung*, 33; *The Divine-Human Encounter*, 31. The German phrases are to be translated as "God who approaches humanity" and "humanity which comes from God".

God is conceived, not as an abstract object of cognition, but as the initiator of a relationship with humanity. God is the one who approaches and addresses humanity; humanity derives its origins from God. "The full truth of both is only knowable [*erkennbar*] in Jesus Christ."[64]

This Christological focus leads Brunner to make a move which must be regarded as marking a significant departure from the dominant Enlightenment approach. "In the Bible, this double-sided relationship between God and humanity is not developed as a doctrine, but as it happened in a story [*Geschichte*]".[65] Where the Enlightenment minimized the significance of both the literary genre of narrative and any notion of truth disclosed through history,[66] Brunner sought to reclaim a more authentic biblical way of thinking. "Abstract formulas" are incapable of expressing the fundamental relational nature of the biblical understanding of truth, which requires "narration [*Erzählung*] as the proper form" of its expression.[67] The content of the Bible could be expressed as the "narrative about the relationship established by God towards humanity".[68]

Brunner's emphasis on the relational nature of truth is, however, open to a misunderstanding. Although the relationship between humanity and God is indeed "two-sided", this does not mean that the two parties to the relationship are to be regarded as possessing equal significance or weight.[69] God is the one who initiates the relationship, and determines its scope and nature. In this sense, it is a relationship of grace. Humanity can only know God in the manner and to the extent that God chooses to be known.[70]

The nature of this knowledge requires further consideration. Brunner points out that the "idealistic-mystic" approach to knowledge understands this, not as revelation or a decision, but as an "awareness of something that has always been there", accessible to human scrutiny and perception.[71] He argues that any such position is theologically indefensible. A proper knowledge of God must be understood in terms of "an event, an act of decision". Where the Enlightenment saw knowledge in terms of a "timeless, static 'knowing'", the Bible understands such knowledge as God's gracious decision to be known in and through a relationship with humanity, which in turn requires a response – a *decision* (*Entscheidung*) – on the part of humanity. "God wills to be known as Lord";[72] the human response to this thus demands both intellectual and relational acceptance of God's nature. "The

---

[64] *Wahrheit als Begegnung*, 33–4; *The Divine-Human Encounter*, 31.
[65] *Wahrheit als Begegnung*, 34; *The Divine-Human Encounter*, 31.
[66] See the classic study of Hans Frei, *The Eclipse of Biblical Narrative: A Study in Eighteenth and Nineteenth Century Biblical Hermeneutics*. New Haven, CT: Yale University Press, 1977.
[67] *Wahrheit als Begegnung*, 34; *The Divine-Human Encounter*, 32.
[68] *Wahrheit als Begegnung*, 38; *The Divine-Human Encounter*, 35.
[69] *Wahrheit als Begegnung*, 35; *The Divine-Human Encounter*, 33.
[70] *Wahrheit als Begegnung*, 34; *The Divine-Human Encounter*, 34.
[71] *Wahrheit als Begegnung*, 37; *The Divine-Human Encounter*, 34.
[72] *Wahrheit als Begegnung*, 47; *The Divine-Human Encounter*, 44.

will of God is fulfilled only when humanity's answer in response to the Word of God has been given."[73]

Brunner describes this "personal response of self-giving to the Word of God" as *Vertrauensgehorsam* – a "trusting obedience" – seeing this as a suitable paraphrase of the Greek word *pistis*, as this is used in the New Testament.[74] God's "voluntary act of self-giving love" (which Brunner characterizes as *agapē*) elicits the corresponding human "reception of this self-giving love" (which Brunner designates as *pistis*). Yet this response to God's self-disclosure must not be interpreted purely as an unaided human action. "While God comes to meet humanity, God also makes it possible for humanity to meet him."

The Implications of Brunner's Notion of "Truth as Encounter"

We must now consider Brunner's formulation of his notion of "truth as encounter" in more detail, and explore how it impacts on his understanding of the theological task, as well as certain of its outcomes. Brunner argues that the most fundamental insight of the Christian faith is that "Jesus Christ is the content of faith and of truth".[75] This, he points out, is inconsistent with the classic Greek notion of truth as something timeless and changeless.[76] For biblical writers, truth is something that *happened*. It is something that God *does*. It does not designate a Platonic world of permanent truths lying beyond humanity, but a divine interposition within the world of human history and experience.

So what are the implications of Brunner's approach to truth for an understanding of theology itself? He concedes that it is not easy to extricate theological thinking from the "Object-Subject" dichotomy. This "pair of tongs" has become such an integral part of western thought that it seems impossible to undertake critical scientific reflection without making use of its core assumptions.[77] So how can theology engage the question of what is objectively true, independent of the observer? Picking up on a theme which has been characteristic of Christian theology and spirituality since patristic times, Brunner suggests that the theologian is a "wanderer between two worlds". Like the traditional *viator mundi* – the pilgrim who is caught up in the tension between the present age and the age to come – Brunner

---

[73] *Wahrheit als Begegnung*, 112; *The Divine-Human Encounter*, 107.
[74] *Wahrheit als Begegnung*, 51; *The Divine-Human Encounter*, 48–9.
[75] *Wahrheit als Begegnung*, 105; *The Divine-Human Encounter*, 100.
[76] *Wahrheit als Begegnung*, 105–6; *The Divine-Human Encounter*, 100–1. For further comment on the classical Greek notion of truth, see Jan Szaif, "Die Geschichte des Wahrheitsbegriffs in der klassischen Antike." In *Die Geschichte des Philosophischen Wahrheitsbegriffes*, ed. Markus Enders and Jan Szaif, 1–32. Berlin: de Gruyter, 2006.
[77] *Wahrheit als Begegnung*, 59–62; *The Divine-Human Encounter*, 56–8.

argues that the theologian is both an "objective thinker" and a "believer" who is concerned with *discerning* an entirely specific truth, which lies beyond the "Object-Subject" antithesis.[78]

Brunner insists that revelation cannot be understood merely as being about "something". "God does not communicate 'something' to me, but 'himself'." Revelation is about God's self-disclosure. There is no analogy for this way of thinking other than that which is provided by "an encounter between human beings, the meeting of one person with another person".[79]

Furthermore, God's revelation is addressed to a "Thou", not an "It". Revelation is about the enabling of a relationship, not simply the communication of intellectual content. God's self-disclosure is a gracious act in which God ceases to be an "It" and becomes a "Thou". Where the Enlightenment regarded God as an object of knowledge at human disposal, Brunner argues that God's self-disclosure as a "Thou" subverts human autonomy, placing us at God's disposal. God addresses us to call us into a relationship, in which we abandon our solitariness – Brunner here seems to hint at Ebner's *Icheinsamkeit* – and are transformed through the resulting changed relationship.

> God does not speak "something" in his Word, but himself – and thereby changes the mode of "speaking". God himself speaks to myself. That is to say, his *speaking* constitutes an *address*. . . . God does not deliver us a course of lectures in systematic theology; God does not submit or explain to us any confession of faith. He says to me: "I am the Lord, your God". God's Word is claim and promise, gift and demand [*Gabe und Aufgabe*].[80]

Brunner does not, however, hold that revelation is contentless.[81] While Brunner emphasises that revelation is primarily about the calling forth of a relationship through "correspondence", he makes it clear that it is far from being intellectually or conceptually vacuous. The Word of God, Brunner insists, both "establishes fellowship with us", yet "contains doctrine in some form". "God addresses us in order that we ourselves may respond to him in faith".[82] While God addresses us, God nevertheless says

---

[78] *Wahrheit als Begegnung*, 61–2; *The Divine-Human Encounter*, 58. There are parallels here with Karl Barth's critique of Heinrich Scholz's proposal for theological method to be subsumed under a generalized methodology: Arie L. Molendijk, "Ein heidnischer Wissenschaftsbegriff: Der Streit zwischen Heinrich Scholz und Karl Barth um die Wissenschaftlichkeit der Theologie." *Evangelische Theologie* 52 (1992): 527–45; Alister E. McGrath, "Theologie als Mathesis Universalis? Heinrich Scholz, Karl Barth, und der wissenschaftliche Status der christlichen Theologie." *Theologische Zeitschrift* 62 (2007): 44–57.

[79] *Wahrheit als Begegnung*, 62–3; *The Divine-Human Encounter*, 59.

[80] *Wahrheit als Begegnung*, 65; *The Divine-Human Encounter*, 62.

[81] As suggested, for example, by William C. Placher, *The Domestication of Transcendence: How Modern Thinking About God Went Wrong*. Louisville, KY: Westminster John Knox Press, 1996, 181–7. William Temple developed a similar idea when he asserted that revelation is "not truth concerning God, but the living God himself." William Temple, *Nature, Man and God*. London: Macmillan, 1934, 322.

[82] *Wahrheit als Begegnung*, 80; *The Divine-Human Encounter*, 76.

"something" to us. Revelation includes "personal and non-personal elements", just as faith entails knowledge.[83] So how does Brunner negotiate this relationship between divine self-impartation and the disclosure of something that is true?

Brunner resolves this difficulty through understanding doctrine as a "sign [*Zeichen*] and framework [*Fassung*], which is indissolubly connected with the reality that it represents".[84] While maintaining that the notion of truth which is entailed by the "Object-Subject antithesis" is "foreign" to faith, Brunner insists that there is a "conjunction of reality and sign" within the act of revelation itself, which necessitates and legitimates both *relational* and *rational* understandings of theology.

> Faith is not ultimately faith in something – something true, a doctrine. It is not about "thinking something", but about a personal encounter, trust, obedience, and love. Yet this personal event is indissolubly connected with conceptual and rational content – with truth in the general sense of the word, truth as doctrine, and knowledge as awareness of facts. God speaks and gives himself to us in no other way than speaking truth about himself; and we cannot enter into fellowship with him in a fully trusting obedience other than by believing "what" God says to us.[85]

This becomes a *Leitmotif* of Brunner's later thought, tending to be amplified rather than modified. In his discussion of the "biblical understanding of revelation" in *Reason and Revelation* (1941), Brunner recapitulates the main themes of his Uppsala lectures, while tidying up some loose ends. Revelation is about divine self-disclosure. Unlike objects, which are passive entities requiring active human investigation, God takes the initiative in revelation – and what is "revealed" does not take the form of abstract and impersonal *information*, but a personal *address*, which calls humanity into relationship with its creator and redeemer.

> We can investigate things on our own; they are objects, which do not meet us through their own active agency or by their making themselves known. We can learn to understand these things through our processes of investigation and thought. But *persons* are not an enigma [*Rätsel*] of this kind; a person is a mystery [*Geheimnis*] which can be grasped only through self-disclosure [*Selbstkundgebung*]. Through this self-disclosure, we encounter it as a person for the first time; previously, it was an "Object", a "something", to us.[86]

Such lines of thought allow Brunner to correct what he regards as the errors of Protestant Orthodoxy (and, by implication, those of Neo-Orthodoxy). Brunner's personalism provides him with a conceptual framework which reinforces several of his core theological insights.

[83] *Wahrheit als Begegnung*, 68; *The Divine-Human Encounter*, 64.
[84] *Wahrheit als Begegnung*, 83; *The Divine-Human Encounter*, 78.
[85] *Wahrheit als Begegnung*, 84–5; *The Divine-Human Encounter*, 80.
[86] *Offenbarung und Vernunft*, 25; *Revelation and Reason*, 24.

1. God is not a passive object awaiting human discovery, but takes the initiative in and through revelation.
2. Although revelation entails the disclosure of information, its primary focus is the self-disclosure of a personal God. God is primarily disclosed through a person, not in a text.
3. This self-disclosure is focused on the historical event of the incarnation, in which grace and truth "happened" in Jesus Christ.
4. The primary function of God's self-disclosure is not to educate or inform humanity, but to call it into an encounter and relationship with its creator and redeemer.

Yet one theme must be noted in more detail: Brunner's increasing interest in mission and evangelism, which sets him at some distance from Barth. Theology as a didactic undertaking has its proper place within a "confessional community [*Gemeinde*]", in which the concern is not with "establishing a believing community" but with "strengthening faith and deepening knowledge".[87] But is a didactic approach "the best way of leading young people to faith"? Brunner argued that "the *missionary* proclamation of the apostles bears only a distant relationship to what takes place in our preaching".[88] The "false identification of doctrine and the Word of God" has impaired the church's tasks of mission and evangelization.

Brunner's growing conviction of the importance of mission and evangelism is evident, though not pronounced, in the Uppsala lectures. In 1949, he commented that he had increasingly "come to the view that the church nowadays speaks not chiefly to Christians, as it did in the Middle Ages and at the time of the Reformation and even a hundred years ago; it must speak primarily to 'heathen'".[89] This insight underlies Brunner's increasing realization of the importance of apologetics, which becomes more marked in his post-war works of theology.

America: The Call to Princeton Theological Seminary, 1937–1939

On 26 November 1934, Karl Barth was suspended from his position at the University of Bonn for refusing to swear allegiance to Adolf Hitler. Barth had moved to Bonn in 1930, before the rise of Nazism.[90] On 22 June 1935 Barth was dismissed. The University of Basle immediately offered him a chair in theology. He returned to Switzerland. His international profile was

---

[87] *Wahrheit als Begegnung*, 135; *The Divine-Human Encounter*, 128.
[88] *Wahrheit als Begegnung*, 134; *The Divine-Human Encounter*, 127.
[89] "Toward a Missionary Theology", 817.
[90] For this period in Barth's career, see J. F. Gerhard Goeters, "Karl Barth in Bonn, 1930–35." *Evangelische Theologie* 47 (1987): 137–50.

now such that he was regarded as the leading Swiss Reformed theologian. Brunner was now overshadowed in his homeland as a result of Barth's homecoming.

Was it because of this that Brunner was willing to consider a major new academic position, outside his native Switzerland? He was well known in America, and able to express himself well in English. Perhaps it was inevitable that some would have seen his ultimate destination as lying in the United States, far from the storm clouds beginning to envelop Europe in the late 1930s.

On 2 February 1937, John Alexander Mackay (1889–1983) was formally installed as the third president of Princeton Theological Seminary, New Jersey.[91] This leading American seminary had been through a major crisis as a result of the fundamentalist-modernist debates of the 1920s,[92] which led to a number of traditionalist Presbyterian faculty – most notably, John Gresham Machen (1881–1937) – leaving Princeton in protest against its "apostasy". Machen went on to found Westminster Theological Seminary in Philadelphia, aiming to establish a theologically orthodox Reformed seminary, along the lines of the Old Princeton School. Princeton was the leading seminary of the Presbyterian church in the United States, and was in urgent need of both a new sense of direction and an injection of morale.[93] The appointment of Mackay was seen as an important step in the process of restoring the reputation and morale of Princeton.[94]

In his inaugural address as president, significantly entitled "The Restoration of Theology",[95] Mackay called for a renewal of confidence in theology, aware that some in his audience regarded theology as ecclesially divisive. Without serious theological engagement and scholarship on their part, Mackay argued, the churches would be powerless against the "weak, undogmatic and invertebrate faith" that was becoming widespread within American Christianity. The Reformed theological tradition, he declared, was alive and well. While Princeton Theological Seminary had some golden memories from the past, it also had a great future ahead of it. The churches needed theologians – and Princeton would supply them.

Significantly, Mackay cited two theologians who seemed to him to exemplify the qualities that the situation demanded – Karl Barth and Emil

---

[91] For a biography, see John Mackay Metzger, *The Hand and the Road: The Life and Times of John A. Mackay*. Louisville, KY: Westminster John Knox Press, 2010.

[92] Bradley J. Longfield, *The Presbyterian Controversy: Fundamentalists, Modernists and Moderates*. New York: Oxford University Press, 1991, 162–80.

[93] For the best analysis of the situation at Princeton around the time of Mackay's appointment, see James H. Moorhead, *Princeton Seminary in American Religion and Culture*. Grand Rapids, MI: Eerdmans, 2012, 370–421.

[94] For a contemporary evaluation, see Henry Snyder Gehman, "John Alexander Mackay as President." *Princeton Seminary Bulletin* 52, no. 4 (1959): 3–14.

[95] John A. Mackay, "The Restoration of Theology." *Princeton Seminary Bulletin* 31 (1937): 7–18.

Brunner.[96] Mackay wasted no time in implementing his vision for the theological consolidation of Princeton. He met Brunner at the "Church, Community, and State" conference, held at Oxford during the period 12–25 July 1937, which was attended by 425 international delegates.[97]

This conference is now regarded as a landmark in the development of the ecumenical movement. It met at a time of growing international tension, amid anxieties about Nazi Germany and reports of the active persecution of Christianity in the Soviet Union. The final resolution of the conference on the role of the state echoed themes already found in the writings of Brunner, which he would develop further during the wartime period.

> We recognize that the state, as a specific form and the dominating expression of man's life in this world of sin, by its very power and its monopoly of the means of coercion, often becomes an instrument of evil. Since we believe in the holy God as the source of justice, we do not consider the state as the ultimate source of law but rather its guarantor. It is not the lord, but the servant of justice. There can be for the Christian no ultimate authority but very God.[98]

Yet despite this common position on the moral ambiguity of the state, the delegates at the conference were unable to agree on a common position concerning the practical Christian response to the challenge of war in the face of a rising tide of totalitarianism.

Brunner had been invited to make a major presentation on the Christian understanding of humanity by J. H. Oldham (1874–1969) and the organizing committee.[99] This decision was not welcomed by some American Christian leaders, particularly those linked with Union Theological Seminary in New York – such as Henry P. van Dusen, Roosevelt Professor of Systematic Theology at the seminary – who regarded the secular positions that Brunner critiqued as somewhat more attractive and interesting than those which he affirmed.[100]

Mackay and others, however, regarded Brunner rather more highly, seeing him as an orthodox Reformed theologian who had a track record of engaging with contemporary issues. Mackay's conversations with Brunner in Oxford convinced him that he had found someone who could play a leading role in the consolidation of Princeton as a centre of Reformed theology, and help with its institutional reconstruction.[101]

---

[96] For the reference to Brunner, see Mackay, "The Restoration of Theology," 15–16.
[97] For an account, see K. W. Clements, *Faith on the Frontier: A Life of J. H. Oldham*. Edinburgh: T&T Clark, 1999, 307–31.
[98] *The Churches Survey Their Task. The Report of the Conference at Oxford, July 1937, on Church, Community and State*. London: Allen & Unwin, 1937, 79.
[99] Clements, *Faith on the Frontier*, 315–20.
[100] It is worth noting that van Dusen and Brunner were both critics of the doctrine of the virgin birth of Christ.
[101] For the details, see Jehle, *Emil Brunner*, 355–80.

On 30 July 1937 Mackay wrote to Brunner, inviting him to consider coming to Princeton Theological Seminary as the Charles Hodge Professor of Systematic Theology. Brunner gave the possibility serious consideration, while noting its implications for his family life. Would his wife be agreeable to such a major move, which would mean leaving so much behind? What would his responsibilities be? And his salary? Mackay's answers to these questions appear to have proved satisfactory, including the salary offer of $6,000. Brunner indicated that he was interested in taking things further.

Princeton might have seemed an attractive option to Brunner, from the safe distance of Zurich. Yet not all at Princeton were sympathetic to the idea of him joining their faculty. Brunner's views on the theological authority of the Bible and the place of biblical criticism in theology were seen by some as provocative, especially given the recent history of the seminary. His denial of the virgin birth of Christ was viewed with suspicion. Perhaps it was unfortunate that Brunner's *Philosophy of Religion from the Standpoint of Protestant Theology* should have appeared in English in 1937.[102] As noted earlier (p. 36), this work was severely critical of Protestant Orthodoxy, especially any suggestion that the Bible could be identified with the "Word of God".

Many at Princeton regarded its Reformed theological identity as having been defined and safeguarded by Orthodox confessions of faith, particularly the Westminster Confession of Faith (1646). It was inevitable that news of Brunner's proposed appointment to such a senior and influential chair of theology would cause controversy. Furthermore, various gifts of capital and land had been made to the seminary on the condition that it should not depart from the teaching of the Westminster Confession. If such a condition were violated, the land and capital were to return to the donors or their successors.[103]

On 17 September, John E. Kuizenga (1876–1949), who had taken up the chair of apologetics and Christian ethics in 1930, wrote to Mackay, pointing out that the calling of Brunner raised certain awkward questions in the light of the seminary's commitment to the Westminster Confession. Kuizenga was not a lone voice on this issue. There was growing pressure for a deferral of Brunner's election until certain matters had been clarified, including his understanding of the relation between the Bible and the Westminster Confession. On 14 October, Mackay wrote to Brunner, explaining that some complications had arisen. Brunner's reply of 23 October clearly indicated some irritation at these developments.[104]

In the meantime, Mackay garnered support for his proposal, eventually winning over doubters and dissenters. On 21 December he wrote to Brunner,

---

[102] The American edition was published by Charles Scribner's Sons in New York.
[103] See William K. Selden, *Princeton Theological Seminary: A Narrative History, 1812–1992*. Princeton, NJ: Princeton University Press, 1992, 39, 57–65.
[104] Jehle, *Emil Brunner*, 360–1.

formally inviting him to become the Charles Hodge Professor of Systematic Theology. By then, however, Brunner's initial enthusiasm about going to Princeton on a permanent basis had faded. On 11 January 1938 he wrote to Mackay, proposing an alternative arrangement: he would come to Princeton for a year, to see how things worked out. This was not what Mackay had wanted; it was, however, what he got. Despite some criticism of the appointment in the American religious press, Brunner arrived at Princeton with his wife as "visiting professor" on 25 September 1938.

After an encouraging start, things began to go wrong. His wife returned to Switzerland towards the end of 1938, leaving Brunner on his own to face opposition from conservative students who were critical of his views on the Bible. One of the most dramatic confrontations took place when Carl McIntyre (1906–2002), a former student of Princeton who had migrated to Westminster Theological Seminary, and subsequently founded his own fundamentalist Bible Presbyterian Church in 1937, attended one of Brunner's lectures, and challenged him publicly over his theological positions, especially on the nature of the Bible.[105] It became increasingly clear to Brunner that his presence at Princeton was compromising its standing within the conservative American Presbyterian constituency.

Brunner increasingly felt intellectually isolated and personally lonely. On 7 January 1939 he wrote to his wife complaining that he had nobody to talk to. He was tempted to return to Zurich. However, the political situation in Europe was changing rapidly. On 12 March 1938, Austria had been annexed by Hitler's Third Reich, in effect becoming a province of Germany. This annexation (often referred to using the German term *Anschluss*) was confirmed retrospectively by a plebiscite a few months later.[106] Would the same thing happen to Switzerland?[107] It was no idle question. Hitler's expansionist policies were partly based on the motif of the unification of the German peoples – a significant number of whom lived in the German-speaking parts of Switzerland.[108] And as the Wehrmacht's archives were opened up after the end of the Second World War, it became clear that detailed plans – known as "Fall Schweiz" – had been laid for a German invasion of Switzerland.

In late January 1939, Brunner set out his decision: he would return home to Zurich at the end of the academic year – unless, of course, Nazi Germany annexed Switzerland. While he would be pleased to come to Princeton regularly each year for a few weeks of teaching, he would not accept a formal

---

[105] Jehle, *Emil Brunner*, 369–70.
[106] See Otmar Jung, *Plebiszit und Diktatur: Die Volksabstimmungen der Nationalsozialisten*. Tübingen: Mohr, 1995.
[107] For the political issue, see Rolf Zaugg-Prato, *Die Schweiz im Kampf gegen den Anschluss Österreichs an das Deutsche Reich, 1918–1938*. Bern: Peter Lang, 1982.
[108] For the issues, see Hans Rudolf Kurz, *Operationsplanung Schweiz: Die Rolle der Schweizer Armee in Zwei Weltkriegen*. Thun: Ott, 1974; Stephen P. Halbrook, *Target Switzerland: Swiss Armed Neutrality in World War II*. Cambridge, MA: Da Capo Press, 2003, 45–64.

invitation to a permanent position at the seminary.[109] This relatively clear decision was made more complex by an unexpected development. Princeton University began an exploratory conversation to see if he was open to accepting a special chair that would be created for him. This, Brunner realized, would extricate him from the confessionally complex situation that had developed at the seminary, and would also offer him a larger salary (the figure mooted was rumoured to be $10,000). Yet nothing came of this development.[110] On 22 April 1939, Brunner sailed from New York to Cannes. After spending some days in southern France with his wife, he returned to Zurich on 6 May.

Brunner's account of his decision to return to Switzerland in his "Intellectual Autobiography" offers a slightly different perspective on this matter.

> Shortly before the outbreak of World War II, I was on the verge of emigrating to the United States to accept the tempting offer of a combined professorship at the university and the theological seminary at Princeton. But my love and responsibility for our homeland and for our church made it impossible to leave at a time when my country was so threatened.[111]

There is, however, no doubt that Brunner felt uneasy about being a Swiss voice in theology who was dislocated from his own cultural, historical, and ecclesial situation. His interest in – and contribution to – English-language Protestant theology from the 1930s to the early 1960s was considerable, exceeding that of any other European theologian. Yet this contribution ultimately reflected Brunner's grounding in his Swiss context. It is open to question whether he would have developed his work – especially his ecumenical concerns – with the same success if he had relocated to Princeton.

Yet it is entirely reasonable to suggest that, had Brunner settled in Princeton, his impact on English-language theology would have been far greater than it in fact was. The only other major Protestant theologian in North America at the time was Paul Tillich, also an émigré from Europe, who had yet to achieve the fame that would come his way after the Second World War. Reinhold Niebuhr, who came to be seen as the leading North American representative of "neo-Orthodoxy", secured attention primarily on account of his social ethics, and only secondarily on account of his theology.[112] Brunner would have dominated North American Protestant

---

[109] Jehle, *Emil Brunner*, 374.
[110] Harvard University later created such a chair for Paul Tillich, who had previously taught at Union Theological Seminary. As a result of Brunner's refusal, Princeton University later approached the Scottish theologian Thomas F. Torrance – who had spent the academic year 1938–9 lecturing at Auburn Theological Seminary – to see if he would be interested in the position.
[111] "Intellectual Autobiography", 20.
[112] Daniel F. Rice, *Reinhold Niebuhr and His Circle of Influence*. Cambridge: Cambridge University Press, 2012.

theology, and secured a public and ecclesial profile that could well have impacted significantly on the post-war North American reception of the writings of Karl Barth. History cannot be rewritten; however, it is entirely reasonable to point out that Brunner achieved a significant impact on the post-war American theological renaissance from his base in faraway Switzerland. Had he been a resident presence and voice in the United States, embedded within such a significant institution as Princeton and able to lecture widely at other leading American and Canadian theological institutions, his impact could only have been greater.

In the event, the outbreak of the Second World War in Europe in September 1939 put an end to any thought or possibility of relocation. Brunner remained in Switzerland. He would play a leading role in formulating the responses of Swiss Protestant churches to the wartime situation, and in their subsequent renewal.

Part II

Consolidation: Brunner's Vision for Post-War Theological Reconstruction

7
Brunner's Vision for the Christian Community: The Church, State, and Culture

By the time the Second World War broke out in Europe, Brunner had clarified both his own theological position and agenda, and his cultural and social location. He would remain in Switzerland, helping his nation and church cope with the trauma of the Second World War, and the process of theological reconstruction which followed its ending.[1] The main phase of his theological development was essentially complete with the publication of *Truth as Encounter*. What lay ahead was the implementation of his theological vision, especially in relation to the church and state.

One of Brunner's main concerns in the late 1930s was the rise of the totalitarian state. As Stalinism gained ascendancy in the Soviet Union and Nazism in Germany, Brunner came to the conclusion that the totalitarian state represented the "greatest threat to humanity today". This development, he came to realize, rested on a false understanding of human nature and identity.

> Totalitarianism is something much more momentous than any form of government. It is the "state-izing" of the whole of human existence, the lordship of the state over man, body and soul, whatever its governmental form. The totalitarian state is essentially irreconcilable to the nature of man as understood from the Christian point of view.[2]

The rise of Hitler, Brunner argued, showed that western civilization ultimately depended on certain core beliefs and values, which had to be

---
[1] Frank Jehle, *Emil Brunner: Theologe im 20. Jahrhundert*. Zurich: Theologischer Verlag, 2006, 381–406.
[2] "Toward a Missionary Theology", 817.

Emil Brunner: A Reappraisal, First Edition. Alister E. McGrath.
© 2014 John Wiley & Sons, Ltd. Published 2016 by John Wiley & Sons, Ltd.

articulated and defended in the face of ideological and political threats. During the 1940s and early 1950s, Brunner set himself the agenda of laying the theological foundations for a recovery of Christian civilization from the threats posed by the totalitarian state. This agenda extended beyond the realm of politics, embracing the relation between church and state, the place of natural law, and the foundations of ethics. In this chapter I shall consider Brunner's theologically grounded vision for church and society, and explore some of its themes.

The Ideological Origins of Totalitarianism

In 1933 the Nazis seized power in Germany, and promptly set about using the law to impose totalitarian rule. Laws established for an essentially democratic purpose were subverted to other ends.[3] The traditional Protestant idea that law was somehow grounded in the objective realities of the world or in social consensus proved utterly incapable of responding to the arbitrary enforcement of power by the Third Reich.[4] What could be done? What intellectual opposition could be offered to these developments?

Brunner began to give these issues serious attention in an article of 1933, as the gravity of the changing political situation in Germany became clear.[5] Political absolutism (*Staatsabsolutismus*) posed a clear threat to the identity and mission of the church. At this early stage, Brunner suggested three ways in which the church could protest against such absolutism, as a way of acknowledging the ultimate authority of Christ as Lord.

1   It was necessary to insist on the provisional, not the absolute, authority of the state. "Unconditional authority and obedience belongs to God alone, and is not delegated to any individuals or human institution."[6]
2   The church needs to ensure that the state is aware that it is not the only authority in the sphere of secular existence. Underlying the state is a *Rechtsordnung* – a legal framework, which gives legitimacy to the authority of the state.
3   The rights of an individual must never be eclipsed by the needs of the state.

In the event, Brunner's most significant contribution to the critique of totalitarianism lies in the second of these lines of argument, as will become clear later in this chapter.

[3]   Peter L. Lindseth, "The Paradox of Parliamentary Supremacy: Delegation, Democracy, and Dictatorship in Germany and France, 1920s–1950s." *Yale Law Journal* 113 (2004): 1341–1417.
[4]   Ernst Wolf, "Zum protestantischen Rechtsdenken." In *Peregrinatio II: Studien zur reformatorischen Theologie, zum Kirchenrecht, und zur Sozialethik*, 191–206. Munich: Kaiser Verlag, 1965.
[5]   "Der Staat als Problem der Kirche": *Ein offenes Wort*, vol. 1, 289–307.
[6]   "Der Staat als Problem der Kirche": *Ein offenes Wort*, vol. 1, 293.

Brunner reiterated this point in 1938, before leaving for the United States. While addressing the situation in Switzerland, he clearly had developments further north in mind.

> Since the state derives its authority from God, it is not sovereign . . . The state cannot say or do anything that it likes, but is bound by the divine will. That applies above all in the case of justice. Let there be no talk about justice being what the state defines as justice! What the unrighteous, godless state defines as justice is therefore not justice, but merely injustice that is defined and enforced by the state.[7]

Some argued for the need for Christians to take up arms against totalitarianism. Brunner resisted any such notion, holding that this confused the role of Christians as citizens, and as believers.[8] Where others in the late 1930s sought to counter totalitarianism through a reassertion of fundamental democratic values, Brunner argued that the most effective way of challenging it was to understand its origins as a prelude to depriving it of its intellectual oxygen. He traced the origins of totalitarianism to the Enlightenment. "The totalitarian State is nothing other than unrestricted legal positivism in political practice, the abrogation in actual fact of the classical and Christian idea of a divine 'law of nature'."[9] For Brunner, justice is not something constructed by humanity, but something discerned, corresponding to a deeper order of things. He therefore mounted a critique of forms of naturalism which regarded justice as a mere social invention. If there is no deeper moral reality, then we are free to invent whatever moral values we please – such as those of totalitarian states.[10] Yet if there is some deeper moral order, we are under an obligation to reflect in it political and social life.

Brunner's argument here shows an implicit knowledge of the intellectual roots of Fascism in 1920s Europe. The Italian dictator Benito Mussolini (1883–1945) argued that the rise of moral and legal relativism in the 1920s prevented anyone from rebutting falsehoods by asserting their untruth. Since "all ideologies are of equal value", in that they are "mere fictions", the modern relativist concludes that "everyone can create their own ideology, and attempt to enforce it with all the energy of which they are capable".[11] Like Niccolò Machiavelli in the sixteenth century, Mussolini noted that power to enforce a notion of truth or justice would ultimately triumph –

---

[7] *Die reformierte Staatsauffassung*, 17.
[8] See the typescript "Zur Besinnung Karl Barths Aufruf": cited Jehle, *Emil Brunner*, 390–1.
[9] *Gerechtigkeit*, 7; *Justice and the Social Order*, 15. I have translated the German "Gerechtigkeit" as "justice" throughout this chapter; at points, the cognate term "righteousness" conveys Brunner's intentions slightly better.
[10] For the critical role of an authoritarian state in early Fascism, see Giovanni Gentile, "The Philosophic Basis of Fascism." *Foreign Affairs* 6, no. 2 (1928): 290–304.
[11] Benito Mussolini, *Diuturna, 1914–1922: Scritti polemici*. Milan: Casa editrice Imperia, 1924, 376–8. I have translated the Italian term *mentalità* as "ideology"; it could also be translated as "mentality" or "intellectual outlook".

especially if there was no eternally valid notion of truth or justice on the basis of which to challenge such a development. Mussolini thus drew the conclusion that his Fascist ideology would triumph in Italy, partly because the cultural outlook of the age would erode any attempt to criticize it,[12] and partly because he reckoned he could create the political momentum necessary to impose it.

The anti-religious moral relativism of the culture of the Weimar era, which arose partly in reaction against the Great War (see pp. 63–4), must also be regarded as having played a significant role in eroding any serious intellectual resistance to Nazism. While many academics were angered and distressed by the Nazification of the German educational system at every level in the 1930s, the foundations of this development were laid in the 1920s, especially through critiques of traditional moral values and their theological underpinnings.[13] "The Weimar period has entered history as the age in which all the major questions were posed and none was solved."[14] One of the more interesting paradoxes of the rise of Nazism is that intellectuals who fled Germany during the 1930s often ended up in *émigré* communities which perpetuated the cultural norms of the Weimar period, which contributed so significantly to the triumph of Hitler in the 1930s.[15]

Having deconstructed traditional moral values and ways of thinking, Weimar culture found it had little to put in their place. Some welcomed this as a period of immense artistic creativity and intellectual freedom; others viewed it with deep foreboding, a harbinger of chaos and loss of cultural identity and stability. The poet Hermann Hesse wrote of the "longing [*Sehnsucht*] of our time for a worldview" within German culture.[16] That cultural vacuum would be filled by Nazism, not simply as a political philosophy, but as a metanarrative of German identity.[17]

Brunner's analysis of the emergence of this relativistic cultural mood in the inter-war period tends to focus on its deeper background, rather than

---

[12] See further Zeev Sternhell, "Fascism: Reflections on the Fate of Ideas in Twentieth Century History." *Journal of Political Ideologies* 5, no. 2 (2000): 149–62.

[13] For important studies of Weimar culture, see Peter Gay, *Weimar Culture: The Outsider as Insider*. New York: W. W. Norton, 2001; Heinrich August Winkler, *Germany: The Long Road West*. 2 vols. Oxford: Oxford University Press, 2006, vol. 1, 3–107.

[14] Walter Laqueur, "Berlin, Brecht, Bauhaus, and a Whole Generation of Isherwoods." *New York Times*, 24 November 1968.

[15] See the brilliant study of Ehrhard Bahr, *Weimar on the Pacific: German Exile Culture in Los Angeles and the Crisis of Modernism*. Berkeley, CA: University of California Press, 2007.

[16] Hermann Hesse, "Die Sehnsucht unser Zeit nach einer Weltanschauung." *Uhu* 2 (1926): 3–14. *Uhu* was one of Germany's most popular illustrated magazines during the period 1924–33, advocating a modernist vision of life and thought. Its publisher, Hermann Ullstein, insisted it was a *Magazin*, not a *Zeitschrift*. See further Paul Knoll, "Die Anzeiger-organization des Ullstein Verlages." In *Der Verlag Ullstein zum Welt Reklame Kongress Berlin 1929*. Berlin: Ullstein, 1929, 124–5.

[17] For the lingering influence of this metanarrative, see Siobhan Kattago, *Ambiguous Memory: The Nazi Past and German National Identity*. Westport, CT: Praeger, 2001, especially 11–34.

more recent developments, especially in the Weimar period. His concern was to locate its intellectual roots in the Enlightenment, not engage its more recent cultural manifestations in Germany. Brunner wished to identify the roots of the trend – and sever them. He saw the solution as lying in the Christian idea of the "law of nature" – an "eternal, supernatural [*überirdischen*] and absolutely valid justice [*Gerechtigkeit*]".[18] This came to be undermined during the Age of Reason, robbing Germany of the resources it need to challenge National Socialism. Brunner argued that a number of stages can be identified within this overall development.

1 An "objective, superhuman standard of justice" was reduced to the essentially subjective perception of individuals.
2 All concepts of justice were declared to be historically located, and thus lacking permanent validity. Brunner regarded this development as taking place during the nineteenth century, which proclaimed "the relativity of all views of justice". As a result, the idea of some "eternal standard of justice" was generally abandoned. Justice was what dominant power groups believed or wished it to be.

Brunner's historical analysis is somewhat sketchy and impressionistic, and lacks scholarly character.[19] However, the general themes he identifies can be seen in the emergence of modern attitudes towards the power of the state,[20] and deserve to be given due weight.

So what is Brunner's solution to this development? Brunner did not need to invent a new answer to the rise of totalitarianism; he had already laid the foundations for this in his writings of the early 1930s. In what follows, I shall consider his analysis.

An Antidote to Totalitarianism: The Renewal of Natural Law

The notion of "natural law" has played a central role in western thinking since classical times. The Sophists regarded nature (*physis*) as embodying the ultimate basis of morality, which was to be contrasted with purely human convention (*homologia* or *symbola*). Aristotle also argued for a deeper order of nature as the basis of human morality and law.[21]

---

[18] *Gerechtigkeit*, 6; *Justice and the Social Order*, 15.
[19] His analysis is actually somewhat simplistic, mainly because it ignores sociological factors. See, for example, the material gathered in H. M. Scott and Brendan Simms, eds., *Cultures of Power in Europe during the Long Eighteenth Century*. Cambridge: Cambridge University Press, 2007.
[20] See, for example, Raimondo Cubeddu, *The Philosophy of the Austrian School*. London: Routledge, 1993, 107–55.
[21] Fred D. Miller, *Nature, Justice and Rights in Aristotle's Politics*. Oxford: Clarendon Press, 1995, 27–66.

The idea can also be found, expressed in carefully nuanced ways, in the Old Testament. The notion of "conformity to a norm" lay behind at least some of Israel's reflections on the nature of righteousness (*sdq*).[22] The world is understood to be ordered in a certain way as a result of its divine creation; to act "rightly" is thus to act in accordance with this divine patterning of structures and events. The "ordering of the world", established by God in creation, acts as a theological bridge between natural righteousness and the "righteousness of the law".[23]

The basic idea of natural law remained important at the time of the Reformation. Despite their misgivings about many aspects of mediaeval theology, most mainline Protestant reformers held that human morality was ultimately grounded in the divinely ordained structures of reality, including the operations of the human mind. John Calvin held that, despite sin, the human conscience was still able to discern the fundamental structures of natural law.[24] "The law of God", he wrote, "is nothing else than that natural law and that conscience which God has engraved within the human mind."[25]

Brunner frequently emphasized that his theological programme was both biblical and grounded in the theology of the Reformation. It is therefore to be expected that at least some of the classical themes of natural law would be found in his writings. As we shall see, this is indeed the case. It is important to appreciate that Brunner's argument for a return to natural law would have been seen as somewhat anomalous by many. In the first place, there was growing scepticism within both European and American intellectual circles over the viability of the notion of natural law. For example, Oliver Wendell Holmes argued that the real issue was to understand how the courts administered law; there was nothing to be gained from philosophical or metaphysical speculation of any kind. Law was simply about "the prediction of what the courts will do". His 1918 essay "Natural Law" argued that those jurists who "believe in natural law" existed in a rather "naïve state of mind that accepts what has been familiar and accepted

---

[22] See, for example, Otto Kaiser, "Dike und Sedaqa. Zur Frage nach der sittlichen Weltordnung. Ein theologische Präludium." *Neue Zeitschrift für systematische Theologie und Religionsphilosophie* 7 (1965): 251–75; Heinrich H. Schmid, *Gerechtigkeit als Weltordnung: Hintergrund und Geschichle des alttestamentlichen Gerechtigkeitsbegriffs*. Tübingen: Mohr, 1968.

[23] An important issue explored in David Novak, *Natural Law in Judaism*. Cambridge: Cambridge University Press, 1998.

[24] See further Irena Backus, "Calvin's Concept of Natural and Roman Law." *Calvin Theological Journal* 38 (2003): 7–26.

[25] Calvin, *Institutio Religionis Christianae*, IV.xx.16. For detailed discussion of this important affirmation of natural law, discerned through the conscience rather than through the reason, see Susan E. Schreiner, "Calvin's Use of Natural Law." In *A Preserving Grace: Protestants, Catholics, and Natural Law*, ed. Michael Cromartie, 51–76. Grand Rapids, MI: Eerdmans, 1997. Older studies remain valuable: see, for example, Gunter Gloede, *Theologia naturalis bei Calvin*. Stuttgart: Kohlhammer, 1935, 103–34; Jürgen Baur, *Gott, Recht und weltliches Regiment im Werke Calvins*. Bonn: Bouvier, 1965, 46–9.

by them and their neighbors as something that must be accepted by all men everywhere".[26]

In the second place, Karl Barth's theological programme of the 1930s regarded any attempt to establish either a knowledge of God or a vision of goodness on the basis of nature as contrary to a properly Reformed understanding of divine revelation. I have already considered his severe and substantial criticisms of natural theology; much the same line of critique could be – and was – directed against the notion of natural law.[27] For Barth, an understanding of Christian morality must be grounded on God's self-revelation in Christ, not on the basis of an appeal to nature.

Yet the rise of Nazism in Germany in the 1930s convinced many within and beyond the Reformed tradition that there was a need for a ground of moral judgement that lay beyond arbitrary human convention and declaration. In 1936, the German Catholic lawyer Heinrich Rommen (1897–1967) published a pamphlet entitled *Die ewige Wiederkehr des Naturrechts* ("The Eternal Return of Natural Law").[28] Rommen pointed out that the Nazis proved able to use the German legal and judicial systems to pursue and impose their own political agendas. Germany's legal professionals, Rommen argued, were so used to thinking about law in purely positivist terms that they were left intellectually defenceless in the face of the imposition of an alien notion of justice by force. The only way of countering this was to appeal to a higher authority than the Nazi state – namely, a divinely ordained moral order,[29] which existed independent of human judgement and arbitration.

Brunner made a similar point in 1943. The rise of the totalitarian state, he argued, made it imperative that the false turn taken at the time of the Enlightenment should be corrected. Brunner states the alternatives in a starkly dichotomist manner, clearly believing that the urgency of the situation and the importance of the issues permitted a certain rhetorical overstatement of the principles:

> Either there exists a valid criterion [*ein Gültiges*], a justice which is presented to us, not by us, a standard which is binding on every state, every "law" and legitimate rule of justice – or there is no justice, but only power, organized in some way or other, which presents itself as law. . . . Either there is a sacred law, to which one can appeal against every inhuman and unjust social order, against any arbitrariness or cruelty on the part of the state, or that sacred law

---

[26] Oliver Wendell Holmes, *Collected Legal Papers*. New York: Harcourt, Brace, and Howe, 1920, 312.
[27] Stephen John Grabill, *Rediscovering the Natural Law in Reformed Theological Ethics*. Grand Rapids, MO: Eerdmans, 2006, 21–38; David VanDrunen, *Natural Law and the Two Kingdoms: A Study in the Development of Reformed Social Thought*. Grand Rapids, MI: Eerdmans, 2010, 333–47.
[28] Heinrich Rommen, *Die ewige Wiederkehr des Naturrechts*. Leipzig: Hegner, 1936.
[29] Rommen, *Die ewige Wiederkehr des Naturrechts*, 32–4.

is nothing but a dream, and law is nothing but another name for the arbitrary outcomes of the actualization of power in the political domain of force.[30]

In the absence of such a transcendent foundation for positive law, Brunner argues that moral and legal decisions are ultimately reduced to matters of taste or prejudice. We cannot say "this is wrong", but only "this is not convenient for me", or "I don't like this".[31]

Brunner had already laid out the foundations of a Christian doctrine of natural law in his debate with Karl Barth over natural theology in 1934 (pp. 113–27). The basic principles were already in place, and indeed had already been deployed in Brunner's subsequent discussion of the foundations of Christian ethics. In what can reasonably be seen as an "eristic" strategy, Brunner mounted a critique of moral relativism, which bears remarkable parallels to that set out around the same time in Great Britain by C. S. Lewis (1898–1963), followed by a demonstration that the Christian tradition is able to offer a viable and defensible concept of justice which is not contingent on arbitrary human conventions or enforcement by the state.[32] For Brunner, the political situation in Nazi Germany and the Soviet Union during the late 1930s rested on the proclamation of the "will of the ruling power as the sole ground of appeal in matters of law".[33]

Brunner's general theological position, as this developed in the late 1920s and early 1930s, was intellectually hospitable to a notion of natural law. His subversion of the autonomy of secular ethics was counterbalanced by his affirmation of the "orders of creation" – an essentially Lutheran theological conception that was easily harmonized with the traditional notion of natural law,[34] which Brunner developed in his own style. Brunner does not endorse the Thomist notion of *lex aeternae*, arguing that positive laws belong to the transient created order. His point is rather than God is the ultimate God of human law, and that human notions of justice must reflect the nature and will of God.

Yet at one point Brunner departs radically from some traditional presentations of natural law. Classical accounts of natural law, including their reformulations during the period of the Enlightenment, placed considerable

---

[30] *Gerechtigkeit*, 8; *Justice and the Social Order*, 16.
[31] *Gerechtigkeit*, 9; *Justice and the Social Order*, 17.
[32] The best study remains Ivar H. Pöhl, *Das Problem des Naturrechtes bei Emil Brunner*. Zurich: Zwingli Verlag, 1963. For Lewis's approach, see Gilbert Meilander, *The Taste for the Other: The Social and Ethical Thought of C. S. Lewis*. Grand Rapids, MI: Eerdmans, 1998, 182–234.
[33] *Gerechtigkeit*, 6–7; *Justice and the Social Order*, 15.
[34] Pöhl, *Das Problem des Naturrechtes bei Emil Brunner*, 33–43. On the Lutheran position, see the analysis of Mark Mattes, "The Thomistic Turn in Evangelical Catholic Ethics." *Lutheran Quarterly* 16 (2002): 65–100. For the earlier discussion within Lutheranism as to whether Martin Luther or Philip Melanchthon initiated the use of the concept of *lex naturae*, see Lauri Haikola, *Studien zu Luther und zum Luthertum*. Uppsala: Lundequistska Bokhandeln, 1958; Gerhard O. Forde, *The Law-Gospel Debate: An Interpretation of Its Historical Development*. Minneapolis: Augsburg Publishing House, 1969.

emphasis upon the notion of conscience.[35] Natural law manifests itself in the human conscience. Brunner departs from this tradition. "Conscience is not, as the theology of the Enlightenment and popular natural theology have held, the voice of God. Nor is it an awareness of the moral law." It is a "flaming sword", which "drives us away from the presence of God".[36]

If the human conscience hears any voice, it is not the voice of God, but the voice of a society or culture. Conscience (*das Gewissen*), Brunner declares, "has nothing to do with God at all".[37] In his later writings, Brunner intensified his critique of a moral appeal to the conscience, arguing that it was vulnerable to a psychological or sociological explanation as "the product of mere social convention".[38] A Christian context might well give rise to a "Christian" conscience; radical social engineering, however, could easily manipulate this to create alternative moral defaults.

This does not mean that Brunner secularizes either theology or ethics. Rather, his concern is to ensure that humanity does not become entrapped in a socially constructed matrix of ideas and values – what we might now call a "social imaginary"[39] – which it erroneously assumes to have divine authority, or at least the potential for divine signification. For Brunner, the primary source of our knowledge of God is divine revelation,[40] not internalized social conventions and attitudes. He thus offers the possibility of theological reconstruction for those whose "social imaginaries" have been moulded by extended periods of totalitarianism – as in Nazi Germany, or the Soviet Union. By offering a theological framework which challenges the self-evidential authority of such moral intuitions, Brunner provides an escape route from an institutionalized totalitarian mindset.

So what positive vision of personal and social morality does the Christian faith commend and defend? Brunner is properly cautious at this point, noting that the New Testament does not set out a positive legal code. The concept of "secular justice" is essentially "incidental to the gospel".[41] While the theme of the "righteousness of God" is closely linked with such major theological concerns as the doctrine of atonement, it is only "indirectly connected" to issues of social justice, in that it is not articulated primarily in terms of social conventions and values.

---

[35] For example, see Timothy Hochstrasser, "Conscience and Reason: The Natural Law Theory of Jean Barbeyrac." *Historical Journal* 36, no. 2 (1993): 381–400; Ian Harris, *The Mind of John Locke: A Study of Political Theory in Its Intellectual Setting*. Cambridge: Cambridge University Press, 1994, 302–3. More generally, see Knud Haakonssen, *Natural Law and Moral Philosophy: From Grotius to the Scottish Enlightenment*. Cambridge: Cambridge University Press, 1996.
[36] *Das Gebot und die Ordnungen*, 140–1; *The Divine Imperative*, 156–7.
[37] *Das Gebot und die Ordnungen*, 140; *The Divine Imperative*, 156.
[38] *Dogmatik III*, 290; *Dogmatics 3*, 255.
[39] For the sense of this term, see Charles Taylor, "Modern Social Imaginaries." *Public Culture* 14 (2002): 91–123.
[40] See the discussion in Pöhl, *Das Problem des Naturrechtes bei Emil Brunner*, 88–127.
[41] *Gerechtigkeit*, 10; *Justice and the Social Order*, 18.

Nevertheless, Brunner argues that careful reflection on the fundamental themes of the Christian faith can lead to a moral vision which can serve as the basis of a restoration of Christian civilization after the catastrophe of the Second World War. In what follows, I shall outline some of the major themes he develops.

The Need for Theological Reconstruction: *Revelation and Reason* (1941)

Every theologian operates within a historical context, which impacts upon both the questions to be addressed and the answers to be given. Brunner's writings of the 1940s clearly presuppose a crisis, which has unsettled and destabilized the Christian churches in Europe and beyond. A process of rethinking and renewal is required, in order to begin the reconstruction of both churches and theology in a period of uncertainty.

Yet it was not merely the rise of Nazism and the outbreak of war in Europe that signalled the need for theological reconstruction. Despite the restrictions imposed by wartime conditions, the German Gesellschaft für evangelische Theologie (Society for Protestant Theology) was still able to meet. The society was founded in 1940, mainly to encourage dialogue between academic theology and church ministry, particularly in the light of the challenges posed by the National Socialist state ideology. Rudolf Bultmann delivered a lecture entitled "The New Testament and Mythology", initially at its regional conference at Frankfurt am Main on 21 April 1941, and subsequently at the society's national conference at Alpirsbach on 4 June.[42] Bultmann gave his Alpirsbach lecture at 9 a.m. The discussion it provoked lasted for the remainder of the day.

Rumours of the lecture and its impact reached Brunner in Zurich, and contributed to his sense of crisis. Bultmann had been a somewhat peripheral member of the "Dialectical Theology" movement in the 1920s,[43] and it is easy to imagine how Brunner must have felt a sense of loss, perhaps even betrayal, at the radical direction in which Bultmann's thought was now developing.[44] It was clear that a reaffirmation of the foundations of theology

---

[42] For details, see Konrad Hammann, *Rudolf Bultmann: Eine Biographie*. 3rd edn. Tübingen: Mohr Siebeck, 2012, 307–16. Bultmann actually gave two addresses at Alpirsbach. The second, on "Theology as a Science", was somewhat overshadowed by the reaction to the first. See Klaus W. Müller, "Zu Rudolf Bultmanns Alpirsbacher Vortrag über 'Theologie als Wissenschaft'." *Zeitschrift für Theologie und Kirche* 81 (1984): 470–1.

[43] Hammann, *Rudolf Bultmann*, 134–47.

[44] Brunner's discussion of "myth" in *Offenbarung und Vernunft* does not refer specifically to Bultmann's lecture: *Offenbarung und Vernunft*, 392–408; *Revelation and Reason*, 396–412. Bultmann tends to be referenced primarily in relation to issues concerning biblical criticism. Bultmann and Brunner both tend to use the term "mythical" to mean "non-historical": for the richer connotations of the term, see Alister E. McGrath, "A Gleam of Divine Truth: The Concept of Myth in Lewis's Thought." In *The Intellectual World of C. S. Lewis*, 55–82. Oxford: Wiley-Blackwell, 2013.

was required. In the end, Brunner did not deal with the theme of "demythologization" at this time, returning to it at a later point.[45]

Brunner's reassertion of the intellectual legitimacy of both the Christian faith and the theological enterprise was set out in *Revelation and Reason*. A working draft was complete by the end of July 1941. He sent a copy to Max Huber, asking for his comments, noting that the typescript was "nearly ready".[46] Huber was delighted with the quality of the writing, and the manner of its engagement with fundamental questions. Yet it seems that the bottom had fallen out of the market for a book which raised such basic theological issues. It sold poorly in Switzerland, and hardly at all in Germany – not surprisingly, given the wartime situation, which had drastic consequences for international trading.[47]

Nevertheless, *Revelation and Reason* remains an important work, setting out Brunner's case for a robust theology that is not dependent on human reason, yet is able to engage human reason effectively on its own terms.[48] It is, in effect, a prolegomenon to dogmatics, clearing the ground for an exposition of the fundamental themes of the Christian faith.[49] Where Brunner's earlier engagements with the question of faith and reason tend to be polemical in tone, *Revelation and Reason* is constructive, laying the foundations for an approach to theology which was capable of responding to the intellectual challenges thrown up by the turmoil of the 1930s.

The opening of the work captures the intellectual mood of the age, and defines a key question that theology must engage. "In the midst of a world whose only axiom is the relativity of all knowledge of truth", the Christian community takes its stand on the truth that it has received. Its task is to reflect on this revelation, and express its truth in human language. "Divine revelation alone is the foundation, criterion, and content of its message."[50] The church must take its stand against the moral and epistemological relativism of western European culture – and Brunner clearly has the culture of Weimar Germany in mind. The fundamental task of theology is thus dogmatic – to allow the church to grasp what it believes, the reasons for believing it, and to express this in appropriate terms.

Yet Brunner once more insists that there is a second task of theology. Where once he used the term "eristics" to refer to this task (see pp. 66–74),

---

[45] His best engagement with it is found in the section of the second volume of his *Dogmatics*: see *Dogmatik II*, 283–8; *Dogmatics 2*, 263–70.

[46] Jehle, *Emil Brunner*, 423–4. For comment on the relation of faith and reason, see Horst Beintker, "Verstehen und Glauben: Grundlinien einer evangelischen Fundamentaltheologie." *Kerygma und Dogma* 22 (1976): 22–40.

[47] Jehle, *Emil Brunner*, 431.

[48] See the assessments in Lorenz Volken, *Der Glaube bei Emil Brunner*. Freiburg: Paulusverlag, 1947; Pietro Braido, *La ragione verso la fede nella teologia di Emilio Brunner*. Turin: Società Editrice Internazionale, 1950.

[49] The 1961 second edition of the work in effect positions it as laying the foundations for the three volumes of Brunner's dogmatics, which were published after the first edition of the work (1946, 1950, 1960). See Jehle, *Emil Brunner*, 431.

[50] *Offenbarung und Vernunft*, 3; *Revelation and Reason*, 3.

he now conceptualizes it primarily in terms of the "apologetic" task of theology.

> Christian theology is under an obligation to the world to demonstrate that we do not believe in revelation because we ignore its objections, but because we are aware of them and have engaged with them seriously.[51]

This, Brunner concedes, is a potentially dangerous undertaking, which runs the risk of "accommodating the truth of revelation to the truth of human reason". He hints that this concern is not unjustified, if the track record of the early church's "Apologists" is considered.[52] Brunner further concedes that there is little sign of any interest in apologetics on the part of the reformers of the sixteenth century. Yet these considerations, he argues, are not of decisive importance. The situation faced by the churches demands the reinstatement of a theologically rooted apologetics.

In developing this argument, Brunner notes that "apologetics" was not restricted to the relatively small group of second-century writers known as the "Apologists." It was implicitly assumed to be part of the task of theology, and an integral element of the ministry of the churches. Augustine of Hippo and Athanasius of Alexandria both saw "theological engagement with the unbelieving and pagan world as a necessary function of the church".[53] And the reformers of the sixteenth century challenged what they saw as the threat of their age – the threat of a semi-pagan humanism, the errors of radical Anabaptism, and the Papacy. But times had changed. "If atheism, or a pagan humanism, had been dominant at that time, the reformers would have fought these."

The cultural situation of the day, Brunner declares, requires that theology should respond appropriately to its challenges. It must combat error and ignorance within the community of faith, and engage and challenge the unbelief of its cultural context.[54] The church is not in a position to pick and choose what it teaches and defends – that is shaped by situations, as and when they arise. Furthermore, the church is not locked into past precedents, which require it to offer the same responses throughout its history. Rather, the church must continually respond appropriately to challenges, in the light of the specific issues and informed by a deep theological foundation.

With the agenda of *Revelation and Reason* in mind, Brunner suggests that there is a third task of theology – the need to explore the relation

---

[51] *Offenbarung und Vernunft*, 13; *Revelation and Reason*, 13. See Brunner's note in which he remarks that his earlier term "eristics" emphasized the offensive – rather than defensive – aspects of theology: *Offenbarung und Vernunft*, 15 n. 20; *Revelation and Reason*, 15 n. 20.
[52] Brunner does not develop the point, but it may be assumed that he has in mind Justin Martyr's tendency to Platonize Christianity in order to make it intellectually acceptable and accessible to second-century Platonism.
[53] *Offenbarung und Vernunft*, 14; *Revelation and Reason*, 14.
[54] *Offenbarung und Vernunft*, 15; *Revelation and Reason*, 15.

between divine revelation and human reason.⁵⁵ Anyone studying theology stands on the borderlands of faith and reason, and is caught up in a dialectical process which seeks to express faith reasonably without reducing faith to reason. "Jesus Christ is not the enemy of reason, but only of an irrational intellectual arrogance or an anti-rational self-sufficiency of reason."⁵⁶

Brunner sees this kind of intellectual arrogance in traditional attempts to "prove" the existence of God. While not dismissing their value, he suggests that these were deficient, both in terms of the type of knowledge that they produced and the concepts of God that they yielded.

> The "God" of the proofs of the existence of God is not the living God of faith, but an abstract intellectual substitute . . . a concept that can perhaps be brought into agreement with faith, but which never evokes it.⁵⁷

If such "proofs" persuade anyone, it is limited to those who are already convinced through faith of the existence of God.

Developing themes found in his *Truth as Encounter*, Brunner argues that a "truth of reason" concerns the correlation of thought and existence. This form of truth is something that can be discovered; and once discovered, it becomes "timeless", in that the truth no longer depends upon discovery for its validation.⁵⁸ The "truth of revelation" is something that *happens*. The knowledge of this truth cannot be dissociated or decoupled from the historical process through which it was mediated. "What we receive through Jesus Christ is something *given*, which is simultaneously the *Logos*, the eternal Word of God, given to us personally and in time."⁵⁹

This emphasis on the personal nature of the truth of revelation is of fundamental importance to Brunner. The truth of revelation is not an "impersonal, objective, 'It' truth", but a "'Thou' truth". It is something that "cannot be appropriated in a single act of objective perception, but only in an *act of personal surrender and decision*".⁶⁰

So what is the relation between the "truth of reason" and the "truth of revelation"? Between the "impersonal conception of reason" and the "personal conception of revelation"? Brunner refuses to reject one and affirm the other. It is not, he insists, a case of either-or. They are to be regarded as two separate "levels of existence" (*Seinstufen*). Brunner here appears to echo the language of stratification of reality found in writers such as Erich Rothacker (1888–1965), which recognizes different "levels" or "strata"

---

[55] *Offenbarung und Vernunft*, 15–17; *Revelation and Reason*, 15–17.
[56] *Offenbarung und Vernunft*, 17; *Revelation and Reason*, 17.
[57] *Offenbarung und Vernunft*, 336; *Revelation and Reason*, 340–1.
[58] *Offenbarung und Vernunft*, 364–7; *Revelation and Reason*, 369–72.
[59] *Offenbarung und Vernunft*, 366; *Revelation and Reason*, 370–1.
[60] *Offenbarung und Vernunft*, 367; *Revelation and Reason*, 371 (emphasis original).

within reality itself, or within the human representation of that reality.[61] For Brunner, the "truth of reason" is a lower "level of existence", which is taken up into the higher-level "truth of revelation".

> The relation between the two kinds of truth is the same as that between the levels of existence: the higher includes the lower, but not the converse. The personal truth of revelation, faith, and love includes within itself the impersonal truth connected with things and abstractions.[62]

Brunner's theological strategy thus avoids those forms of intellectual bifurcation which force believers to choose between the "truths of reason" and "truth of revelation". The Christian theologian has a higher-level understanding of "truth" which embraces, without being limited to, the objective truths of reason. The Christian faith articulates a profoundly personal and transformative notion of truth, which creates intellectual space for its impersonal counterparts. In effect, Brunner offers an account of the Christian faith which provides believers with a platform from which to engage with the non-Christian world without being reduced to its level.

One aspect of the non-Christian world that Brunner chose to engage merits closer attention: his reflections on non-Christian religions.[63] He rejects the notion that there is some generic concept known as "religion", of which Christianity is simply one example. For Brunner, Christianity is *sui generis*, and cannot be reduced to one variant or manifestation of a more generalized phenomenon. The Christian revelation provides a standpoint from which other religions may be evaluated, both in terms of their approaches to revelation and salvation.

Brunner insists that a vantage point is required in order to consider the question of religion. Christianity provides such a viewpoint, as a result of revelation in Christ. "Jesus Christ is both the fulfilment of all religion and the judgement upon all religion. As the one who fulfils, he is the truth which these religions have sought in vain."[64] After listing some core issues which he believes to be essential to religion, Brunner declares that other religions only "know these in a fragmentary or distorted form, as if they were relics of some original revelation".

Although Brunner adopts a critical attitude towards non-Christian religions,[65] he takes them seriously, and insists that their individuality and

---

[61] Erich Rothacker, *Die Schichten der Persönlichkeit*. 4th edn. Bonn: Bouvier, 1948. For the best study, see Ralph Stöwer, *Erich Rothacker: Sein Leben und seine Wissenschaft vom Menschen*. Göttingen: Vandenhoeck & Ruprecht, 2012.
[62] *Offenbarung und Vernunft*, 368; *Revelation and Reason*, 371.
[63] The best discussion is *Offenbarung und Vernunft*, 215–69; *Revelation and Reason*, 218–73.
[64] *Offenbarung und Vernunft*, 267; *Revelation and Reason*, 270.
[65] As noted by Hendrik Kraemer, *Religion and the Christian Faith*. Philadelphia: Westminster Press, 1957, 182–5. Brunner's discussion of the issue of other religions has generated little interest or discussion: see its virtual absence, for example, from Veli-Matti Kärkkäinen, *An Introduction to the Theology of Religions: Biblical, Historical, and Contemporary Perspectives*. Downers Grove, IL: InterVarsity Press, 2003.

complexity be respected, rather than reduced for the purposes of theoretical simplification and accommodation. Although some writers advocated seeing Christianity as the fulfilment of other religions – a particularly important theme at the Edinburgh Missionary Conference of 1910[66] – Brunner rejects this, arguing that other religions are, at heart, "religions of self-redemption" which do not know or acknowledge "the self-revelation of the holy and merciful God".[67]

Brunner's *Revelation and Reason* is a theological manifesto for cultural engagement, providing a robust platform for the churches to interact with their context confidently and critically. We have already seen how this platform allows Brunner to make theological sense of the existence of totalitarianism, and offer an antidote to its absolutization of the power of the state. But what vision of a Christian society does he propose in its place?

The Christian State: A Modest Theological Proposal

Brunner's response to the rise of totalitarianism can be considered to have two main components. In the first place, he offered a theological account of how this development took place, highlighting the way in which it reflected an inadequate understanding of human nature. Second, he offered a political alternative to totalitarianism, grounded in his vision of Christian theology. Although Brunner did not consider it to be theologically or practically defensible to treat the Bible or Christian theology as providing a template for a Christian society, he nevertheless set out some fundamental themes which he considered to be integral to the shaping of a Christian society. In what follows, I shall consider his proposals, set out in *Justice and the Social Order* (1943).

Brunner argued that the modern state was characterized by its tendencies towards totalitarianism, atheism, and collectivism. Although Brunner's concerns here partly arose from the Nazi experience, they also reflect tendencies in Stalinism. Although most Christian social theorists declined to critique the Soviet Union after the Second World War, Brunner maintained his criticisms of these trends, risking being dubbed a "cold warrior".[68] For Brunner,

---

[66] Kenneth R. Ross, "Edinburgh 1910: Scottish Roots and Contemporary Challenges." *Theology in Scotland* 17, no. 1 (2010): 5–21. This "fulfilment" approach was especially associated with John Nicol Farquhar (1861–1929): see Eric J. Sharpe, *Not to Destroy but to Fulfil: The Contribution of J. N. Farquhar to Protestant Missionary Thought in India before 1914.* Lund: Gleerup, 1965. For this theme in recent Catholic thought, see Adam Sparks, "The Fulfilment Theology of Jean Daniélou, Karl Rahner and Jacques Dupuis." *New Blackfriars* 89 (2008): 633–56.

[67] *Offenbarung und Vernunft*, 268; *Revelation and Reason*, 271.

[68] For example, his later comment (1948) that the Soviet Union was "not only the first, but also the most consistent, of all embodiments of the totalitarian principle": *Christianity and Civilisation*, vol. 1, 115. Most mainstream Christian theologians avoided criticism of the Soviet Union in the 1950s and 1960s, apparently believing it would lead to them being branded as "right-wing."

a Christian society should be rooted in a biblical framework, especially as this was developed during the period of the Reformation. He was puzzled by those who criticized National Socialism for being totalitarian yet refused to criticize other totalitarian regimes. For Brunner, "the whole family of totalitarianisms as such are an enormity to which the Christian Church can only say No – unconditionally, passionately and beyond any possibility of misrepresentation".[69]

Although Brunner argues that human law and authority must be recognized as grounded in – and hence ultimately accountable to – natural law, this does not lead him to bypass either the biblical witness or the Christian theological tradition. Nor does he hold that the recognition of some natural law entails a single legal or judiciary implementation of this law, valid and binding for all times and places. He insists that how justice is to be implemented is specific to historical contexts,[70] and cannot be universalized.

Brunner begins by insisting that the state has only limited authority. God has ordained certain "orders of creation" as a means of providing an appropriate environment within which human beings can flourish. These "orders of creation" ensure that "all institutions [*Ordnungen*] exist for the sake of human beings; human beings never exist for the sake of institutions".[71] A refusal to acknowledge human individuality, Brunner suggests, lies at the heart of totalitarianism. "Whenever people talk about 'collective persons', the way to the totalitarian state lies open." God addresses individuals; this must, Brunner holds, lead to affirming the "primacy of the individual over all collective considerations".

To assert the "primacy of the individual" does not, however, imply that a just society is characterized by radical individualism. Human beings are called to fellowship. The individual thus finds fulfilment in relationships and communities – such as the family.[72] The family is the "primal community" whose "rights take absolute precedence" over every other institution.[73] Yet between the family and the state, Brunner suggests, there must be a number of "intermediate links" that God has ordained as "as integral part of human life". It is not essential to human life that the state should exist; it nevertheless brings benefits – within limits. "The State is only necessary to human life in that there must be a supreme, encompassing union of all the primary forms of community."[74] The state has two primary responsibili-

---

[69] Brunner's criticisms were particularly directed against Karl Barth at this point. See his open letter to Barth, "Wie soll man das verstehen? Offener Brief an Karl Barth." *Kirchenblatt für die reformierte Schweiz* (1948): 59–66. See Jehle, *Emil Brunner*, 453–61.
[70] *Gerechtigkeit*, 147–54; *Justice and the Social Order*, 114–29. For further comment, see Jehle, *Emil Brunner*, 432–48.
[71] *Gerechtigkeit*, 159–60; *Justice and the Social Order*, 120.
[72] *Gerechtigkeit*, 161; *Justice and the Social Order*, 121.
[73] Brunner's ideas need to be set in context here: see Paul Ginsborg, "The Politics of the Family in Twentieth-Century Europe." *Contemporary European History* 9 (2000): 411–44.
[74] *Gerechtigkeit*, 162; *Justice and the Social Order*, 122.

ties to these "links". In the first place, it should never seek to usurp them. And in the second, it should positively preserve and protect them.[75]

A similar dialectic emerges in Brunner's reflections on economics. At the economic level, Brunner envisages a parallel between capitalism and radical individualism on the one hand, and communism and collectivism on the other. "The individualism of an unlimited right of disposition [*Verfügungsrecht*] in relation to private property results in economic anarchy, while communism just as inevitably results in totalitarian tyranny."[76] Brunner called for the formulation and implementation of a middle way between capitalism as unrestrained economic individualism and communism as a collective economic order that robs individuals of their rights and freedom.[77]

Community is not to be identified with the state.[78] God created human beings to be social, "predestined to community". Brunner argues that these "orders of creation" include human communities in the "economic, technical, purely social, and intellectual spheres". These communities are "antecedent to the state", and can exist without it. "The State is only the final link in the chain of these associations."[79] The state, he argues, is something that is to be "built up from below",[80] not imposed from above. Brunner extends this to the economic sphere, arguing that employers and employees should see themselves as part of a company community, working for its common good.[81]

Brunner only sketches an outline of his *Rechtsstaat*, his "ideal state". Yet it is clear immediately from his discussion that he regards the state as limited in its authority. It is charged with the responsibility of fostering communities, and thereby enhancing human wellbeing through the forging of a society in which humans can be the relational creatures which God intended. Although Brunner warmly commends democracy, he cautions against the innate tendency to absolutism – what we might call demagogy – that can so easily emerge within a democratic society, without the application of appropriate checks and balances. "Neither State nor people is sovereign;

---

[75] Note Brunner's later (1948) comment that "the state is created for the protection of those human rights which man has not from the state but from God." *Christianity and Civilisation*, vol. 2, 111.
[76] *Gerechtigkeit*, 212; *Justice and the Social Order*, 160.
[77] *Gerechtigkeit*, 207–13; *Justice and the Social Order*, 156–60.
[78] For a discussion of Brunner at this point, see Tim Petersen, "Emil Brunner's Social Ethics and Its Reception in Ordoliberal Circles." In *60 Years of Social Market Economy Formation, Development and Perspectives of a Peacemaking Formula*, ed. Christian L. Glossner and David Gregosz, 43–68. Berlin: Konrad-Adenauer-Stiftung, 2010. For a helpful analysis of "ordoliberalism" in the German context, see Razeen Sally, *Classical Liberalism and International Economic Order: Studies in Theory and Intellectual History*. New York: Routledge, 1998, 105–30.
[79] *Gerechtigkeit*, 163; *Justice and the Social Order*, 123.
[80] *Gerechtigkeit*, 159; *Justice and the Social Order*, 120.
[81] *Gerechtigkeit*, 205–7; *Justice and the Social Order*, 154–6.

both stand under a law which is binding upon them, which sets limits on their rights."[82]

Brunner therefore argues that it is "not democracy but federalism which is the bulwark against the totalitarian state".[83] Federalism is a form of community which is built from below, safeguarding and affirming the importance of local communities and personal identity. Such a political order, of course, existed in Brunner's native Switzerland.[84] Others, however, believed that the future peace of Europe depended on some form of European state. Brunner called for an "end to all impulsive unification and centralization as a matter of principle" in Europe, which might well preserve its life, but would ultimately cause it to lose its soul.[85]

Brunner's ideas were taken seriously by many concerned with the reconstruction of post-war Europe, and represent a relatively rare case of theological influence over recent economic thinking.[86] Wilhelm Röpke (1899–1966), who became Professor of Economics at the University of Geneva in 1937, regarded Brunner's *Justice and the Social Order* as a significant contribution to the debate over the role of the state in politics and economics,[87] citing it appreciatively in several works of the late 1940s. Röpke was one of the leading theorists of a social market economy, which played a significant role in the economic regeneration of the post-war German economy.[88]

Walter Eucken (1891–1950), who also played a significant role in laying the intellectual foundations for the post-war recovery of the German economy, argued that that the role of the state was essentially to provide a political framework for economic freedom. Like Röpke, Eucken interacted with Brunner,[89] considering him to offer a defensible account of the economic role of the state, even if he considered that Brunner lacked sufficient knowledge of economic theory to make some of his points persuasively.

Yet Brunner's vision for a reconstructed Europe involved more than the recalibration of social norms and institutions in the light of fundamental Christian motifs. He also believed that the churches themselves had a sig-

---

[82] *Gerechtigkeit*, 88; *Justice and the Social Order*, 71.
[83] *Gerechtigkeit*, 159; *Justice and the Social Order*, 120.
[84] For its distinctive features, see François de Capitani and Georg Germann, eds., *Auf dem Weg zu einer schweizerischen Identität 1848–1914*. Fribourg: Universitätsverlag Freiburg Schweiz, 1987; Lidja R. Basta and Thomas Fleiner, eds., *Federalism and Multiethnic States: The Case of Switzerland*. Fribourg: Institut du Fédéralisme, 1996.
[85] *Gerechtigkeit*, 295; *Justice and the Social Order*, 218.
[86] See Tim Petersen, "Theologische Einflüsse auf die deutsche Nationalökonomie im 19. und 20. Jahrhundert: Drei Fallbeispiele." *Zeitschrift für Wirtschafts- und Unternehmungsethik* 12, no. 2 (2011): 318–30.
[87] Petersen, "Emil Brunner's Social Ethics and Its Reception in Ordoliberal Circles," 53–5. For Brunner's relationship to Röpke, see Jehle, *Emil Brunner*, 438.
[88] See Sally, *Classical Liberalism and International Economic Order*, 131–49.
[89] Petersen, "Emil Brunner's Social Ethics and Its Reception in Ordoliberal Circles," 57–8.

nificant role to play as communities. In what follows, I shall consider his commitment to ecumenism, and its implications.

Rediscovering the Church as Community: Brunner's Ecclesiology

Brunner had always appreciated the importance of ecumenism, and was perhaps the most ecumenically engaged German-speaking Reformed theologian of his age. Brunner began to become involved in ecumenical activities at an early state in his career. In 1909 he attended the World Student Christian Federation meeting at Oxford from 15 to 19 July, at which he made the acquaintance of some leading figures in the international ecumenical movement, such as John R. Mott (1865–1955). Yet the matter became increasingly important to him during the 1930s, as the deteriorating international situation convinced him that the churches had a critical role to play in catalysing reconciliation and lessening tensions between nations. Brunner actually had relatively little interest in "organizational unity", and valued such encounters primarily because of the opportunities they provided for the "exchange of ideas and sharing of experiences".[90]

Brunner's most significant ecumenical experience was the "Church, Community, and State" conference at Oxford in July 1937 (see pp. 173–4). He had formed a high regard for J. H. Oldham, who played a significant role in the International Missionary Conference at Edinburgh in 1910,[91] and an arguably greater role in convening the Oxford conference of 1937. Although Brunner found this a worthwhile experience, the event nevertheless raised some concerns. One obvious difficulty was the lack of any significant outcome from the conference, which served to expose differences within the world Christian community rather than harness them for united action in the face of an increasingly uncertain and dangerous international situation.

Yet Brunner formed the impression that the politics and concerns of Christian institutions were compromising genuine theological dialogue and ecumenical collaboration between Christians. The 1910 Edinburgh conference had been organized by laity, who were aware of the dangers of entangling such ventures with denominational politics. The Ecumenical Missionary Conference, held in New York in 1900, was generally judged to have achieved little in the way of active proposals for the future, partly because of the predominance of clerical organizers and attendees. The 1937 conference attempted to avoid such institutional difficulties, while at the same time providing a resource for the major Protestant churches.

[90] "Intellectual Autobiography", 10–11.
[91] K. W. Clements, *Faith on the Frontier: A Life of J. H. Oldham*. Edinburgh: T&T Clark, 1999, 73–99.

Brunner sensed that the 1937 conference was the high point in an ecumenical movement which was increasingly coming to be dominated by questions of harmonizing institutional structures, rather than encouraging grass-roots collaboration and solidarity. Brunner remained firmly committed to the vision of Oldham himself. As he recalled appreciatively, Oldham "kept reminding us theologians that the Church of Jesus Christ is founded on the priesthood of all believers and must beware of becoming a clerical institution".[92]

This concern appears to lie behind Brunner's increasingly non-institutional approach to ecumenism and ecclesiology, perhaps best seen in his 1951 work *Das Missverständnis der Kirche* ("The Misunderstanding of the Church"). Yet these concerns are evident earlier, as in a 1939 paper reflecting on Zurich church law.[93] In a discussion of the development of the notion of the church, Brunner reflected on the move away from a New Testament conception towards the institutionalized concept which became dominant in the Middle Ages.[94] The reformed church of Zurich, Brunner pointed out, was set up by a decree of the Zurich city council, and was thus the product of a human agency.[95] But what relation did this historical church have to the New Testament church?

Some of the themes of Brunner's increasingly non-institutional understanding of the church echo concerns expressed elsewhere, particularly in England, as a result of the wartime experience. The lay Anglican writers Dorothy L. Sayers (1893–1957) and C. S. Lewis both argued for greater ecumenical understanding and collaboration during the Second World War.[96] Writing in 1944, Lewis argued for a "standard of plain, central Christianity ('mere Christianity' as Baxter called it) which puts the controversies of the moment in their proper perspective".[97] The wartime situation seemed to demand a recalibration of denominational sensitivities and agendas, which was best served by the reaffirmation of a consensual form of Christian belief shorn of its denominational specifics – an idea that the English Puritan theologian Richard Baxter (1615–91) expressed in the phrase "mere Christianity", which Lewis appropriated for his own purposes.

---

[92] "Intellectual Autobiography", 11.
[93] "Zürcher Kirchengesetz und christliche Kirche": *Ein offenes Wort*, vol. 2, 43–58.
[94] "Zürcher Kirchengesetz und christliche Kirche": *Ein offenes Wort*, vol. 2, 45–9.
[95] *Das Missverständnis der Kirche*, 123; *The Misunderstanding of the Church*, 107.
[96] On Lewis, see Alister E. McGrath, "A 'Mere Christian': Anglicanism and Lewis's Religious Identity." In *The Intellectual World of C. S. Lewis*, 147–61. Oxford: Wiley-Blackwell, 2013. On Sayers, see Giles Watson, "Dorothy L. Sayers and the Oecumenical Penguin." *Seven* 14 (1997): 17–32.
[97] C. S. Lewis, "On the Reading of Old Books." In *Essay Collection and Other Short Pieces*. London: HarperCollins, 2000, 439. For Lewis's dependence on Baxter at this point, see N. H. Keeble, "C. S. Lewis, Richard Baxter, and 'Mere Christianity'." *Christianity and Literature* 30, no. 3 (1981): 27–44.

Brunner's post-war ecclesiology shows him to have considerable sympathy with institutionally minimalist understandings of the church. His fundamental concern is that the New Testament notion of the church has become reified, and has thus lost its fundamental emphasis on the church as an organic community of believers.

> The *ekklesia* of the New Testament, the community of Christ, is precisely not what every "church" is at the least – an institution, a "something". The community of Christ [*Christusgemeinde*] is nothing other than a fellowship [*Gemeinschaft*] of persons . . . As the Body of Christ, it is not an organization, and has nothing of an institutional character about it.[98]

As a matter of historical fact, Brunner concedes, the word "church" has come to have strongly institutional associations, especially in Roman Catholicism. An inexorable process of historical development over 1,500 years has led to the "replacement of a communion of persons [*Persongemeinschaft*] by a juridical [*rechtliche*] institution".[99] Yet this development was a matter of historical contingency, not theological propriety. As the Reformation made clear, it was reversible.

Brunner is open to criticism at this point, not least in that he offers what is probably best described as a Romantic idealization of the early church, inattentive to the realities of imperial Roman politics before the conversion of Constantine, and a failure to give due weight to the importance of institutions in consolidating movements. Yet we may allow that the early church offers a template for ecclesial existence which is helpful in some respects, not least in challenging the predominant ecclesial models that arose, under very different social and political conditions, in western Europe during the Middle Ages. Brunner is clear that the reformers of the sixteenth century achieved only a partial reversal of this damaging trend towards an institutionalized conception of the church, which became normative during the medieval period. Calvin, he suggests, retained rather more of an institutional understanding of the church than Luther.[100] It is important to continue the process of completing what the reformers began. Institutional understandings of the church tend to subordinate the laity to a sacralized caste of priests, which bears little relation to what we know of the New Testament Christian communities.

Brunner's critique of institutional conceptions of Christianity mirrors his analysis of the state. Just as he argued for the need for a middle way between individualism and collectivism in society by means of "communities" (pp. 197–8), so he argues that "Protestant individualism" and "Catholic collectivism" must be overcome in a similar manner. The church is "the Body of Christ, consisting of nothing but persons", possessing both vertical and

---
[98] *Das Missverständnis der Kirche*, 12–13; *The Misunderstanding of the Church*, 10–11.
[99] *Das Missverständnis der Kirche*, 19; *The Misunderstanding of the Church*, 16.
[100] *Das Missverständnis der Kirche*, 115–21; *The Misunderstanding of the Church*, 101–5.

horizontal dimensions: fellowship between persons and God, and between persons themselves. "The fellowship of Christians is just as much an end in itself as is their fellowship with Christ".[101] Fellowship with Christ (*Christusgemeinschaft*) entails a mutual fellowship of believers.[102] Brunner argues that the stratification of church institutions is to be resisted. The *ekklesia* is not a hierarchically structured society, but a community of fellow believers.

So how does Brunner interpret the four traditional "notes" or "marks" of the church – one, holy, catholic, and apostolic? He inverts his order of discussion for presentational reasons, arising from his extended discussion of the "communion of the saints" – or "fellowship of believers". In what follows, I retain the traditional order, as I explore Brunner's discussion of these themes in the light of his non-institutional concept of the church.[103]

1   The church is *one*. Where many Protestant theologians regarded the multiplicity of churches as a problem which required solution, Brunner tended to the view that these different implementations of the church provide a welcome diversity of possibilities. Given a "considerable measure of generous toleration", each individual church could celebrate its distinctiveness, while at the same time conceding the potential merits of other approaches. The real problem, for Brunner, is "not the existence of different Christian bodies, but the failure to acknowledge the *ekklesia* as a spiritual fraternity, not an institution".[104]

2   The church is *holy*. Once more, Brunner insists that this is not to be understood as referring to the institution of the church, but to the fellowship of believers. The institution of the church is not to be thought of as conveying grace. The church is "holy" in that it is a "church which is founded on the sanctifying act and word of God in Jesus Christ, that can only be received through faith".[105]

3   The church is *catholic*. Brunner takes this to refer to the universal scope of the church, and its appeal to all people at all times. The church is charged with proclaiming the gospel to all peoples. In order to do this, it must be immersed within the world, without losing its own distinct identity. The church must "lay aside its sacred garments" in order to enter into the world, as Christ entered that world in the incarnation.[106]

4   The church is *apostolic*. Brunner opposes any notion that the authenticity of the church's mission and teaching is safeguarded *institutionally* – for example, by the "legitimacy of episcopal succession". Any church

---

[101] *Das Missverständnis der Kirche*, 14; *The Misunderstanding of the Church*, 12.
[102] *Das Missverständnis der Kirche*, 20; *The Misunderstanding of the Church*, 17.
[103] *Dogmatik III*, 141–58; *Dogmatics 3*, 117–33.
[104] *Dogmatik III*, 154; *Dogmatics 3*, 129.
[105] *Dogmatik III*, 151; *Dogmatics 3*, 126.
[106] *Dogmatik III*, 146–9; *Dogmatics 3*, 121–4.

"which considers its institutional apparatus to be essential to its nature" has fallen victim to a "false ecclesiasticism".[107] To be "apostolic" is not about identifying an institutional foundation, but a spiritual criterion.

One of the factors that shaped Brunner's non-denominational approach to the *ekklesia* was his experience of working with Christian organizations, such as the Student Volunteer Movement for Foreign Missions under John Mott, and the Oxford Group (see pp. 85–7).[108] Indeed, he suggested that many Christians found a fellowship in this and other organizations which was lacking in churches. The parallels between "fellowships" and "churches" are perhaps most evident in American Christianity, where the ideas and values of "voluntary organizations" – such as mission organizations – have played a major role in shaping attitudes and expectations.[109] Brunner's experience of American Christianity allowed him to point to examples of churches in which the generation of Christian community took priority – such as Harry Emerson Fosdick's interdenominational Riverside Church in New York, which Brunner identified as a prime example of a church which recognized the importance of fellowship over institutional concerns.[110] For Brunner, traditional churches that were defined and constituted primarily as institutions appeared to show a reduced capacity to connect up with the concerns for community and fellowship within post-war society.

So can a church exist without being or becoming an institution, at least in part? Brunner's concern for the future of traditional churches reflects his belief that institutional agendas and interests were hindering many churches from identifying and articulating the vision that lay at the heart of the New Testament *ekklesia*. He recognized that it was a sociological inevitability that "fellowships" should become "institutions", but nevertheless insisted on the importance of avoiding being *defined* by institutional markers.[111] As he puts it, an institutional form of the church is the "covering, shell, and agency" of the *ekklesia*.[112] The institution enfolds, protects, and propagates the *ekklesia*. But it is not part of its essence, which Brunner believed he had seen in movements such as the YMCA and the Oxford Group, which

---

[107] *Dogmatik III*, 145–6; *Dogmatics 3*, 121.
[108] *Dogmatik III*, 129–40; *Dogmatics 3*, 106–16. Brunner distanced himself from the Oxford Group after it reconstituted itself as "Moral Re-Armament" in 1938, seeing this as marking the adoption of an ideology that was alien to its original intentions.
[109] See, for example, Ben Harder, "The Student Volunteer Movement for Foreign Missions and Its Contribution to 20th Century Missions." *Missiology* 8 no. 2 (1980): 141–54.
[110] *Dogmatik III*, 131; *Dogmatics 3*, 108. On Riverside Church, see Robert Moats Miller, *Harry Emerson Fosdick: Preacher, Pastor, Prophet*. New York: Oxford University Press, 1985, 200–42.
[111] Brunner was particularly impressed by the Mukyōkai ("Not-Church") movement, founded in Japan in 1901 by Kanzō Uchimura (1861–1930), and which was still active fifty years later, when Brunner was reflecting on these themes. See the comments in his 1959 article "Die christliche Nicht-Kirche-Bewegung in Japan."
[112] *Dogmatik III*, 141–58; *Dogmatics 3*, 117–33.

positioned themselves at a distance from church institutions. Brunner's own reflections on the nature and purpose of the YMCA suggested to him that it had a legitimate claim to be considered an *ekklesia*, in the New Testament sense of the term.[113]

Alongside Brunner's concerns to ensure that the churches were able to grow through connecting up with contemporary societal concerns, we find a further layer of analysis which is clearly of importance to Brunner's theological vision: the role of the churches in creating and sustaining society. Brunner's federal vision of society allowed a significant place for "fellowships" such as the churches, which can work to ensure a Christian presence and voice within society. His non-institutional approach to the church encouraged ecumenical collaboration, precisely by its de-emphasis of the importance of institutional issues, and focus on the shared spiritual values and beliefs of Christians, irrespective of their denominational allegiance.

Brunner offers an approach to the doctrine of the church which de-emphasizes (without denying) its institutional elements, and focuses on the creation of a Christ-centred fellowship. While his views of the New Testament *ekklesia* may indeed involve a degree of theological idealization, perhaps stimulated by his frustration at the very specific social and cultural roles demanded of – and imposed upon – the Swiss Reformed church in the canton of Zurich, it is clear that his emphasis on the essentials of the church resonates with contemporary concerns of the 1940s, and their continuation in the twenty-first century.

Brunner's understanding of the church creates theological space for entrepreneurial individuals, discouraged by the institutional concerns and agendas of traditional Protestant denominations, to develop forms of the church which retain its essential theological characteristics yet which are able to create Christian community and fellowship in a more effective manner than traditional denominations can now achieve. Brunner's suggestion that "voluntary societies" – such as the YMCA – can be regarded as an *ekklesia* offers an important theological lifeline to experiments designed to explore how the church can adapt to rapidly changing cultural situations.[114]

From what has been said in the present chapter, it will be clear that Brunner's writings during the period of the Second World War show him to have had a vision of theology as a resource for church and society. This naturally leads us to consider his role as a public intellectual, which became particularly significant around this time.

---

[113] Jehle, *Emil Brunner*, 507–11.
[114] For reflections, see Alister E. McGrath, *Christianity's Dangerous Idea: The Protestant Revolution*. San Francisco: HarperOne, 2007, 278–85.

8
Teacher and Preacher: Brunner as a Public Intellectual

By 1930 it had become clear that Brunner was one of the leading Protestant theologians of his age. By 1950 it was equally clear that he had emerged as one of Protestantism's most significant public intellectuals. Alongside his substantial academic output during the Second World War, for example, we find a stream of articles in the *Neue Zürcher Zeitung* and pamphlets, both journalistic and scholarly, dealing with topics such as the death penalty, issues of social justice, coping with the social and ethical problems of the war, the rise of totalitarianism, and the longing for peace. Brunner's reflections on the theological foundations of social justice led to him being awarded an honorary doctorate in law (*Doctor Juris*) by the Faculty of Law at the University of Berne.[1]

Perhaps more importantly, Brunner was awarded the Grosse Verdienstkreuz (Grand Merit Cross) by Eugen Gerstenmaier (1906–86), president of the Bundestag of the Federal Republic of Germany, at a ceremony at the German embassy in Zurich on 14 May 1960.[2] In his congratulatory speech, Gerstenmaier – one of those who had been involved in the plot to assassinate Hitler in July 1944 – acknowledged the seminal role that Brunner had played in creating the intellectual environment in which the catastrophe of Nazi Germany had given way to a democratic federal state. During a visit to Zurich during the Second World War, Gerstenmaier had asked himself how Germany could ever be rebuilt after such a catastrophe. Then Brunner had presented him with the manuscript of his book *Gerechtigkeit* by night at the Hotel Glockenhof in Zurich. "When morning dawned after I had taken it from you", Gerstenmaier declared, "I knew that I had read the foundations for the rebuilding of Germany." Brunner's work provided "a new beginning for Germany".[3]

---

[1] Frank Jehle, *Emil Brunner: Theologe im 20. Jahrhundert*. Zurich: Theologischer Verlag, 2006, 442. The degree was awarded on 29 May 1948.
[2] Jehle, *Emil Brunner*, 435–6.
[3] Jehle, *Emil Brunner*, 435.

Emil Brunner: A Reappraisal, First Edition. Alister E. McGrath.
© 2014 John Wiley & Sons, Ltd. Published 2016 by John Wiley & Sons, Ltd.

Few theologians – let alone Swiss theologians – were singled out for such commendation by a leading German political figure. Yet Gerstenmaier's is but one of many voices pointing to the major role that Brunner played as a public intellectual during the 1940s and beyond. In this chapter, I shall consider some aspects of that role, and reflect on its wider significance.

Rector of the University of Zurich, 1942–1943

Brunner's academic prestige was both manifested and extended when he was elected rector of the University of Zurich in 1942. His rectoral address on the theme of the relation of faith and scholarship – "Glaube und Forschung" – was delivered on 23 April 1943. It is a vigorous and spirited defence of the place of theology within the university community, and a challenge to theology to ensure it connected with the broader world of research, scholarship, and debate. This neglected speech sets out Brunner's vision of a public theology, confident in its own foundations yet willing to engage other disciplines in a generous and critical manner. Writing against the backdrop of a pan-European war, Brunner argued for the creative engagement of the disciplines that a university context – such as that of Zurich – made possible and necessary.

> The resounding question of the last century was: can a scholar [*Forschender*] believe? Today we must ask: can scholarship survive without faith? The catastrophe of western culture and humanity, of which we are witnesses today, compels us to ask questions about this disintegration – and that also means about the most profound assumptions of our culture.[4]

For Brunner, the war raised some disturbing questions about human nature, above all its disturbing tendency to be enthralled by ideologies and lose sight of its greater good and higher goals.[5] In the end, the "fundamental questions of our culture" concern values and goals that do not belong to the "realm of a world of objects", but to the world of persons – a world which lies beyond empirical verification, and which needs to be received through faith.

> This faith is unprovable, and lies completely outside the scope of scientific investigation. That is the essence of faith; indeed, it is the essence of personality. Morality is also unprovable. Proof is only possible in the realm of objects, not of persons. Here, decisions about trust and love take the place of proof.[6]

Brunner's argument remains important far beyond its original context. Proof simply cannot be given for most of the fundamental beliefs and values which

---

[4] "Glaube und Forschung": *Ein offenes Wort*, vol. 2, 134–49; quote at 139.
[5] "Glaube und Forschung": *Ein offenes Wort*, vol. 2, 140–1.
[6] "Glaube und Forschung": *Ein offenes Wort*, vol. 2, 143.

undergird western civilization, including religious faith. The great upheaval of the Second World War had exposed the *fragility* – not the *implausibility* – of these beliefs and values. Brunner ended his address with a plea to his academic colleagues to work for the restoration and renewal of such beliefs and values. "No university can flourish on nihilistic foundations."[7]

Brunner had become isolated during the Second World War. He was unable to travel beyond Switzerland, and experienced considerable difficulty in sending and receiving foreign correspondence.[8] As a result, he tended to focus on debates and issues within his Swiss context. The ending of the war in 1945 gradually led to an easing of travel and correspondence restrictions, and allowed Brunner to lecture abroad. During a return visit to the United States in the autumn of 1946 he spoke at several major YMCA conventions.[9]

Brunner also became a significant presence in Great Britain. He was invited to deliver the prestigious Gifford Lectures at the University of St Andrews in the spring of 1947 and 1948, giving him the opportunity to address the theme of "Christianity and Civilization" at some length. In March 1952 he addressed the National Congress of the Free Church Federal Council, meeting in the Welsh capital city, Cardiff, speaking of the place of the church in a "new social order". In this wide-ranging address, Brunner explored the implications of a non-institutional vision of the *ekklesia* for the contemporary situation. The *ekklesia* generated community – and a sense of community was essential to the new social order. "What we need now is a new social Gospel, but different from that of the last generation in that it does not strive for a social *order* but for personal community."[10]

In previous chapters I considered Brunner's theological development, and some aspects of his mature theological vision. In the present chapter I shall focus on the manner in which Brunner established himself, not merely as a systematic theologian, but as a public intellectual – someone who engaged multiple audiences in the academy, church, and society. To begin with, I shall look at an earlier work in which Brunner established a reputation as someone who could deploy theological insight in the service of ecclesial pedagogy.

The Catechist: *Our Faith* (1935)

In 1935 Brunner published a short, highly accessible introduction to the main themes of the Christian faith, considered from a Protestant perspective.[11] In a preface to the second edition of this work (1951), Brunner

---

[7] "Glaube und Forschung": *Ein offenes Wort*, vol. 2, 149.
[8] Jehle, *Emil Brunner*, 475.
[9] For Brunner's involvement with the YMCA, see the analysis in Jehle, *Emil Brunner*, 499–514.
[10] *The Church in the New Social Order*, 28–9.
[11] Jehle, *Emil Brunner*, 323–4.

declared that of all the books that he had written it was his "favourite" and the "most useful". The work had its origins in a series of thirty-five short articles that he published during the period 1930–5 in a local Swiss religious periodical.[12] These articles were intended for an audience of laity and pastors, and made no presumption of any familiarity on the part of their readers with contemporary or classic theological debates. The talks on which they were based arose from Brunner's involvement with the Oxford Group, which helps us understand their disinclination to become involved in matters of theological contentiousness or ecclesiological tension. Brunner brought these articles together in a single volume, entitled *Unser Glaube: Eine christliche Unterweisung* ("Our Faith: A Christian Catechism").

Theologically, Brunner's book is positioned within a classic Protestant framework, predominantly Reformed, but with Lutheran tinges. Yet what is most important about this work is not its theological orientation, but the pedagogical presentation of its material, clearly reflecting Brunner's experience as a pastor in Obstalten. He tends to use short sentences, to avoid complex terms and theological jargon, and to use illustrations and analogies to make otherwise inaccessible theological points.

Consider this example. How is the Word of God conveyed in the Bible? What is the relation of God's word and human speech? Brunner approaches this important theological question using a homely illustration. In translating this, I have tried to retain the sentence structure and tone of the original German text.

> On every street you see posters for the gramophone company "His Master's Voice". So the gramophone company tells us that, if you buy the record, you will hear the Master – Caruso's – voice. Is that true? Of course! But is it really his voice? Certainly! And yet the gramophone makes its own noise. That's not the Master's voice – it's just the scratching of the record. But don't get impatient with the record! It is only through the record that you can hear "The Master's Voice". Look, it's the same with the Bible. It makes the real Master's voice audible. It's really his voice, his words, and what he wants to say. But there's some background noise, because God speaks his word through a human mouth.[13]

This beautifully contextualized analogy would have made perfect sense to Brunner's readers in Switzerland during the 1930s. The international marketing campaign by the Victor Talking Machine Company used a trademark image of a dog (a fox terrier named Nipper) listening to a wind-up gramophone. These posters, with their slogan "His Master's Voice", were a familiar sight in Swiss cities. The Italian tenor Enrico Caruso (1873–1921) was

---

[12] The journal was *Kirchenboten für den Kanton Zürich*, which began publication in 1915, aiming to reach a local audience of Reformed Christians and their pastors in the canton of Zurich. The journal ceased publication in its original form in 2008.

[13] *Unser Glaube*, 11–12; *Our Faith*, 19. The English translation of this text is unreliable.

the first opera singer to realize the importance of commercial recordings,[14] and made nearly 300 for the Victor Talking Machine Company. Caruso's recordings were highly popular during the 1920s and 1930s. No other classical recording artist even approached his high public profile in Europe or America. The audio technology of the 1930s was prone to precisely the problem Brunner describes. The phonograph discs of the 1930s were made from the resin shellac (Brunner refers to this as *Hartgummi*). Sound reproduction was achieved by a steel needle tracking the grooves containing the audio recording as the disc rotated. Imperfections in the recording and pressing process meant that extraneous scratching and hissing accompanied the playback process. Gramophones were so widely used that this phenomenon would have been familiar to Brunner's readers. The theological interpretation and application of the analogy would have seemed entirely natural to his readers at the time.[15]

Or consider Brunner's reflections on the question of why we find it so difficult to make sense of things. How can we discern God's purposes in history? Or discover the secret pattern which lies behind the seemingly random events within the world? Once more, Brunner uses an analogy which would resonate with the experience of his envisaged original readership within the canton of Zurich.

> Anyone who looks down on the city in the evening darkness from the heights of the Zurichberg sees a narrow strip in the sea of light beneath their feet which is densely packed with bright lights – a bundle of lights. It is beautiful and extraordinary to look at, although we don't understand what this cluster of lights means. It is the region around the railway station. Each of the hundreds of lights is in its place, but someone looking down from above knows nothing about this ordering. Only the director of the railway station knows why this arrangement has been made, and not some other. He has the plan, and can see the whole thing. His insight and will direct the whole thing.[16]

Brunner here draws on the popularity of Zurich's local mountain – often known as the Züriberg – a wooded hill rising to about 2,000 feet (650 metres) above the city. It was easily ascended in the 1930s by means of the Rigiblick and Dolderbahn funicular railways, and was a popular site for walks. The area around Zurich's main railway station (*Hauptbahnhof*) emerged as the main shopping area in Zurich in the twentieth century, and was a familiar city landmark at night on account of its street lights. Brunner's analogy would thus be familiar to his readers. The interpretation that he places on the analogy is natural and unforced. We see a complex and seemingly incomprehensible world, whose structure and ordering lie beyond our grasp. But that doesn't mean that there is no underlying structure or plan.

---

[14] A point emphasized by Michael Scott, *The Great Caruso*. New York: Knopf, 1988.
[15] Brunner mentions this analogy elsewhere in his writings: see, for example, *The Scandal of Christianity*, 25; *Das Ärgernis des Christentums*, 23.
[16] *Unser Glaube*, 22; *Our Faith*, 27.

The importance of this theological primer, aimed mainly at lay people, does not lie in its theology. It does not break new ground in terms of its ideas. The work's significance lies in its accessibility, and Brunner's ability to use carefully chosen analogies to explore its theological themes. This is the gift of a preacher. So how do we find Brunner's theology expressed in his sermons?

The Fraumünster Sermons: Brunner as Preacher

Brunner began his career as a pastor in the village of Obstalten in February 1916, and remained there – apart from a year spent at Union Theological Seminary in New York – until the autumn of 1924, when he moved to Zurich to take up the chair of systematic and practical theology at the University of Zurich. Although he no longer had pastoral responsibilities, he nevertheless continued to be actively engaged in the life of the church. "It is totally absurd", he wrote to Eduard Thurneysen in January 1926, "to be a theologian without preaching."[17] Part of Brunner's duties as Professor of Systematic and Practical Theology at the University of Zurich was to teach his students to preach. And what better way of doing this than to lead by example?

Brunner and his wife became members of the congregation of the Fraumünster, a parish church in the city of Zurich.[18] Since 1970 the church has become a tourist attraction on account of the installation of five stained glass windows by the artist Marc Chagall (1887–1985). Brunner's association with the Fraumünster began at his ordination in the church on 27 October 1912. On his return to Zurich from Obstalten, he resumed his connection with the church, and preached regularly there from 1925,[19] generally once a month. Visitors formed the distinct impression that the congregations were substantially larger when Brunner preached.[20]

The Brunners now lived at 47 Hirslanderstrasse, Zurich 7, several kilometres from the centre of the city. Although other churches were closer, the Brunners clearly regarded this city-centre church as their spiritual home. As Brunner's reputation as a theologian and public intellectual grew, his sermons attracted increasing attention – especially during the years of the

---

[17] Jehle, *Emil Brunner*, 205.
[18] The best English translation would be "Lady Minster" – i.e. a church dedicated to the Virgin Mary. The church was originally attached to a Benedictine monastery, which was suppressed in 1524, and finally demolished in 1898. Brunner also became involved with other Zurich churches around this time, preaching at Fluntern (near Züriberg) and Oberstrass in 1925.
[19] Jehle, *Emil Brunner*, 204.
[20] For example, J. Robert Nelson, "Emil Brunner – Teacher Unsurpassed." *Theology Today* 19, no. 4 (1963): 532–5. Nelson was one of Brunner's students at Zurich during the academic year 1948–9.

Second World War, when his attempts to make sense of the wartime situation to his Zurich audience clearly won him a substantial following.

Three volumes of Brunner's sermons were published. The first, and in some ways the most interesting, took the form of a collection of twelve wartime sermons on the Apostles' Creed. Brunner here mingled theological exposition with reflection on the fears and concerns of Swiss citizens during the period of the Second World War.[21] What would the future hold? Would Switzerland continue to exist? Where was God in the chaos they saw around them?

One of the great strengths of these sermons is that Brunner articulated the anxious thoughts of many, which they feared to articulate lest the answers should be unbearable. Might the clash of totalitarianisms around them lead to the persecution, even extinction, of Christianity? "Will Christian congregations have to crawl into the catacombs again, because the powers on earth are enemies of Christianity and belief in God?"[22] In his discussion of the character and providence of God, Brunner sought to reassure as much as to inform, to bring out the deeper existential meaning of the Creed's often terse statements and apply them to the uncertainty of his age. These sermons reveal Brunner as an interpreter of the classic Christian theological tradition, able to make connections with contemporary situations.

Perhaps the most poignant of these sermons engages the topic of "Christ in despair".[23] Brunner here expounds the ideas of the suffering and death of Christ, and his descent into hell. It is a powerful exploration of the theme of the incarnation and atonement for humanity in its present predicament. We feel that we have been abandoned by God. Yet God has entered into the darkest places of our world, to reassure us that we have *not* been abandoned. Once more, Brunner makes an existential application of a classic Christian doctrine.

> God is with me, so that there is no longer any despair for me. God has done what needed to be done, so that there is nothing in this world, not even its darkest aspects, that he has not himself gone through; no place which he has not visited.[24]

In Christ, God has come to where we are – not to leave us there, but to get us out of its darkest places.

> Surely you know that, just as [Christ] carries the burden of guilt for you, so that you can come to God once more, as if you had no guilt, so he also comes

---

[21] *Ich glaube an den lebendige Gott.* The English translation of these works removes some "dated material that might have distracted the reader"; *I Believe in the Living God*, 9. While this makes this translation easier to read, it means that the reader does not always fully grasp Brunner's ability to speak to the very specific situation of this Zurich congregation in a time of uncertainty and anxiety in terms they could easily appreciate and understand.
[22] *Ich glaube an den lebendige Gott*, 9; *I Believe in the Living God*, 17.
[23] *Ich glaube an den lebendige Gott*, 69–79; *I Believe in the Living God*, 75–85.
[24] *Ich glaube an den lebendige Gott*, 76; *I Believe in the Living God*, 82.

into your despair. Even there, he will find me, for that was not for him too far from God. Even there, one can hold fast to God through him. So Jesus Christ has entered into everything that is human, even the most dreadful, so that there may be no human place, no human experience, no difficulty, no situation, in which there is no relationship with God.[25]

Brunner's ability to interpret the Christian tradition to engage the dark developments and anxieties of the age won him many admirers.

Once the war was over, Brunner was able to revert to a more traditional approach to preaching, relating biblical texts and theological themes to the concerns of his congregation. In 1955 he published a collection of sermons delivered over a period of five years at the Fraumünster, from 1948 to 1953, in response to demands from the congregation.[26] These sermons deal with a wide range of topics, anchored (sometimes, it must be said, a little loosely) to biblical texts and (more rigorously) to theological motifs – but always seeking to make connections with the human soul.

This is perhaps most striking in Brunner's sermon for Christmas Day 1952.[27] This sermon takes as its theme the gospel text set for Christmas Day: "There is born to you this day in the city of David a Saviour, who is Christ the Lord" (Luke 2:10–11). Brunner develops this point in a number of ways, including the affirmation of the solidarity of God with believers. "In the midst of a frightening and dark world, we can be joyful and have light."[28] Yet Brunner insists that the birth of Christ in the past must lead to the rebirth of the believer in the present. "Jesus Christ has been given to us in order that we might become something else." For Brunner, faith is not simply belief, but an active embracing of Christ – "to be incorporated into the eternal life of Christ, and to grow into it" – and, as a result, to behave in a new way.[29]

The third volume of sermons, published in 1965, brought together sermons from Brunner's later years. These sermons are undated, making them difficult to correlate with events in Switzerland or the wider world. They are often dark in tone, reflecting Brunner's anxieties about the failure of post-war Europe to deal with the political and military threat of the Soviet Union, and a sense that the west is losing its moral compass.

This is particularly clear in a sermon entitled "The Light of the World", preached on Trinity Sunday. The background to Brunner's sermon is not clear. The presumption is that something has happened which will cause the congregation anxiety.

---

[25] *Ich glaube an den lebendige Gott*, 77–8; *I Believe in the Living God*, 84.
[26] *Fraumünster-Predigten*, 5; *The Great Invitation*, 5.
[27] *Fraumünster-Predigten*, 117–22; *The Great Invitation*, 142–8.
[28] *Fraumünster-Predigten*, 120; *The Great Invitation*, 146. Brunner here uses the Swiss German term *gfürchig*, an idea rendered in German as *beängstigend* or *angsterregend*.
[29] *Fraumünster-Predigten*, 121; *The Great Invitation*, 147.

> We come together in church, terrified and made anxious by all the happenings in the world, by the darkness that lies over the world, terrified by confusion and hostility. We can't cope any more. We can see no clear way ahead. One person says one thing, another says something different – even in the church.[30]

Brunner interprets this as a failure of the Enlightenment's vision of knowledge, and more fundamentally of human nature. Yes, knowledge can help us understand things. But it cannot make us better people. Indeed, it could make things worse. "What use is it, if humanity becomes even more powerful, and can thus cause even more chaos in the world?" Echoing themes found in some philosophical critiques of modernity, Brunner concludes that "Despite all Enlightenment and all light of science, it is darker in the world than before."[31]

It is to this world that the word is spoken: "I am the light of the world" (John 8:12). Yet, Brunner points out, this is not "Enlightenment" in the modernist sense of the term, which thinks of life and the world as an "it". The knowledge that the Christian faith brings is *personal*. God addresses us in a majestic "I", and invites us to respond. The key to a better world lies in the personal transformation that lies at the heart of the Christian gospel, not in the increasingly impersonal and technocratic knowledge made possible by the sciences.

Since this sermon was preached on Trinity Sunday it would have been unthinkable for Brunner not to comment on this doctrine. In bringing his sermon to its close, he set out what really mattered about the doctrine of the Trinity.

> Dear Friends, today is Trinity Sunday. What I have said about the "I" of God who speaks to us through the "I" of Jesus Christ is all that needs to be said about what we need to know about the mystery of the Trinity. This "I" of God speaks to us clearly only in Christ. For that reason, Christ is one with God. The Holy Spirit is present when someone believes this in their heart. From this faith, the Spirit of God comes into our lives – even the light of life. It is pointless to speculate about the unity of three persons in one God. It is enough for us to live in Christ as the Word of God, and then experience something of what the presence of the Holy Spirit is.[32]

We see here Brunner's characteristic anti-speculative and anti-metaphysical theological concerns, expressed in a pastoral form.

Yet Brunner's theological concerns were better expressed in his public lectures, which offered him a platform to engage a wide audience, reflecting the academy, church, and society at large. In what follows, I shall consider

---

[30] *Fraumünster-Predigten: Neue Folge*, 92.
[31] *Fraumünster-Predigten: Neue Folge*, 93.
[32] *Fraumünster-Predigten: Neue Folge*, 97. The precise date of this sermon is uncertain; it is likely to date from the late 1950s, after Brunner's return to Zurich from Japan.

what were probably his most successful lectures, on the theme of the "scandal of Christianity".

The Public Lecturer: *The Scandal of Christianity*

In October 1946 Brunner delivered the Zenos Lectures at McCormick Theological Seminary in Chicago, on the theme of the "Scandal of Christianity". The same lectures were subsequently given as the Robertson Lectures at Trinity College, Glasgow, Scotland, in March 1948. The lectures, which were published in English in 1951, and in German in 1957,[33] generated much interest and comment. For example, the leading evangelical theologian Carl F. H. Henry (1913–2003) sent a detailed report of the Zenos Lectures to the trustees of Wheaton College, Illinois, commenting on the perceptivity of Brunner's analysis, while raising questions about his approach to the authority and theological status of the Bible.[34] Henry's comments were of some importance, as a recent review of Brunner's work by the American evangelical theologian Cornelius van Til (1895–1987) had been highly critical of his theology.[35]

These lectures show Brunner at his best, mingling cultural analysis, theological reflection, and apologetic engagement. What are the barriers to the proclamation of the Christian faith in post-war culture? What are their origins? And how may they be addressed? Brunner notes that the post-war cultural mood has created opportunities and openings for the Christian faith. The rise of totalitarian states and the trauma of the Second World War has, he suggests, discredited the hitherto dominant "complacent picture of optimistic evolutionism".[36] Yet other factors have caused difficulty for faith – such as the growing "rejection of dogmatic religion" and a hankering for the securities of metaphysical certainty, as opposed to the contingencies and uncertainties of historically mediated knowledge.[37]

[33] It is unclear which is to be regarded as the primary text. The 1951 English text was revised by Ronald Gregor Smith (1913–68), editor of SCM Press from 1947 to 1956, who subsequently became Professor of Divinity at the University of Glasgow: see Keith W. Clements, *The Theology of Ronald Gregor Smith*. Leiden: E. J. Brill, 1986, 49–69. Smith was competent in German, and translated Buber's *Ich und Du* into English in the 1930s: Clements, *The Theology of Ronald Gregor Smith*, 11–16. The German text of 1957 clearly shows Brunner's style, and does not give any indication of being a translation from English, suggesting that it is to be regarded as the (possibly modified) original on which the English lectures were based. At multiple locations, the German text diverges from the English. I have decided to treat the German text as primary, while providing references to the English text, as modified by Smith. I do not believe that this uncertainty causes any difficulty in ascertaining Brunner's meaning at any point of importance.
[34] Carl F. H. Henry, "Theological Views of Emil Brunner", unpublished typescript (3 pages); Billy Graham Center Archives, Wheaton College, Illinois; collection 628.
[35] Cornelius van Til, *The New Modernism: An Appraisal of the Theology of Barth and Brunner*. Philadelphia: Presbyterian & Reformed Publishing Company, 1946.
[36] *Das Ärgernis des Christentums*, 8; *The Scandal of Christianity*, 10.
[37] *Das Ärgernis des Christentums*, 10–12; *The Scandal of Christianity*, 12–14.

Although Brunner does not develop the idea quite as forcefully as might be expected, his fundamental point is that a modernist mindset, inherited from the Enlightenment, continues to haunt western culture, raising concerns for faith. This, he suggests, impacts especially on five areas of Christian thought, each of which raises its own distinct "scandal" for a modernist mindset.

The first is the notion that God should choose to be disclosed in the contingencies of history, rather than the certainties of human rationality. Echoing, without acknowledging, the concerns of G. E. Lessing (1729–81) about the "scandal of particularity", Brunner notes how modernity finds itself scandalized by the historical particularity of divine self-disclosure in historical events. For Lessing, it was inconceivable that the contingencies of history could become the basis for the necessary truths of reason.[38] Brunner counters this by pointing out that the biblical notion of a personal God is most naturally expressed in terms of this God entering into history, and engaging with human existence under its own limiting conditions.[39] The rationalism of our age takes offence at the idea of historical revelation precisely because of the challenge this poses to its own rationalist notion of God.

This leads Brunner into the second "scandal" – the doctrine of the Trinity. For Brunner, the doctrine of the Trinity separates Christianity from other monotheistic faiths, on the one hand, and from philosophical and rationalist ideas of God on the other.[40] After a brief reflection on philosophical notions of God, Brunner makes his core point: a rationalist notion of God is simply a human invention, whereas Christianity seeks to respond to a self-disclosing God. Rationalism believes in "a God who arises from human thought, who is grounded in thinking"; in other words, to put this negatively, it does not believe "in a God who reveals himself in history".[41] The God of philosophy is by definition "an ideogram [*Gedankengebilde*] of our own thinking". It is "an object of human thought"; but it is not a "living God", a "God who addresses us".[42] God's self-revelation breaks open "the immanent structure of human thought", in effect liberating it from a rationalist prison and enabling it to discover a "transcendent reality", to which the human mind is otherwise closed.[43]

---

[38] "Zufällige Geschichtswahrheiten können der Beweis von notwendigen Vernunftwahrheiten nie werden." G. E. Lessing, *Über der Geweis des Geistes und der Kraft* (1777). In *Werke*, ed. H. G. Göpfert. 8 vols. Munich: Hanser Verlag, 1970–9, vol. 8, 12.
[39] *Das Ärgernis des Christentums*, 13–26; *The Scandal of Christianity*, 15–28. On Lessing's views on revelation and history, see Gordon E. Michalson, *Lessing's Ugly Ditch: A Study of Theology and History*. University Park: Pennsylvania State University Press, 1985.
[40] *Das Ärgernis des Christentums*, 29; *The Scandal of Christianity*, 31. Brunner's analysis here should be set against the historical backdrop presented in works such as Barry Nisbet, "The Rationalisation of the Holy Trinity from Lessing to Hegel." *Lessing Yearbook* 41 (1999): 65–89.
[41] *Das Ärgernis des Christentums*, 31; *The Scandal of Christianity*, 33. The German text makes the point much more clearly than the English.
[42] *Das Ärgernis des Christentums*, 33; *The Scandal of Christianity*, 35.
[43] *Das Ärgernis des Christentums*, 34; *The Scandal of Christianity*, 36.

The point that Brunner develops in this important lecture could be summarized as follows (and here I depart from his own way of expressing himself). The doctrine of the Trinity is both the theological *consequence* and theological *articulation* of the fundamental "givenness" of divine revelation. It contradicts reason precisely because it challenges both the authority of autonomous human reason and the legitimacy of the worldview that it creates to reinforce its own self-evidential correctness – a false assumption that is called into question by God's act of revelation.

Having called the autonomy of human reason into question, Brunner proceeded to challenge a further element of the Enlightenment's optimistic vision of humanity. His third lecture engaged the "scandal" of original sin. Brunner interprets this primarily in terms of a denial of the autonomy of humanity. We are created in order to relate to God. "Humanity alone is created to hear God's word. It alone is intended to live in fellowship with God."[44] This involves a reorientation of humanity, to recognize that its true destiny, in the first place, lies outside itself, and in the second, cannot be achieved unaided, without divine grace.

Brunner then explores what happens if humanity refuses to accept its place within the created order. The origins of human evil, he argues, lie in the fact that "human beings want to be their own god". Instead of being "free in God", people long to be "free from God".[45] For Brunner, sin is not merely an existential possibility; it is a reality. It is not as if there is a "bad" part of human nature that corrupts what is otherwise healthy.[46]

Brunner argues that the Christian understanding of human nature represents a viable and necessary middle way between the "negation of all human dignity" and the "boundless exaggeration of human divinity" spawned by the Enlightenment – namely, a view that "sees the greatness and misery of humanity together in a way that chimes with experience".[47] For Brunner, this is the way things are, and no realistic account of human identity, human possibilities, or human social life which ignores this truth can be sustained.

Brunner's fourth lecture, on the scandal of "The Mediator", deals with a cultural reluctance to incorporate the person of Jesus Christ into belief in God, or attendance at church. Brunner, however, insists that a Christological focus must be maintained, not least because of its importance for belief in a personal God – and hence for sustaining human personality in an increasingly impersonal age, characterized by the "the depersonalization of the modern understanding of life".[48] The Christian way of thinking, Brunner

---

[44] *Das Ärgernis des Christentums*, 56; *The Scandal of Christianity*, 58.
[45] *Das Ärgernis des Christentums*, 59; *The Scandal of Christianity*, 61.
[46] *Das Ärgernis des Christentums*, 62; *The Scandal of Christianity*, 64.
[47] *Das Ärgernis des Christentums*, 68; *The Scandal of Christianity*, 70–1; The English translation at this point is poorly expressed; the German text makes it clear that the issue is not so much the "divinity" of humanity, but an attempted "divinization" (*Vergottung*) of humanity.
[48] *Das Ärgernis des Christentums*, 71; *The Scandal of Christianity*, 73.

insists, is not about Jesus Christ making possible "union" with God, but rather "communion" with God – that is to say, God's intention is for humanity to exist in a community, characterized by love. "Unity makes for the impersonal, community for the personal."[49]

Having defended the notion of sin in the previous lecture, Brunner insists that God's forgiveness of sin is anchored, not simply to the person of Jesus Christ, but to his death. "The cross of Christ and the message of atonement or redemption is nothing but the last phase of incarnation, which in itself is the final phase of God's coming to man."[50] Where some portrayed Jesus Christ as essentially a prophetic figure who became incorporated into a Pauline doctrine of redemption, Brunner insists on the continuity of the gospel according to Jesus Christ with the gospel of Jesus Christ.

Finally, Brunner turned to deal with the scandal of the resurrection. His concern here is not so much Enlightenment critiques of the historical actuality of the resurrection of Jesus Christ as an understanding of the transhistorical significance of Christ, and its implications for our understanding of history. Brunner contrasts the New Testament idea of "hope" with the secular notion of "progress", arguing against the "pseudo-Christian" idea of advancement towards a Christian society characterized by peace and social justice.[51] Rather than indulge in such utopian thinking, Christians are called upon to struggle in hope, whatever their situation. Brunner uses an analogy familiar from the Second World War:

> Just as there was a D-Day on which the dark powers were broken on the cross, so there will be a V-Day on which this victory, which is hidden until then, breaks into visibility – a real day of victory.[52]

Brunner's achievement in these lectures was to demonstrate that his five chosen topics were not isolated ideas but were, rather, interwoven and interconnected aspects of the Christian faith. That they were "scandalous" to modernity was not because they were ungrounded or irrational, but because they challenged prevailing understandings of reason and human nature, offering an alternative vision of reality. As a public intellectual, Brunner offered a vigorous defence of the theological reliability of core Christian beliefs in the face of cultural anxiety about their credibility and hostility towards their implications.

---

[49] *Das Ärgernis des Christentums*, 73; *The Scandal of Christianity*, 75.
[50] *Das Ärgernis des Christentums*, 83; *The Scandal of Christianity*, 86. The English version glosses the German term *Versöhnung* as "atonement or redemption".
[51] *Das Ärgernis des Christentums*, 103–4; *The Scandal of Christianity*, 109–10.
[52] *Das Ärgernis des Christentums*, 100; *The Scandal of Christianity*, 105. "D-Day" (6 June 1944) marked the Allied landings in Normandy that proved a turning point in the Second World War, leading to "V-Day" (strictly speaking, "VE-Day", 8 May 1945), when Nazi forces surrendered, bringing to an end the war in Europe. The war in the Pacific continued until 15 August 1945.

Theological Education: Brunner's *Dogmatics*

The twentieth century saw a number of major works of Protestant dogmatics – that is to say, a systematic presentation of the core themes of Christian theology.[53] The most famous is Karl Barth's *Church Dogmatics*, which tends to overshadow its rivals. If pressed to identify others, most would mention Paul Tillich's *Systematic Theology* and Emil Brunner's *Dogmatics*. The first two volumes of Brunner's *Dogmatics* appeared in 1946 and 1950; the third and final volume did not appear until 1960.[54] Yet few would now consider Brunner's three volumes as having anything approaching the status of Barth's major work. Indeed, this judgement seems to have been anticipated by his readers in the 1960s. Why?

Brunner's *Dogmatics* were based on his Zurich lectures on Christian theology, which he began to plan in 1924, and continued to teach until his retirement from Zurich some thirty years later.[55] Brunner wrote to Barth on 23 January 1924, setting out four possible approaches to the teaching of dogmatics, and asking for Barth's advice.[56]

1. The exposition of a confession (*Auslegung eines kirchlichen Bekenntnisses*). This, for Brunner, had the distinct advantage of demonstrating that theology was ecclesially anchored and grounded.
2. Biblical theology.
3. The teachings of Christianity, considered as a section of a more general theory of religion.
4. A speculative theology, which establishes from the outset that it will lead to Christian outcomes.

Brunner's inclination at that time was to develop a confessional approach, paralleling in certain ways that of Calvin's *Institutes*. Barth's response indicated a degree of convergence with him, indicating that he was at that time considering mingling a "prophetic" approach like Calvin's with a dogmatic approach, echoing Christian confessions while finding their ultimate grounding in Scripture.[57]

Barth, however, saw the production of successive works of dogmatics as a means of developing his own thinking. Brunner preferred to develop his theology through monographs, focusing on specific theological issues, rather

---

[53] For an overview of the genre, see Dietrich Ritschl, "Systematic Theology." In *The Encyclopaedia of Christianity*. 5 vols., vol. 5, 286–97. Grand Rapids, MI: Eerdmans, 2008. Note the issues raised by Colin Gunton, "A Rose by Any Other Name? From 'Christian Doctrine' to 'Systematic Theology'." *International Journal of Systematic Theology* 1, no. 1 (1999): 4–23.
[54] Jehle, *Emil Brunner*, 493–7.
[55] For the early lectures, see Jehle, *Emil Brunner*, 203–12. The three sets of lectures on systematic theology were entitled "Christliche Theologie im Zusammenhang I–III".
[56] Letter to Barth, dated 23 January 1924; *Karl Barth–Emil Brunner, Briefwechsel*, 87–93.
[57] Barth to Brunner, 26 January 1924, *Karl Barth–Emil Brunner, Briefwechsel*, 94–6.

than propounding a particular overall "dogmatic" framework. As I noted earlier (p. xi), Brunner's period of intense theological reflection and creativity can be located primarily within the years between the two world wars. During this period, Brunner tended to develop his ideas through theological monographs, such as *The Mediator* and *Truth as Encounter*, allowing himself ample space to explore issues, and develop answers that he believed were satisfactory. Where Barth's *Church Dogmatics* were an instrument of theological exploration and development, Brunner's *Dogmatics* were essentially summative rather than innovative, bringing together ideas that had already been developed and explored elsewhere. Brunner makes this clear in his preface to the first volume of the *Dogmatics*, pointing out that these volumes re-cast material that he had developed over many years in the form of "single monographs".[58] The re-casting of the material is new; the substance of that material is, however, primarily hewn from his substantial exploratory monographs.

As noted, the three volumes of Brunner's *Dogmatics* were published after the Second World War. By this time, Brunner's creative powers were on the wane. Frank Jehle, Brunner's most recent and most thorough biographer, notes that "Brunner's creativity, his gift to raise new questions and give new answers to old questions, declined in the years after the Second World War."[59] Yet Jehle rightly notes that this creative decline was not of critical importance to the *Dogmatics*, which had no intention of being "original or new, but were rather the basics of a concentrated textbook". Brunner's *Dogmatics* arose out of his lectures at the University of Zurich over many years, and are strongly pedagogical in their orientation.

The superficially attractive and plausible comparison with Barth's *Church Dogmatics* does not really work; a far better comparison can be made with Calvin's *Institutes of the Christian Religion*.[60] Like Calvin – who in turn, of course, followed the great twelfth-century theologian Peter Lombard – Brunner believed that a formal presentation of theology was to be divided into four sections, preceded by some introductory comments setting the context for the work. Brunner's *Dogmatics* is structured as follows:

Prolegomena: The Meaning and Task of Dogmatics
Part 1: The Eternal Foundation of Divine Self-Communication
Part 2: The Historical Outworking of the Divine Self-Communication
Part 3: The Self-Communication of God as Making Himself Present through the Holy Spirit
Part 4: The Consummation of the Divine Self-Communication in Eternity

---

[58] *Dogmatik* I, 8; *Dogmatics* 1, vi.
[59] Jehle, *Emil Brunner*, 494.
[60] Many have pointed out how Brunner's *Dogmatics* follow the traditional approach of pre-Kantian Reformed dogmatics: see, for example, Richard A. Muller, "Christ – the Revelation or the Revealer? Brunner and Reformed Orthodoxy on the Doctrine of the Word of God." *Journal of the Evangelical Theological Society* 26 (1983): 307–19.

Like Calvin before him, Brunner's concern was to present a systematically organized account of Christian doctrine.[61] Both Barth and Brunner have opening sections dealing with "prolegomena". Yet while Barth's prolegomenon provides both a foundation and clarification of the tasks of dogmatics, Brunner's is much more concerned with pedagogical concerns – in effect, clearing up some preliminary issues, such as the place of dogmatics in the life of the church, before beginning the task of dogmatics itself. Like Barth, Brunner includes historical analysis within his dogmatic exposition; unlike Barth, he separates the two, placing his historical analysis in a series of "Excurses", which do not disrupt the flow of his dogmatic reflections.

One point must be noted before we proceed further. Brunner's reflections on the tasks of theology led him to draw a distinction between its "dogmatic" and "eristic" or "apologetic" roles (see pp. 66–74, 191–2). Brunner's reflections on the post-war situation led him to emphasize the missionary challenges confronting the churches,[62] and to ensure that the churches were resourced theologically as they engaged in the missionary task. It is therefore significant to note that he included a section entitled "Missionary Theology" in the prolegomena to his *Dogmatics*,[63] which emphasized the role of theology in "removing the obstacles which lie on the road between the gospel and its audience – namely, those obstacles which are amenable to intellectual reflection".

Brunner thus distinguishes between two aspects of "eristic theology". Negatively, it is about challenging the intellectual "spirit of the age"; positively, it is about presenting the gospel in forms adapted to the situations of its audiences. "Missionary theology is such an intellectual unfolding of the gospel of Jesus Christ, which sets out from and addresses the spiritual situation of its audience."[64] For Brunner, Protestant theology has failed to appreciate the importance of such a "missionary theology", tending to "ignore it, and even to subvert it".[65]

Brunner seems to have envisaged his *Dogmatics* as a resource for students and pastors seeking to develop their own theological positions. Yet his tendency to recapitulate what had already been discussed and developed elsewhere in his works inevitably reduced their appeal. The manner in which Brunner arranged his material was of interest; yet there proved to be limited novelty value in such a limited "re-casting" of theological topics. Where Barth's *Church Dogmatics* were – and continue to be – seen as magisterial

---

[61] See the points made in Alister E. McGrath, "The Shaping of Reality: Calvin and the Formation of Theological Vision." *Toronto Journal of Theology* 25 (2008): 187–204; Günter Frank, "Gläubige Vernunft – Vernünftigen Glaube: Luther, Melanchthon und Calvin und die Frage nach einem vernünftigen Glaube." In *Calvinus Clarissimus Theologus*, ed. Herman J. Selderhuis, 141–57. Göttingen: Vandenhoeck & Ruprecht, 2012.

[62] See especially "Toward a Missionary Theology".

[63] *Dogmatik I*, 108–9; *Dogmatics 1*, 101–3.

[64] *Dogmatik I*, 108; *Dogmatics 1*, 102.

[65] *Dogmatik I*, 109; *Dogmatics 1*, 103.

discussions of theological questions of abiding importance, Brunner's *Dogmatics* have long since ceased to be read.

Are we to see this as a failure on Brunner's part? Perhaps. Yet Brunner himself does not appear to have been entirely enthusiastic about his *Dogmatics*. The slow pace of writing the volumes over more than fifteen years inevitably suggested that he saw other projects as taking priority. The uneven quality of the third volume – reflecting Brunner's declining health in the final phase of his life – led its readers to feel there was a lack of sparkle and originality suggesting that the work was not of great significance.

In any case, Brunner was caught up in new developments after the Second World War, which may well have distracted him from his work on his *Dogmatics*. In what follows, I shall consider his growing connections with Asia, and their implications for his future career.

Tokyo: Brunner's Engagement with Asia

Relaxation of travel restrictions in the post-war period made it possible for Brunner to reconnect with his colleagues in Europe and America. It also allowed him to travel to Asia for the first time. He had long been involved in the work of the YMCA (known as the Christliche Verein Junger Menschen, or simply CVJM, in Germany and Switzerland). In the late 1940s, Tracy Strong (1887–1968) invited Brunner to play a leading advocational and advisory role for the movement as it developed its connections with Asia.[66] To mark his twenty-five years as professor, the University of Zurich granted Brunner extended leave of absence, allowing him to lecture in Japan, Korea, and China in August and September 1948, and in India in February and March 1949.[67]

Brunner's visit to Japan clearly had a considerable impact on him. To the surprise of some, he accepted the offer of a "Professorship of Christianity" at the newly established International Christian University in Tokyo in December 1952. This school, which began its teaching programme in April 1953 with 400 students, was established partly to rebuild relationships between the United States and Japan following the tensions of the Second World War. It had extensive support from the American National Council of Churches. Significantly, the teaching programme would be delivered in English.

In a sermon preached in Zurich's Fraumünster on 30 August 1953, a week before his departure for Asia, Brunner made it clear that he saw this invitation from Tokyo as a "call from God".

---

[66] Jehle, *Emil Brunner*, 515–43.
[67] For a report of this visit, see Lloyd Lorbeer, "Brunner Meets Indian Queries." *The Christian Century*, 25 January 1950, 121–2.

> I can only say that the circumstances are such that I have to recognize the call from the International Christian University in Tokyo as the call of God, and as my wife shares this perception, I have ventured to accept this call. What will come of this, I have placed in God's hand. I do not know. I do not go with particularly high expectations. But I cannot be disobedient to this call.[68]

It remains unclear what led Brunner to resign from his chair at Zurich at the age of 64, and set out on this new phase of his career. He would receive a generous salary by the standards of the time ($6,650) at Tokyo. The death of his son Thomas (born 1926) on 1 August 1952 may well have precipitated reflection about his future. It is also possible that Brunner may have realized that his star was fading in Europe, suggesting that a move "to fresh woods, and pastures new" (John Milton) might give him a new lease of life. Work on the third volume of his *Dogmatics* – which was eventually published in 1960 – had stalled.

Brunner's arrival in Japan in September 1953, to lecture on Christian philosophy and ethics to students of all faculties at the International Christian University in Tokyo, was greeted with widespread acclaim. Initially, the Brunners shared this sense of excitement. Margrit Brunner's letters to friends and family at home in Switzerland were upbeat; Brunner found himself lionized by Christian groups across Japan, and called upon to speak at major events. Yet within a few months of their arrival, it was clear that things were going wrong.[69] Margrit stopped writing home. Her friends and family now received circular letters from Brunner himself. In one such letter, dated 5 May 1954, Brunner reported that Margrit had broken her wrist as a result of a fall, and was no longer able to paint. It proved a turning point. Brunner was now calling into question the wisdom of his decision to go to Japan.

In a circular letter of 11 November 1954, Brunner disclosed that Margrit was now suffering from depression. It was, he remarked, very common among western women in Japan. Brunner's intention had been to remain in Japan until he was 70. But the deteriorating health of his wife threw his plans into turmoil. While Margrit was well enough to accompany Brunner to California in February 1955 to deliver the Earl Lectures at the Pacific School of Religion in Berkeley, it was clear to the Brunners that they would have to return to Switzerland. On 11 July, they set out for home. At an early stage on the long sea journey, Brunner suffered from a stroke, which required him to be hospitalized in Colombo for two weeks. The Brunners eventually arrived in Zurich on 4 September 1955.[70]

Brunner never regained his health. He suffered a second stroke almost exactly a year later, which led to him being confined to bed and prevented

---

[68] "Dienst": *Fraumünster-Predigten*, 151–6; quote on p. 155.
[69] Jehle, *Emil Brunner*, 538–9.
[70] Jehle, *Emil Brunner*, 540–3.

him from working. In September 1955 he wrote to his close friend Max Huber, telling him that a "weakness" in his left hand was making it difficult for him to write.[71] His last lecture course on "Freedom and Justice", delivered during the winter semester of 1955–6 was a considerable success – but not one that would be repeated.[72] He struggled to complete his writing projects, including the final volume of his *Dogmatics*, which eventually appeared in 1960. The work draws on earlier writings published before his move to Japan, especially *The Misunderstanding of the Church* (1951) and *Eternal Hope* (1952). Now unable to write, he had to dictate the text, which was transcribed by a family friend, Hanni Guanella-Zietzschmann.[73]

Final Illness and Death

Brunner's delicate health finally collapsed in early 1966. The signs were there for everyone to see. He was deteriorating. Few of his friends or family had any doubts about the inevitable outcome of the process they could see unfolding before their eyes. He could not be expected to remain alive much longer. Some of his closest friends took the view that there was unfinished business that needed to be sorted out – Brunner's dysfunctional relationship with Karl Barth.[74]

On 2 April 1966, Peter Vogelsanger (1912–95), pastor of the Fraumünster in Zurich,[75] and one of Brunner's closest friends, wrote to Barth, apparently without Brunner's knowledge. Vogelsanger informed Barth that Brunner was seriously ill in hospital, and had not long to live. Barth replied immediately, in some distress.

> Your letter with its concluding two lines about Emil moved me *very much*. … If I myself were able to get about after more or less two years of illness, I would get on the next train, so that I could hold Emil Brunner's hand. Tell him from me, if he is still alive and if it is possible, that I yet again commend him to *our* God. And tell him *most certainly* that the time when I felt that I had to say "No!" against him is long past, and that we all live only because a great and merciful God speaks his gracious "Yes" to us all.[76]

[71] Jehle, *Emil Brunner*, 546 n. 3.
[72] For a good account of Brunner's final years, see Jehle, *Emil Brunner*, 545–67.
[73] Jehle, *Emil Brunner*, 556–8.
[74] I. John Hesselink, "Karl Barth and Emil Brunner – A Tangled Tale with a Happy Ending." In *How Karl Barth Changed My Mind*, ed. Donald K. McKim, 131–42. Grand Rapids, MI: Eerdmans, 1986. Hesselink arranged a meeting between Brunner and Barth in Basle on 19 November 1960; this did not, however, lead to a "reconciliation" between the two men.
[75] See his masterly study of the history of the Fraumünster: Peter Vogelsanger, *Zürich und sein Fraumünster: Eine elfhundertjährige Geschichte (853–1956)*. Zurich: NZZ Libro, 1994.
[76] Although Barth's letter was addressed to Vogelsanger, it is included in the collected edition of the Barth–Brunner correspondence: *Karl Barth–Emil Brunner, Briefwechsel*, 391. Barth's phrase "*Unserm* Gott befohlen!" (emphasis in original) parallels the French *Adieu*, and is not easily rendered in English.

Barth's letter arrived on the morning of 5 April. Vogelsanger cycled to the clinic at Zollikerberg, and informed Brunner that "Karl Barth sends his greetings!"[77] He then read Brunner this letter by his bedside. Brunner smiled, pressed his hand, and shortly afterwards lapsed into an unconsciousness from which he never reawakened. He died at noon on Wednesday, 6 April 1966 at the Neumünsterspital at Zollikerberg, near Zurich. His funeral at the Fraumünster in Zurich on 12 April 1966 was led by Vogelsanger.

So what is Brunner's legacy? What have later generations made of his theological project? In the final chapter, I shall reflect on his longer-term importance for Christian theology.

---

[77] *Karl Barth–Emil Brunner, Briefwechsel* 391 n. 4.

9
Legacy: The Contemporary Significance of Emil Brunner's Theology

The task of assessing the significance of a theologian is not easy, not least because of the need for historical depth and perspective, and a certain degree of critical distance. Many theologians of the twentieth century who were regarded as outstanding in their own day and age have failed to persuade subsequent generations of their merits. The reception of theology is a complex and poorly understood process, in which later generations review and revise the judgements of their forebears. Karl Barth was regarded as a theological colossus at the time of his death in 1968; that judgement remains the dominant view in the first decades of the twenty-first century. But what of Emil Brunner?

At the time of his death in 1964, Brunner was celebrated as one of the greatest theologians of the twentieth century.[1] His impact on both European and American Christian thinking – especially in the field of theology and political thought – was substantial.[2] Yet interest in him stalled in the 1970s, and declined dramatically thereafter. Where once there had been a torrent of publications and doctoral theses concerning Brunner, both in English and

---

[1] For particularly important assessments, see J. Robert Nelson, "Emil Brunner – Teacher Unsurpassed." *Theology Today* 19, no. 4 (1963): 532–5; Frank Jehle, *Emil Brunner: Theologe im 20. Jahrhundert*. Zurich: Theologischer Verlag, 2006, 569–82. For other assessments, see Franco Ronchi, "Emil Brunner: 1889–1966." *Protestantismo* 21 (1966): 104–7; Gerhard Ebeling, "Die Beunruhigung der Theologie durch die Frage nach den Früchten des Geistes: Vortrag in einer akademischen Festschrift für Emil Brunner in der Universität Zürich." *Zeitschrift für Theologie und Kirche* 66 (1969): 353–68; Hans Wildenberger, "Emil Brunner: Sein Leben und Werk." *Reformatio* 31, no. 4 (1982): 85–102; Eckhard Lessing, *Geschichte der deutschsprachigen evangelischen Theologie von Albrecht Ritschl bis zur Gegenwart*. 2 vols. Göttingen: Vandenhoeck & Ruprecht, 2000–4, vol. 2, 43–8.
[2] See particularly the influential collection of essays from 1962: Charles W. Kegley, ed., *The Theology of Emil Brunner*. New York: Macmillan, 1962.

Emil Brunner: A Reappraisal, First Edition. Alister E. McGrath.
© 2014 John Wiley & Sons, Ltd. Published 2016 by John Wiley & Sons, Ltd.

German, this rapidly declined to a trickle.[3] He now tends to be recalled (inaccurately) only as someone who (unsuccessfully) defended natural theology against Karl Barth in 1934.

Brunner needs to be reconsidered and rehabilitated – not in his totality, but certainly in relation to some of his methods and approaches, which retain validity and significance, especially in the theological and cultural climate which has developed in the west in the twenty-first century. In this chapter I shall map out some areas in which Brunner's ideas have relevance for this new situation. But first, we must consider why he has been neglected since his death.

In one sense, Brunner has been the victim of a historical happenstance, over which he had no control. Karl Barth towers over twentieth-century Protestant systematic theology in general, and Swiss theology in particular.[4] Brunner always stood in Barth's shadow, and was gradually eclipsed by him, even during his lifetime. With the publication of the final volume of Brunner's *Dogmatics* in 1960, it was obvious that his depth of theological exposition was inferior to that of Barth.[5] Brunner's decline in the face of Barth was thus neither unexpected nor unmerited.

Yet Barth was not the sole reason for the decline in Brunner's reputation after the 1960s. Brunner, it must be conceded, contributed significantly to his own eclipse. A number of weaknesses are evident to the attentive reader of his writings.

First, Brunner's engagement with the Bible is often shallow, suggesting that he adapts and incorporates it at will into his dogmatic reflections. A particularly luminous example of this is found in his distinction between the "formal" and "material" aspects of the *imago Dei* (see pp. 118–20), which rests on a superficial engagement with a biblical theme which has been the subject of intense discussion by biblical scholars.[6] Brunner's sermons tend to use biblical texts as their point of departure rather than as their expository foundation. His only major work of biblical exegesis is his 1938 commentary on Paul's letter to the Romans, which is best seen as a catechetical rather than a scholarly work. The contrast with Barth is striking; even those who disagree with Barth's interpretation of the Bible, or his

---

[3] See the thorough analysis in Mark G. McKim, *Emil Brunner: A Bibliography*. Lanham, MD: Scarecrow Press, 1996.
[4] Note the title of a 1945 collection of Barth's pieces: Karl Barth, *Eine schweizer Stimme, 1938–1945*. Zurich: Evangelischer Verlag, 1945. Switzerland produced a disproportionate number of outstanding theologians in the twentieth century, including the Catholic writers Hans Urs von Balthasar (1905–88) and Hans Küng (born 1928).
[5] For a more sympathetic account of Brunner's dogmatics, see Gabriele Lunghini, *Emil Brunner*. Brescia: Editrice Morcelliana, 2009, 105–16.
[6] For examples of the modern scholarly discussion relevant to Brunner's approach, see Peter Schwanz, *Imago Dei als christologisch-anthropologisches Problem in der Geschichte der alten Kiche von Paulus bis Clemens von Alexandrien*. Halle: Niemeyer, 1970; A. Jónsson Gunnlaugur and S. Cheney Michael, *The Image of God: Genesis 1:26–28 in a Century of Old Testament Research*. Stockholm: Almqvist & Wiksell International, 1988; Gerald Kruhöffer, *Der Mensch – Das Bild Gottes*. Göttingen: Vandenhoeck & Ruprecht, 1999.

understanding of its theological authority, can hardly overlook the major role that biblical engagement plays in his theological project.[7]

Second, Brunner's decision to develop his theology through weighty monographs on focused topics – evident in such works as *Truth as Encounter* – had the advantage of allowing him to engage with topics in substantial detail. His readers are left in little doubt as to the depth and quality of his engagement with the issues. Yet Brunner does not make it easy for his readers, who are often overwhelmed with detail and – especially in some of his works of the 1920s and 1930s – forced to cope with a difficult analytical style. Brunner can write easily and accessibly, as *Our Faith* (1935) makes abundantly clear. Yet the dogmatic works in which he develops his own approach do not reward readers with stylistic vibrancy or verbal elegance. With some exceptions, their style is pedestrian and workmanlike rather than polished and eloquent.

Third, Brunner tends to dismiss his opponents somewhat peremptorily, often denigrating theological categories or approaches as a result of concerns about their individual representatives. His 1924 work *Die Mystik und das Wort*, for example, dismissed Schleiermacher in an almost cavalier manner, failing to show any concern for, or attentiveness towards, the specific limitations of the intellectual context in which Schleiermacher developed his theological approach. It is little wonder that Barth – himself a critic of Schleiermacher – felt that this work was far too shrill in its tone, and superficial in its analysis.[8] Barth never ruled out the possibility of some kind of theological *rapprochement* with Schleiermacher,[9] believing that Brunner's dismissal of any such possibility was premature. Similarly, Brunner's somewhat peremptory dismissal of the doctrine of the virgin birth of Christ was seen as contentious, contrasting with the more nuanced and appreciative approach of Barth.[10]

This troubling aspect of Brunner's approach caused him difficulties during his time at Princeton Theological Seminary during 1938–9. His somewhat simplistic dismissal of Reformed Orthodoxy's doctrine of the "Word of God" raised hackles among many conservative Presbyterians in the United States. He rejected many of their ideas as *Bibelglaube* (a "faith in the Bible",

---

[7] See, for example, Bruce McCormack, "Historical Criticism and Dogmatic Interest in Karl Barth's Theological Exegesis of the New Testament." In *Biblical Hermeneutics in Historical Perspective*, ed. Mark Burrows and Paul Rorem, 322–38. Grand Rapids, MI: Wm. B. Eerdmans, 1991; idem, "The Being of Holy Scripture is in Becoming: Karl Barth in Conversation with American Evangelical Criticism." In *Evangelicals and Scripture: Tradition, Authority and Hermeneutics*, ed. Vincent E. Bacote, Laura C. Miguélez, and Dennis L. Okholm, 55–75. Downers Grove, IL: InterVarsity Press, 2004.

[8] Karl Barth, "Brunners Schleiermacherbuch." *Zwischen den Zeiten* 7 (1924): 49–64. Note especially Barth's comments about respecting Schleiermacher's cultural, apologetic, and ethical intentions.

[9] Bruce L. McCormack, "What has Basel to do with Berlin? Continuities in the Theologies of Barth and Schleiermacher." *Princeton Seminary Bulletin* 23, no. 2 (2002): 146–73.

[10] Dustin Resch, *Barth's Interpretation of the Virgin Birth: A Sign of Mystery*. Farnham: Ashgate, 2012.

rather than in the one to whom the Bible bears witness) or a mere *Fürwahrhalten* (the "holding of certain beliefs to be true").[11] The regrettable outcome of this was that the *tone* of Brunner's theological pronouncements alienated many who might otherwise have been sympathetic to the substance of his approach, and willing to consider where it might lead – even if this appeared to take them beyond their theological comfort zone.

It is a matter for regret that Brunner seems to have played a significant role in his own decline. Yet this is not to say that his theological contribution can – or should – be ignored. There are good reasons for suggesting that he has bequeathed a useable legacy to the twenty-first century. In bringing this work to a close, I shall briefly explore some significant points at which Brunner deserves to be brought back into contemporary theological discussions.

The Reformed Tradition: A Richer Range of Possibilities

The Reformed tradition is rightly recognized as representing one of the most intellectually rigorous and productive approaches to theology, philosophy, and spirituality. Many – such as myself – who are not confessionally Reformed take this tradition with the greatest seriousness, recognizing its significance and value across a wide range of disciplines.[12] Yet the Reformed tradition is not monolithic, culturally or theologically.[13] Some would argue that, since the 1960s, the tradition has come to define itself increasingly with reference to Barth,[14] who has come to be seen as a standard-bearer for Reformed theological convictions across many constituencies which would earlier have considered him of questionable Reformed provenance and orthodoxy.[15]

Yet the Reformed tradition is open to redirection and redefinition, in the light of ongoing dialogue with its own past and the new cultural situations that it faces. It cannot be frozen into a set of doctrines and attitudes. In

---

[11] Brunner's attitude here reflects a Kantian context: see Axel Hesper, "Wahrheit und Fürwahrhalten." *Synthesis Philosophica* 50, no. 2 (2010): 317–32.

[12] For example, Reformed philosophy has come to play a major role in contemporary debates: see Dewey J. Hoitenga, *Faith and Reason from Plato to Plantinga: An Introduction to Reformed Epistemology*. Albany, NY: State University of New York Press, 1991.

[13] See the diversity within David Willis-Watkins and Michael Welker, eds., *Toward the Future of Reformed Theology: Tasks, Topics, Traditions*. Grand Rapids, MI: Eerdmans, 1999. More specifically, see Yung Han Kim, "The Identity of Reformed Theology and Its Ecumenicity in the Twenty-First Century." In *Reformed Theology: Identity and Ecumenicity*, ed. Wallace M. Alston and Michael Welker, 1–19. Grand Rapids, MI: Eerdmans, 2003.

[14] See the points made by Bruce L. McCormack, "The End of Reformed Theology: The Voice of Karl Barth in the Doctrinal Chaos of the Moment." In *Reformed Theology: Identity and Ecumenicity*, ed. Alston and Welker, 46–64.

[15] Evangelicalism is a case in point: Sung Wook Chung, *Karl Barth and Evangelical Theology: Convergences and Divergences*. Grand Rapids, MI: Baker Academic, 2006.

speaking, for example, of a "Reformed objection to natural theology",[16] contemporary scholarship has allowed certain views within the tradition to assume normative or privileged status. Brunner unquestionably represents a Reformed voice in theology. Yet in terms of its presuppositions and its outcomes, Brunner's method differs from that of Barth. Brunner gives priority to Calvin over later interpreters of Calvin,[17] and offers readings of the Reformed tradition which diverge from that of Barth – most notably on natural theology.

Barth and Brunner were both strongly committed to the Reformed theological community and churches, and saw their theologies as being ecclesially embedded. There is a need for the Reformed tradition to recreate theological space for Brunner's method and approaches. In what follows, I shall note how in four areas his approaches would further enrich the Reformed tradition, as well as a wider Christian theology. In each case, Brunner has something significant to say that need to be heard – not least in relation to natural law and natural theology.

A Theology of Nature: The Basis of Natural Law, Theology, and Science

Brunner's flawed 1934 debate with Karl Barth is often framed in terms of "natural theology", despite the fact that its focus clearly lies elsewhere. Nevertheless, Brunner's theological approach unquestionably mandates a new appreciation for the significance of nature. Brunner never departed from his fundamental assertion that, as a consequence of its created character, the natural order possessed some "permanent capacity for revelation" (*dauernde Offenbarungsmächtigkeit*).[18] As we have seen, Brunner was emphatic that the human ability to discern this revelation was attenuated, and that it was only alleviated in the case of those whose "blindness had been healed by Christ".[19] This is not a "natural theology" in the sense of offering rational proofs for God's existence, but more in the sense of intuiting God's presence and character from reflection on the created order, and finding such knowledge confirmed, extended, and above all transformed through divine self-disclosure (see pp. 121–7). Brunner was emphatic that a proper knowledge of God results only from "self-disclosure, a self-manifestation of God – that is, when there is revelation".[20]

---

[16] Laura L. Garcia, "Natural Theology and the Reformed Objection." In *Christian Perspectives on Religious Knowledge*, ed. C. Stephen Evans and Merold Westphal, 112–33. Grand Rapids, MI: Eerdmans, 1993.
[17] For the issues, see Richard A. Muller, *After Calvin: Studies in the Development of a Theological Tradition*. Oxford: Oxford University Press, 2003.
[18] "Natur und Gnade", 345; "Nature and Grace", 27.
[19] "Natur und Gnade", 344; "Nature and Grace", 26–7.
[20] *Dogmatik I*, 24–31; *Dogmatics 1*, 14–21.

Yet there is little doubt that Brunner's understanding of the doctrine of creation gives a new theological impulse to attentiveness towards the natural order. For Brunner, this creates conceptual space for certain forms of natural law, natural theology, and an understanding of the natural sciences.

> The world created by God as a creature is a limited, dependent being, which is fundamentally different from the being of God . . . Yet this creature, as the work of the creator, is *not without likeness* to the Divine Being, who chooses to exalt and communicate himself through it. God manifests himself, his "everlasting power and divinity", in his work of creation.[21]

In the first place, Brunner sees such an understanding of creation as mandating the natural sciences, both as an intellectual enterprise in itself and as a legitimate calling for a Christian believer. Indeed, he offers a theology of creation which indicates that a believer will engage the natural world to greater effect than others: "The world is only knowable as something created by *God* through divine revelation; but, as *created* by God, it is the subject of legitimate scientific investigation."[22]

The creation of the world by God undergirds "the mathematical order of the material world, which bears witness to the thought of the creator".[23] Brunner's theological anthropology – especially his understanding of the *imago Dei* – gives added weight to his affirmation of the legitimacy of the natural sciences.

> Just as God has created a world which is not himself, but a second thing as his counterpart, so also he has given reason to humanity, which is capable of knowing what is in the world. Therefore there is, according to the will of God, a "natural knowledge, which really knows (that is, finds the real truth), even if this truth is never the ultimately valid and complete truth, but only something that is in the process of being discovered.[24]

Brunner's theological framework creates conceptual space for dialogue between theology and the natural sciences. In this respect, he differs significantly from Karl Barth, whose suspicions about any such conversations are well known.[25] Brunner's careful calibration of the scientific disciplines (see pp. 137–40) allowed him to offer a positive theological mandate for the interaction of Christian theology and the natural sciences, which respected their respective limits, precommitments, and methods. Despite his anxieties about the naturalist precommitments of psychology, for example, Brunner was nevertheless able to note its potential importance for theological reflection.

[21] *Dogmatik II*, 32; *Dogmatics* 2, 21.
[22] *Dogmatik II*, 40; *Dogmatics* 2, 29.
[23] *Dogmatik II*, 32; *Dogmatics* 2, 21.
[24] *Dogmatik II*, 42; *Dogmatics* 2, 30–1.
[25] Hans Schwarz, "Das Verhältnis von Theologie und Naturwissenschaft als systematisch-theologisches Problem." *Neue Zeitschrift für systematische Theologie und Religionsphilosophie* 11 (1969): 139–53.

Brunner's contribution to the dialogue between Christian theology and the natural sciences was not especially significant in terms of its substance. His importance lies more in the theological angle of approach that he advocates, which is hospitable towards a theologically legitimate and intellectually enriching exploration of themes and methods. Barth's weakness in this area indicates the need for alternative approaches. Brunner's lies to hand, and remains a viable option in the twenty-first century.

Although Brunner was not an exponent of a "natural theology" in the traditional sense of the term as "knowledge of God obtained independently of God's revelation", there is no doubt that he affirms the notion of a natural knowledge of God, paralleling in most respects Calvin's exposition of this notion. Brunner does not see this as "proving" anything, least of all the existence of God; he does, however, see it as an important element of a broadly apologetic strategy, through which the Christian churches can connect their proclamation with the world of their audiences.

Yet perhaps Brunner's reconnection with the Reformation's reflections on natural law is to be considered as his most significant contribution to a theology of nature. His careful analysis of human justice was based on his belief that humanity, left to its own devices, constructed notions of justice which were subservient to the vested interests of the powerful. His experience of the rise of totalitarianism led him to emphasize that the will of God was the ultimate foundation of human notions of justice, no matter how imperfectly they reflected this foundation. It is clear that there is renewed interest within Protestantism in the notion of "natural law";[26] Brunner's theological reflections on this theme remain relevant, and have considerable potential for catalysing further development, especially within the Reformed tradition.

Cultural Engagement: The Theological Foundations of Apologetics

Brunner's theological legitimation of apologetics remains of landmark importance, especially given the new challenges faced by the churches in secularizing cultures. By 1929 it was clear that Brunner was aware of the need for the churches to engage the culture of their day – not in an intellectually opportunistic manner, but using approaches which were deeply rooted in Christian theology. Although Brunner initially used the term

---

[26] For example, see J. Budziszewski, *Written on the Heart: The Case for Natural Law*. Downers Grove, IL: InterVarsity Press, 1997; Michael Cromartie, ed., *A Preserving Grace: Protestants, Catholics, and Natural Law*. Grand Rapids, MI: Eerdmans, 1997; Stephen John Grabill, *Rediscovering the Natural Law in Reformed Theological Ethics*. Grand Rapids, MI: Eerdmans, 2006; David VanDrunen, *Natural Law and the Two Kingdoms: A Study in the Development of Reformed Social Thought*. Grand Rapids, MI: Eerdmans, 2010; Robert C. Baker and Roland Cap Ehlke, *Natural Law: A Lutheran Reappraisal*. St. Louis, MO: Concordia, 2011.

"eristic" to designate the "second task of theology", it is clear that the general approach he adopted is better understood in terms of "apologetics" – understood both as the challenging of prevailing cultural assumptions and the identification and exploitation of ways in which the Christian proclamation can be brought into contact with contemporary cultural concerns.[27]

Brunner was convinced that this was not an arbitrary or illegitimate approach, but that it was mandated and endorsed by the nature of the Christian faith itself. At a time when ideologically driven political movements were gaining traction in western Europe, Brunner offered the churches a theological platform from which such developments could be interpreted, engaged, and potentially redirected. On 13 December 1932, he wrote to Barth, setting out a theme that he was coming to realize was of critical significance: theology, it now seemed to him, was "fundamentally nothing other than a specific form of evangelization – namely, the struggle against pagan thought [*der Kampf gegen das heidnische Denken*]".[28]

Disappointed at what he increasingly regarded as Barth's tendency merely to say "No" to culture (see pp. 11–12, 14–15), Brunner offered an approach which allowed the critical evaluation and appropriation of cultural trends. Although Brunner saw theology as having a critical role in facilitating and resourcing cultural engagement, he never understood this as a simple affirmation or rejection of cultural trends, concerns, or norms. His approach of critical appropriation and engagement is easily pilloried as inconsistent, in that it offers neither a uniform "Yes" or "No". Yet his achievement is to demonstrate how a theological framework can be used to evaluate or "filter" culture, identifying appropriate modes of approach and engagement. Theology allows judgement of individual cultural themes, rather than the prejudgement that all are to be rejected.

By providing theological criteria for cultural engagement, Brunner's approach enables the church to take a principled and consistent approach to its context. The church is not required to offer an unconditional "No!" or "Yes!" to culture, but is able to filter and evaluate developments, and respond to them as appropriate. This enables the churches to avoid becoming cultural ghettos, disconnected from wider culture on the one hand, or merely cultural clones with a religious or spiritual patina on the other.

Personalism: The Defence of Relational Identity

Brunner's Uppsala Lectures of 1937 (see pp. 161–72) set out a style of theology that was deeply concerned with analysing relations – relations between human beings, but above all between human beings and God.

---

[27] Peter Vogelsanger, "Theologie als Apologie des Glaubens: Ein Anliegen Emil Brunners." In *Der Auftrag der Kirche in der modernen Welt*, ed. Peter Vogelsanger, 75–88. Zurich: Zwingli Verlag, 1959.
[28] Brunner to Barth, 13 December 1932; *Karl Barth–Emil Brunner, Briefwechsel*, 212.

Writers such as Martin Buber and Ferdinand Ebner had earlier sought to reaffirm the importance and distinctiveness of individual human identity in terms of relationships. We establish ourselves as individual humans by transcending whatever generalized accounts we might use to define humanity in general. Ebner and Buber were both concerned about the depersonalizing tendencies of reductionist accounts of human nature that appeared to be gaining ground after the Great War in the Weimar Republic.[29] Buber's critical distinction between the realms of the "I" and the "It", between *Erfahrung* and *Begegnung*, succinctly expresses the manner in which a human being – a *someone* – can be reduced to *something*, to an abstraction, to a mere chemical formula or biological role.[30]

Brunner developed such "personalist" approaches,[31] partly to clarify the nature of truth, yet also to defend the Christian understanding of God against metaphysical abstraction and to secure a robust understanding of human nature that was secured in and through being "addressed" and loved by God. Although Karl Barth expressed concern that Brunner was making his theology dependent on a freestanding philosophy of existence, Brunner saw the loose philosophical framework provided by Buber and Ebner as essentially heuristic and descriptive, offering an angle of approach that enabled certain core themes, already known to Christian theology, to be articulated and examined more rigorously.

It is no accident that Brunner came to see anthropology as being of central importance to the theological task. While he had some good theological reasons for this judgement (see pp. 134–40), the cultural backdrop to this development is the growing trend towards "depersonalization" which he saw in the rise of the totalitarian state, of whatever political complexion. Brunner came to see the notion of a "personal God" who addressed humanity as safeguarding the uniqueness of each individual human being. *Man in Revolt* remains one of the finest works of theological anthropology of the twentieth century, and continues to provide insights about "authentic existence" which go beyond the rather bland formulae of existential theologies.

Brunner's approach and concerns resonate strongly with more recent theological trends. The Russian *émigré* theologian Vladimir Lossky (1903–58) is one of many who emphasize the importance of being a "person",

---

[29] For such developments, see Lars Koch, "Die Depotenzierung des Menschen im kollektivistischen Denken der Weimarer Republik." In *Totalitarismus und Literatur*, ed. Hans Jörg Schmidt and Petra Tallafuss, 39–54. Göttingen: Vandenhoeck & Ruprecht, 2007.

[30] For such concerns in the writings of Martin Heidegger during the 1930s, see S. Emmanuel Faye, "Der Nationalsozialismus in der Philosophie: Sein, Geschichtlichkeit, Technik und Vernichtung in Heideggers Werk." In *Philosophie im Nationalsozialismus*, ed. Hans Jörg Sandkühler, 135–55. Hamburg: Meiner Verlag, 2009.

[31] For the general trend, see Bernhard Langemeyer, *Der dialogische Personalismus in der evangelischen und katholischen Theologie der Gegenwart*. Paderborn: Verlag Bonifacius-Druckerei, 1963. On Brunner, see especially Roman Rössler, *Person und Glaube; Der Personalismus der Gottesbeziehung bei Emil Brunner*. Munich: Kaiser Verlag, 1965.

while at the same time cautioning against interpreting this in terms of conformity to a template.[32] The political and cultural implications of such an approach are considerable,[33] not least in that it leads to social and political structures which are capable of affirming and supporting individual human beings, while at the same time discouraging social fragmentation in the form of isolated and disconnected individuals. Brunner's personalism led him to commend federal political structures, which he regarded as achieving a judicious balance of power between social structures and individual human beings. For Brunner, humanity always stands in the midst of a network of relations; the negotiation of their centres and limits stands at the heart of political and social existence.

Yet Brunner's personalism also safeguards important theological themes – such as the fundamental idea that God is able to address humanity; that God's revelation is neither mystical (that is to say, contentless) or intellectual (taking the form of mere information), but fundamentally *personal*; and that humanity is challenged, by being addressed in this manner, to make a decision as to how to respond. Humanity's identity is thus constituted *relationally* – initially, in the relationship established by being part of God's created order, and subsequently through a new relationship resulting from the decision to respond to God's address.

Brunner's explorations of the notion of "person" offer a rigorous theological framework for understanding the nature of revelation as both the disclosure of information about God and the self-communication of a personal God, which is to be embraced in an act of personal decision rather than mere intellectual acceptance. In an age in which depersonalization remains a serious threat, Brunner's theological defence of God as the ultimate ground and guarantor of personal identity remains significant, and ought to be allowed to feed into contemporary discussions.

The Trinity: A Plea for Theological Modesty

Although the doctrine of the Trinity played a major role in the work of some leading Protestant writers of the early modern period – such as the American Puritan theologian Jonathan Edwards (1703–58)[34] – it came increasingly to be relegated to the margins of Protestant systematic theology in the era prior to the Great War, partly on account of anxieties concerning

---

[32] Vladimir Lossky, "The Theological Notion of the Human Person", in *In the Image and Likeness of God*. New York: St Vladimir's Seminary Press 1974, 111–23.

[33] See the important essay by Vasilios N. Markides, "Gemeinschaftlichkeitsvorstellungen in Ost- und Südosteuropa und die Rolle der orthodox-christliche Tradition." In *Kulturelle Orientierungen und gesellschaftliche Ordnungsstrukturen in Südosteuropa*, ed. Joachim von Puttkamer, 111–35. Wiesbaden: Harrassowitz, 2010.

[34] Steven M. Studebaker and Robert W. Caldwell, *The Trinitarian Theology of Jonathan Edwards: Text, Context, and Application*. Farnham: Ashgate, 2012.

the rational foundations and theological utility of the doctrine.[35] Karl Barth's innovative reading of the theological utility of the doctrine in the late 1920s is widely regarded as having been of critical importance in bringing about a revival of Trinitarian theology, which saw the doctrine moving from the periphery to the centre of Christian theological reflection.

By the beginning of the twenty-first century, the doctrine of the Trinity can reasonably be said to have returned to centre stage,[36] playing a major role in Christian reflections on a substantial range of issues. This recovery of confidence in the characteristically Christian understanding of God is to be welcomed, particularly as the theological reinstatement of Trinitarianism has been accompanied by a growing understanding of its roots in the theology of the patristic age, which has corrected misunderstandings which have hindered proper reflection on contemporary reformulations of the doctrine.[37]

The resurgence in Trinitarian thought has, however, been accompanied by a number of less welcome developments which have indicated its potential limitations. The development of social models of the Trinity is open to criticism, partly on account of its inflated conceptualities, and perhaps more significantly on account of its tendency to read culturally dominant anthropological categories into a doctrine of God.[38]

Brunner offers an alternative reading of the theological *function* of the doctrine of the Trinity, which serves as an important counterbalance to the current tendency towards Trinitarian inflationism. He does not treat the doctrine as the foundation of anything – such as the possibility of revelation. For Brunner, God's capacity for self-revelation depends on the divine self-identity, which may be articulated in terms of the doctrine of the Trinity.

> It is obvious that the starting point for the doctrine of the Trinity is not something speculative, but the plain witness to faith of the New Testament. It is not concerned with the God of reason, but with the God who makes his name known. He makes his name known as the name of the Father; he makes the name of the Father known through the Son; and he makes the Son known as the Son of the Father, and the Father as the Father of the Son through the

---

[35] For these concerns in early modern England, see Paul Chang-Ha Lim, *Mystery Unveiled: The Crisis of the Trinity in Early Modern England*. New York: Oxford University Press, 2012.

[36] Christoph Schwöbel, "Introduction: The Renaissance of Trinitarian Theology: Reasons, Problems and Tasks." In *Trinitarian Theology Today*, ed. Christoph Schwöbel, 1–30. Edinburgh: T&T Clark, 1995; Roderick T. Leupp, *The Renewal of Trinitarian Theology: Themes, Patterns, & Explorations*. Downers Grove, IL: InterVarsity Press, 2008.

[37] An excellent example is Lewis Ayres, *Nicaea and Its Legacy: An Approach to Fourth-Century Trinitarian Theology*. New York: Oxford University Press, 2004.

[38] For example, see Alan J. Torrance, *Persons in Communion: An Essay on Trinitarian Description and Human Participation*. Edinburgh: T&T Clark, 1996, 164; Sarah A. Coakley, "'Persons' in the 'Social' Doctrine of the Trinity: A Critique of Current Analytic Discussion." In *The Trinity: An Interdisciplinary Symposium on the Trinity*, ed. Stephen T. Davis, Daniel Kendall and Gerald O'Collins, 123–44. Oxford: Oxford University Press, 2002.

Holy Spirit. These three names form the actual content of the New Testament message.[39]

Brunner insists that the doctrine of the Trinity is not itself part of the New Testament proclamation, but is the outcome of theological reflection on that proclamation.[40] The Bible does not speak of a "triune God", nor can one speak of the doctrine of the Trinity as a revealed truth; this way of speaking – which Brunner insists is legitimate – arises from "reflection on the truth given in revelation".[41] It is essential, he argues, to be able, not simply to distinguish between "what is 'given' in revelation and reflection upon it", but also to be clear about what criterion is to be used in making such a distinction.[42]

For Brunner, hostility towards the doctrine of the Trinity is not entirely due to the "rationalistic rigidity of the theology of the Enlightenment";[43] it reflects a deeper unease about forms of speculative theology which have become detached from the biblical proclamation of revelation and redemption. "How often, and at how many points, has the dogmatism of orthodox theology driven people, who would otherwise have been open to a truly biblical theology, into its opposite – rationalism!"[44] Reflecting on the concerns raised by the Swedish theologian Anders Nygren (1890–1978) about the rationality of the doctrine, Brunner remarks on the danger "of allowing our thinking to focus mainly on the nature of the Triune God, considered apart from the historical revelation of God in Christ".[45] Barth, he comments, did not fall victim to this danger, which confirms the essentially biblical character of his thought.

Brunner thus offers an approach to the Trinity which is anti-speculative, seeing it as the outcome of reflection on the core themes of the Christian proclamation – the actuality of divine revelation and salvation in Jesus Christ.

> The church's doctrine of the Trinity, established by the dogma of the early church, is not a biblical *kerygma*, therefore it is also not the *kerygma* of the church, but is a theological defensive doctrine [*eine theologische Schutzlehre*] for the core faith of the Bible and of the church. It therefore does not belong to what the church has to preach, but it belongs to theology, in which it is the purpose of the church to scrutinize its message, in the light of reflection on the Word of God given to the church.[46]

---

[39] *Dogmatik I*, 209; *Dogmatics 1*, 206.
[40] M. A. Schmidt, "Der Ort der Trinitätslehre bei Emil Brunner." *Theologische Zeitschrift* 59, no. 1 (1949): 46–66.
[41] *Dogmatik I*, 241; *Dogmatics 1*, 236.
[42] *Dogmatik I*, 242; *Dogmatics 1*, 237.
[43] *Dogmatik I*, 243; *Dogmatics 1*, 238.
[44] *Dogmatik I*, 243; *Dogmatics 1*, 238.
[45] *Dogmatik I*, 244; *Dogmatics 1*, 240.
[46] *Dogmatik I*, 209; *Dogmatics 1*, 206.

It is not necessary to have a firm grasp of the complexities of intra-Trinitarian relationships; indeed, Brunner indicates scepticism about the merits of any such speculation. The New Testament writers had no intention of developing a doctrine of the Trinity. The doctrine is a development of the ideas of the New Testament "which the church places before the faithful in her theology".[47] The "mystery" at the heart of the New Testament is not the "intellectual paradox" of the doctrine of the Trinity, but the proclamation that "the Lord God became incarnate and endured the cross for our sake". We may indeed maintain an "attitude of reverent silence" in the face of the mystery of God; instead of "constructing a *mysterium logicum*" we ought to renounce any attempt on the part of human reason to "penetrate a region that is too high for us".[48]

Brunner's approach counters the metaphysical inflationism and conceptual complexity of much recent thinking about the Trinity; above all, it reconnects the doctrine of the Trinity with the world of the New Testament, and the life and witness of the church. By presenting the doctrine as the outcome, not the presupposition, of faith, Brunner renders the apologetic task of the church easier. There is a need for his modest – yet theologically defensible – account of the Trinity to be brought back into play in contemporary discussion, not least on account of a resurgence of cultural concern about the intrinsic rationality of faith.

Conclusion

This study has not set out to be either a biography of Brunner or a synopsis of his theology. It is, in effect, both an exploration of the emergence of his theological vision, set against its cultural context, and an assessment of its continuing relevance. In the course of this analysis, a number of important issues of historical theology have been considered, including the origins and character of "dialectical theology", and the manner in which theology impacts upon questions of wider public importance. Yet in the end a plea must be made for Brunner to be recovered, and taken seriously. Whatever his weaknesses, Brunner offers a theological platform with considerable potential for the engagement of contemporary cultural concerns. It would be madness not to make better use of it.

For Brunner, the gospel demanded and deserved constant rearticulation and restatement, without losing sight of its changeless and timeless relevance. "There is indeed an *evangelium perennis* but not a *theologia perennis* ... The gospel remains the same, but our understanding of the gospel must ever be won anew."[49] The notion of some permanently valid theological

---

[47] *Dogmatik I*, 230; *Dogmatics 1*, 226.
[48] *Dogmatik I*, 231; *Dogmatics 1*, 227.
[49] "Toward a Missionary Theology", 816.

formulation seemed pointless to him, in that it would amount to the petrification of something that was meant to be dynamic and living. For Brunner, theology was an activity, rather than an outcome – a process of reflection, engagement, and connection. He offers us a vision of theology as a dynamic discipline, constantly seeking to ensure that the gospel is faithfully and effectively articulated in contemporary cultural contexts.

Brunner saw it as being theologically important to "maintain a conversation" in his theological monographs "with people, in the present and the past, who have already thought about these questions", so that his readers might listen in on their discussion.[50] He surely deserves to enter our theological conversations once more. His presence can only enrich our discussions.

---

[50] *Das Gebot und die Ordnungen*, viii; *The Divine Imperative*, 12.

Works by Emil Brunner Cited in This Study

1 Originally Published in German

Books

Das Ärgernis des Christentums: Fünf Vorlesungen über den christlichen Glauben. Zurich: Theologischer Verlag, 1957.
Dogmatik I: Die christliche Lehre von Gott. Zurich: Zwingli Verlag, 1959.
Dogmatik II: Die christliche Lehre von Schöpfung und Erlösung. 3rd edn. Zurich: Theologischer Verlag, 1972.
Dogmatik III: Die christliche Lehre von der Kirche, vom Glauben, und von der Vollendung. Zurich: Zwingli Verlag, 1960.
Erlebnis, Erkenntnis und Glaube. 3rd edn. Tübingen: Mohr, 1923.
Das Ewige als Zukunft und Gegenwart. Zurich: Zwingli Verlag, 1953.
Fraumünster Predigten. Zurich: Zwingli Verlag, 1955.
Fraumünster Predigten: Neue Folge. Zurich: Zwingli Verlag, 1965.
Das Gebot und die Ordnungen: Entwurf einer protestantisch-theologischen Ethik. Tübingen: Paul Siebeck, 1932.
Gerechtigkeit. Eine Lehre von den Grundgesetzen der Gesellschaftsordnung. Zurich: Zwingli Verlag, 1943.
Gott und Mensch: Vier Untersuchungen über das personhafte Sein. Tübingen: Mohr, 1930.
Die Grenzen der Humanität. Tübingen: Mohr, 1922.
Ich glaube an den lebendigen Gott: Predigten über das altchristliche Glaubensbekenntnis. Zurich: Zwingli Verlag, 1945.
Karl Barth–Emil Brunner, Briefwechsel 1911–1966. Zurich: Theologischer Verlag, 2000.
Die Kirchen, die Gruppenbewegung und die Kirche Jesu Christi. Berlin: Furche Verlag, 1936.
Der Mensch im Widerspruch: Die christliche Lehre vom wahren und vom wirklichen Menschen. 4th edn. Zurich: Zwingli Verlag, 1965.

Emil Brunner: A Reappraisal, First Edition. Alister E. McGrath.
© 2014 John Wiley & Sons, Ltd. Published 2016 by John Wiley & Sons, Ltd.

Das Missverständnis der Kirche. Zurich: Theologischer Verlag, 1951.
Der Mittler: Zur Besinnung über den Christusglauben. 4th edn. Zurich: Zwingli Verlag, 1947.
Die Mystik und das Wort. 2nd edn. Tübingen: Mohr, 1928.
Natur und Gnade: Zum Gespräch mit Karl Barth. 2nd edn. Tübingen: Mohr, 1935.
Offenbarung und Vernunft: Die Lehre von der christlichen Glaubenserkenntnis. Zurich: Zwingli Verlag, 1941.
Ein offenes Wort: Vorträge und Aufsätze 1917–1962. 2 vols. Zurich: Theologischer Verlag, 1981.
Die reformierte Staatsauffassung: Vortrag vor der neuen helvetischen Gesellschaft in Zürich. Zurich: Rascher Verlag, 1938.
Religionsphilosophie evangelischer Theologie. Munich: Leibniz Verlag, 1948.
Der Römerbrief. Kassel: Oncken Verlag, 1956.
Das Symbolische in der religiösen Erkenntnis: Beiträge zu einer Theorie des religiösen Erkenntnis. Tübingen: Mohr, 1914.
Unser Glaube: Eine christliche Unterweisung. Zurich: Zwingli Verlag, 1947.
Wahrheit als Begegnung: Sechs Vorlesungen über das christliche Wahrheitsverständnis. Zurich: Zwingli Verlag, 1938.
Vom Werk des heiligen Geistes. Zurich: Zwingli Verlag, 1935.

Articles

"Die christliche Nicht-Kirche-Bewegung in Japan." *Evangelische Theologie* 4 (1959): 147–55.
"Christlicher Glaube nach reformierter Lehre." In *Der Protestantismus der Gegenwart*, ed. G. Schenkel, 343–74. Stuttgart: Friedrich Bohnenberger Verlag, 1926.
"Das 'Elend der Theologie.' Ein Nachwort zum Zürcher Fereinkurs, zugleich ein Vorwort." *Kirchenblatt für die reformierte Schweiz* 35, no. 50 (1920): 197–9.
"Gesetz und Offenbarung: Eine theologische Grundlegung." *Theologische Blätter* 4 (1925): 53–8.
"Das Grundproblem der Philosophie bei Kant und Kierkegaard." *Zwischen den Zeiten* 6 (1924): 31–46.
"Der Römerbrief von Karl Barth: Eine zeitgemaß-unmoderne Paraphrase." *Kirchenblatt für die reformierte Schweiz* 34, no. 8 (1919): 29–32.
Other articles are referred to in the collected edition *Ein offenes Wort: Vorträge und Aufsätze 1917–1962.* 2 vols. Zurich: Theologischer Verlag, 1981.

2 Originally Published in English

Christianity and Civilisation. 2 vols. New York: Scribner's Sons, 1948.
The Church in the New Social Order. London: SCM Press, 1952.
"A Great Time for the Preacher." *Christian Century* 68, no. 28 (1951): 816–18.
"Intellectual Autobiography." In *The Theology of Emil Brunner*, ed. Charles W. Kegley, 3–20. New York: Macmillan, 1962.
"Reply." In *The Theology of Emil Brunner*, ed. Charles W. Kegley, 325–52. New York: Macmillan, 1962.

The Theology of Crisis. New York: Charles Scribner's Sons, 1929.
"Toward a Missionary Theology." *Christian Century* 66, no. 27 (1949): 816–18.
The Word and the World. London: SCM Press, 1931.

3 English Translations

The Divine-Human Encounter. London: SCM Press, 1944.
The Divine Imperative: A Study in Christian Ethics. London: Lutterworth Press, 1937.
Dogmatics 1: The Christian Doctrine of God. London: Lutterworth Press, 1962.
Dogmatics 2: The Christian Doctrine of Creation and Redemption. London: Lutterworth Press, 1952.
Dogmatics 3: The Christian Doctrine of the Church, Faith, and the Consummation. London: Lutterworth Press, 1962.
Eternal Hope. London: Lutterworth Press, 1954.
God and Man: Four Essays on the Nature of Personality. London: SCM Press, 1936.
The Great Invitation: Zurich Sermons. London: Lutterworth Press, 1955.
I Believe in the Living God: Sermons on the Apostles' Creed. London: Lutterworth Press, 1961.
Justice and the Social Order. London: Lutterworth Press, 1945.
The Letter to the Romans: A Commentary. London: Lutterworth Press, 1959.
Man in Revolt: A Christian Anthropology. London: Lutterworth Press, 1939.
The Mediator: A Study of the Central Doctrine of the Christian Faith. London: Lutterworth Press, 1934.
The Misunderstanding of the Church. London: Lutterworth Press, 1952.
Natural Theology, Comprising "Nature and Grace" by Professor Dr. Emil Brunner and the Reply "No!" by Dr. Karl Barth. London: Geoffrey Bless, 1946.
Our Faith. London: SCM Press, 1949.
The Philosophy of Religion from the Standpoint of Protestant Theology. London: Nicholson and Watson, 1937.
Revelation and Reason: The Christian Doctrine of Faith and Knowledge. London: SCM Press, 1947.
The Scandal of Christianity. London: SCM Press, 1951.

Index

Althaus, Paul, 39, 109, 128
Anknüpfungspunkt, 12, 69, 92, 119, 123–4, 145–8
anthropology, 84–5, 91, 132, 133–53, 233
Augustine of Hippo, 72, 95, 144

Bachofner, Heinrich, 1
Barmen Theological Declaration (*Barmer theologische Erklärung*, 1934), 112–13
Barth, Karl, x, 4, 9, 9–12, 13–16, 22–5, 38–9, 51–2, 70, 88–9, 96, 101–5, 108–9, 109–10, 113–20, 126–7, 135–6, 165–6, 172–3, 187, 218–19, 223–4, 225, 229, 235
Baxter, Richard, 200
Bergson, Henri, 17
Beza, Theodore, 98
Blumhardt, Christoph, 166
Bolshevik Revolution, 62–3
Bonhoeffer, Dietrich, 20, 108

BRUNNER, EMIL
biography
  birth, 1
  education at Zurich, 2–4
  pastor at Leutwil (canton of Aargau), 4–5
  schoolteacher in England, 5–6
  military service in Great War, 6
  pastor at Glarus (canton of Glarus), 8–9
  marriage to Margrit Lauterburg, 9
  pastor at Obstalten (canton of Glarus), 9
  early relationship with Karl Barth and Eduard Thurneysen, 9–12
  visiting scholar at Union Theological Seminary, New York, 12–13
  emerging tensions with Barth and Thurneysen, 14–16
  discovery of the writings of Søren Kierkegaard, 15–16
  granted *pro venia legendi* (right to lecture) at University of Zurich, 16–18
  delivers *Habilitationsvorlesung* at the University of Zurich, 22–5
  appointed chair of systematic and practical theology at University of Zurich, 27
  major themes of his *Antrittsvorlesung* ("inaugural lecture"), 32–4
  anxiety over Barth's possible return to Switzerland in 1927, 35
  delivers Schwander Lectures at Lancaster Theological Seminary, Pennsylvania, 54–60

Emil Brunner: A Reappraisal, First Edition. Alister E. McGrath.
© 2014 John Wiley & Sons, Ltd. Published 2016 by John Wiley & Sons, Ltd.

lectures on "dialectical theology" at King's College London, 74–8
becomes involved with the "Oxford Group", 85–7
lectures at Copenhagen on the Holy Spirit in 1934, 87–9
controversy with Karl Barth over "natural theology", 90–127
lectures on objectivity and subjectivity in theology at the University of Uppsala, 154–72
invited to become Charles Hodge Professor of Theology at Princeton Theological Seminary, 172–8
declines invitation to Princeton and remains in Switzerland during the war, 176–8
elected rector of the University of Zurich 1942–3, 206–7
delivers Zenos Lectures at McCormick Theological Seminary in Chicago, 214
delivers Gifford Lectures at the University of St Andrews, 207
accepts Professorship of Christianity at International Christian University in Tokyo, 221–2
returns to Zurich, 222
awarded the Grosse Verdienstkreuz (Grand Merit Cross) by the President of the Federal Republic of Germany, 205
final illness and death, 223–4
decline in influence, 225–8
major publications
"Die andere Aufgabe der Theologie", 66–74
The Divine Imperative, 78–85
Dogmatics, 218–21
Erlebnis, Erkenntnis und Glaube, 16–18, 21
Justice and the Social Order, 195–9
Man in Revolt, 133–53
The Mediator, 25, 39–50
The Misunderstanding of the Church, 200–2
Die Mystik und das Wort, 25–6, 227
Nature and Grace, 113–21
"Die Offenbarung als Grund und Gegenstand der Theologie", 32–4
Our Faith, 117–18, 207–10, 227
The Philosophy of Religion from the Standpoint of Protestant Theology, 36–9
Revelation and Reason, 33, 121–7, 190–5
The Scandal of Christianity, 214–17
Das Symbolische in der religiösen Erkenntnis, 3, 5
Truth as Encounter, 154–72
The Word and the World, 74–8
theological issues
on anthropology, 84–5, 91, 132, 133–53, 233
on apologetics *see* on the eristic aspects of theology
on the Bible, 36–8
on Christian faith and academic research, 206–7
and Christian pedagogy, 207–10, 218–20
critique of the doctrine of the Virgin Birth, 45
critique of Protestant Orthodoxy, 36–8, 164
on "Dialectical Theology", 9–12, 14–16, 35–6, 39–40, 41–2, 74–6, 165–6
on the doctrine of the Trinity, 44, 50–4, 213, 215–16, 234–7
on ecclesiology, 77–8, 89, 182–3, 199–204, 207
on ecumenism, 199–204
on the eristic aspects of theology, 34, 66–74, 81, 148, 191–2, 220, 231–2
on ethics, 39, 49–50, 60, 78–85, 185–90
on faith as a "leap", 47–8
on the Holy Spirit, 87–9
on the human capacity for revelation, 118 n. 24, 124–5, 131, 135–6, 229
on the human conscience as a moral authority, 188–9

theological issues (cont'd)
  on the image of God in humanity,
    92, 118–20, 130–1, 145–8,
    152–3
  on the incarnation, 33, 39–50, 75,
    122, 193–4, 211–12, 216–17
  on the "law of the closeness of
    relation" (*Gesetz der
    Beziehungsnähe*), 15, 137–40
  on the limits of human reason,
    22–5, 32–4, 67–8, 140–2, 190–5,
    215
  on mission, 77–8, 123
  on modernism, 58–9
  on natural law, 185–90, 229–30
  on natural theology, 71, 90–127,
    229–30
  notion of *Anknüpfungspunkt*, 12,
    38, 69, 92, 119, 123–4, 145–8
  on objectivity and subjectivity in
    theology, 155–72
  on the "orders of creation", 34, 39,
    78–80, 82–3, 92, 109, 114,
  on the "other task of theology",
    66–74, 231–2
  as preacher, 209–14
  on the psychology of religion,
    18–20, 73
  on reason and theology, 22–5, 32–4,
    67–8, 140–2, 190–5, 215
  relation to Lutheranism, 34, 39,
    78–80
  on religions, 194–5
  as a representative of the Reformed
    tradition, 36, 228–9
  on revelation, 23–5, 32–4, 35–8,
    41–2, 43–4, 46–7, 74–7, 122–3,
    169–72, 190–5
  on the role of narrative in theology,
    168
  on the role of the state, 195–9
  on science and theology, 229–31
  on sin, 49, 143–5, 216
  on Social Darwinism, 148–53
  on subjectivity and objectivity in
    theology, 155–72
  on the tasks of theology, 32–3,
    66–74, 161–2, 190–3
  on the "theology of crisis", 39–40,
    54, 92–3
  on totalitarianism, 182–90, 195–7

Brunner, Peter, 128
Buber, Martin, 21, 158–9, 233
Buchman, Frank, 85–6
Bultmann, Rudolf, 24, 151, 190–1

Calvin, John, 34, 35, 98, 99–101, 118,
  186, 218–19
Caruso, Enrico, 208–9
Chagall, Marc, 210
Cicero, Marcus Tullius, 94–6
Coe, George Albert, 19, 166
Cole, George Douglas Howard, 6
conscience as a moral authority,
  188–9
Cullberg, John Olof, 159

Darwinism, 134, 148–53
Dewey, William, 20
dialectical theology, 9–12, 14–16,
  35–6, 39–40, 41–2, 74–6, 165–6

Eberhard, Johann August, 97
Ebner, Ferdinand, 21, 26–7, 70, 76,
  157–8, 233
ecclesiology, 77–8, 89, 182–3,
  199–204, 207
ecumenism, 199–204
Edwards, Jonathan, 235
Elert, Werner, 39
eristic aspects of theology, 34, 66–74,
  81, 148, 191–2, 220, 231–2
ethics, 39, 49–50, 60, 78–85,
  185–90
Eucken, Walter, 198
Eusebius of Caesarea, 47

Faith Movement of German Christians
  (Glaubensbewegung deutsche
  Christen) *see* German Christians
Farrer, Austin, ix
Fezer, Paul, 128
Fichte, Johann Gottlieb, 155
Fosdick, Harry Emerson, 203
Fraumünster, Zurich, 210–14, 224

Freud, Sigmund, 134
fundamentalist controversies in North America, 57–9

Galen of Pergamum, 95
German Christians (Glaubensbewegung deutsche Christen), 107–8, 110–11, 128
German Faith Movement (Deutsche Glaubensbewegung), 106–7
Gerstenmaier, Eugen, 205
Gifford Lectures, University of St Andrews, ix, 207
Glarus (canton of Glarus), 8–9
Gleichschaltung, as Nazi policy, 108–9, 110–12
Goebbels, Joseph, 65
Gogarten, Friedrich, 16, 21, 24, 39, 110, 135
Grundmann, Walter, 111
Guild Socialism, 6
Gustloff, Wilhelm, 65

Hall, G. Stanley, 19
Harnack, Adolf von, 3, 44, 63
Hartmann, Nicolai, 150
Hauer, Jakob Wilhelm, 107
Hazlitt, William, 142
Heidegger, Martin, 157
Hitler, Adolf, 65, 105–6
Holl, Karl, 101
Holmes, Oliver Wendell, 186
Holy Spirit, 87–9
Huber, Max, 191
human nature, 84–5, 118 n. 24, 124–5, 131, 132, 133–53, 229, 233

ideology, rise of within Germany following Great War, 62–6
image of God in humanity, 92, 118–20, 130–1, 145–8, 152–3
incarnation, 33, 39–50, 75, 193–4, 211–12, 216–17

James, William, 19, 166
Jaspers, Karl, 157
Jehle, Frank, xii, 219

Jena, University of, 110–12
Justin Martyr, 72

Kant, Immanuel, 3, 97, 155
Keller, Adolf, 12
Kierkegaard, Søren, 15–16, 21, 47, 70, 156–7
King's College London, 61
Köhler, Walter, 2, 18
Krause, Reinhold, 110
Künneth, Walther, 39
Kutter, Hermann, 2, 7

Lake, Kirsopp, 58
Lancaster Theological Seminary, Pennsylvania, 55–7
Lenin, Vladimir Ilich, 62–3
Lessing, Gotthold Ephraim, 215
Leuba, James H., 19
Leutwil (canton of Aargau), 4–5
Lewis, C. S., 188, 200
limits of human reason, 22–5, 32–4, 140–2, 190–5, 215
Lossky, Vladimir, 233–4
Luther, Martin, 34, 78, 80–1, 113, 143
Lutheranism, 34, 39, 47–8, 78–80
Luxemburg, Rosa, 63

McConnachie, John, 54
MacDonald, Ramsay, 6
Machen, J. Gresham, 58, 173
McIntyre, Carl, 176
Mackay, John Alexander, 173–5
Mackintosh, Hugh Ross, 27, 54
mission, 77–8, 123
Moore, Aubrey, 148
Mott, John R., 2, 86, 199, 203
Mukyōkai ("Not-Church") movement in Japan, 203 n. 111
munus triplex Christi, 47
Mussolini, Benito, 64, 183

National Socialism, 65–6, 105–13, 182–3
Natorp, Paul, 21, 26
natural law, 185–90, 229–30
natural theology, 71, 90–127, 229–30
Nazism, Nazis *see* National Socialism

New College Edinburgh, 61
"Not-Church" (Mukyōkai) movement in Japan, 203 n. 111
Nygren, Anders, 236

objectivity and subjectivity in theology, 155–72
Obstalten (canton of Glarus), 9, 13–14, 22, 210
O'Donovan, Oliver, 132
Oldham, J. H., 174, 199
orders of creation, 34, 39, 78–80, 82–3, 109, 114
"other task of theology", 66–74, 231–2
Otto, Rudolf, 33 n. 7
Overbeck, Franz, 14
"Oxford Group" (later "Moral Rearmament"), 85–7, 203

Pauck, Wilhelm, 55
pragmatism in American theology, 20, 57–8
Princeton Theological Seminary, 173–8
Protagoras, 133
psychology of religion, 18–20, 73

Rad, Gerhard von, 109–10
Rade, Martin, 63
Ragaz, Leonhard, 2–3, 4, 7, 10, 17
Rauschenbusch, Walter, 3
Reinhold, Karl Leonhard, 155
revelation, 23–5, 32–4, 35–8, 43–4, 74–7, 122–3, 169–72, 190–5
Ritschl, A. B., 3, 25, 44
Rommen, Heinrich, 187
Runestam, Arvid, 154

Safenwil (canton of Aargau), 9
Sayers, Dorothy L., 200
Schleiermacher, F. D. E., 3, 25–7, 44, 102, 135

Schmiedel, Paul Wilhelm, 18
sin, 49, 143–5, 216
Snowden, Philip, 6
Social Darwinism, 148–53
Spengler, Oswald, 62
Spoerri, Theophil, 86
subjectivity and objectivity in theology, 155–72
Switzerland, crisis of identity in Great War, 6–8

tasks of theology, 32–3, 66–74, 161–2, 190–3
Temple, William, 6
"theology of crisis", 39–40, 54, 92–3
threefold office of Christ, 47
Thurneysen, Eduard, 4, 6, 9, 9–12, 13–16, 39–40, 115, 210
totalitarianism, 182–90, 195–7
Trinity College Glasgow, 61
Trinity, doctrine of the, 50–4, 213, 215–16, 234–7
Troeltsch, Ernst, 63, 103

Uchimura, Kanzō, 203 n. 111
Union Theological Seminary, New York, 12–13, 166

Virgil, 95
Virgin Birth, 45
Vogelsanger, Peter, 223–4

Wall Street Crash (1929), 13, 55–6, 64–5
Walser, Paul, 26
Weimar Republic, 105–7, 184
West Leeds High School, Yorkshire, 6
Winchester House School, Norfolk, 4–6
Wolf, Ernst, 114, 128
Wyon, Olive, 40, 142

Zwingli, Huldrych, 34, 35